TRUE TO LIFE

ELEMENTARY

Joanne Collie
Stephen Slater

TEACHER'S BOOK

CAMBRIDGE
UNIVERSITY PRESS

PUBLISHED BY THE PRESS SYNDICATE OF THE UNIVERSITY OF CAMBRIDGE
The Pitt Building, Trumpington Street, Cambridge, United Kingdom

CAMBRIDGE UNIVERSITY PRESS
The Edinburgh Building, Cambridge CB2 2RU, UK
40 West 20th Street, New York, NY 10011–4211, USA
477 Williamstown Road, Port Melbourne, VIC 3207, Australia
Ruiz de Alarcón 13, 28014 Madrid, Spain
Dock House, The Waterfront, Cape Town 8001, South Africa

http://www.cambridge.org

© Cambridge University Press 1995

First published 1995
Seventh printing 2002

Printed in the United Kingdom at the University Press, Cambridge

ISBN 0 521 42142 X Elementary Teacher's Book
ISBN 0 521 42141 1 Elementary Personal Study Workbook
ISBN 0 521 42140 3 Elementary Class Book
ISBN 0 521 42143 8 Elementary Class Cassette Set
ISBN 0 521 42144 6 Elementary Personal Study Cassette
ISBN 0 521 48574 6 Elementary Personal Study CD

CONTENTS

INTRODUCTION

Who this course is for

True to Life is a three-level course designed to take learners from elementary to good intermediate level.

The course is specifically designed for adult learners. Topics have been chosen for their interest and relevance to adults around the world, and activities have been designed to provide adults with the opportunity to talk about their experiences, express opinions, use their knowledge and imagination to solve problems and exchange ideas so as to learn from one another.

True to Life Elementary is for learners who have had some exposure to English but may feel they have forgotten a lot. It is designed to take them from near beginner level to the lower intermediate level. It provides approximately 72 hours upwards of classroom activity, depending on the time available and the options used.

Key features

True to Life incorporates the best of current classroom methodology by providing varied teaching materials to meet the needs of different learners and learning styles, but particular attention has been paid to the following:

1 Learner engagement and personalisation

We believe that learning is most effective when learners are actively engaged in tasks which they find motivating and challenging. Moreover, it is essential for learners to have opportunities to see the relevance of new language to their own personal circumstances. We have, therefore, provided a very large number of open-ended and interactive tasks which allow learners to draw on their knowledge of the world and to be creative. These tasks are used not just for fluency work but also in quite controlled activities designed to activate specific language areas (vocabulary, grammar and functions).

2 Speaking and listening

It has been our experience that adult learners place great emphasis on oral/aural practice in the classroom, often because it is their only opportunity to obtain such practice. We have, therefore, decided to limit the amount of reading material in the Class Book (but increase it in the Personal Study Workbook) so that we can devote more time and space to speaking and listening. Users should find that opportunities for speaking practice are present in most stages of the lessons.

3 Recycling and checking

We have decided to employ the 'little and often' approach to revision. Instead of sporadic chunks, we have devoted one page in every unit to revision. This section is called *Review and development*; it gives learners a chance to review material while it is still relatively fresh in their minds, and ensures that material from every unit is formally recycled on two separate occasions, excluding the tests in the Teacher's Book. For example:

Unit 10

Lesson 1	Lesson 2	Lesson 3	Lesson 4
input	input	input	Review and development of Units 8 and 9

Unit 11

Lesson 1	Lesson 2	Lesson 3	Lesson 4
input	input	input	Review and development of Units 9 and 10

4 Quick Checks

Photocopiable Quick Checks for each lesson are included in the Teacher's Book. These allow learners to check their own mastery of the structures and vocabulary learnt, as well as to reflect upon specific areas of language that may have been practised but not overtly highlighted during the lesson.

The Quick Check can be used as personal practice, thus helping learners to build their confidence and take responsibility for their own learning.

5 Flexibility

It is important that learners know what they are learning and can see a clear path through the material. It is also important, though, that teachers can adapt material to suit the needs of their particular class. We have provided for this with the inclusion of further activities in the Teacher's Book (called Options). In addition, each unit offers worksheets which may be photocopied. This, then, gives teachers a clear framework in the Class Book, but with additional resources to draw upon in the Teacher's Book for extra flexibility.

6 Vocabulary

In *True To Life*, vocabulary is not treated as a separate section because it forms an intrinsic and fundamental part of every unit, and a wide range of vocabulary activities is included throughout the three levels. Moreover, great importance is attached in these activities to spoken practice of newly presented lexical items, so learners have the opportunity to use new words and phrases in utterances of their own creation.

7 The Personal Study Workbook

This aims to be as engaging on an individual basis as the Class Book is on a group basis. Personalisation is, therefore, carried through to the Personal Study Workbook, which provides a range of activities, both structured and open-ended, designed to motivate learners to continue their learning outside the classroom.

Special features include:

Visual dictionary: one illustration for each unit, for learners to label. That is, a personal dictionary which is easy to compile, and allows genuine self-access with the aid of a bilingual dictionary.

Components and course organisation

At each level, the course consists of the following:

Class Book and Class Cassette Set
Personal Study Workbook and Personal Study Cassette or CD
Teacher's Book

The Class Book and Class Cassette Set

The Class Book contains 24 units, each one providing three to four hours of classroom activity. Each unit is divided into four lessons and each lesson is designed to take 45 to 60 minutes. Teachers are, of course, free to explore the material in different ways (indeed we have indicated ways of doing this in the following teacher's notes), but each lesson has been designed as a self-contained, logical sequence of varied activities, which can be used as they stand.

The first three lessons contain the main language input. This consists of:
– a clear grammatical syllabus
– an emphasis on lexical development
– key functional exponents
– listening and reading practice
– speaking and writing activities.

The final section of each unit provides review and development activities based on the two previous units; e.g. the final section of Unit 4 revises Units 2 and 3; the final section of Unit 5 revises Units 3 and 4.

At the back of the book there is:
– a Grammar Reference section
– a list of irregular verbs
– the phonemic alphabet

The listening material on the Class Cassette Set is very varied – scripted, semi-scripted and unscripted – and a particular feature is the regular inclusion of dual-level listening texts. These provide two versions of a listening passage, one longer and more challenging than the other. This feature allows teachers to select the listening material that best meets the needs of their particular learners, but it also gives more scope for exploitation. In some cases, the content of the listening in each version is slightly different, so teachers may start with the easier listening and then move on to the more difficult one; in other cases where the content is the same but more challenging, the teacher could (if facilities permit) split the group and give a different listening to different learners. And there is nothing to stop a teacher doing version 1 at one point in the course, and then returning to do version 2, days, weeks or even months later.

The Personal Study Workbook and Personal Study Cassette or CD

The Personal Study Workbook runs parallel to the Class Book, providing 24 units which contain further practice and consolidation of the material in the Class Book.

The exercises at the beginning of each unit concentrate on consolidating grammar and vocabulary; later exercises focus on skills development.

The Personal Study Cassette or CD provides further material for listening practice, and there is a tapescript at the back of the Workbook along with an answer key for most of the exercises.

An additional feature is the visual dictionary, which provides illustrations at the back of the book for learners to compile their own personal dictionary. The material is linked to the units in the Class Book, so learners complete it at regular intervals during the course.

The Teacher's Book

This offers teachers a way through the activities presented, but also provides a wide range of ideas that will enable them to approach and extend activities in different ways. Each unit offers supplementary worksheets which may be photocopied and distributed in class.

In addition, the Teachers' Book provides:
– guidance on potential language difficulties
– a complete answer key to the exercises in the Class Book.
– four photocopiable tests, each test covering six units of the Class Book
– tapescripts of the Class Book recordings which may be photocopied and given to the learners.

FINDING OUT

CONTENTS

Language focus: the verb *to be*: positive, negative, question forms
there is, there are
articles: *a, an, any*
adjectives
sentence structures

Vocabulary: names, addresses, jobs
buildings and facilities

INTRODUCTION TO THE UNIT

This unit encourages a lot of interaction from the very beginning, so that teachers and learners can get to know each other and build up some confidence. A lot of language is covered, but your learners will probably know quite a bit of it. The activities will help them to remember and practise it. If, however, learners need more explicit presentation of the language, you could use the exercises in the Personal Study Workbook in class, before you start using the Class Book with them. Appropriate exercises from the Personal Study Workbook are mentioned in the notes to the activities. There are also additional exercises in the Starter Unit to help learners who may be 'false beginners' to revise some basics. These include practice with the alphabet and numbers (Starter Unit, Exercises 1 and 2), saying the time (Starter Unit, Exercises 3 and 4), expressing dates, months and days (Starter Unit, Exercise 5), revision of personal pronouns and possessive adjectives (Starter Unit, Exercise 7).

A

Breaking the ice

If this is your first lesson with the learners, you will want to start with greetings and responses to them, thereby revising one area of assumed knowledge.

Greet the learners in turn, using a range of expressions: *Hello, how are you? How's it going?* Encourage the learners to repeat this model to you, and offer them a range of responses, e.g. *Fine, Fine, thanks, Good, Great, OK, Not bad, So so, Terrible!* At the end, you may want to write the expressions up on the board.

Option 1

If your learners need practice in the intonation patterns of greetings, draw three faces on the board.

Ask the learners to greet you. Give a response and ask them to say which face to write it under. Make sure your intonation is appropriate for the face. Then greet the learners and ask them to respond. Point to the appropriate face to remind them of intonation differences.

Option 2

Bouncing orange (or ball). This is a well-known icebreaker, which can be used after the first modelling of greetings. Bring in an orange (or ball), say a greeting and throw the orange to a learner. They reply, then greet another learner and throw the orange to them, and so on. Encourage the learners to vary their greetings and responses as much as possible.

Example: T: *Hello, how's it going?*
JUAN: *Great.* (throwing orange to third learner) *Hello, how are you?*
REIKO: *Fine, thanks.* (and so on)

1 Excuse me, what's your name?
asking and giving names, addresses, telephone numbers

This activity gets the learners circulating and using English while making contact with each other. It's often a good idea for learners to know each other's names, addresses and phone numbers. They can keep the completed list and it can be used to create conversation pairs or phone practice, e.g. by asking the learners to phone each other occasionally, for homework, to chat in English.

To model the three questions, you can prepare a recording of them in advance, gapped for your responses. Play the recording and answer the questions yourself, like this:

(on recording) *What's your name?*

Reply with your name and write it on the board at the same time:

(on recording) *What's your address?*

Reply with your address, and write it on the board … etc.

> ### Language Point: telephone numbers
> Phone numbers in English are given individually; 0 is usually pronounced /əʊ/; 33 is usually given as 'double three'.

Get the learners to ask you the three questions again. Reply, pointing to the board.

Option 1

If the learners don't remember numbers, or letters of the alphabet, revise with flash cards, or with a simple number/letter game like bingo. Learners draw a grid with nine squares and write either a number or a letter in each square. Call out numbers or letters in random order. Learners cross them out as they hear them. The first person to cross out all their numbers or letters wins.

Option 2

To revise alphabet and spelling, you can use Personal Study Workbook Starter Unit, Exercise 1. For numbers, you can use Personal Study Workbook Starter Unit, Exercise 2. If your learners don't know how to say their telephone numbers in English, you can use Personal Study Workbook Unit 1, Exercise 7.

For multilingual groups or for learners who already know basic name and address questions, this offers an extension of forms. Model the forms if necessary or simply draw the learners' attention to them.

Suggested steps

Tell the learners to make a list like the example in the book. They should copy the headings *Name*, *Address*, and *Telephone* into their notebooks or on paper. You can show them how to do it by writing the headings on the board, and filling in the information for yourself. If you haven't modelled the questions yet, demonstrate by going through the three questions with one student.

Let the learners mill around to obtain names, addresses and numbers. Circulate, giving support, or join in the task using a class list yourself. If the class is a large one, ask the learners to get five names only. (They can complete the task during breaks, or copy missing information from each other's worksheets.)

The completed lists can be used for oral revision and extension. Point to one learner and ask another: *Who's this? What's her/his telephone number?* etc., thus revising third person forms. They answer by referring to their list.

A completed list can be displayed in the class for reference. Other categories could be added later as you progress through other units, for example adding a column for hobbies, favourite colours, likes, dislikes, etc.

Personal Study Workbook
8: meeting and greeting people

2 He's a waiter. What do you do?
vocabulary and articles; question forms

Option

If you feel your learners need more explicit presentation of job words, you can use Personal Study Workbook Starter Unit, Exercise 6, or Unit 1, Exercise 5 in class, before moving on to the matching activity.

Suggested steps

If this is their first exposure to the vocabulary, model the sound of the words by discussing the illustration with your learners, e.g. *What's this? It's an office. It's a restaurant.* This gives an opportunity to show the difference between *a* and *an*.

If the learners have done the Personal Study Workbook exercises, they can go straight into doing the matching exercise in pairs.

When you check answers, you have another opportunity to draw the learners' attention to the difference between *a* and *an*. You could write the three words on the board: *an office, an electrician, an accountant*, underlining the first vowel. You could also make a list of the vowels: *a, e, i, o, u*, with an in front of them.

Answer key

a restaurant: a waiter, a waitress
an office: a secretary, an accountant, a lawyer, a
  businessman, a businesswoman
a van: an electrician, a plumber
a school: a teacher
a surgery: a doctor, a dentist
a garage: a mechanic

Before doing the miming activity, draw the learners' attention to the example to remind them of the question form. Write the statement form and the question form on the board, to show the contrast between them:

Are you a waiter? You are a waiter.

Choose another job from those given and mime it.

Get the learners to mime their own jobs to each other in groups of three or four. If they need words they don't know, encourage them to use a dictionary or show their mime to you.

If your learners don't have jobs, they can mime a job they would like to do.

Ask a few individuals to mime to the whole class. Model the question *What do you do?* and ask them to respond: *I'm a … .*

If time is available, the learners can enter the jobs on their class list at this point, otherwise it can be done at the start of the next lesson as a memory game or warm-up. If there is time, the learners write the sentences in class or they can be given out as homework.

Personal Study Workbook

Unit 1, Exercises 5 and 10: jobs
Unit 2, Exercise 3: question forms

3 Where are you from? ⚏
listening; speaking

Suggested steps

Before listening, establish *I'm from …*, by saying where you are from. Then go round the class and ask the learners: *Where are you from?* Model the weak form /ə/.

Establish the countries by working with the illustration: *This is Denmark, this is Japan,* etc.

First listening: the learners listen, then answer the questions. The tapescript is on page 217.

Answer key

Is Arturo from Mexico?   Yes, he is.
Is Helga from the United States?   No, she isn't. She's from Denmark.
Is Kenji from China?   No, he isn't. He's from Japan.

Encourage the learners to practise the forms during feedback. Ask: *Is Arturo from Mexico?* and help the learners use the short form: *Yes, he is.*

Get the learners working in pairs. Encourage them to ask as many questions as possible, using the vocabulary they have learnt or revised, e.g. the vocabulary in the Help section in Exercise 2.

Personal Study Workbook

1: short and long forms

Quick Checks

There is a photocopiable Quick Check for the end of each lesson. They are on pages 202 to 216 of this Teacher's Book. The aims are:

1. to enable learners to practise the structures or the language learnt in a quick, simple way;
2. to get learners to think about language forms that have been practised but perhaps not highlighted during the interactive activities. For example, the Quick Check often gives examples, then asks learners to make deductions about items such as long forms and short forms.
3. to help learners build their confidence in actually using the language. For this reason, this kind of exercise is not usually very difficult.

The Quick Check can be used for personal practice after the interactive practice of the lesson. Learners can be allowed to do it by themselves, perhaps as homework. This helps them to take responsibility for their own learning. Alternatively, you may wish to use some of

them as short tests of the material learnt in the lesson or the unit.

Quick Check answer key

(i)
a secretary   **an** accountant
a doctor   **an** engineer
a parent   **an** optician

(ii)

Short forms	Long forms
What's your name?	What is your name?
I'm a waitress.	I am a waitress.
He's a mechanic.	He is a mechanic.
She's a nurse.	She is a nurse.

Is your name Lee? Yes, it is.
Is she a teacher? Yes, she is.

A: What's your name?
B: Juanita. And is your name Paul?
A: Yes, it is. What's your address?
B: It's 34 South Parade.
A: What do you do?
B: I'm a dentist. What do you do?
A: Oh, I'm an electrician.

QUICK NOTES

This went well:

....

....

This didn't quite work:

....

....

Things to think about:

....

....

B

1 Where are you now? ⚏
listening

This is a warm-up activity for the vocabulary presented/revised in the next exercises. It is also an opportunity to practise the prepositions of place: *in a classroom*, *in an office*, but *at home*, *at work*.

Suggested steps

Before listening, establish the three places: *in a classroom* – by showing the room if you are in one (or using a picture if you are not in a 'formal' classroom). You can use the illustration for Lesson A, Exercise 2 to establish *in an office*, (*at work*).

Option

If you feel your learners need more practice with these location expressions before you start the activity, use illustrations – either magazine pictures, or pictures on an OHP. Superimpose the picture of a man onto the picture of a classroom. Ask: *Where is he? He's in a classroom.* Then a picture of a woman, in an office. *Where is she? She's in an office ... She's at work.* (This pre-teaches some of the expressions they will need to talk about their friends in the second part of the exercise.)

Let the learners listen to the sounds and indicate their guesses by ticking the right column. They can then check their guesses, either in pairs, or the whole class together.

Answer key

Person 1 is in an office (at work).
Person 2 is in a classroom.

Set up the pair activity by doing it with the class. Tell them the name of one of your friends. Elicit *Where is he now?* or *Where is she now?* and answer: *She's at work. He's at home*, etc. Then get the learners doing the activity in pairs.

Personal Study Workbook

Starter Unit, Exercise 8: prepositions of place

2 In the room, there's a carpet ▭

there's (there is), there are; vocabulary and writing

Option

If you feel your learners need more explicit presentation of the words they are going to hear in the listening exercise, use the room that you are in to pre-teach some of the vocabulary. Point to an item, e.g. a chair, a table, etc. and see if any learner remembers the word for it. You can build up a list of items in the room on the board:

In the classroom, there's a door.
There's a board.
There are four windows.
There are ten chairs. etc.

You can also pre-teach the negative forms, e.g. by writing up:

There's a car. (Cross *car* out and elicit or supply *No, there isn't a car.*)
There are two plants. (Cross *two plants* out and elicit or supply *No, there aren't any.*)

Suggested steps

Work with the illustration. Unless the learners are quite confident with the vocabulary, it may be a good idea to go quickly over the items that they can see in the picture, using the form *In the room, there's a ...* (elicit *table*) *... and there are ...* (elicit *two chairs*).

Let the learners listen and complete the sentences, in pairs or by themselves. The tapescript is on page 217.

Answer key

There isn't a light. There aren't any windows.

Set up the pairwork by using one of the learners as your 'partner' to show turn-taking. You can go round the pairs helping them if they have difficulties, and extending their practice by asking questions which will encourage use of the negative forms, e.g. *Is there a painting?* (Elicit *No, there isn't.*)

Work with the example to show the learners how to tackle the writing/guessing activity. If necessary, write an example of some possible sentences on the board and get the class to say what's wrong. If the class is large, the activity can be done in pairs or even small groups, with each group reading their description to another group.

Personal Study Workbook

3, 4: the vocabulary of rooms and what they contain
9: *there is, there are*

3 Is there a lift in the building? ▭

question forms; short answers

Suggested steps

The first exercise can be done as pairwork if the class is confident with the vocabulary, or as a whole-class activity, if the learners need more overt presentation (leading to further pair practice if there is time). Work with the illustration, draw the learners' attention to the examples, and then ask the first question: *Is there a lift in the building?* Learner A answers, then asks Learner B the next question, and so on.

If the listening is likely to prove demanding for your learners, you can do it in two stages. First, a whole-class exercise: the class listens to the questions and you pause after each question and elicit answers for the building in which you are working.

As the second stage, the learners choose another building in the town. Make sure everyone understands that they are choosing one building, but not telling the other learners which one. An alternative is to get the learners to choose one building in pairs, so that they can consult each other about their answers. Answers can be given orally, in pairs, or written down.

To facilitate the next part of the activity, you could write the key words on the board as the learners listen to the recording; e.g. for the first question, write *a lift?* For the second, write *any parking spaces?* etc. Alternatively, if there is time, do the first one as an example, then ask the learners to listen again and write down the key words. They then ask their partner questions, using the key expressions. e.g. *Is there a lift?* and guess the building their partner is thinking of. The tapescript is on page 217.

4 How good is your memory?
review of *a, an, any,* and vocabulary

Suggested steps

Allow some time for the learners to study the example. They can then write in the missing words by themselves, or with a partner. When checking answers, highlight the singular/plural distinctions, if it seems that the learners need reminding of this point.

Answer key

Are there any escalators?
Is there a lift?
Are there any public telephones?
Are there any parking spaces?
Is there an information desk?

Write the two headings *Things in rooms* and *Things in buildings* on the board. The learners can be encouraged to look through the lesson while you are doing this. When they close their books for the memory quiz, try to make it fun. The learners can try to remember as many items as they can in pairs. The lists can be established orally instead of being written down (there are opportunities here to practise again the forms *There is … There are …*).

Option

If your group enjoys competitions, you could do this as a gentle team game. Divide the class into two and get them to write down the words for the above activity in their notebooks. They then get together as a team and make sure that they have got the spelling and articles right (*a carpet, an information desk,* etc.). Each team can then either write their lists on the board, or call out one word in turn.

Quick Check answer key

(i)
Short forms
There's a light.
There isn't a light.

(ii)
A: Is there a computer in the building?
B: Yes, there is.
A: Is there an information desk?
B: No, there isn't.
A: Are there any parking spaces?
B: Yes, there are.
A: Are there any public telephones?
B: No, there aren't.

 C

The skill focus in this lesson is reading. The text is slightly adapted from a newspaper article and can be a bit challenging at this level, though it is very short, and the main potential difficulties are pre-taught in the first two activities.

The exploitation of the text encourages learners to read for interest; it helps them to extract information, and tolerate some unknown language. These reading strategies are useful ones to develop from the very start in the new language.

1 The important things in a good workplace
vocabulary; adjectives

There are two aims in this pre-reading task:
1. to personalise the theme for the learners, so that they are motivated to read the text;
2. to pre-teach some of the potentially difficult words or concepts that they will need to interpret the passage.

Suggested steps

Work with the illustrations. If necessary, go over each item, modelling sounds and making sure that both concrete items like *workplace* and abstract ideas like *nice people* are understood.
Write down three choices of your own. After the learners have indicated their preferences, draw their attention to the example, then model the conversation with your own choices before asking them to talk about their own choices with others.

Personal Study Workbook
10: reading and writing

2 The important things in life
reading; subject–verb–adjective

The first part of this exercise again highlights the theme of the passage and encourages the learners to express their own opinions about it. The warm-up exercise is framed so that they can show that opinion visually, as a 'sum' in mathematics. This is fluency practice, with the aim being to get the learners to express their own convictions, even if they have to use fairly minimal language. It helps motivation if you accept all attempts at communication, limiting correction or modelling for the time being. You can always jot down any mistakes you hear and do some specific work on them with the class at a later point.

Suggested steps

You can help the learners get started by giving them your own 'sum' as an example. Help them with any difficult terms and supply missing vocabulary they might need. Encourage them to compare their 'sums' with as many others in the class as possible.

Tell the learners that they are going to read the text quickly, without using dictionaries, looking for the answers to two questions:

1. How many jobs are mentioned in the text? 4, 5, or 6?
2. From the text, can they tell whether the three expressions the key thing, the important thing, and the main thing have the same or a similar meaning?

Answer key

5 jobs: nurse, engineer, waitress, teacher, economist
the key thing = the important thing = the main thing
(True: the three expressions have a similar meaning.)

It often helps to set a time limit for the first reading. Adjust this according to the composition and nature of your own class. Many teachers like allowing the learners to read the text quietly on their own to start with, then the teacher reads it out loud while the learners re-read.

The learners can answer the post-reading questions by themselves, then compare their answers with others.

Answer key

Petra: the happiness of her children
Ben: learning new things at work
Luisa: meeting new people
Zoran: having a lot of free time

The final question (comparing what people in the text think and what the learners themselves think) provides another chance for the learners to use any language they have to give personal opinions.

3 What about learning a new language? What's important?
speaking

This exercise recycles some of the structures and words learnt through the reading text.

Suggested steps

Work with the illustration. You can complete your own pie chart as an example. Encourage the learners to use their own ideas and then to compare them with others.

Quick Check answer key

(i)
Adjectives: good, comfortable, main, free, new, interesting, important
Nouns: chair, thing, people, time, job

(ii)
1. The main/important/interesting thing in my life is my family.
2. A comfortable chair is important in an office.
3. A lot of free time is important to my happiness.
4. What about my job? It's interesting/good/important.

(iii)
The subject in sentence 2 is *people*.
The subject in sentence 3 is *job*.
Two verbs: *is, work*
Sentence 3

QUICK NOTES

This went well:

....

....

This didn't quite work:

....

....

Things to think about:

....

....

D   REVIEW AND DEVELOPMENT

The last section of each unit is normally devoted to review and development of previous units. However, in this first unit, Part 1 focuses on classroom language, and Part 2 reviews and practises assumed knowledge about numbers, times and saying where things are.

PART 1 – focusing on classroom language

Warm-ups

Start by getting the learners to carry out simple spoken instructions to establish the context of instruction words, e.g. *Open your book. Put your book on the table/floor/chair. Close your eyes/book. Stand up. Sit down.*

Many teachers know the game Simon Says. Give a series of rapid instructions, some preceded by the words 'Simon says'. The learners carry out the instructions, except when the instruction is not preceded by the words 'Simon says'.

To get the learners to give instructions as well as understand and carry them out, use a chain technique. All the learners stand up. You begin by giving one instruction to a learner. The learner carries it out, gives a different instruction to another learner and then sits down. Continue until everyone is sitting.

Mime instructions and get the learners to supply the words.

1 Language for the English class
instructions for learners

Suggested steps

Get the learners working in pairs for the matching and sentence completion activities.

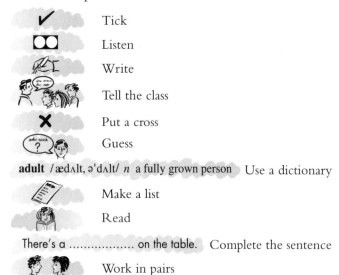

✔	Tick
CD	Listen
	Write
	Tell the class
✗	Put a cross
?	Guess
adult /ˈædʌlt, əˈdʌlt/ *n* a fully grown person	Use a dictionary
	Make a list
	Read
There's a .... on the table.	Complete the sentence
	Work in pairs

Encourage them to compare lists and sentences by writing them on the board or pinning them up.

Answer key

1. Compare your charts in groups, p. 11
2. Put a tick in the table, p. 8
3. Work with a partner, p. 7
4. Read your description to others, p. 8
5. Ask questions and write down the answers, p. 6

Option

The language introduced here could form the basis of a mini dictionary of classroom language, with students adding new items to the dictionary as they arise.

2 What does *salary* mean? CD
questions; listening

Suggested steps

If these questions are new to your learners, practise them using words from Exercise 1, e.g. *What does tick mean? How do you spell 'dictionary'? Could you write 'guess' on the board, please?* etc.

After the first listening, check the questions ticked, and the one not in the list. The tapescript is on page 217.

Answer key

The learners should have ticked questions 1, 2 ,4, 5 and 6.

The question that is not in the list is: What page is it on?

Ask one learner to write it on the board. You can play the recording a second time and ask them to retrieve *pay phone* and *dictionary* (the two words being asked about on the recording).

The learners can continue to practise these question forms while at the same time revising vocabulary from Unit 1.

Example: Learners work in small groups of three or four. Learner A chooses a word from the unit and asks the others: *What does* escalator *mean? How do you spell it?* The others, if necessary, say: *Could you repeat that, please?* etc.

PART 2

The focus here is on saying where things are inside a building.

1 Where's the computer room? It's next to the lift. CD
reviewing expressions of location; listening

Warm-up

If the expressions of location in this exercise are likely to be unknown to your learners, it might be better to establish them using the building in which you are working, before using the illustration in the book.

First, quickly revise the vocabulary the learners have learnt in Lessons B and C: *first floor, second floor, public telephones (pay phones)*.

Mime, then write on the board, vocabulary needed to locate these facilities in your building, e.g. *along, up one floor, opposite, corridor*, etc. Then ask a learner to ask the question *Where's the toilet?* Reply to the question in full, e.g. *Up one floor, along the corridor, opposite room 5.* (Mime at the same time.)

Suggested steps

If you have already introduced the vocabulary through a warm-up, simply allow the learners to do the first part of the activity, then check the answers with them. Otherwise, use the first exercise to establish the expressions of location: *opposite, next to, at the end of.*

Answer key

The incorrect sentence is: Room C is opposite Room B.

Work with the cut-away plan of the school. Introduce the polite form, *Excuse me, where's the lift?* and the plural form, *Where are the toilets?* Get the learners to tell you where the labelled items are in the school, using *It's …* and *They're …*

Let the learners listen to the whole recording. Then play it again, pausing after each speaker, to let them consult each other, write down their answers, etc. The learners can check their answers with each other before the class check. The tapescript is on page 217.

Answer key

The computer room is on the first floor, opposite Room A.

The library is on the ground floor next to Room 1 (opposite Room 2).

To show the learners how to do the guessing game, do it with them yourself to start with. Get them to guess where you have placed one of the items listed. Then get them to choose two items, place them on their plan, and then work in pairs to guess locations.

Worksheets

Supplementary practice with giving directions and saying where things are is provided in the two photocopiable worksheets (Worksheets 1A and 1B) on page 163. You can use them either immediately after you have finished the unit, to revise the vocabulary and structures acquired, or a bit later, to check that the knowledge has been retained. The two worksheets are of the kind that most of you will be familiar with. Learners work in pairs. Each one has the plan of a conference centre with some of the items missing. Without showing each other their plan, they have to label the missing items on their plans by asking their partner questions.

END OF UNIT NOTES

How's the class getting on?

....

....

Language that needs more work or attention:

....

....

My learners:

....

....

2

WHAT HAVE YOU GOT?

CONTENTS

Language focus: *has got / have got*
some (some/any)
subject pronouns and possessive adjectives
contractions

Vocabulary: families and countries
homes and possessions

INTRODUCTION TO THE UNIT

This unit introduces and practises *have got*, using all the pronoun subjects, including *it's got*. The subject pronouns and possessive adjectives which were introduced in Unit 1 (and exemplified overtly in the Personal Study Workbook, Unit 1 Exercise 2) are now practised with both *to be* and *have got*. Unit 2 also begins to make learners aware of areas of meaning covered by *some* and *any*. The two main lexical areas may be fairly demanding in terms of sheer memory work. If your learners have not met the vocabulary before, or have forgotten it, you may want to spend more time familiarising them with it. You can use the more explicit exercises in the Personal Study Workbook to do this, as suggested below. Another possibility is to work with the visual dictionary in class, if there is time.

1 He's got two daughters

have got / has got; vocabulary; discussion

Warm-ups

Many learners at this level will already have been exposed to the vocabulary of the family and may well remember many of the key words, like *mother, father, sister, brother*. If this is the case, you can start directly with the first exercise. (See the suggested steps below.)

If you feel that your learners need more explicit presentation of the vocabulary, you can pre-teach the vocabulary, using yourself as an example, then go on to use Personal Study Workbook Exercise 4 in class.

Option

Indicate to the learners that you are talking about your own family. Draw yourself on the board, labelled 'me' (or your name). Draw your own family tree – at least

one set of grandparents, mother, father, any sisters or brothers, sons, daughters, etc.

Having established the basic vocabulary, get the learners working in pairs to do Personal Study Workbook Exercise 2. In the whole-class checking of the exercise, you can use *have got* or *has got*, e.g. *What've you got for number 4, Jan? Yes, that's right, he's got …*

Suggested steps

Work with the illustrations. Talk about each family group, pointing to the mother, father, etc. Encourage the learners to work in pairs to find the missing words. They then check with other learners before the whole-class checking session.

The learners stay in pairs. They have to identify the person in the paintings who is described in each statement. If necessary, do the first statement with the whole class to show them how to proceed: *Let's do number 1. 'She's got a little sister and a brother.' Is it this person? No? No, that's not a 'she'! Is it this person, then?* etc. Then the learners do the following statements.

Option

Alternatively, in small classes, the activity can be done by the whole group working together.

Answer key

She's got a little sister and a brother: The older girl in Picture A.
He's got two daughters. He hasn't got a wife: The man in Picture B.
She's got two granddaughters and a grandson: The old woman in Picture A.
'We've got a son and daughter': The man and woman in Picture C or Picture D.
He's got one daughter: The man in Picture C, D or E.

Personal Study Workbook

4: vocabulary of families (if not used as a warm-up)

2 Have you got any friends in other countries? 🎧

Have you got ...? questions with short answers

Suggested steps

Introduce the question form and short answers by working briefly with the vocabulary the class has just learnt or revised. Write on the board: *Have you got any brothers or sisters?* and the answers: *Yes, I have. No, I haven't.* Ask the learners about their own family situation: *Have you got any brothers, Juan?* Elicit the short answers: *Yes, I have. I've got one.* or *No, I haven't*, etc.

Talk about the illustration. You can introduce the first question they are going to hear on the recording: *Have you got any brothers or sisters in another country?* Get the learners to ask you the question. (If they find it difficult, write it in full on the board.) Answer it with the short answer only at this point.

Tell the learners to listen to the questions, then tick the right answer for them: either *Yes, I have* or *No, I haven't.* The tapescript is on page 218.

Go over the answers the learners have jotted down before moving to the next part of the activity. This can be done either as pairwork, or in small groups. The learners can start this in pairs, then, when they have finished, encourage them to exchange partners and continue their questioning with other members of the class. Go over the possible questions with the class, showing them the next step for *yes* answers. If you feel they need it, give a demonstration of the kind of exchanges required by getting a learner to ask you the questions, and answering them for yourself.

To prepare for the next activity, it is useful to ask the learners to make notes on their conversations. For example, you could jot down notes of your own answers on the board – (Your name): 2 sisters in ..., no brothers, a friend in England, etc.

Personal Study Workbook

6: vocabulary of families; listening

3 He's got a cousin in Rio de Janeiro

writing a short paragraph

After the interaction of the previous activity, this writing task allows for some quiet consolidation of the material practised. It also shifts the language focus from *I've got, you've got* to *he's got, she's got.*

Suggested steps

Go over the example with the class. Explain that each one is to write a similar paragraph about someone else in the class. (Encourage them to consult their notes if they have taken some in the previous activity.)

To demonstrate the guessing activity, read a short paragraph to the class and get them to guess who it is about. In large classes, learners can do this activity in groups of three or four.

Personal Study Workbook

2: *has got / have got*

Quick Check answer key

(i)
Example: We've got some friends in the U.S.A.
Use *some* with plural nouns, in positive sentences.
Example: Have you got any friends in Mexico? We haven't got any friends in Mexico.
Use *any* with plural nouns, in negative sentences and in questions.

(ii)
Have you got a sister in another country? Yes, I have.
Have you got any cousins in another country? No, I haven't.
He's got a brother in Rio.
She's got a sister in Italy.
We've got a friend in Brazil. We haven't got any friends in Africa.
They've got some friends in America. They haven't got any cousins in Europe.

(iii)
1. She's got some friends in Canada and a pen friend in Edinburgh.
2. He hasn't got any daughters but he's got two sons.
3. They've got cousins in America and in New Zealand.
4. They've got a lot of friends but they haven't got any cousins.

```
QUICK NOTES

This went well:
.........................................................
.........................................................

This didn't quite work:
.........................................................
.........................................................

Things to think about:
.........................................................
.........................................................
```

B

1 He's got some money 🎧

vocabulary: possessions

Warm-ups

Before you use the book, it is a good idea to model the structure and pre-teach some of the vocabulary using realia.

Option 1

Bring a bag of some sort to class with you (handbag, briefcase, shopping bag, etc.). Elicit guesses from the learners as to the contents of your bag, e.g. *What's in the bag?* or *What have I got in my bag?* In small classes, you could ask them to feel the bag and make guesses: *It's a … or Is it a …?*

They may not have the vocabulary yet to make oral guesses, but they can mime them – e.g. they might guess *comb* by miming the action of combing their hair. When they do that, put the words *a comb* on the board and confirm the guess by using the structure: *Yes, I've got a comb* (taking it out) or *No, I haven't got a comb.*

Option 2

Since part of the grammatical focus in this unit concerns *some* and *any*, write guesses on the board in two columns, one for singulars, headed *a: a pen*, etc; the other headed *some*, for plurals or non-count words: *some money, some keys*, etc. This also introduces *some* before the learners hear the recording.

It will probably speed up the first book activity if the words missing in it are pre-taught here: *a pen, money, car keys* and *a mobile phone.*

Suggested steps

Get the learners working in pairs to match the pictures with the words that are missing. In checking the answers, make sure you give a spoken model of any vocabulary that has not been pre-taught during the warm-up. Then let the pairs guess the contents of the handbag and briefcase.

> **Language Point: possessive adjectives**
> Knowledge of possessives has been revised in the Personal Study Workbook, Unit 1, Exercise 2. But if the learners query the possessive form used, briefly explain *my* by showing something of yours: *a key, my key*, etc.

Let them listen for confirmation. As they listen, they could tick the items mentioned on the list that they've filled in. The tapescript is on page 218.

Answer key

She's got a comb, a pen, a handkerchief and her credit card.
He's got some money, his car keys, his house keys, his mobile phone and a handkerchief.
The mirror, the calculator and the portable computer are not on the recording.

Feedback: see how many guesses the learners got right. Check that they caught the items not mentioned on the recording.

Personal Study Workbook

7: more vocabulary of possessions; listening

2 Have you got any car keys?
have got, some and *any*

This activity asks the learners to use the form *we* for the first time. You may wish to establish this before the activity starts, for example by miming *I've got* – then with another person, *We've got.*

Suggested steps

It may be useful to start by giving a model of the two questions that the learners are going to ask by putting examples on the board, like this:

We've got a pen.   *We've got some keys.*
Have you got a pen?   *Have you got any keys?*

Option

If you feel your learners need it, you can have a quick revision/practice of the two questions at this point, using flash cards. Show a picture of a pen, and get the learners to ask you: *Have you got a pen?* Show keys and get them to ask you: *Have you got any keys?* Answer with the short form in both cases: *Yes, I have* or *No, I haven't.*

Get the learners working in pairs and writing lists together. Circulate, and help with the vocabulary needed to make the lists.

Join two pairs together and get them practising questions and answers. You may wish then to have a final whole-class feedback: you ask the first group one question, which they answer; they then ask the second group one question, and so on.

Personal Study Workbook

3: *some* and *any*

3 How many plants have you got? ⟐
vocabulary

The aim of this activity is to revise some of the vocabulary practised in Unit 1 Lesson B, Exercise 2 and extend it by introducing or revising the vocabulary of the different rooms in a home and what they have in them.

The activity introduces the question form *How many …?*

Warm-ups

Pre-teaching the new vocabulary of rooms and revising words like *plants, books, television* will probably make the activity easier for most learners.

Option 1

You can present *How many …?* and simultaneously introduce or revise the vocabulary by using the illustration in the book, or, alternatively, using single, large magazine pictures or overhead transparencies, e.g. *This is a … yes, a sofa. How many sofas are there in the picture? There are two.*

Option 2

After presenting the vocabulary, have a rapid-fire quiz to practise it, e.g. *What have we got in the classroom? Have we got any chairs? How many have we got? Have we got any sofas? How many have we got? Have we got any beds/lamps, etc.?*

The learners can be asked to reply in a variety of ways, either using the short forms: *Yes, we have / No, we haven't*, or simply *Yes/No*. Or they can show *yes* or *no* in non-verbal ways, e.g. *Raise your hands for yes. Clap your hands for no. (Clap once for yes, twice for no.)* The non-verbal form makes a change and allows a bit a movement as well, without becoming chaotic.

Option 3

A variation on the rapid-fire quiz is to start the quiz off yourself, then get the learners to add one new question in turn.

Suggested steps

Make sure the learners understand that they are to fill in the first column of the questionnaire for themselves, (*How many … have you got?*). Then they listen to the recording and fill in the columns about Peter and Sheila. If you prefer your learners not to write in the book, get them to copy the questionnaire onto a sheet of paper.

Answer key

	Peter	Sheila
phones	3	2
radios	none	lots
plants	lots	lots
beds	5	3
books	lots	lots

If you are running short of time, you can continue directly on to Activity 4. If there is time, a general feedback after this activity gives valuable additional practice. The tapescript is on page 218.

Option

Ask the learners the questions, e.g. *How many phones have you got, Pinar?* etc.

You could then tell the learners you've got a certain number (1, 2, 3, 4 or 5) of the things on the questionnaire. Can they guess which ones? Get them to ask you the questions on the questionnaire, and confirm their guesses.

4 Has she got a phone in the bathroom? ⊂⊃
listening

This is a continuation of the previous activity.

Suggested steps

Ask the learners first to answer about themselves, writing *Yes, I have* or *No, I haven't* in the first column of the table.

Play the recording, pausing after each set of questions to allow the learners to fill in their answers about Peter and Sheila. It might be best to check the answers to each one before continuing. The tapescript is on page 218.

Answer key

	Peter	Sheila
a phone in the bathroom?	No, he hasn't.	No, she hasn't.
a television in the bedroom?	No, he hasn't.	Yes, she has.
any plants in the kitchen?	Yes, he has.	Yes, she has.
any beds in the sitting room?	No, he hasn't.	No, she hasn't.

Option

If you would like the learners to get extra practice using *they*, organise a general feedback on the two speakers: *What have they got in their homes? They've got …*

Organise the follow-up conversations which are modelled on the recording. The learners start with one partner, then change partners and report the answers they have just heard. At the end, ask a few learners to report to the class. In smaller groups, the second reporting part could be done as a whole-class 'chain' activity.

Here is a follow-up idea for revising the vocabulary and structures learnt in this lesson. It is a memory game which you can use to round off Lesson B, or for quick revision at the start of the next class.

This is an easy game which incorporates a lot of revision of the structures: *I've got, he's got* and *she's got*. Learners play it in turns, each one remembering what has been said before, and adding one item of their own.

The teacher can start: *I've got a pen.*

Learner 1: *He's got a pen and I've got a pencil.*
Learner 2: *He's got a pen, she's got a pencil, and I've got a comb.*

And so on, going round the class. In larger classes it might be better to play this in two medium-sized groups. Alternatively, one half of the class plays the game, listing things they have with them. The second half then plays the game, listing things they have at home, e.g. a television, a radio, some plants, etc.

Personal Study Workbook

1,2: grammar focus on *have got*
9: vocabulary of rooms and furniture

Quick Check answer key

(i)
Use *a* with a singular noun.
Use *some* with plural nouns – and with the noun *money*.
(ii)

Singular noun	Plural noun	Singular noun	Plural noun
child	children	family	families
sister	sisters	woman	women
country	countries	son	sons
radio	radios	man	men
knife	knives	computer	computers

(iii)

What have you got in your bag? I've got a pen and some money.

How many phones have you got? I've haven't got any.

How many plants has he got? He's got three.

How many books has she got? She's got lots.

I have got is the long form. *I've got* is the short form.

She has got is the long form. *She's got* is the short form.

They have got is the long form. *They've got* is the short form.

QUICK NOTES

This went well:

....

....

This didn't quite work:

....

....

Things to think about:

....

....

C

1 It's got a nice little kitchen
it's got; reading and discussion

This activity extends the practice of *have got* by using *it's got*. Because it revises vocabulary learnt in the first two lessons, there is no formal pre-reading task. It might be a good idea, however, to establish the theme of a motorhome before reading, by working with the illustration or a magazine picture. If anyone in the class has a motorhome, they could have a first go at talking about it – how big it is, what it's got in it, etc.

Suggested steps

Give the learners time to read the text silently. Encourage them to read without a dictionary. They can be told to ask one or two other learners in the group for help if they have difficulties, before asking the teacher. (In some classes, learners work well together if they are placed in small groups and told to help each other with the text.) You may then want to read the text out loud as a way of getting the learners to re-read before they start their tasks.

Get the learners, working in pairs or small groups, to compile their lists. For feedback, you can set up an oral chain. One learner from each group says one thing which the motorhome has got. A learner from another group says one thing which the motorhome hasn't got. And so on, for as long as possible around the class.

Option

Alternatively, the feedback can be linked in to the discussion that follows. Make two columns on the board, one with a happy face symbol (good idea) one with a sad face symbol (bad idea). One learner records reasons for considering the motorhome a good idea or a bad idea. Start with what the motorhome has got, e.g. *It's got a shower* (the learner writes *a shower* under good idea). *It hasn't got a bath* (good idea? bad idea?). Then if possible go on to more general reasons, e.g. *It's cramped* (bad idea); *it gives cheap holidays* (good idea) and so on.

Personal Study Workbook

8: vocabulary of bedrooms; reading

2 My bedroom's my favourite room
vocabulary

Having worked with the vocabulary of rooms in a more limited way, the learners are now invited to try a more extensive description of their favourite rooms. They will use the learnt vocabulary, but extend it with some new qualifiers: *favourite, old/new, small/big*.

Warm-up

It could be useful to pre-teach the new vocabulary before the activity starts. You can do this simply by telling the learners about your favourite room, eliciting questions, and miming to help with vocabulary, e.g. *My favourite room is … . In it I've got … . It's old/new big/small* (put on board). *And I've got …* Get the learners to ask you questions about it: *Is it old? Is it big?* etc.

Suggested steps

Get the learners to list the things in the room under the headings given. If your learners are already familiar with these adjectives, you could add other columns: *interesting things, comfortable things*, etc.

Encourage the learners to make simple plans of their favourite rooms. If they seem to find this daunting, exemplify by drawing a very simple outline on the board and describing your own room: *This is my favourite room. It's my kitchen. It's got a table, here* (point to drawing, or add table symbol to plan on the board), and so on. The learners can add the furniture in the form of small symbols, drawings or words. Having a visual plan to refer to often helps learners when they are describing the room to someone else.

If time is short, you can give this task as homework, or start it in class and get the learners to finish it at home. The oral work arising from it can then be done in the next class.

Quick check answer key

1. What has your motorhome got?
2. It's got a big bed and four little beds.
   (*or* It's got a little bed and four big beds.)
3. My favourite room is the kitchen.
4. We've got some plants over the sink.

For more practice with rooms and furnishings, see Worksheets 2A and 2B on page 164.

D REVIEW AND DEVELOPMENT

REVIEW OF DATES, MONTHS, YEARS

1 When's your birthday? ▭
listening; vocabulary; conversation

Warm-up

Use the chart in the Class Book for a very quick oral revision of the months of the year. Learner A starts with *January*, Learner B says the month opposite in the wheel – *July*, then Learner C continues with *February*, Learner D with *August*, and so on. The aim is to speak as quickly as possible.

Suggested steps

Set the scene by telling the learners when your birthday is, using the structures given: *My birthday's in* (month). *It's on … When's your birthday, Lee?* Elicit a few birthdays from people in the class.

Play the recording once through, then once again, pausing after each one of the speakers to allow the learners to copy the information onto their charts. The tapescript is on page 218.

Answer key

Sam: the second of December
Alex: the third of March
Penny: the sixth of August

Get the learners to put in their own birthdays, then form groups of four to ask each other about their birthdays and mark them on the chart. Circulate and help with difficulties.

Personal Study Workbook

Starter Unit, 5: dates, months, days

2 Favourite months
vocabulary; discussion

This can be done as pairwork or, if your class is small, as a whole-class activity. Do the activity for the class, giving your own favourite month, or perhaps two months, with reasons. Show your reasons by miming or drawing, e.g. *August's my favourite month, because it's hot* (draw a sun on the board).

Learners can use their dictionaries, or ask others or the teacher for help.

The comparison of ideas can be done in groups of three or four.

REVIEW OF UNIT 1

1 The car park is at the end of the street
saying where things are; writing sentences and guessing

The aim here is to revise prepositions and location expressions as a warm-up to the listening activity which follows.

Circulate and help the learners with the first writing activity. Then demonstrate the reading part by reading out four sentences of your own. Depending on timing, you could ask the learners simply to say whether each sentence is true or false. If they seem to need more practice with these forms, you could ask them to offer a correct sentence when they identify one that is false.

2 Where's the Director's office, please? ▭
listening; creative writing

In this listening activity, the learners will hear a man asking his way in a building and trying to find the Director's office. If you think it is necessary, do a quick revision of direction words to set the scene. You could ask the learners to go back to the illustration of the building in Unit 1, and have a rapid-fire quiz (with verbal or non-verbal responses), e.g. *Is the lift next to the exit door? Is Room 3 opposite the toilets?* etc.

Option

Alternatively, revise the nine expressions using things in the classroom or school building.

The listening activity is in four parts, with a pause in between them. Play the recording in parts, and check comprehension and answers at the end of each. The tapescript is on page 218.

Answer key

along the corridor   next to   opposite   one floor down
at the end of the corridor   on the left

Get the learners working in pairs to continue the story. Ask them to write one more part. Provide a framework by writing on the board the last words of the recording:

WOMAN: *No of course not. He's much further on. (Where?)*
Where does Mr. Lee go next? Look at the example.
Knock, knock.
Come in!
What happens next?

Ask the learners to read out their endings, either in small groups, or to the whole class. Each learner takes one part. This is an opportunity to practise meaningful intonation. Learners often read their dialogues in a monotone. If they do this, go over the sentences with them. Give them a model to show how the sentence carries an emotional part that is expressed through intonation. (For example, *of course not* can have a strong stress on *course* to show that the Director is *obviously* not there.) You can even exaggerate the stress a bit, to add to the enjoyment – this is not a very serious dialogue, after all, and reading the ending can be a lot of fun.

Worksheets

As with Unit 1, the worksheets for this unit contain a well-known type of pairwork activity, designed to get learners actually using the vocabulary they have learnt in the unit. This time, each learner chooses from a set number of items, and places them in their plan of a house. This activity can be used at any point in the unit, once the vocabulary of household items has been introduced, in Lesson B, Exercise 3. The worksheets are on page 164.

END OF UNIT NOTES

How's the class getting on?

....

....

Language that needs more work or attention:

....

....

My learners:

....

....

3

WHAT WOULD YOU LIKE TO EAT?

CONTENTS

Language focus: present simple question forms
the verb *to have* (used with meals, food and drink)
asking what people would like and saying what you'd like
countable and uncountable nouns

Vocabulary: food and meals, prices

INTRODUCTION TO THE UNIT

The central theme is food and meals. Although the vocabulary presented is quite extensive, it may be easier for learners to assimilate because it is practical and related to most people's daily lives. Structurally, the unit covers a range of question forms, some of which introduce the simple present tense. Plenty of opportunities are offered for learners to practise asking and answering questions. Exercises in the Personal Study Workbook provide additional stress and rhythm practice to help with fluent pronunciation of questions. There is also a focus on countable and uncountable nouns. These aren't usually a barrier to communication at this level, but it is probably easiest to start establishing control over the forms from the start. The unit does this by asking learners to work deductively with the forms and to reflect upon the rules that govern them.

Warm-ups

Say: *For breakfast, I have …* (mime drinking from a cup and elicit guesses from learners) *and …* (mime spreading and eating a piece of toast and elicit guesses again).

Write on board, for example: *For breakfast, I have a cup of coffee and some toast.*

Option

As above, but use flash cards instead of mime. Let the learners try to guess what's on the flash cards first.

A

1 What do you have for breakfast? 📖
vocabulary; discussion;

Suggested steps

Use the illustrations in the unit to build vocabulary. Finding the four missing words can be a whole-class activity.

Answer key
1. Milk 2. Eggs 3. Coffee 4. Bananas

Option

If there is time, you could also use the illustrations to revise prepositions of place, as in: *Where is the jam, Pedro?* (*next to the …*), or: *What is next to the yoghurt, Rie?*

Listen to the recordings, one speaker at a time, pausing after each. The tapescript is on page 218.

Encourage the learners to check their answers with each other, then have a class feedback.

Answer key

Speaker 1: Table B; Speaker 2: Table C
Speaker 3: Table A; Speaker 4: Table D

The three things in the picture but not on the recording are orange juice, jam and noodles.

Start the interactive exercise by asking the learners: *What about you? Do you have other things for breakfast? What do you have for breakfast? Croissants? Fruit? Yoghurt?* Introduce the question: *What time do you have breakfast?* going quickly round a few members of the class. Model reduced forms as in: *What do you have for breakfast? Coffee and toast.* (As opposed to *I have coffee and toast.*) Then get the learners working in pairs or small groups.

Let the learners ask and answer the full range of questions. Circulate, listening and gently assisting. Show stronger learners the additional questions in the help section.

A short class feedback can act as a link to the more general questions that round off this activity. Ask a few individuals: *What do you have for breakfast, Pedro/Olga?* Then ask each group to choose one breakfast that they think is good. They write it on the board. Compare answers from different groups. What is a good breakfast for adults? Is it good for children also? What is a good breakfast for children? Ask for suggestions and write them on the board.

2 Room Service 🔲 🔲🔲

What would you like? /
What time would you like breakfast? I'd like …

This activity presents and practises *What would you like?*
and *I'd like* as set formulas for requests. At this early
stage, there is not usually any need to analyse the forms,
though it may be useful to signal the long form *I would*
for the short form *I'd*.

Warm-up

Pre-teach the notion of Room Service, by asking
learners: *What are the names of some hotels in …?* (your
town, or the town where they live) *Is the … a good hotel?*
What is room service in a hotel? Use the illustration to help.
Elicit and accept all guesses e.g. *telephone for food / food in
your room / telephone for service.*

Suggested steps

Check that the learners understand the listening task by
eliciting examples of a room number, order and time.

There are two versions of the recording: a simpler
version in which the order is repeated at the end of the
phone call, so that the learners can listen to it a second
time and pick up any details they missed; and a more
difficult version with no repetition of the guest's order.

Option

As in all dual listening activities throughout the book,
you can choose, according to the level of your learners,
either to use only one of the versions, or to use the
simpler one first, followed by the more difficult one.
The tapescripts are on page 219.

Encourage the learners to compare their notes from the
listening.

Answer key

Room number: 308.
Breakfast order: orange juice, scrambled eggs with
    tomato, toast, coffee with cream.
Time: (about) 7.30.

Get the learners working in pairs to practise a similar
order. Circulate, and help with pronunciation and
intonation.

For further communicative practice, another interactive
Room Service exercise is available in the worksheets for
this unit on page 165.

Personal Study Workbook

5: *What would you like?* and *I'd like …* (pronunciation)

3 I'd like some sugar, please

countable and uncountable nouns

Countable and uncountable nouns present problems for
many groups of learners, and this is the reason for
highlighting them at this point.

Warm-up

It is a good idea to focus on the difference between the
two types of noun by using realia to illustrate the first
statements in the book. For example, bring in a few
items that can be counted (e.g. eggs, oranges, carrots,
etc.) and a quantity of something that is not counted
(e.g. sugar, rice, etc.). Go over the statements in the
book, illustrating them with the realia.

Option

Instead of realia, use pictures (e.g. magazine pictures) of
various types of food. Set the scene for the exercise by
asking the learners to say whether each picture is of a
countable or an uncountable noun.

Suggested steps

Let the learners do the matching exercise (putting the
nouns in the right group) alone, or in pairs. Ask them to
check with others before the general class feedback.

Answer key

Countable nouns
apple, peach, banana, noodle, orange
Uncountable nouns
sugar, rice, water, milk, cheese, tea, toast, cereal, butter,
yoghurt, fruit juice, bread

> ### Language Point:
>
> Learners studying in English-speaking countries
> may well have heard exceptions to the rule that this
> activity teaches. For example, they may know that
> English speakers quite often order *Two teas, please*
> when they mean *Two cups of tea, please.* Or they
> may have heard: *How many sugars do you take in your
> coffee? Two, please.* Here the word *two* is a short cut
> for *two spoonfuls of sugar* or *two sugar cubes.* This kind
> of short cut expression is explained in the
> Grammar Reference section, and learners who
> enquire can be told to study the relevant part.
> However, in this first presentation, we have kept to
> the general rule, on the principle that the general
> distinction between countable and uncountable
> nouns is difficult enough for learners at this
> elementary level.

The learners can do the next part of the exercise
(studying the examples and deducing the rules) by
themselves. They then join another person or a small
group to check answers before the whole-class feedback.

Answer key

With countable nouns, use: *a* or *an*, numbers or *some.*
Countable nouns are singular or plural.
For questions, use: *How many?* with countable nouns.
With uncountable nouns, use: no article or *some.*
Uncountable nouns are never plural.
For questions use: *How much?*

Option

If you have time, you might like to try this way of organising the feedback. Divide the class into two (or four in large classes, to produce two sets for each rule). Check their answers quickly, then ask each group to create a poster presenting the rules: one group for countable nouns, the other for uncountable nouns. One or two people can be responsible for showing the rules in a clear, memorable way. The others can work on the examples, trying to find a way to make them visual and striking. You can then display the posters in the class as a reminder of this language point.

Personal Study Workbook

2: countable and uncountable nouns

4 What would you like for breakfast, madam? ▭

speaking practice; writing

Suggested steps

Working in pairs often makes this kind of activity more fun. But if your learners prefer doing it on their own to start with, let them do so and then join a partner to compare answers, before listening to the recording. If some pairs finish early, you can ask them to copy the corrected dialogue into their notebooks.

The recording is short enough to be played through without pausing. The learners should listen and check their corrections.

Answer key

WAITER: What would you like for breakfast, madam?
MOTHER: I'd like some cereal, and some coffee. With hot milk, please. And my daughter would like two eggs, an apple, some toast with butter and a glass of water.
DAUGHTER: No, no, mother. No eggs, please. I'd just like a banana and some rolls – with jam.

You may wish to play the dialogue again to give a model for intonation patterns. Role play it with one learner, then get the pairs practising it together.

If your learners find it hard to think of a dialogue to write, you can suggest various frameworks. The learners can imagine, for example:

– a person phoning room service to order breakfast in a hotel; the staff reply that it's too late for breakfast. The person continues to order …
– a couple ordering breakfast in a café. They are very hungry, but one of them is worried about the cost …
– a parent trying to get a teenager to eat a good, healthy breakfast. The teenager prefers … chocolate? cake?
– one person (a wife or husband?) offering a huge breakfast to someone who is still very sleepy and doesn't want to eat any food at all …

Circulate and help the learners with the writing task. Make sure they understand that they are supposed to

incorporate two mistakes in their dialogue. (Suggest incorrect use of countable or uncountable nouns!)

Note:
Teachers sometimes worry about asking learners to write mistakes. Will the learners not remember the mistakes instead of the correct form? We feel that in this exercise, where learners are creating the mistakes deliberately, then asking others to spot them, they are clearly focusing on the correct form as much as, or probably more than, the incorrect. The mental processing involved in writing, then guessing and reading the correct version, must help in making the particular language point more memorable.

As soon as two pairs complete their dialogue, get them together reading each other's work, spotting mistakes and reading out the correct version. Encourage them to read with emotion! Each pair can then join other pairs as they finish, and do the exercise again.

If you like, and there is time, it is often enjoyable to get one or two of the more amusing dialogues read out loud (in a correct version) to the class.

Option

Another feedback possibility is asking the pairs to write out their corrected versions (perhaps as homework) and put them all up for the class to read during breaks, etc.

Personal Study Workbook

5: *I'd like …*

Quick Check answer key

A: What do you have for breakfast?
B: Just some coffee and some toast. What about you?
A: I have tea and some cereal.
C: What time would you like breakfast?
D: At eight, please.
C: What would you like?
D: I'd like some coffee and toast, please.

QUICK NOTES

This went well:

....

....

This didn't quite work:

....

....

Things to think about:

....

....

This section is designed to build up more food vocabulary, get the learners to use it to talk about their own preferences, and last but not least, help them to become more aware of their own learning patterns. One of the great problems of learning a language is, of course, remembering words, and adults especially often find this particularly difficult. By experimenting with different methods of memorising vocabulary, learners not only see that different people learn in different ways, but they become more confident as they realise that they can take positive steps to influence their own progress.

1 Today, we've got onions, lettuce and cucumber ☐☐
learning vocabulary

Warm-up

In classes with a common first language that you also speak, you can preface this first task by talking about some of the difficulties that learners have in remembering new language, and eliciting how they go about the task of doing so. Listen and accept all comments. At this point, it is best simply to let them state their own opinions. Then explain that they are going to experiment with different methods to see which one suits them best. After the activity, have a feedback to compare notes and discuss whether any of the methods might be useful for them personally.

Suggested steps

Look at the illustration with the class before listening to the recording, or get the learners in groups discussing the various arrangements of food. Ensure that they understand the category words: fruit, vegetables, fish, salad and meat. (They can use their dictionary for any unknowns, or ask their partners.)

If the learners don't come up with them, point out the various types of mnemonics (a device used to help memorisation) used:

1. In the fruit group, the initial letters of each word are used to create a new word, BAPS, which provides a 'hook' to help recall the individual names.
2. In the vegetable group, the initial letters form not a word but a rhythmical and rhyming 'expression', p–b–p–c, which is easy to repeat and also acts as a spur to remembering the names.
3. In the fish group, pictures and names are disposed around a clock, thus providing a visual 'hook' to jog the memory.
4. In the salad group, a 'real-life' situation is used, with dialogue, to make the names more memorable.
5. The meat group offers no mnemonics at all, as a 'control group' against which to test the other methods.

Play the recording once. (Play it again if you think it useful.) The tapescript is on page 219.

Get the learners to study the words and pictures for exactly two minutes. (Time them.) Then get them to write down the names they remember.

Ask the learners to form small groups. They should now put the names they jotted down into categories, according to the methods (1 to 5) in which the food is placed. They then decide whether they remembered more foods from one category than the others.

Encourage them to compare their 'best' categories with others in their group.

Personal Study Workbook

3, 4: the vocabulary of food (and food containers)

2 My favourite food's ice cream ☐☐
vocabulary; conversation

Suggested steps

The first activity can be done by the learners on their own, or in pairs. Feedback can be:

- in groups: get the learners comparing their additions. Go round the groups helping with pronunciation.
- as an oral 'chain': (Learner A: For fruit, *I've/we've got cherry/cherries. What about you, Lena? What have you got?*)
- as a blackboard exercise: write the five categories on the board. Learners add their items to the categories. Go over the pronunciation of the items with them.

> ### *Language Point:*
>
> In the original list, several of the countable nouns are given as plurals, whereas the nouns in the dictionary will of course be singulars. If there is time, you can make this into a teaching point by establishing two lists on the board: *singular nouns*: a pineapple, an apple, a peach, a strawberry, etc. and *plural nouns*: pineapples, apples, peaches, strawberries, etc.
>
> Nouns that are usually considered uncountable include: tuna, salmon, chicken, lamb, beef and duck when the meaning is food, not the animals themselves.

Establish the idea of 'favourite food' (in multilingual classes, mime pleasure) and also the idea of food which is 'good for you', i.e. healthy.

Option

Take in one of your favourite foods. Say to learners: *What is this?* (elicit the answer, e.g. *chocolate*) then continue: *Chocolate is my favourite food, my number one food.* Show pictures of other foods; mime dislike accompanied by, for example: *Butter's not my favourite food.* Ask individuals, using pictures or flash cards as the choices: *What is your favourite food?* Elicit replies (supply the name if necessary) and give the appropriate picture to the learner.

In the listening exercise, the learners are asked to extract a number of food items. If you think your learners can cope, simply play the recording once or twice and then get them comparing answers. The tapescript is on page 219.

Answer key

Speaker 1: pasta, rice, potatoes, tomatoes, strawberries
Speaker 2: spicy food: Indian food, food from Thailand,
Malaysian food; very sweet things: ice cream, cakes
with cream, chocolate cake, chocolate biscuits,
chocolate bars

Option 1

If you think the items are likely to present problems for
your learners, the best solution is to write them on the
board in muddled order. The learners copy them into
their notebooks, then make sure they understand them
by using their dictionaries or checking with others.
Check that they have understood *spicy*. They then listen
to the recording, and write 1 (for Speaker 1) or 2 above
each item.

Option 2

If you wish to make the listening more challenging, add
a few 'distractors' to the list you write up on the board,
e.g. Chinese food, French food, spaghetti, grapes,
melon, duryan, aubergine, etc.

Begin the conversation activity by drawing the learners'
attention to the example. Get one (or all the learners
together) to ask you the question: *What is your favourite
fruit?* Answer it, then ask one of them: *How about you?*
Organise them into small groups so that they can
practise asking questions and answering them with their
own preferences.

Option 1

After the 'guided' conversation on their favourite food,
encourage a more open discussion of international food.
Mention any restaurants in your town or city that
specialise in dishes from other countries. Keep your
language simple, e.g. *Is the Acropolis restaurant good? What
is your favourite Spanish/English dish? What's that? What
things are in it? Is it healthy?* Encourage confident
participation by not correcting unless absolutely
necessary. Make a note of particular difficulties your
learners have when trying to speak freely at this level on
this topic.

Option 2

If your learners show interest in the topic of
'international food' (and if you have time) you might
like to do the Personal Study Workbook reading exercise
on Asian food (Exercise 8) with them in class.

Personal Study Workbook

1: plurals of foods
7: favourite foods from different countries

3 What would you like to drink?

vocabulary practice; discussion

Suggested steps

Get the class to form small groups. You can then set the
scene for the activity by working with the first question.

Give the groups a few minutes to decide, then ask each
one to say where their special meal is: in a restaurant,
etc.

Get the learners to list the food and drink that they
would like the meal to consist of. It is sometimes useful
to impose a time limit, so that the group sharing starts at
the same time for all groups.

Option

Depending on the level of the class (and on the time
available), you may wish to get the learners to complete
the whole activity (imagining the meal; discussing how
to describe food to English guests, etc.) before the
whole-class feedback.

Alternatively, encourage another whole-class feedback at
the end of the first discussions. The learners can
compare their meals by joining other groups, or by
writing 'menus' up on the board first.

They then go on to think of the English expressions
they need to explain the food to English guests, and to
ask guests what they would like to eat or drink. Refer
them to the Help section for some examples of useful
expressions. If time is short, they can prepare this last
part individually, as homework, and report back to the
group (or the class) at the beginning of the next lesson.

Optional Follow-up

If there is time, you can play a food vocabulary version
of Bingo. This can be set up simply by asking the
learners to create a grid of 9 or 12 squares, and to write
the name of one food on each square. You (or a learner)
then call out foods from the unit at random and the
learners cross out words on their grids as they are called
out. The winner is the first person to cross out all the
words on their grid.

Quick Check answer key

1. vegetable   2. fruit   3. fish   4. meat

```
QUICK NOTES

This went well:
.................................................................
.................................................................

This didn't quite work:
.................................................................
.................................................................

Things to think about:
.................................................................
.................................................................
```

1 How much is milk in your country?
talking about prices ...

Warm-up

Take some food items or pictures of them into the classroom. Ask: *How much is this?* Elicit some guesses. Ask: *Are you sure?* Use doubt to establish the concept of *about*, meaning approximately. If you have a group which is not likely to know the price of everyday food items, use other examples to establish the difference between countables (*How much are newspapers? Cigarettes?*) and uncountables (*How much is petrol? Caviar?*).

Suggested steps

Ask the learners to add items to the list, then demonstrate the Question/Answer routine with another learner.

With multilingual groups, it may be necessary to convert currencies into, for example, dollars or pounds if the learners answer in their own money. Make sure the learners know the meaning of your question: *How much is that in (dollars/pounds)?* and write approximate conversion tables on the board if that helps.

2 Is food cheap in your country, or expensive 💿
listening; discussion

In this activity, the learners are going to listen to two extracts from unscripted conversations, in which the language is not kept down strictly to this book's level. It is important that they should not feel too worried about the fact that they will probably not understand everything they hear. The main thing for them is to try to pick out some of the information in the extracts. In monolingual classes, you may wish to discuss this with them before listening. Reassure them that they are not expected to understand everything. (This parallels the experience of beginners trying to understand conversations in English-speaking countries. At first, they can only pick out one or two familiar words. Gradually, more of the message comes through.)

Suggested steps

Before the listening activity, make sure the class knows the meaning of *cheap* and *expensive*. Hold up either a real item that is cheap, e.g. a paper clip, or a picture of one, and ask: *How much is this?* Do the same with something expensive, e.g. a ring, some other piece of jewellery or a watch. Write two columns, *cheap* and *expensive* on the board, and under the appropriate one: *paper clip* and *ring*. Continue: *Is a Mercedes cheap or expensive? Is a glass of water cheap or expensive?* Add them to the list.

Explain that the speakers talk about prices in two different countries, Malaysia and Chile. Try to elicit guesses from learners as to cheap and expensive food items in the two countries.

Here are the answers to the listening exercise. Depending on the level of your learners, you could get them to pick out the more difficult expressions in brackets, or simply omit them and concentrate on the other, simpler words. If your learners have difficulty picking up information from listening, help them by listing the items on the board (use the same procedure as in Lesson B, Exercise 2).

Answer key

Speaker 1: *cheap food*: (food grown in the country); fish, vegetables, rice; *expensive food*: (imported food); strawberries, apples, pears (all European types of fruit and vegetables)

Speaker 2: *cheap food*: all food (especially fresh produce), (fruit grown in the country), vegetables, meat, fish, wine

The first extract is in two parts: first cheap food, then expensive; the second lists only cheap items. Play the recording once or more times if the learners request it. The tapescript is on page 219.

After the learners have compared their answers to the listening activity, you could let them listen again without a task, for relaxation. Then encourage free discussion of expensive and cheap items in your (and/or their) country. With multilingual groups, you will need to be careful not to get too embroiled in converting from one currency to another, though useful revision of numbers could occur. Watch out also that you don't get too drawn into use of comparative forms at this stage.

3 I'm sorry, we haven't got any
role play

This is a familiar type of role play, which learners quite often enjoy. It allows them to practise their new language in an unstressful, game-like atmosphere. If the class is still very hesitant in using the language, the 'shoppers' can simply ask for items on their list, and 'sellers' say whether or not that item is available. Otherwise, make the role play more challenging by getting the 'sellers' to put prices on their items, and asking the 'shoppers' to ask for the price of the items they want.

Option 1

If there is time, this may be the right place for a quick revision of *this*, *that*, *these* and *those*, which are quite useful in a shopping situation.

Before starting the role play, put out one item (e.g. an apple or a pencil) on one side of your desk or table, at the front. Put another single item at the back of the table. Demonstrate *How much is this?* by pointing and contrasting with *How much is that?* Then do the same for two or more items, to demonstrate: *How much are these?* and *How much are those?*

Option 2

Another way of revising *this*, *that*, *these* and *those* is to use Personal Study Workbook Exercise 6 in class.

Option 3

If many groups in the class chose a restaurant as the meal venue in Lesson B, Exercise 3, the role play can be adapted to ordering food in a restaurant.

Suggested steps

Before the role play starts, build up or revise additional language by acting as a shop keeper, and encouraging learners to come to your shop. (Give out flash cards with the food item they want written on it.) Use language like: *I'm sorry, we haven't got any, Yes, they're very fresh, We've got some very nice meat today.*

Then divide the class in two large groups, and into pairs within these large groups. Get them making their lists in pairs. Circulate, and encourage them to list as many things as possible.

It might be a good idea to organise the classroom like a market or a group of shops for the role play.

Organise the 'sellers' on one side of the class, with 'shoppers' circulating and trying to find the items they want.

Encourage the shoppers to talk while they are queuing. While the role play is in progress, monitor the language the learners use, for a quick repair session later.

Personal Study Workbook

6: *this, that, these* and *those* (if not used as a warm-up)

Quick Check answer key

How **much** is milk?
It**'s** about 50 pence a pint.
How much **are** eggs?
What about rice? **Is it** cheap **or** expensive?

```
QUICK NOTES

This went well:
...................................................
...................................................

This didn't quite work:
...................................................
...................................................

Things to think about:
...................................................
...................................................
```

D REVIEW AND DEVELOPMENT

REVIEW OF UNIT 1

1 He's a dentist, and she's an engineer ▭
vocabulary – jobs; pronunciation – sentence stress

Suggested steps

You can go through the list of occupations with your learners or let them use dictionaries to clarify any new items.

The aim of writing the sentences is to check/revise the use of *a* or *an*. The learners then work with whole sentence stress and intonation patterns.

Answer key

I'm an actor.	I'm a waiter.	I'm an engineer.
I'm an actress.	I'm a waitress.	
I'm a doctor.	I'm a lawyer.	
I'm a teacher.	I'm a dentist.	
I'm a builder.	I'm a salesperson.	

Stress pattern ● ● **●** ●: I'm an actor. I'm an actress. I'm a doctor. I'm a teacher. I'm a builder. I'm a waiter. I'm a waitress. I'm a lawyer. I'm a dentist.
Stress pattern ● ● **●** ● ●: I'm a salesperson.
Stress pattern ● ● ● ●: I'm an engineer.

The learners compare their ideas, then listen to the recording for confirmation. They can then listen again and repeat to practise the intonation patterns. The tapescript is on page 219.

2 Are dentists very expensive? ▭
discussion; listening

This activity revises the vocabulary of jobs while extending it by using words learnt in Unit 3, *cheap/expensive*, and adding *free*.

Establish the concepts by whole-class discussion, for example, elicit the meaning of *quite cheap* by indicating that it's not very cheap, but not expensive.

Option

You could draw a line on the board going from *expensive* to *free*. Get the learners to draw the same line and place on it: *dentists, lawyers, doctors, plumbers, builders, car mechanics, handymen*. (They should know all the jobs from the previous activity except for plumber, car mechanic and handyman. Explain these through mime or translation. You can explain handyman as 'someone you get in to come and help with all the chores in your house' which pre-teaches the expression they are going to hear on the recording.)

Ask them to compare their lines with others. In classes of learners from the same country, you could try to negotiate an agreed class line on the board.

Get the learners making guesses about the three countries mentioned in the listening activity. This is simply to motivate them to listen, and to orient them to what they are going to hear.

Answer key

Speaker 1 (United States): doctors E, dentists E, lawyers E, car mechanics, builders, etc. (not mentioned)

Speaker 2 (Sri Lanka): doctors E, dentists E, lawyers E, car mechanics, builders, etc. C

Speaker 3 (Northern Ireland): doctors C, dentists C, lawyers (not mentioned), car mechanics, builders, etc. QC

Emphasise that they do not need to understand everything in the recording. (The speakers use phrases like *system of national health, medical needs*, etc. that do not need to be taught overtly at this point.) All the task requires is for the learners to decide whether the speakers think the various jobs are expensive, quite cheap, or cheap in their countries. If you like, you can give the learners extra help before listening by pointing out that some jobs in the table are not mentioned on the recording. You can even tell them which jobs are going to be mentioned (or alternatively, which jobs are not mentioned).

As they listen, or immediately afterwards, they fill in the yellow boxes to show the speakers' opinions. The tapescript is on page 220.

After feedback from the listening task, you can ask the learners about other services that are cheap or expensive, e.g. private English lessons, computer courses, driving lessons, etc.

REVIEW OF UNIT 2

1 Some change for a phone call ▢▢
group dictation; structure review; sound discrimination

This activity reviews *some* and *any* with a focus on accurately reproducing short dialogues. It is a variation on the well-known technique of dictation.

Suggested steps

Tell the learners they are going to hear a conversation between two people standing near a public phone. The first speaker speaks four times, the second speaks three times. Can they write down as much of the conversation as possible while they listen?

After the first listening, organise the learners into groups of three, tell each group to compare notes and try to write the exact conversation they heard. Remind them that they are to try to write every word and spell each word correctly. Set a time limit (about 5 minutes).

Play the recording again, reminding the learners that they should try to listen for any missing words, or to check what they have written. Different members of each group can be assigned different listening tasks, if the groups think that is a good idea.

The groups continue to refine their written versions of the dialogue.

Option

One member from each group can visit other groups and compare versions, then return to their own group and report on differences and discuss changes to be made.

Play the recording for a final listening and then ask the groups to write out a final version.

Provide the groups with a copy of the tapescript (which you will find on page 220). Each group compares its reconstructed dictation with the original tapescript.

2 Where are the ...? ▢▢
group dictation

Suggested steps

This is a similar activity, slightly longer and more difficult; it can either be done additionally to Exercise 1, or instead of it if the group has strong listening skills. The tapescript is on page 220.

An additional task after this dictation can be to guess where the speakers on the cassette are (in a large office building or a hotel).

Worksheets

Worksheets 3A and 3B (on page 165) allow the learners to recycle the vocabulary they have learnt in the first lesson, as well as the structures *What would you like?* and *I'd like …* They can be used as revision and for extra practice at any point after the end of Lesson A.

Suggested steps

Get the learners working in pairs. One of them has Worksheet 3A and is the hotel guest. The other plays the part of the waiter at Room Service, using Worksheet 3B. When they have finished, first get them to check that the waiter got the order right, then ask them to change worksheets and reverse roles.

Circulate and help with any pronunciation or intonation difficulties. Make notes of any problems for further correction work later on.

END OF UNIT NOTES

How's the class getting on?

....

....

Language that needs more work or attention:

....

....

My learners:

....

....

4

A SENSE OF COLOUR

```
                          CONTENTS

 Language focus:    more question forms with present simple verbs:
                       Where do you ...? Why do you ...?
                       How often do you ...? + present simple verb
                    introduction to present simple verbs in positive
                       sentences: 1st and 3rd person forms

    Vocabulary:     clothing, colour
                    time expressions: never, once a year, twice a year
```

INTRODUCTION TO THE UNIT

This unit extends questions to cover both 2nd person and 3rd person forms, and a variety of *Wh-* questions; a lot of practice of these is provided, and the learners start using the present simple tense in positive sentences, with a few verbs like *to buy, to mean, to give* and *to receive*. The vocabulary focus is clothing, with related areas of colour, fabric, etc. Once again, as with food, the actual number of items presented is quite high, but the words are practical and useful, and there is extensive recycling to help with the learning process.

A

1 100% cotton made in Portugal ▭
vocabulary and conversation; listening

Warm-ups

Model the word for one of your own items of clothing, e.g. *jacket.* Point to your jacket. Ask the learners: *What is it?*

Then say another word, e.g. *socks.* Ask: *Where are they?*

Let the learners guess by pointing. When they point correctly, revert to: *What are they?* to elicit *socks* again. Build up clothes items in this way, using items worn by the learners.

Revise colours and link them to the vocabulary of clothes by saying: *I've got a blue jacket* (pointing to your jacket). Then ask *Who's got a green jacket? I've got brown shoes. Who's got black shoes in the class?* etc. Write up the clothes items to reinforce new words.

If you feel your class needs more overt presentation of clothes items, you could use the first matching exercise in Personal Study Workbook Exercise 5 in class before starting the unit. If you feel they need overt presentation

of colours, use Personal Study Workbook Exercise 4 in class.

Suggested steps

Work with the illustration. Point to a label, or show a copy of one on an overhead or drawn on the board. Ask the learners questions, e.g. *Which country is it from?* Elicit as much language as possible, by asking questions, e.g. *What words are on the label? Are there any other things on the label?* Let them guess which article of clothing it is from by referring to the illustration in the book, asking: *Is it from the jacket? Is it from a pair of socks?* etc. You can introduce *because* here to give reasons for thinking the label belongs to one particular item of clothing, e.g. *It's the label from the jeans. Why? Because it says 100% cotton.*

> **Language Point:**
> Remember to indicate the use of *pair of* as in *a pair of shoes, a pair of jeans.* You can say *one shoe* (a shoe is a separate item), but not *one jean!*

Get the learners working in pairs. They make their list, count the number of examples in the class, and write colours. Circulate and help with any difficulties.

Before listening to the recording, establish the names of one or two materials and the difference between *made of* and *made in*. Use one or two learners from the class and convenient clothes items, e.g. *jacket, tie, skirt* (the words which are on the recording). Ask them questions, elicit (or supply, to start with) answers. Using learners enables you to alternate between the forms: *Where is your jacket from?* and (turning to other learners) *Where is her or his jacket from?* Alternatively, you can use pictures or flash cards.

Tell the learners they can hear the recording twice if they like. Play the conversation through once and encourage them to start filling in the grid. The tapescript is on page 220.

The learners can then compare their answers, or listen once more, then compare.

Answer key

	Clothes mentioned	Colour	Made in	Made of
Julia	jacket	blue	Scotland	wool
Mark	tie	green	China	silk
Suheila	skirt	green	Egypt	cotton

The conversation that follows probably needs no further introduction. You can draw the learners' attention to the example. Except in small classes, it is probably best to get the learners working in groups of about three or four to do this exercise.

Personal Study Workbook

5: clothes (do the second part, if the first has been used as a warm-up)

6: *made in / made of* and pronunciation

2 Are some of your clothes old?
vocabulary; conversation

Suggested steps

If you can actually link this lesson to an international appeal, that will give it added authenticity. Bring in newspaper cuttings showing an appeal for help for a disaster of some kind. If not, work with the illustration in the book to establish the notion of an international appeal.

Establish *summer* and *winter* by miming, or using a calendar. Then ask individual learners this question: *Is your jacket new or old? Are your shoes new?* Ask: *Have you got any old clothes at home? Give me some examples.* Elicit answers from several learners by saying: *What about you, Jorge? How about you, Anna?*

List some of the examples they give under the appropriate heading on the board: *summer clothes, winter clothes,* or *children's clothes*.

The learners then make a short list for themselves.

For the feedback, get the learners to work together in pairs. Draw their attention to the example, and ask them to compare their lists.

Option

If your class finds it difficult to imagine giving their own clothes away for an appeal, adapt the exercise. Ask them: *What kind of clothes are good to collect for an appeal?* e.g. *A coat is good for people in an emergency – let's write that under 'winter clothes',* etc. Then get them, in small groups, to choose one category and write good kinds of clothes to collect under that heading. For feedback, get each group to write their list on the board.

3 Pink uniforms for the police
vocabulary of colours; discussion

This activity is an opportunity for learners to revise colours and start associating them with clothing and other items in their own lives. It also allows a bit of fantasy to emerge in the choice of unusual colours for uniforms.

Suggested steps

Tell the learners to choose clothes and colours that they themselves would like. They can make their choices by themselves, or in pairs, then form small groups to compare with others. Draw their attention to the example, which recycles the structure: *I'd like …*

The learners can remain in their groups to choose and discuss 'good colours'.

Ask the class to consider the colour of the uniforms of the police, traffic wardens and nurses in their country. In multilingual situations, compare the colours in different countries and your country (if different). Ask if they think the colours are nice, OK, smart, etc.

Before the learners choose new colours for uniforms in pairs, go through an example with them first, e.g. a policeman, and elicit suggestions for new colours (white uniformed policemen for peace?). If you have a class where interest in clothes is low (this is sometimes the case in mainly male groups), use other examples like the national flag, national airline, police cars, sports team outfits (e.g. for the Olympics).

During the activity, you can teach and encourage the use of reaction expressions such as: *That's interesting. That sounds terrible. That's a good colour. That's a good idea.*

To set up the last part of this exercise, think of something you own which is an unusual colour. Ask the class to try to guess its identity, by saying, for example: *I have something at home in my kitchen. It's pink. What is it?* Indicate whether guesses are 'warm' or 'cold'. The learners can have a turn asking others to guess, once they understand that it must be something of their own, which is an unusual colour.

Personal Study Workbook

4: (if not used as a warm-up) colours

Quick Check answer key

(i)
1. from; in
2. of; It's
3. in; of; of

(ii)
1. men's clothes
2. a man's tie
3. Mark's shirt
4. women's clothes
5. a woman's dress
6. Suheila's shoes

B

1 Where do you buy your clothes?
listening; question forms: *Where do you buy?*
Where does she/he buy?

Your learners by now should be quite comfortable with clothes vocabulary and should be able to concentrate on the structures practised, especially the fairly complex question form *Where do you ...?*

Warm-ups

Option 1

Take into class three magazine pictures – one showing an impoverished student; a second showing a wealthy-looking woman, and the third showing a wealthy-looking man. Tell your learners that these three people come from your town or city. Give them names if you like.

Hold up the picture of the woman and ask the learners: *Where does she buy her shoes?* Write down their answers or suggestions, but try to elicit particular shop names to increase the scope for exchanges between yourself and the group, e.g. *M and S? Where's that? Is it expensive?* etc.

Continue with the other pictures, then ask the learners to ask and answer similar questions about the other clothes the three people in the pictures are wearing. They can use the answers written on the board for the replies. Practise the question form chorally to build good rhythm, flow and stress.

Option 2

In this warm-up you use yourself as the example. Say to your learners: *Ask me about my clothes. Ask me: Where do you buy your clothes? Where do you buy your shoes?* Write the questions on the board. Give appropriate answers. Then ask one or two learners about their clothes.

Suggested steps

Use the illustration to pre-teach the names of different kinds of shops: *market (stalls), boutique, department store,* etc.

Explain the listening task and check understanding by asking a learner to repeat the task.

This is a dual listening task. First there is a simplified, scripted version, then a more difficult, unscripted version. Choose the first if your class finds listening difficult. The second version has a lot of unknown words and structures; but if your learners are confident with listening tasks, you can use it, reassuring them that they do not need to understand everything, just pick out the information needed for the table.

As in all dual listening tasks, you can play the more simple one first, and check the learners' answers. Afterwards, they could listen to the more difficult version without a task, simply to get more practice in listening.

If your learners are not confident at listening work, stop after each speaker and let them check in pairs. The tapescripts are on page 220.

Answer key

See the tapescripts on page 220.

Get the learners to check their answers with others, then ask for feedback.

If the learners wish, play the recording again and let them listen to all three speakers again, with no task.

Personal Study Workbook

1, 2: present simple questions

2 How often do you buy shoes?
present simple questions and answers; time expressions; *because*

Suggested steps

Go over the question form with the class. Remind them of the change from *do* in *Where do you ...?* to *does* in *Where does she/he ...?*

The time expressions can be demonstrated quickly by drawing lines on the board. The first line goes from January to December. Put one cross on the line, explain this is *once a year*. Two crosses on the line mean *twice a year*, etc. Another line can be drawn for months, if you would like the class to extend their vocabulary consciously to *once a month, twice a month*.

Divide the class into groups of three. Circulate during groupwork to help and to note mistakes for later correction. The help section gives learners an option of what to say if they don't buy their clothes personally very often.

Allow a short feedback to practise the *you* and *I* forms. The next activity will focus more particularly on the 3rd person, *he* or *she*. Get a learner to ask you one of the questions from the exercise. When you answer, 'bounce' the question back to someone: *What about you, Sandra? How often do you buy dresses?* They then ask you a further question.

3 She buys her blouses in a department store

present simple: 3rd person

The Class Book suggests an oral feedback for the previous exercise, which can be done either as a whole class, or in groups (for example, in a large class, two groups could be formed).

Option

If you feel your class needs more writing practice, ask them to write one or two sentences about someone else, from the conversation they've just been having in their groups. You can then either get them to read the sentences out, or compare them with a partner. Alternatively, collect them in and repair major errors to the present simple 3rd person structure that is being highlighted. Next class, use the descriptions for a guessing game that revises the forms at the same time: *She buys her shoes at the market. She never buys hats. Her husband buys her dresses. Who is she?*

Personal Study Workbook

3: 3rd person forms, using the verb *prefer*

4 Where does Alex buy clothes? ▭

practice with the 3rd person form; listening

The last exercise in this lesson offers a more conventional kind of 'fill in the blank' writing practice. This allows the learners to consolidate the patterns that they have practised in the oral exchanges that have preceded.

As the learners have been doing a lot of interacting, you can let them have a change of pace by asking them to do the task quietly by themselves. Ask them to compare their answers with a partner before listening for confirmation. The tapescript is on page 220.

Answer key

1. Where *do* you buy your ties, Lee?
   I *buy* them at the market, because they're cheap and colourful.
2. I *buy* my shoes from a department store, but my mother *buys* her shoes at the market.
3. How often *does* Leah buy jackets?
   She *buys* jackets twice a year – in the summer, and in the winter. I sometimes *buy* a jacket in the winter – never in the summer.
4. Where *do* your parents *buy* their clothes?
   They *buy* clothes from Marks and Spencer's, but they *buy* shoes from a little shoe shop near their house.
5. Do you and your friend *buy* your hats at the same shop, Franz?
   No, of course not! I *buy* my hats at the supermarket. She *buys* her hats at a hat shop, or sometimes at the market.

Option – Follow-up

With classes that enjoy project-type work, the topics just examined can lead to a variety of follow-up activities.

The advantage of this kind of work is that it extends the use of the new language from the learners' classroom to their own environment and lives. Learners can get very involved in the slightly different, more self-directed tasks. Finally, working collaboratively on them often reinforces solidarity within groups.

1. Clothes and fashion. As homework, ask the learners to look through current newspapers and magazines. They should cut out and bring to class some pictures of clothes that they find striking. In groups, they prepare descriptions of the fashions to present either orally to the class, or in the form of a poster, or as a fashion 'magazine' with pictures and short written descriptions.
2. In multinational classes, the learners might like to do a more extended piece of work on their own national dress patterns, historical costume and/or everyday dress. Exercise 7 in the Personal Study Workbook could be a starting point here. The learners could write a short description of clothes people wear in their own countries, illustrating it if at all possible with photos, magazine pictures or pictures from tourist brochures, etc.
   In single nationality classes, you could adapt this exercise and ask the learners to research the national dress of a country quite different from their own. They then write descriptions of their own clothing patterns, comparing and contrasting with the other country, and illustrating with pictures.
3. Shops. Get the learners, perhaps in pairs, investigating the various places to buy clothes (or other goods, if you wish to extend their vocabulary range) in their town (or nearest town). They can take notes about prices, variety and range of items offered. The worksheet for this unit on page 166 gives help with the structuring of this third project, on shops, and also gives suggestions for feedback.

Quick Check answer key

1. b   2. a   3. d   4. c

QUICK NOTES

This went well:

....

....

This didn't quite work:

....

....

Things to think about:

....

....

The focus in this reading-oriented lesson shifts away from clothes to the topic of colour, and what colours can signify. Even at this early stage, we feel that it is useful occasionally to move slightly away from the very functional, 'survival-language' approach that is the necessary core of elementary courses. Here the learners are asked to personalise the topic of colour, focusing upon the non-literal, metaphorical connotations that are related to individual preferences, but also to different cultural contexts.

Warm-ups

Bring in realia of different colours, e.g. a bouquet of flowers of different colours; small articles of clothing in different colours, e.g. scarves or ties; jewellery, small ornaments, pens, etc. in different colours. Set them out on a table and ask the learners to react to them (facial expression can be exploited here!) and choose their favourite. In this way, words that might present difficulties can be pre-taught, e.g. *flowers*.

Option 1

The same activity can be done with pictures – either magazine pictures or reproductions of paintings that have a strong central colour atmosphere.

Option 2

Since the learners are going to be asked to draw out the emotional and cultural implications that colours have for them, a strong warm-up with classes that like imaginative activities is the identification of colours with music. Bring in recordings of at least three or four different types of 'mood' music, e.g. slow and romantic, martial, swinging, down-to-earth folk song, passionate, etc. Play the music and ask the learners to shut their eyes (if they are willing to do this). They 'visualise' the colour that comes into their mind and is associated with the music. They can either compare their impressions with others immediately after each piece, or jot the colour down and compare after all the music has been played.

1 Red means money or good luck
3rd person singular; means; writing

If your learners enjoy working together, get them working in groups to discuss these sentences and write one set of answers for their group. Otherwise get them to write their answers individually (tell them they need choose only two or three of the colours) before comparing their ideas.

Depending on the time available, get the learners or groups to read out their sentences, or pin them up for the class to read and compare.

Personal Study Workbook

7: the meaning of colours in different countries

2 What colour are roses?
speaking; reading

This activity is in three parts – the pre-reading task, the reading itself, and two post-reading tasks, the first focusing on response to the text, the second on extending understanding of language and meaning.

Suggested steps

For the pre-reading task, ensure that the learners know the meaning of *roses*, *songs*, and *receive*. This can be done rapidly with the whole class, with concrete examples (realia, pictures) and gestures. Alternatively, you can simply write the three words on the board and get the learners to check their meaning by using dictionaries or asking others in the class.

Encourage discussion of the questions, as these set the scene for the text they are about to read.

Ask the learners to read the text through once by themselves. Encourage them to read for gist, without dictionaries, to get a general impression of what the text is about. It is very important for them to develop the confidence to do this without feeling they need to understand every single word before they can get the general meaning. They can then compare their ideas with others, asking them about any difficulties they have encountered. As with other reading tasks, you may wish to read the text aloud after this is completed. Read it with a lot of feeling (especially the part about giving roses to family and friends). This often helps the learners understand the emotional colouring of a text.

After reading the text, ask the learners to write down one interesting thing about it, individually. This stimulates re-reading in a focused way. It also gives a concrete point around which discussion of reactions to the text can be organised. Encourage the learners to try to say why they do or don't like the idea of the new rose. (Some may like innovation, others may not like 'tampering' with nature, some may have reservations about the artificiality of the process.)

The final exercise gets the learners to revisit the text and consider its language more closely. You can see from the answers, and also from how difficult your learners find this exercise, how well they have understood the text. It could be set for homework if time is running short.

Answer key

1. Roses are favourite gifts from men to their girlfriends or wives, and women also give roses to their family and friends.
2. Cut flowers are an important business – many billions of dollars worldwide.
3. … it's not so easy to change the colour of songs!
4. The rose is a very popular flower all over the world.
5. Roses mean many things: *I love you, thank you, I'm sorry.*

Personal Study Workbook

8: reading
9: reading and writing

Quick Check answer key

1. gives   2. say   3. means   4. receive

```
┌──────────────────────────────────────────┐
│             QUICK NOTES                    │
│                                            │
│  This went well:                           │
│  ........................................  │
│  ........................................  │
│                                            │
│  This didn't quite work:                   │
│  ........................................  │
│  ........................................  │
│                                            │
│  Things to think about:                    │
│  ........................................  │
│  ........................................  │
│                                            │
└──────────────────────────────────────────┘
```

D   REVIEW AND DEVELOPMENT

REVIEW OF UNIT 2

1   Lost and found ▭▭ ▭▭
listening

Suggested steps

Before listening, establish the idea of a Lost and Found office. Monolingual classes could provide a translation in their own language.

The listening task is in two stages. The first set of exchanges which the learners hear are short, and they merely extract the information they need to fill in the missing parts of the table. After the first listening, get them to check their answers with each other. The tapescript is on page 221.

Then they listen to the longer exchanges. Tell them they may not understand everything. If they wish to, they can hear it a second time. All they need to catch is the kind of bag in each case: a suitcase, a briefcase, or a handbag. In the first exchange for example, they may not know *a sort of fabric* but they have learnt *made of*, so they can at least deduce that the expression means some kind of material that is dark blue.

Get the learners to check their answers with others before you confirm them for the whole class.

Answer key

Speaker	Colour	Made of	Kind of bag
1:	black	leather	briefcase
2:	red, with a white strap	plastic	handbag
3:	dark blue, with some brown	fabric, with a bit of leather	suitcase

2   At home, I've got a very big suitcase
writing sentences; speaking

Suggested steps

It may be helpful for you to go through the three questions with the whole class before starting this activity. Tell them about a bag you have at home, e.g. a suitcase, a briefcase, a shopping bag. Write your own answers on the board. Then get the learners to write their answers. For the question *What's in it?* get them to imagine the bag as it usually is, or when it's being used, and encourage them to keep the answers simple, e.g. *My briefcase has papers, a pen,* etc. *My shopping bag has food, bottles of water,* etc.

Collect all the papers, mix them up, and divide them into piles of three or four. Hand the piles out to some of the learners. The learners without piles start asking questions to find their bags. The learners with the piles consult their papers and reply.

For example in a class of twelve, make four piles of three answers, give the piles to four learners. The eight without piles start questioning the four with piles.

As soon as a learner finds their own bag, they take over the pile and the learner who was holding it has to begin questioning to find their own bag. Learners who have found their bag and handed on their pile to someone else sit down.

Large classes can be divided into two groups, to reduce the time taken. A time limit can be set – see how many people can manage to find their bags in, say, five minutes.

REVIEW OF UNIT 3

1   What is good with rice? ▭▭
vocabulary; listening

This exercise revises and builds on food vocabulary, and gives further practice with simple ordering (*What would you like? I'd like …*)

Suggested steps

Draw a simple picture of a fish. Ask: *What's this?* Elicit *fish.* Ask general questions like: *Is fish popular in your country / in your family? Is fish good to eat? What things are good to eat with fish?* Build up a list on the board. Help with pronunciation.

Let the learners work in pairs to find other things that are good with chicken and rice.

Have a plenary feedback briefly, by asking pairs: *What have you got for chicken/rice?* Encourage the learners to build up their description of any unusual choices.

Suggest that the learners look at the menu. Ask them: *From which country is curry / kebabs / roast chicken?* (Accept all answers, since strict accuracy is not really the point.) *What are they?* (Review unknown words that are on the recording, like *plum sauce.*) *Are they good to eat? What is a dessert?*

To prepare the learner for the listening task, ask them what the waiter says when he comes to the table to take your order from the menu. Elicit: *What would you like?* Ask one or two students to order from the chicken menu (Elicit *I'd like chicken curry …*)

Tell the learners that on the recording, someone is in a restaurant with the chicken menu but there is a problem. Guess: *What is it?*

Play the recording and ask for feedback about the problem (many of the things on the menu are not available – the restaurant doesn't have them). Ask: *What does he have to eat?* (Mime *eat.*) The tapescript is on page 221.

Play the recording again to confirm the answer.

Answer key

He has chicken and egg custard.

When the learners write their own menus, you might like to prepare a decorative menu card as a template, for added realism. (Or give the learners a menu-sized card and ask them to decorate it.) These cards can then be used in the role play as props.

If your group is confident, they might like to change pairs, so that one of the pair receives a menu that they haven't seen before, and has to improvise. With a less confident group, build up a model role play with the whole class first, using a menu from one of the pairs.

With a small class, the learners can rotate so that sometimes they are waiters, sometimes customers in different restaurants.

Worksheets

The worksheet for this unit is on page 166.

The aim here is to encourage the learners to work together to find out more about shopping facilities in their own town (or their nearest town). It is usually a good idea to start by explaining the format of the feedback, so that the learners think about it right from the beginning.

The feedback can be in the form of:

− a report (made orally to the class, or handed in as a written assignment);
− the creation of a 'brochure' (for visitors to the area) giving details of the various shopping facilities;
− a visual presentation on a poster (with photos, if the learners enjoy taking them) and short descriptive texts, comparison graphs, etc.

The last two feedback options involve slightly more lengthy preparation, but they are often highly motivating for learners.

Get the learners working either in pairs, or small groups of three or four at the most. (This allows them to put in more individual effort.) Give each member of the group a copy of Worksheet 4, and encourage them to discuss it together in class. The actual research, writing down notes, etc. is done out of class, usually as homework

(although in some classes an expedition into the shopping areas of the town during lesson hours, if there is time, can sometimes provide a welcome change and be very motivating). Allow some class time for them to prepare the feedback format that you (or they) have chosen.

Display the results (the written passages, the posters or 'brochures') in the class and let the learners mill around and view them.

END OF UNIT NOTES

How's the class getting on?

....

....

Language that needs more work or attention:

....

....

My learners:

....

....

5

GOOD HABITS, NEW ROUTINES?

CONTENTS

Language focus: present simple verbs: positive, negative, questions
frequency adverbs

Vocabulary: daily routines
habits and customs

INTRODUCTION TO THE UNIT

This unit gives the learners a lot of opportunities to practise verbs in the simple present, and to link them with adverbs of frequency. Present simple question forms have already been previewed in Units 3 and 4, but here a wider range is presented, with emphasis on *Do you …?* and *How often do you …?* The unit begins by presenting the verbs with *I* and *you*, with the third person form being introduced at the end of the first lesson. The topic areas create a setting which exemplifies the fact that this tense is used for actions that happen regularly or repeatedly (daily routines) or that are customary or habitual.

1 Are you a morning person?
present simple verbs: 1st, 2nd person

Warm-ups

You may feel that with your particular learners it would be useful to pre-teach some of the many verbs they are going to meet in the questionnaire, by using mime or illustrations of some kind, flash cards, magazine pictures, OHP pictures, etc. A problem with this procedure is that it naturally leads to the present continuous, (e.g. *In this picture she's having breakfast*), which may be confusing for the learners. One way of avoiding the confusion is to present the vocabulary initially as your own description of what you do *every morning*. In multilingual classes, the concept of *every morning* and *usually* may usefully be established here by showing a calendar: *on Mondays, Tuesdays, Wednesdays, every day, usually, …* Mime or indicate the picture: *Every morning, the alarm rings, I …* (miming or showing an illustration) *… Yes, I wake up* (write on board). Build up a step by step sequence of what you do every morning.

You can have a quick confirmation by getting the learners to ask you questions, e.g. *Do you get up?* which

is a way of introducing the short answer forms: *Yes, I do. I usually do. No, I don't.*

Another lead-in to the questionnaire is through an exploitation of the illustration. *What's this? An alarm clock. What time is it? Yes, it's seven thirty. Is it morning?* etc.

Suggested steps

Go through the items with your learners. Imitate the sound of an alarm clock ringing and ask the learners: *What do you do …? Do you …?* Mime the verbs that have not been pre-taught in the warm-up. Indicate that the learners should make a choice and tick it.

It is often fun for the learners if the teacher does the activity as well. If you have the facilities, you could photocopy your answers onto an OHP transparency, so that you can use it as a basis for comparison with the learners' own answers.

When the learners have made their choices, encourage comparison of the results, and give them their 'Profiles':

Four or more ticks in column A – you are definitely a morning person.

Four or more ticks in column B – you are definitely not a morning person.

Same number of ticks in A and B – you are sometimes a morning person, sometimes not.

Your class might like to find out how many of them are 'morning persons'.

Personal Study Workbook
4: daily routines

2 First thing in the morning
present simple practice

This is really pairwork feedback and practice using the material from Exercise 1. Depending on the time available to you, you could set the learners a minimum number of questions for them to ask each other, with faster pairs moving on to further questions.

The question about the weekend is designed to allow some feeling of extension, of more genuine communication with the pattern the learners are using.

The help section gives additional expressions useful for an interactive situation.

Personal Study Workbook

1: more practice with questions

3 She has a cup of coffee ▭

present simple: 3rd person

Here the focus is the 3rd person singular form of the present simple. The learners hear the first person form, but the written form they work with is the third person.

Suggested steps

Go over the sentences in the book, modelling them for the class. Ask them to guess the order, then play the first monologue for confirmation. You could have a quick confirmation of the 3rd person form by asking the learners to give you the order: *First she …, then she …, then she …*

Follow the same procedure with the next monologue. Both are unscripted, but this second one is less straightforward, because the speaker goes to the bathroom and has a quick wash before breakfast, then he goes *back* to the bathroom and has a shower after breakfast. As you go through the sentences, you can help the learners by indicating/miming the meaning of *back* – he goes again, he goes a second time.

For either monologue, you can get the learners comparing their guesses, then ask them to write sentences on the board in the order they have decided upon. The monologue can then be played once, for confirmation, and once or twice again as the learners try to get as much of the missing information as they can.

The tapescript is on page 221.

Answer key

Speaker 1
1. She goes straight to the bathroom.
2. She has a bath.
3. She has two cups of coffee.
4. She has a slice of toast.

Speaker 2
1. He goes to the bathroom.
2. He has a quick wash.
3. He goes downstairs.
4. He makes breakfast.
5. He has tea and two slices of toast.
6. He goes back to the bathroom.
7. He has a shower.
8. He gets dressed.
9. He leaves the house.

If you have a spare moment in this or the next two lessons, you might like to try one of the optional quick games that revise the present simple. This will help the learners internalise the new structure.

Option 1

Chain revision. The first person begins by saying one thing that they usually do in the morning (e.g. Learner A: *I have a shower*). Each succeeding player repeats the previous speaker's sentence and adds one of their own (e.g. Learner B: *He has a shower, and I brush my teeth.* Learner C: *She brushes her teeth, and I have a cup of coffee.*).

In small classes, and if there is time, a second round can be played, with each learner giving the previous two sentences before going on to their own.

Option 2

Take out your front door key and tell your class what you do every day when you get home from work, miming if necessary, e.g. *I open the front door, I pick up my mail, I go upstairs, I have a cup of coffee.* Ask them to do the same with their partner.

An extension is to follow this up by saying: *You have a magic key. When you open the door, you can find anything you want. Think about that, then tell your partner what you find when you open the door.*

Another extension is to think about a famous person in your country: a politician, pop star, etc. What does that person do when they get home at night? (This revises the third person form.)

Option 3

The learners stand in a circle. You start the activity by saying one thing you don't do in the morning when you're on holiday, e.g. *When I'm on holiday, the alarm doesn't ring in the morning. I don't get up until eleven. What about you?* Instead of saying the nominated learner's name, throw a ball. The receiver answers, then asks another question, throwing the ball to the person who is to reply.

Option 4

Get the learners to write out a list of five things they do first thing in the morning (e.g. on workdays). They then stand up. Learner A starts by asking a question of Learner B: *Do you have a shower, Patricia?* If Learner B has written I have a shower on her list, she answers *Yes, I do* and sits down. Learner A can then question Learner C. If Learner B hasn't included a shower on her list, she can answer *No, I don't* and she then gets a turn to ask Learner C a question. (In large classes, divide them into two groups.)

Personal Study Workbook

2: vocabulary of daily routines; collocations
3: all the present simple forms

Quick Check answer key

A: wake/get
B: do
A: don't; up; wakes/gets; have; has; gets; have

B

The focus here is on interactive practice of frequency adverbs.

1 How often do you sleep with the lights on?

vocabulary; conversation; frequency adverbs

In this activity, the learners indicate their answers to questions by standing against a wall, instead of writing them down. Apart from the advantage of getting people out of their seats and moving a bit, the fact of indicating opinions so openly can often help stimulate comparison and discussion.

Suggested steps

If necessary, establish the notion of *never*, *sometimes* and *often* by using a weekly or monthly calendar and by telling the learners about your own habits: *I often sleep with the lights on* (Monday, Tuesday, Wednesday, every day); *I never eat in bed* (indicating a negative by miming, shaking your head, etc.).

Establish the two ends of the wall as the two extremes: *never* and *often*. You could put up notices, or write on the board. Draw the learners' attention to the illustration in the Class Book.

Once again, it may be useful for you to go through the questions with your learners, miming them as you go (or using illustrations). It may be fun for your class if you show your own habits by taking up a position on the wall as well.

Each time the learners take up a position, they should then add a sentence to their lists of habits, e.g. if they have replied to *How often do you eat in bed?* by standing at the *often* end, they write: *I often eat in bed.* An alternative is to get people who stand together to write their sentences together, e.g. Mala, Roberto and Sange: *We never smoke at work.*

2 It's a very bad habit! 🎧

writing a conversation; listening; speaking

This activity is a writing and listening activity where the learners extend their stock of present simple verbs and use the models for practice and to start building their own conversations.

Suggested steps

Help the learners get started by exploring the illustrations with them: *What is the situation? Who are these people? Are they happy/sad?* etc.

The next activity can be done in pairs or small groups. The learners order the speech bubbles to create a coherent conversation.

In each case, the last line of the conversation is missing – the empty speech bubble. Each pair or group writes a last line to the dialogues. They might like to read their dialogues to another pair before they listen to the recording. The tapescript is on page 221.

When the learners have listened to the two conversations and put the sentences in order, let them check their answers with another pair or with you. The final line can be taken down as a dictation. Then play the first conversation again, to allow the pairs to practise it.

The short conversation is designed to allow the learners to use whatever vocabulary they can summon up from their lessons so far and use it to communicate. Encourage them to take risks and help them by supplying any missing words they need to express their thoughts.

Personal Study Workbook

6: habits: present simple

3 Language learning habits 🎧

discussion; listening; writing; asking questions

The aim of this activity is twofold: it revises and extends knowledge of present simple verbs, and it also allows the learners to reflect on their language learning habits, increasing their awareness of different possibilities.

Suggested steps

Ask the learners to tick the appropriate sentences by themselves. They can then join others in small groups to compare what they do to learn English. Circulate, helping interaction.

Have a quick whole-class feedback. Ask the learners: *How many of you ticked 'I use my dictionary?'* If you write the sentences on the board (or on an OHP transparency) you can add ticks to record how many learners used each method so that the learners can see which methods are most popular in the class.

Make sure your learners understand the situation they are going to listen to on the recording. Explain that the teacher is talking about her own students, whose names appear on the page. It is also useful to go over the true/false statements with the class before they listen. This increases their familiarity with the topic, and makes comprehension easier. The tapescript is on page 221.

Answer key

1. T   2. F   3. T   4. F   5. T   6. F   7. T   8. F

After the learners have checked and compared their answers, get them working in groups of three. Tell each group that they must write three questions. (You can change this depending on the level of your learners, and how much time you have in the lesson.)

When the groups have written the required number of questions, the learners can either find a partner from another group and ask them the questions they wrote, jotting down the answers, or you can structure this as a milling exercise, with the learners asking as many people as they can the questions, and jotting down the answers.

Personal Study Workbook

5: an exercise to help the learners remember verbs, and become aware of their learning patterns

Quick Check answer key

1. Do you use your dictionary? Yes, I do.
2. Does she listen to English songs? No, she doesn't.
3. Do you write down new words? Yes, I do.
4. How often do you eat in bed? Sometimes.
5. How often does she wash up? Quite often.
6. How often does he sleep with the lights on? Never.

QUICK NOTES

This went well:

....

....

This didn't quite work:

....

....

Things to think about:

....

....

C

This lesson focuses first on national customs, then on shopping habits. Expressions of frequency are extended and practised.

1 People kiss on both cheeks
practice with present simple verbs; conversation

This activity can elicit varied responses in multinational classes, but even learners in monolingual classes often have a surprising diversity and richness of background.

You can often elicit this by seeing how many people in the class have parents or grandparents who come from different countries or relatives who have gone to live in different countries.

Suggested steps

Get the learners to use the illustrations and make guesses. You could start them off with one of the sentences they are more likely to know, e.g. *People eat a special cake for their birthday*, and then let them continue the exercise in pairs.

Answer key

1. D   2. F   3. E   4. C   5. B   6. A

Once again, it is probably more important for the learners to feel they can say something about these customs than it is for them to find 'right' answers. Some possible answers to the question about countries follow, but there are many other possibilities, which may well crop up during the exercise and which can make it much more interesting and enjoyable.

Answer key
Some possible answers:
1. Japan, Malaysia
2. European countries such as France, Belgium, and on formal occasions in the UK and the USA
3. France, Belgium
4. Some Muslim countries such as Pakistan, Malaysia, Arab countries, …
5. European countries, the UK, the USA, Canada, Australia
6. Although sometimes considered a very British feature, queuing is something that happens in different circumstances in many countries over the world.

Encourage your learners to add other customs and talk about them – in groups in large classes, though this could be a general discussion in smaller or medium-sized classes.

2 How often do you go shopping? ⬜⬜ ⬜⬜
more frequency adverbs; listening and speaking

There are two versions of the listening. The first is scripted and fairly simple; the second is unscripted, has more unknown elements, and is slightly more rapid. Use them in the same way as other dual listening recordings.

Suggested steps

The sequence here is: the learners start with a simple statement to complete and compare their answers with others. Next, they listen to other possibilities and then try to extend their conversational range by using a variety of questions.

The second, unscripted extract is designed to help the learners overcome panic when they listen to a flow of English at natural speed. Emphasise that they do not need to understand everything – just picking up the frequency expressions is a good achievement. You can point out that this kind of listening happens outside the classroom when people try to pick out essential information from announcements, for example in railway stations or airports.

The tapescript is on page 222.

Get the learners to check their answers with one or two others, then give a whole-class confirmation.

If there is enough time and the learners are keen, you can let them listen to the exchanges again (or if they have listened to the first, they might try the second) to see how many more details the class as a whole can now supply.

Answer key

Speaker 1 goes shopping once a week.
Speaker 2 goes shopping every day.
Speaker 3 goes shopping on Saturdays / once a week.
Speaker 4 goes to the bakery every day and to the
    supermarket once a week.

3 What do you do in a long queue?
speaking

The frequency adverbs are recycled in this activity. If the notion of queuing needs to be pre-taught, you could do it by working with the illustration and talking about times when you usually queue, e.g. *I queue every morning for the bus. It's very boring. Do you queue?*

The discussion questions after the learners have filled in the table can provide feedback for the class as a whole. An alternative feedback, if you have time, is the following option.

Option

Organise a mini-debate on the question: *Do you think queuing is a good thing or a bad thing?* Get the learners to indicate their opinion in some way, e.g. those who think it's a good thing move to the front of the class, others to the back. They then have a set time, e.g. 5 minutes, to prepare arguments for their point of view. Put some starter ideas on the board:

> *orderly   fair   peaceful   gives you time to think   boring*
> *doesn't work   people get frustrated*
> *other people jump the queue.*

When the time is up, the two teams get into two lines and in turn give their reasons. Each team tries to give a reason to counter the arguments used by the other side. If your class likes competitions, encourage them to go on as long as possible. The group which speaks last is the winner.

4 Q – a poem ▭
reading

Roger McGough is a poet from Liverpool, England. Although the poem has vocabulary and structures which have not been taught yet in the course, the central situation that is outlined is strong and amusing enough to be understood by the learners at this level.

Suggested steps

The poem is meant to be read for enjoyment, simply to round off the lesson. In some classes, you might like the learners just to read it quietly, then listen to it on the recording. They can then compare their reactions, and re-read the poem for homework.

Alternatively, set the scene by exploiting the illustration. The people in the queue are silent. But what are their thoughts? Ask the learners to imagine that they are in the queue. How do they feel? What are they thinking? They read the completed bubble, which pre-teaches one of the expressions they will meet in the poem, then fill in the empty thought bubble with their own thought.

Option 1

Instead of getting the learners to write out their thought bubbles, you can structure this part of the activity in the form of a version of the well-known game, Chinese Whispers. Each person imagines being in the queue, and thinks of one sentence that would form their own thought bubble. Get the learners to stand in a long queue. The first one in the queue whispers their sentence to the one behind, who whispers it in turn to the person behind, and so on to the end of the queue, when the received sentence is compared out loud to the original. The second person then moves to the head of the queue and whispers their sentence.

If the class is large, you might wish to set up two or more whispering queues.

If there is time, another possibility for classes who enjoy drama is the following.

Option 2

Get the learners working in small groups. They are to imagine that they are making a video version of the poem. There may be someone reading the poem, with other people acting out and saying the dialogue parts, or it may be done as a voice-over with mime. They have a set time for preparation and rehearsal, then present their 'video' to another group or to the whole class.

Personal Study Workbook

7, 8: reading practice

Quick Check answer key

(i)
1. How often do you go shopping?
2. Where do you buy food?
3. Do you (often) stand in queues?
4. How often do you buy food?

(ii)
1. I don't talk in English a lot.
2. She doesn't sing English songs.
3. Men don't shake hands in my country.
4. Sven doesn't go shopping every week.

D REVIEW AND DEVELOPMENT

REVIEW OF UNIT 3

1 Visiting someone's home
reading

This exercise reviews Unit 3 by going over some questions forms and extending some food vocabulary.

Warm-up

Establish the notion of a gift by exploiting the illustration. What do the learners think about the gifts? Are they interesting gifts? Who are they for? What is the occasion? Move from that into talking about what you do when you go out to dinner, or go to stay with friends. Then ask the learners what they do. Do they give gifts? Do they give gifts on the first visit? etc. Even in groups from the same country customs may differ widely.

Suggested steps

Get the class to answer and talk about the questions in pairs. Let them use their dictionaries, or ask each other if they encounter difficulties. Circulate, offering help if needed.

Have a quick feedback on the answers given – ask different pairs to exchange their views, and compare them with your own if that is useful.

Some of the potential vocabulary difficulties in the reading text have been dealt with in the pre-reading questions. Direct your learners' attention to the two post-reading questions, telling them that they can start thinking about the questions as they read.

Encourage your learners to have a quick first reading of the article. Although people do read at greatly varying speeds, it is useful for them to read through as quickly as they can on the first encounter, without using a dictionary, but trying to understand as much as they can from the context. If you like, you can then read the article out loud to let them listen to it and re-read at the same time.

When the reading is finished, get them working in pairs to discuss the answers given in the text, and which country the text is about.

Answer key
The country is China.
1. No.
2. An even number.
3. Sometimes.
4. Yes.
5. Yes.
6. Some colours are not OK, e.g. white, blue or black.

When they have checked their answers, encourage the learners to talk about the text, then ask them to study the two situations and talk about what they themselves do when they go out to dinner or to stay with someone. What is a good gift to take in those circumstances? You could ask pairs to write their two gifts on the board and see how many of them have the same ideas.

REVIEW OF UNIT 4

1 I wear jeans at home after work
vocabulary consolidation; discussion

This activity revises the vocabulary of clothes, and develops it by introducing the terms *casual* and *formal*.

Suggested steps

First, the learners write their own choices (or they can work in pairs, if they prefer). They then compare them with others, using the framework given in the example.

The next set of questions extends the topic to a more general area and provides more practice with the verb *to wear*, a verb whose pronunciation many learners find difficult. You can tell them that the word rhymes with *where*. Write the two words on the board, to associate them in their memory.

Depending on the size and level of the class, you can structure this discussion in small groups, or as a whole-class activity.

2 We wear whites and we wear greens ⊏⊐
pronunciation: sentence rhythm; /v/ and /w/

This is the first of a series of 'rhythm raps' included in the book. Their purpose is to get the learners practising whole sentences in a contextualised, rhythmic, enjoyable way. This 'rap' provides plenty of practice with the sounds /v/ and /w/, which many learners find particularly difficult. Even if your class doesn't have this problem, the learners can benefit from the rhythm practice, since this helps them develop whole sentence stress and intonation patterns that are communicative and meaningful.

Suggested steps

Let the class listen to the example on the recording first, or give them the text and get them practising to start with, then let them compare with the group on the recording. The words are in the box below, which may be photocopied.

Divide the class into two halves. Set the rhythm by clicking fingers before you start the chanting. Get each half chanting their part in rhythm. To start with, you will probably have to give them the text, or at least write the key words for each section on the board. Even if you give the class the script, it is helpful to write key words up on the board so that the learners can stand and chant, without having to read from a text. You can help them keep time by clapping or swinging your arms to the beat.

Get the learners to rehearse the chant a few times, then if you possibly can, record them doing it. Classes usually find this a lot of fun and enjoy listening to their chant afterwards.

Worksheets

There are two supplementary worksheets for this unit (on page 167), which you can use to let your class have more practice with present simple verbs used for routines and habitual actions. We have given two so that you can have a choice – different topics appeal to different people! You can either choose one yourself for the class, or let the learners choose. Part of the class could work with one, part with the other.

Both worksheets are surveys – the learners have to ask at least five people the questions. It is best to get the learners to take the surveys and ask people outside class, as this gives more variety and authenticity to their survey.

Suggested steps

In countries which are not English-speaking, the learners will have to translate the questions so that they can ask their friends and family. This first step could be done in class before they start actually doing the survey or alternatively, they could do the translation as homework, to be checked in class next period.

In both surveys there is a space left at the end for additional questions. Encourage the learners to add something – this personalises their work and increases their involvement in it.

Ensure that any difficulties in the language are dealt with and explained, e.g. *spare time* in Worksheet 5B, or *play/watch sports*. The learners can use their dictionaries, ask others, or ask you.

It is usually more fun to carry out the survey in pairs or groups, rather than individually, and groupwork also makes feedback more interesting.

As with most project-type work, feedback is very important, but its format can be varied. See the feedback techniques suggested for the worksheets for Unit 4.

Since the answers to the survey can be tabulated, a particularly appropriate form of feedback for this exercise is the following: a group creates a graph showing the total response to its questions.

END OF UNIT NOTES

How's the class getting on?

....

....

Language that needs more work or attention:

....

....

My learners:

....

....

REVIEW OF UNIT 4

Exercise 2   Tapescript

A: What've you got, oh, what've you got?
   What've you got, oh, what've you got?
B: We've got rhythm, we've got blues,
   We've got a hat and ... brand new shoes.
A: They've got rhythm, they've got blues,
   They've got a hat and ... brand new shoes.
B: What d'you wear, oh, what d'you wear?
   What d'you wear, oh, what d'you wear?
A: We wear whites and we wear greens,
   We wear a shirt and ... our blue jeans.
B: They wear whites and they wear greens,
   They wear a shirt and ... their blue jeans.
A: What d'you wear, oh, what d'you wear?
   What d'you wear, oh, what d'you wear?
B: We are formal, we wear suits,
   We wear coats and ... polished boots.
A: They are formal, they wear suits,
   They wear coats and ... polished boots.
B: What d'you want, oh, what d'you want?
   What d'you want, oh, what d'you want?
A: We want English and we want love,
   We want the earth and ... the stars above!
B: They want English and they want love,
   They want the earth and ... the stars above!

TRUE TO LIFE ELEMENTARY   © Cambridge University Press 1995

Unit 5 GOOD HABITS, NEW ROUTINES?

6

THE WAY YOU LOOK

```
                        CONTENTS

    Language focus:   expressing opinions; agreeing and disagreeing
                          with opinions
                      I'd like for wishes
                      adjectives and modifiers
                      too and not enough

    Vocabulary:       appearance: face and body
                      describing personality
```

INTRODUCTION TO THE UNIT

After the quite strongly structural work on the present simple tense in the previous unit, the learners go on to a more lexically based set of lessons. In this unit, they practise the very useful function of expressing their own opinions, as well as agreeing or disagreeing with others. They have already been exposed to *I'd like*, used when asking for things. Now they encounter a new use, speaking about more hypothetical wishes. The main vocabulary areas are appearance and personality, and in order to describe these, adjectives and modifiers are stressed, as well as the terms and concepts *too* and *not enough*.

Warm-up

The first activity in this unit starts in a rather oblique way, by getting the learners to speculate about how much can be deduced about a person's character simply by looking at their eyes. You may feel you would like a more direct approach, or more overt presentation of the personality words the learners are going to be handling. Here is a choice of warm-ups for that purpose, to use before you turn to the book.

Option 1

Use flash cards, magazine pictures, or OHP transparency drawings to build up the pairs of opposing characteristics that are used in Exercise 1. For example, show a picture of an obviously sad person. With mime and facial expression, reinforce the mood. Elicit or supply: *sad*. Write on the board: *She's sad. She's not happy. Sad* was presented in Unit 4, Lesson C, Exercise 1, but the learners may need reminding of it!

Repeat the procedure with *old*, writing on the board:

He's old. He's not young. Old was also presented in Unit 4 (Lesson A, Exercise 2) but may need revising. For more abstract words like *kind* and *selfish*, show pictures or cartoon drawings of kind or selfish actions (someone helping another person; someone knocking another person out of their way, etc.).

Option 2

Another way of presenting personality words is through mime. Show the learners how to do it by miming *sad* – let your body droop, your facial expression be full of sorrow, wipe a tear from your eye, etc. Ask: *What am I?* Elicit or supply: *I'm sad. I'm not happy.* Write it on the board. Let the learners find the meanings of other unknown words by looking them up in the dictionary. Then give each pair a slip of paper with a set of opposites on it. They prepare a mime – the class guesses which words they are presenting. (If your class is large, you can present some of the other descriptive words used in later activities.)

1 My friend looks serious but he's a lot of fun
vocabulary; speaking; listening

Different ways of indicating thoughts, guesses, hypotheses are practised in this first activity.

Suggested steps

If you have not pre-taught the personality words, give the learners some time to establish meanings, by using the dictionary or discussing the words with others.

Work with all the learners, getting them to make guesses about the three pairs of eyes. Draw attention to the example and model the phrases used to express (uncertain) opinion: *I think ... he looks ...* Encourage all speculation, supplying other words if they are needed. The help section extends communicative ability by highlighting modifiers, which are useful in expressing shades of meaning.

When speculation is at an end, tell the learners they are going to listen to three friends talking about the people whose eyes they have been looking at.

This is a dual listening task. The first version is a simplified and scripted version of the second one, which is the authentic, unscripted recording. Stop the recording before the speakers reveal which are their friends. The tapescripts are on page 222.

Let the learners check the words they wrote down in the table with each other before confirming. Then ask them who they think Speaker A's friend is: 1, 2 or 3, etc.

Answer key

Words in brackets are additional words used in Version 2.

Speaker A's friend: young, (healthy), looks confident, (proud), people think she's serious but she's happy, kind (2)

Speaker B's friend: looks happy (proud), confident, (ambitious), practical, kind (1)

Speaker C's friend: looks serious; is fun, lively, (generous, intelligent, artistic) (3)

Play the final part of the recording to confirm the identity of the friends.

Personal Study Workbook

4: pronunciation of the vocabulary of body and clothes

2 I'm a practical person, really
speaking; adjectives

Many of the activities in this unit are set in the general area of games (the not very serious questionnaire in Lesson A, Exercise 3) or fantasy (the 'computer selection of children' in Lesson B, Exercise 1). The reason for this is that appearance and personality are very personal, often delicate matters. The learners may not wish to speak too much (or too seriously) about their own appearance or personality. As their teacher, you are best placed to decide how to handle this issue.

If your groups are supportive of each other and not likely to cause embarrassment or hurt, then you can simply ask them to carry out the task as described in the book. Encourage the groups to use as many adjectives as they can from the first exercise. Circulate and add your comments to the discussion, e.g. *I think you look artistic, Seni. Are you artistic, really?*

Option

If there is any friction amongst the groups, it might be better to adapt the activity. Elicit the names of some famous people. Write them on the board. Then ask each group to choose one famous person and imagine what they are really like, at home, in private. The groups choose adjectives and then compare their choices with other groups.

Personal Study Workbook

1: adjectives and their place in the sentence

3 Is your hair curly?
vocabulary extension: adjectives; speaking

This is a game type of activity, the content of which is meant to be interesting, intriguing, but not really very serious. The learners are invited to do the questionnaire, then talk about whether or not it is right for them, thus implying that it is clearly not going to be accurate for everybody. Many people enjoy doing questionnaires in magazines, even if they don't take the results too seriously, and it is hoped that they will enjoy this light-hearted way of thinking about physical characteristics and their relation (or lack of relation!) to personality characteristics.

Suggested steps

The first part of this activity is a reading exercise. Many of the words will be unknown, and the learners should work in pairs or small groups to make sure they understand the options before they attempt to tick their own answers.

If you like, you can then go over the eight questions, miming the various characteristics (e.g. a wide forehead – extend your hands on either side of your forehead; a narrow forehead – bring your hands close together on your forehead, and so on) as the class is deciding which option to tick. (Don't forget to tick your own decisions.)

Use your own questionnaire answers to demonstrate how to establish your profile, which is done in two parts. First, establish which adjective corresponds to your answers on the questionnaire.

If, for example, for number 1 you ticked c, a high forehead, this means you put a tick for the characteristic 'shy'. If in number 2 you ticked a, small, you put a tick against 'artistic'. And so on.

Secondly, see how many ticks you have for each of the seven characteristics, and find your personality, as in the example in the book.

Encourage a lot of discussion about the results, first in pairs or small groups, then in the whole class. Express surprise at the results, so that the learners are prompted to say more, recycling the adjectives.

Option 1 – Follow-up

If you did not use the *option* for Lesson A, Exercise 2, you can use a version of it as a quick revision of the adjectives learnt. Write on the board the names of five well-known people that everyone in the class is sure to know (film or TV stars, politicians, especially controversial ones, pop stars, anyone who has recently been in the news, etc.). Ask the learners to choose one personality adjective for each (or two, if you want a more challenging but more time-consuming task).

For feedback, ask Learner A to write their chosen adjective beside name 1, Learner B to write their chosen word beside name 2, etc. Then ask for any other words chosen by the class; add them to the list on the board. Ask how many in the class have got each adjective, so that a 'majority verdict' begins to emerge.

Option 2

Another way to revise personality adjectives without personal embarrassment for the learners is to show pictures of animals: monkeys, bears, tigers, cats, dogs, etc. (If the names are unknown, you can simply number the pictures, unless you wish to extend your learners' vocabulary range at this point.) Ask the learners to choose a 'personality' adjective for each. Use the same feedback procedure as the previous option, if you like.

Personal Study Workbook

3: adjectives and their corresponding nouns

Quick Check answer key

(i)
1. b   2. a   3. b
(ii)
1. confident   2. kind   3. old   4. happy   5. narrow

QUICK NOTES

This went well:

....

....

This didn't quite work:

....

....

Things to think about:

....

....

 B

1 I'd like a child with brown eyes

vocabulary; speaking; listening

This activity recycles the descriptive adjectives introduced in the previous lesson, in a fantasy or futuristic scenario. The structure *I'd like* (in response to the question *What would you like?*) is introduced with a new function, indicating a hypothetical preference rather than an actual order (the use the learners have practised in Unit 3).

Warm-up

You can set the scene by getting the learners to imagine they are in the future. Write on the board: *It's now the year 2095.* Show pictures from science fiction novels or videos, if you have any. Elicit a list of things which are different in the year 2095 – put two lists on the board:

There are some   There aren't any

Elicit guesses to put under the two columns, e.g. *There are some computers, aeroplanes, space ships* (supply

vocabulary if needed)*, people from Mars, etc. There aren't any cars, buses, roads, small houses, etc.*

End up by asking the question: *What about children? What is different now?* Then say *It's possible to choose the way your child looks!* Turn to the illustration in the Class Book and indicate the list of computer choices that parents now have.

Suggested steps

After the warm-up, you can go over the various options for children with the learners. They should know most of the words, but mime any unknown ones, like *strong*. Alternatively, get the learners to study the options and make choices by themselves. Encourage them to add other options if they prefer.

After this, get them comparing their choices with a partner, and talking about them. Draw their attention to the example. Circulate and react to their choices – express surprise, interest, agree or disagree to reinforce reaction expressions like: *Really? Do you think so? Is that right? I think so, too. Oh, no, I don't think so.*

A whole-class feedback can round off the conversations. Get the learners to ask you about your choices. (*What about you? What kind of child would you like/choose?*) Elicit reaction expressions from them.

The hypothetical use of *would like* is extended to the third person (*He/She would like a child*) in the listening activity. The tapescript is on page 223.

Get the learners to check their answers with each other before confirming them. Encourage comparison of the choices heard on the recording with those the learners made in the previous activity. (*Is anyone here like Speaker 1? Yes, Nadine, you'd like a child with brown eyes too.*)

Answer key

Speaker 1 would like a girl with big brown eyes, dark hair and small, artistic hands.
Speaker 2 would like a boy with straight, fair hair and strong legs.

Personal Study Workbook

5: vocabulary of appearance; listening

2 The sleeves are too long!

too and *not enough*; listening; dictation

After the interactive fantasy activity, this will bring a change of atmosphere and pace to round off the lesson. This is a more conventional type of language learning activity, which introduces a structure and gets the learners to practise it in a controlled way.

Suggested steps

Go over the example picture with the class. Model the sentences, emphasising the word *too*.

Then go over the three situations which are shown in the other illustrations. Elicit reactions (facial expression, or expressions like *Oh, dear!*) from the learners.

Play the recording, pausing after each sentence to let the learners write it down. If they can't get the whole sentence after one listening, get them to check with their partner or with others before letting them hear the sentences again. Alternatively, you can let the learners check with others after each sentence, but tell them that all six sentences will be repeated again afterwards.

The tapescript is on page 223.

Answer key

1. My feet are too big. (Picture C)
2. My arms are too short. (Picture A)
3. The shoes are not big enough. (Picture C)
4. My shoulders are too wide. (Picture B)
5. The sleeves are too long. (Picture A)
6. The jacket's not big enough. (Picture B)

Check the six sentences with the learners. In some classes, you could ask different people to write one sentence each on the board. Then get them to do the matching activity by themselves or with others.

Option 1 Follow-up

It is often a good idea to reinforce *too* and *not enough* by using your own real-life situation. Write different aspects of your situation on the board, and ask the learners to write one sentence about them using *too* or *not enough*. Here are some examples for you to choose from:

1. This room: *It's not big enough*, or *It's too tiny* (recycle *tiny* from Unit 2) or *It's not colourful enough* (recycle *colourful* from Unit 4) or *It's too old*, etc.
2. This building: *It's not quiet enough* (recycle *quiet* from Unit 2).
3. This English lesson: *It's not long enough*, or *It's not interesting enough* (recycle *interesting* from Units 1 and 4) or *It's too expensive*.
4. This board
5. These windows
6. These chairs or tables (recycle *comfortable* from Unit 1)
7. Our coffee shop
8. The weather today: *It's not hot/cold enough* (recycle vocabulary from Unit 1).

For feedback, you can get the learners writing their sentences up on the board, or comparing them in groups. Another way of getting feedback is to ask one learner to read out any one of their sentences, e.g. *It's not quiet enough* and the other learners guess what topic was intended by saying the whole sentence, e.g. *The room's not quiet enough?*

Option 2

Alternatively, the exercise can be done orally instead of in writing. Write the topics mentioned above (or any others that you think appropriate) on the board or on an OHP transparency. Point to one at random and ask a learner to say a sentence using *too* or *not enough*. The learner who has answered can then nominate another topic, and another member of the class to give a sentence about it.

Option 3

With classes that are not too inhibited about drawing, ask each person to draw a situation that requires the use of *too* or *not enough*. They can be simple drawings, e.g. a cup beside the much smaller box it is meant to go in, a stick person much bigger than the house beside, etc. You can start by drawing something extremely simple on the board as an example. Set a time limit (so that no one agonises over their drawing, or tries too hard to make it perfect!). Each learner gives their drawing to another person, who writes an appropriate sentence beneath it. Afterwards, have an exhibition of drawings for the learners to see.

Personal Study Workbook

2: *too* and *not enough*

Quick Check answer key

1. a 2. b 3. b 4. b 5. a 6. a

```
QUICK NOTES

This went well:
.............................................................
.............................................................

This didn't quite work:
.............................................................
.............................................................

Things to think about:
.............................................................
.............................................................
```

C

This is a skills lesson, focusing on reading and writing, which recycles and extends the vocabulary of appearance and personality.

1 Is it important for a friend to be lively?
vocabulary and speaking

The first speaking activity introduces the topic: 'qualities that we might look for in a friend', thus acting as a warm-up for the next exercise. *Important* was introduced in Unit 1, but it is now used in a slightly different structure: *It's important for a friend to be ...*

Suggested steps

You can establish the idea of qualities that are important in a friend by talking about a friend of yours. Show a photo if you've got one, to help personalise what you say. You can complete your two sentences on the board as you speak, if you think the learners will find this helpful. (*X is my friend. She's kind, and for me, it's very, very important for a friend to be kind. She's quite practical, but for me that's not important in a friend. She's interested in music, and that's very important too, etc.)*

Use this warm-up to go over any unknown vocabulary that might be a problem for your class, e.g. *an outdoor life.*

Get the learners to complete the two sentences. Help them with any other vocabulary they might need. They can then read their sentences to a partner or in a small group, to compare the choices they have made.

If you like, you can organise a class 'profile' for friends by asking for words that they have used to complete the first sentence. Put the words on the board and ask how many people have chosen each quality. Write a 'class' sentence using the words chosen most often: *For us, it's important for a friend to be …* Do the same for the second sentence, if there is time.

Personal Study Workbook

8: writing descriptions of people

2 Long-haired guy looking for interesting woman

reading

Because the concepts and many of the words have been made familiar by preceding work, there is no pre-reading task set. Many people are familiar with 'want ads' for companions. If your class is not, it would be a good idea to show them an example from a local newspaper or a magazine. Explain that the ads are from people who want to find some friends.

The only expressions you might like to highlight before they start reading are *seeks* and *looking for* which, you can explain, have a very similar meaning.

The texts are taken from authentic examples in the international press. Some words or expressions in them may be unknown, but the learners can often use their previous knowledge to make guesses, e.g. they know *friend* so they can have a shrewd guess about what the phrase *seeks … girl for friendship* could mean.

Encourage the learners to read for gist, without using a dictionary. They can then join others in a small group to ask for help with any problems and to compare their reactions.

They can then work through the 'true or false' questions in their groups, or do them by themselves and compare with others afterwards. The sentences act as a check for comprehension, while reinforcing some of the vocabulary encountered.

Have a whole-class check of the answers before moving on to the next activity.

Answer key

1. T   2. F   3. F   4. T   5. F   6. F   7. F

Personal Study Workbook

6: appearance and fashion; reading

3 In reply to your ad …

writing a letter

This activity uses the context of the previous task to teach some of the vocabulary associated with writing a letter in reply to a newspaper item.

Before they begin to write, if you think it is useful for your particular group, you may wish to go over the format of an English-style letter, as shown in the example. Point out the standard greeting at the beginning: *Dear …,* (fill in a name); the expression *In reply to your …* which can be used in other situations, e.g. *In reply to your letter, In reply to your request;* and finally the standard phrase at the end *Yours sincerely.*

> ### Language Point:
>
> In Britain, the ending *Yours sincerely* is used when the greeting at the beginning includes a name. e.g. *Dear Mr Duffy, Dear John, Dear Mrs Landro.*
>
> If the greeting is more impersonal, without a name, e.g. *Dear Sir, Dear Sirs, Dear Madam,* it is customary in Britain to use a different formula at the end: *Yours faithfully.* A more formal letter example is given in Personal Study Workbook Exercise 7.

The learners complete the letters on their own. They can choose to write about a friend if the idea of answering an ad doesn't appeal to them personally. The letter form gives a framework so that they are supported in the writing task. Circulate and help if needed.

For feedback, get the learners to read their completed letters either in a group, or to the class. Alternatively, you can put them up on a noticeboard and let the class read them.

Personal Study Workbook

7: a letter of application

Quick Check answer key

(i)
1. Me too. / I think so too.   2. Yes, she is.
(ii)
a long-haired man   a non-smoker

```
┌─────────────────────────────────────┐
│            QUICK NOTES                │
│                                       │
│   This went well:                     │
│   ..................................  │
│                                       │
│   ..................................  │
│                                       │
│   This didn't quite work:             │
│   ..................................  │
│                                       │
│   ..................................  │
│                                       │
│   Things to think about:              │
│   ..................................  │
│                                       │
│   ..................................  │
└─────────────────────────────────────┘
```

REVIEW OF UNIT 4

1 How often do you go shopping?
question forms with *do*

Suggested steps

Question forms with *do* present a lot of problems to many beginners. This first activity offers a straightforward check of the form. Go over the example questions with the class, then let them add the missing words on their own.

Feedback: checking in groups, followed by class confirmation.

Answer key

1. How often *do* you buy clothes?
2. *Do* you go shopping at the weekend?
3. When *do* you play football?
4. What do *you* wear in the winter?
5. Where *do* you find good shoes?
6. Do you go *to* the supermarket on Saturday?

REVIEW OF UNIT 5

1 On Sundays, I ...
vocabulary and collocation

Suggested steps

This is a fairly straightforward revision of expressions describing daily routines, and it also revises some of the verbs encountered in Unit 5, e.g. *kiss, eat, smoke, listen to, wash, tidy*. The learners can use their dictionaries for any new (or forgotten) items.

In a feedback session get the learners to read out their completed sentences in groups or to the class.

Answer key

1. I make the bed.
2. I kiss the children.
3. I feed the cat.
4. I eat breakfast.
5. I smoke a cigarette.
6. I listen to the radio.
7. I wash my clothes.
8. I tidy my room.
9. I clean the windows.
10. I watch the TV.

2 I always listen to the radio ▭▭
speaking; listening

Suggested steps

If the feedback for the previous exercise was done in groups, let the learners continue in groups for this follow-up conversation. Otherwise, put them in pairs. Draw their attention to the example. After they have gone through the conversation, tell them to find a new partner so that they can each report what they have found out.

In a whole-class feedback, ask: *Who knows what Juan does on Sundays?* React to the reported activities: *Oh, that's interesting. I do, too. Oh, I don't … That's different.*

Play the recording. Pause after the first speaker to let the class complete their notes. The tapescript is on page 223.

Answer key

For the answers, please refer to the tapescript on page 223.

Get the learners to check their answers and then take it in turns to report to the class. Monitor the change from 1st person to 3rd, especially the final *s* or *es* sounds: *she stays, gets up, has* (not *have*), *cleans, washes, goes, meets,* (but with *they go*, the form is the same as *we go*); *does* (if necessary highlight the changed sound here as well), *buys, asks, watches, doesn't play.*

Worksheets

The worksheets for Unit 6, which are on pages 168 and 169, can be used for communicative pair practice to revise the vocabulary of appearance and personality. The learners each have pictures of six people, and six half paragraphs: one half about each one of the people in the pictures. Each learner has three beginnings, and three continuations. In pairs, they find the right continuations for each beginning. (Hint: beginnings give the name of the person, while continuations end with incomplete sentences.) They then choose, from the box, the right endings for each paragraph.

If they are puzzled, help them by doing the first picture with them. Get them to describe it, mentioning the 'long straight brown hair' which is the clue. Say: *Does any description mention long straight brown hair? Ah, so that's about Shirley. Now let's see, what's the second part of that description?* etc.

Answer key

1. E. g. (v)
F. 2. l. (i)
D. 3. k. (ii)
4. A. j. (iii)
C. 5. h. (vi)
6. B. i. (iv)

```
END OF UNIT NOTES

How's the class getting on?
.................................................
.................................................

Language that needs more work or attention:
.................................................
.................................................

My learners:
.................................................
.................................................
```

7

WHAT CAN WE DO?

CONTENTS

Language focus: *can* for ability, skills or permission: positive, negative
statements, questions
can and *could* for requests
introduction of past simple of *to be*: positive,
negative statements, questions
introduction of past simple: *to have*, *to go*, positive
statements only, and *could* as past tense of *can*

Vocabulary: personal skills and abilities
childhood

INTRODUCTION TO THE UNIT

The first two lessons familiarise the learners with the
concept of *can* used for ability, skills and permission, and
can or *could* used for requests. The learners are given a lot
of opportunity to practise the concept and structure in
questions and statements, thereby associating it with
their own abilities or skills. The third lesson signals a
shift of direction: the learners start using the past tense,
concentrating on the verbs *to have*, *to go* and *could*, now
used as the past tense of *can*. The whole area of the past
tenses in English is a very complex and difficult one for
many learners, especially those whose languages use
different strategies for talking about past events. This
progressive introduction of the tense over the next few
units will, it is hoped, gently ease them into it.

A

1 Can you use a computer?
can, *can't* (ability/skills); vocabulary, reading and speaking

Warm-up

You can present the concept *can* before using the book,
if you like. Demonstrate with some items in the
classroom, e.g. show a book in English (or the first
language of a monolingual group). Say: *I can read this
book*, and write the sentence on the board. Show a book
in another, obviously foreign language. Say: *I can't read
this book*, and write the sentence on the board. Give one
more example, e.g. *I can write with this pencil*.
Demonstrate *I can't write with this pen* (no ink). Give a
learner a book, and ask: *Can you read this book?* The
learner answers, then passes the book to someone else,
asking the question in turn. After a few turns, continue
with the other book, and the pen or pencil.

Option

The same kind of introduction can be done using
pictures. In this case, you may wish to pre-teach the
vocabulary required for the first activity. Show a picture
of a car, and start with the known word *drive*: *I can drive
a car*. Then move on to *I can repair a car* or *I can't repair a
car* (picture of a mechanic working on a car). A picture
of a computer can elicit: *I can use a computer* and *I can
type with all my fingers*. And so on.

Suggested steps

Tell your class that the topic here is: 'useful skills to have'
or 'skills for survival in the modern world'. Explain
useful and *survival* or let them grasp the concepts through
dictionary work. What useful skills can they think of?
Accept all suggestions and write them on the board. Have
a few extra ideas in reserve, in case they can't think of
many, e.g. writing a business letter, driving a car, doing
two things at the same time, speaking another language,
etc. Another way of stimulating the discussion is to think
of unusual or outrageous 'skills' and propose them to the
class, e.g. the skill of getting other people to do your
work for you, the skill of making money easily, etc.

Get the learners working in pairs to understand the
questions in Exercise 1, and write two more questions
themselves.

As soon as some pairs finish, they can start comparing
their questions and answers, while others finish their
writing. Get the pairs to go through their questionnaires,
then choose new partners and do it again. When
everyone has finished, the class can go on to a discussion
of which skills are important for them, either in groups,
or as a whole-class conversation.

As a final check, use a chain technique. Everyone shuts
their books and notebooks. Learner A starts, by asking
Learner B: *Can you …* (any one of the verbs they've just
been learning). Learner B answers *Yes I can* or *Of course, I*

can or *No, I can't*, then asks Learner C another question, and so on.

Personal Study Workbook

1: *can* – grammar focus, long forms/short forms
5: *can* and vocabulary extension

2 What can you do?

practice with *can* in questions; dictation

This is a way of recycling questions with *can* in a guessing game format.

First get the learners to write one of their skills on a slip of paper. It is best if the skill is something they are proud of being able to do – or a funny or unusual skill. Help the learners with new vocabulary if they need it to express their particular speciality. Make sure they do not show their slips to others or talk about them!

Collect all the slips. Get the learners to prepare a sheet of paper with numbers from 1 to X (the number of the learners in the class) down the side of the page. In large classes, divide into two groups. Do the dictation for one group, then for the other.

Dictate the skills from each of the slips. If there are unusual or unknown words, write them up on the board. The learners can ask you to write things on the board if they cannot understand.

For example: *This is number 1. Number 1 can play the piano. Write 'play the piano' for number 1* (write piano on the board). *Now number two … ready? Number 2 can stand on his head. Stand … on his head. Stand? OK, this is stand* (write it on the board). If you like, you can remind the learners that *his* or *her* gives a hint about male or female identity.

When the dictation is done, tell the learners that they must now find out who number 1 is, number 2, etc. Tell them that they can only ask one person one question, then they must move on and ask another person one question. (This is to facilitate milling. The instruction is often disregarded by learners eager to find out more quickly! But as it is a game, remind them lightly that they should really ask only one question at a time.)

Personal Study Workbook

6: *can* + prepositions

3 But can he use a computer?

grammar practice; reading and
writing short dialogues or letters

After the previous two, very interactive, activities, this one introduces a more traditional grammar focus, to be done quietly by the learners working on their own. They then compare answers and write a similar gapped dialogue in pairs.

Suggested steps

Go over the examples with the learners. Draw their attention to the use of *can't* and *cannot* and the use of *can* + verb in contrast to the present simple of the verb.

Language Point:

1. *Can't*, the short form, is contrasted with *cannot*, the long form. *Can't* is often used in speaking, while *cannot* is often used in more formal writing, like business letters. This distinction is illustrated in sentences 1 and 2.
2. *Can play* (*can* + verb) is contrasted with *plays* (the present simple tense of the verb). *Can play* is used to indicate possibility or skill (the same form is used for all persons: *I can play*, *he can play*); while *play* or *plays* indicates the actual doing or performing of the action (there is a change in the 3rd person – *I/you/we/they play*, but *she/he plays*). This distinction is illustrated in sentence 3.

Ask the learners to read the four parts and fill in the blanks. Remind them to be aware of the two grammar points just discussed. Circulate and help them with any difficulties you spot.

Answer key

1. 'Can you read on your way to work, Mat?'
   'No, I *can't* read in crowded buses at all, but my sister *can*. She *reads* a whole magazine on her way to work in the morning.'
2. 'Well, Mr Grestun seems right for the job. But *can* he use a computer?'
   'Oh, yes, he *uses* computers all the time now.'
   'And *can* he type?'
   'Well, he *can't* type very well, I'm afraid. He types with two fingers – but he's very fast!'
3. Dear Mrs Bosak,
   I am very sorry indeed that we *cannot* use your story in our magazine this week.
4. Dear Deni,
   I'm here in Nema with Sam and Lisa. Sam's a wonderful cook. He *can* make lovely meals, but he takes a lot of time. So Lisa makes sandwiches for us at lunchtime.

When the learners have finished, get them working in pairs to check their answers before the class confirmation.

They then write either a dialogue, or a letter, of the kind they have just been working with. It should show some use of *can*, *can't* or the present simple verb. They leave these blank, as in the sentences they have just completed. While they are writing, circulate and make sure that all the pairs have understood the task.

Put pairs together when they have finished, and get them filling in the blanks in each other's pieces of writing.

For feedback, ask the learners to read their completed dialogues or letters to the class.

Option – Follow-up

Here is a way to revise *can* and extend vocabulary whenever you have a few spare minutes in class.

The learners work in two teams (four in larger classes). Each group writes 20 questions – 10 similar to A, where the answer is *Yes, they can* and 10 similar to B, where the answer is *No, they can't*.

A: Can people type with their fingers?
B: Can people type with a chair?

Write these two kinds of questions (and their answers) on the board. (Other examples to supply if the learners can't think of their own: *Can people eat with a fork? Can people drink with a window? Can people drive a house? Can people talk with a door? Can people sit on a chair? Can people repair a sandwich?* etc. The questions requiring the answer *No, they can't* can be as nonsensical or amusing as the learners wish.)

Each team member writes down the 20 questions, in a random order agreed on by everybody in the team. The teams then face each other. Each member in turn 'fires' a question at the opponents. The opponents, in turn, have quickly to give the correct answer (either *Yes, they can* or *No, they can't*) then fire one of their questions. Answering has to be done very rapidly. If people questioned take longer than five seconds (counted by the teacher), or give the wrong answer, they have to sit down. The object is to have as many as possible of the team members still standing when the 20 questions have been fired.

Personal Study Workbook

7: pronunciation of *can*, weak forms and questions

Quick Check answer key

(i)
1. b   2. a   3. b   4. a

(ii)
1. Can he play a musical instrument? / Can he play the drums?
2. Can you cook?
3. Can your mother type? / How fast can your mother type?

QUICK NOTES

This went well:

....

....

This didn't quite work:

....

....

Things to think about:

....

....

Two further uses of *can* are practised in this section: *can* for permission, and *can* (or *could*) for requests.

1 At what age can you get married?

can for permission

Suggested steps

Either let the learners work in pairs with their dictionaries to establish the new vocabulary, or go over it with them, miming, explaining, etc. In countries where it is appropriate, you can add 'buy alcohol' or 'buy cigarettes'. Work with the illustration to reinforce the concept of an age limit at which you can start to do things. If your learners ask analytical questions about language and like to know how it works, explain that *can* here means *you are allowed to; the law lets you do it*, i.e. it is used to express permission, as opposed to ability or skill as practised in the previous lesson. Otherwise, you can just work with this activity as simply further practice for *can*.

> **Language Point:**
>
> *Get married* is a set expression which is used by itself, that is without an object, e.g. *We're getting married. In our country, we can get married at 16.* When there is an object, you can use either *He's getting married to Jane* or *He's marrying Jane*.

In multinational classes, the comparison of ages at which people are allowed to do the various things will probably stimulate more discussion – in that case, encourage some extension into the reason for age limits, what is a 'good' age limit and why, etc. In single nationality classes, the learners simply check that they've all got the same answers (by no means always the case – opening a bank account and getting married are actions that often provoke disagreements about age limits). If you like, you can then ask them whether they think the age limit is a good one, before moving on to the listening task.

The dual listening follows the typical pattern. The first is a scripted version, the second the original unscripted answers (in both cases, the two respondents are an American woman and a French man). You can pause after the first interview in each case to let the learners jot down their notes, and perhaps have a first quick comparison of answers with others in the class.

The tapescript is on page 223.

Confirm answers after group comparisons have been made.

Answer key

Extra information in brackets is in Version 2.

	Speaker 1	Speaker 2
... vote?	18	18
... drive a car?	you can learn at 15½ you can get a licence at 16 (in some farming states 14)	18
... open a bank account?	at any age	18
... get married?	16	18 (16 with parents' permission)

Encourage comparison of the age limits in different countries, and extend the earlier discussion on opinions about them, if it is appropriate.

2 Can I try it on, please?

can and could for requests; anybody and anywhere

This exercise gives a change of pace, with the focus shifting to more functional questions used in everyday situations. There is additional practice in using *can* or *could* for requests in the worksheets at the end of the unit.

Warm-up

You can set the scene by introducing the request form of *can* directly. Ask one learner to do something, e.g. *Can you open the window, please?* (indicate by miming that the learner should do the action). Write the question on the board. Ask: *Could you pass me that book, please?* (indicate by miming that the learner should do the action). Write the question on the board.

Set up a chain: Learner A asks Learner B to do something in the class, using either *can* or *could*. Learner B does it, then asks Learner C to do something. If the learners enjoy playfulness in these types of activities, you can add some impossible requests: *Can you touch the ceiling, please? Could you give me a new car, please?* etc. The respondent replies: *I can't* or *No, of course I can't.*

Suggested steps

Go over the example sentences with the class. Note that no distinction is made in the activity between *can* and *could*, which are used here, as they are by many English speakers, almost interchangeably. If the learners ask, you can say that *could* is considered a slightly more polite form. It is also used for requests that seem less straightforward, more hypothetical. Sometimes people want to give the impression that they know they are asking a favour, that they are apologising for disturbing the other person with their request, etc., and for this they use *could*, or even *could ... possibly*: *Could you help me with this exercise, please? Could you possibly give me a lift home?*

If you need to, explain the all-purpose term *an official* – anyone who has an 'official' position of some authority. Draw the learners' attention to the use of *anybody* and

anywhere which they may wish to use in completing the exercise.

Let the learners answer the questions by themselves, or with others. Get them to check their answers in groups before class confirmation.

Answer key

4. Anybody   At the table, during a meal
5. A teacher   In a classroom (or Anybody; anywhere)
6. An official   In an office, or at an airport, etc.
7. Anybody   Anywhere
8. Anybody (a friend/husband/wife, etc.)   At home, in a café/restaurant/bar, etc.
9. A learner   In a classroom
10. A teacher   In a classroom or other teaching situation

Personal Study Workbook

2: *can* and *could* for requests

Quick Check answer key

1. 1   2. 3   3. 2   4. 1   5. 2   6. 3   7. 2   8. 1   9. 3

+---+
| QUICK NOTES |
| |
| This went well: |
| .... |
| .... |
| |
| This didn't quite work: |
| .... |
| .... |
| |
| Things to think about: |
| .... |
| .... |
+---+

C

This lesson introduces the past simple tense of a few verbs: *to be, to have, to go*, and *could* as the past tense of *can*. The learners work interactively with these, talking about their own childhood, then read a passage which contrasts the present and the past.

1 I was a happy child ⊡

the past simple tense; could as past tense; listening and speaking

Warm-up

If you like, you can present the past directly, before turning to the book. One way of doing this is to bring in a photo of yourself as a child. (If you have a group photo, e.g. a photo of yourself with your primary school class, ask the learners to try to pick you out.) Show the photo and say: *I was (six) years old.* Write two headings at either end of the board: PAST and NOW. Write your sentence under PAST. Say a contrastive sentence: *Now, I'm thirty three or quite old!* or even, humorously, *very old!* Write it under NOW. Continue building sentences about the past, showing the photo when you say them: *I was a student at school.* (Contrast: *Now I'm a teacher.*) *I wasn't a very good student.* (*Now, of course, I'm a very good teacher.*) *I was a thin child.* (*Now I'm not very thin.*) etc. When you have built up five or six sentences, use them for a quick question session with the learners: *What about you, Dora? Were you a thin child?* Elicit *Yes, I was …* or *No, I wasn't …*

Suggested steps

Now is the time to establish a gesture that you can use in class to signal the past. When they speak about things that have happened, the learners often lapse back into the present. If you establish a gesture that means 'we're talking about the past – use a past tense', you can signal to them without interrupting what they say. Many teachers use the conventional gesture of pointing behind them, over their shoulder, to signal past.

Explore the illustration with the whole class, especially if you have not used a warm-up. Compare with your own experience: *I was a happy child, too.* Or: *No, I wasn't really a very happy child. I was ill a lot.* (Mime *ill*.) Ask the learners: *Were you a happy child? Were you very busy? What about now? Are you busy now?* etc.

Let the learners listen to the first conversation, then pause and allow note-taking and comparing. After the second conversation, get the learners working together to check their answers.

The tapescript is on page 223.

Answer key

Speaker	as a child	as an adult
1	happy, loved animals, energetic	happy, loves animals, always tired
2	always on his own	never on his own

Talk about the conversations with the class. Go over the main points of the recording and elicit opinions.

Finally, get the learners working in pairs to talk about their own childhood. They can use the example as a prompt, if they wish, or simply talk about their memories. Circulate and help with the past tenses.

If there is time, ask one or two learners to tell the class either about their own childhood experiences, or about something they have heard in their conversations.

Personal Study Workbook

3: contrasting the present simple and the past simple
4: the grammar of the past simple

2 My father's life

reading; discussion

The text is slightly adapted from an essay written by a Chinese teenager learning English in Toronto, after her family emigrated from China to Canada.

Suggested steps

The first task is a prediction activity. It acts as a warm-up to the topic, and it pre-teaches some of the vocabulary which might otherwise prove troublesome. The learners can do it on their own or with others. Encourage them to guess, and to talk about the reasons for their guesses: *What was the father's life like in China? Would 'language problems' be something in his life in China, or his life in the new country?* and so on. Get the learners to write down their guesses in two columns, under PAST (The father's life in China) and PRESENT (The father's life in Canada). (PRESENT = NOW.)

The learners should be given a few moments to read the essay by themselves. Encourage them to read for gist, looking for specific confirmation of their guesses. Get them together in pairs or small groups to decide the column under which each of the seven expressions should really be placed.

Answer key

PAST	PRESENT
(The father's life in China)	(The father's life in Canada)
an easy life	language problems
a bank manager	pay not very good
restaurant at lunchtime	school in the evening
	a friendly boss

As a second stage, with the learners still in groups, get them to re-read the text and find the four mistakes with *can* or *cannot* in it. Ask them to correct the mistakes, and check their answers with others.

Answer key

The four mistakes are:
line 2: He cannot finds …
Correct: He cannot find …
line 5: … he cannot reading English yet.
Correct: He cannot read English yet.
line 7: … he can studies English.
Correct: … he can study English.
line 8: … how he can find enough energy to listen to the teacher?
Correct: … how can he find enough energy to listen to the teacher?

The learners then answer three comprehension questions on the text. If you prefer, the answers can be done orally, as a whole-class exercise, instead of in writing, as a writing task follows immediately afterwards.

Answer key

1. Why is the father not in the right place? Because he cannot find a good job, a job that is appropriate for him.
2. Why does the father like his job? Because the boss is friendly.
3. Why does he go to school? To study English.

The follow-up questions about other people in a similar situation, and the difficulties of people coming to live in a new country, give the learners an opportunity to recycle the vocabulary they have learnt in the exercise. Most countries have some immigrant populations, and the question is therefore one that many learners will have opinions about. They may themselves have had the experience and be prepared to say a few things about it.

Personal Study Workbook

8: reading about immigrant experience

3 In China he went to a restaurant with his friends
writing

Apart from practising the past tenses, the aim here is to get the learners to work with the text once again, so that they re-read it and become more familiar with the vocabulary and structures. It provides a quiet, individual activity to round off the lesson. If time is short, however, the learners could do the task as homework – to be checked at the beginning of the next class.

Feedback can be in the form of reading out the sentences produced to the class. Alternatively, ask the learners to see how many people they can find in the class who have written at least one sentence that is similar to one of theirs (a milling exercise).

Personal Study Workbook

8: writing a paragraph

Quick Check answer key

1. went   2. went   3. Were; was   4. could   5. had

```
QUICK NOTES

This went well:

.................................................
.................................................

This didn't quite work:

.................................................
.................................................

Things to think about:

.................................................
.................................................
```

D   REVIEW AND DEVELOPMENT

REVIEW OF UNIT 5

1 Annoying habits ⊂⊃
vocabulary and speaking; listening

Make sure the concept *to get annoyed* (to be irritated, to become cross) is understood. Use mime (plus facial expression) or dictionary work. Ensure, also, that the framework used is that of other people's *habits* that we find annoying (not one specific event, but something that happens fairly regularly). This will ensure a natural use of the present simple.

Get the learners to make their choices by themselves or with a partner. (The vocabulary is from Unit 5, so direct them to the unit if they don't remember a particular item.) Encourage them to think about the things that do really irritate them, and add other options to the list.

Have a quick comparison of choices. Ask for any new options that the learners have written, and put those on the board.

For the listening, it is a good idea to get the learners working in pairs. One is responsible for taking notes on Speaker 1, the other on Speaker 2. After a first listening, they can consult each other. Unless the class has got most of the details already, play the recording a second time.

Remind the learners that they don't have to understand everything the first time – they simply have to try to pick out the thing that annoys the speakers. You may wish to pre-teach *flatmate*, which is a colloquial British expression for a friend who lives in the flat (apartment) with you.

The tapescript is on page 224.

Answer key

For the answers, see the tapescript on page 224.

Option – Follow-up

Now that the learners have learnt the form *can*, they can follow up their listening by thinking about solutions to the problems outlined by the two speakers. Ask them: *What can people do about the problem of litter? What can the speaker do about his friend?* Accept all suggestions and write them on the board, e.g. for the first question: *Towns can put out more litter bins / rubbish bins. Pupils at school can learn not to drop litter. People can pick up litter.* For the second: *The speaker can talk to his friend about the problem. The speaker can move to a new flat*, etc.

2 I get to work at three
collocation

Get the learners working in groups, with their dictionaries. Tell them that some of the expressions can go with more than one verb.

Put the three verbs on the board. As soon as the learners are ready, they can come up and write an expression after one of the verbs. Make sure all the options are put up.

With the class sitting in a circle if possible, they take it in turn to use one of the verbs. See how long they can keep going!

Answer key

I get a cup of tea
I get home
I get annoyed
I get to work
I get a phone call
I get up
I have a cup of tea
I have a chat
I have a bath
I have an appointment
I have a rest
I make a cup of tea
I make an appointment
I make a phone call.
(*I make up* is also possible, although the learners are not likely to know it.)

3 That's the way the day goes ▭
pronunciation – rhythm and stress practice; weak form /ə/

This exercise gives some more rhythm work, practising intonation patterns over whole sentences. Rhythm work is especially appropriate to practise the weak forms. This 'rap' is a light-hearted spoof on a 'hard worker'.

Get the class working together, or in pairs, to try to find the missing words in the poem. If they find it difficult, hint: for each missing word, there is a rhyming word two lines up or down.

Answer key

The missing words are *tea*, *rest*, *you* and *eight*.

When the class is ready, let them listen to the poem for confirmation of their guesses. They can correct their sentences if necessary.

On the recording, the poem is now repeated, but with a gap for the learners to say lines 2 and 4. Do the exercise chorally to start with – the learners have to try to keep to the rhythm and get their line said in the space of time left on the recording. Have a first go at stanza one, and if the learners find it difficult, go back and give them another opportunity. If the class enjoys this kind of work, you can go back again after the end of the poem. This time, nominate individual speakers to say lines 2 and 4.

REVIEW OF UNIT 6

1 A beard really changes your face!
vocabulary extension – appearance; speaking

This exercise recycles the vocabulary of appearance from Unit 6, developing it into the areas of cosmetics, jewellery and other things that can be added to change appearance.

Do you enjoy drama? Startle the class by changing your appearance with a wig, sunglasses, a large hat, a false moustache or beard, etc. to set the scene.

Get the learners working together to think of ways of changing one's appearance and add to the list in the book.

Ask pairs to divide the methods listed into good or bad ways of changing appearance. Put two columns on the board and get them to write items under each. If there is disagreement, help them to give reasons for their opinions. Encourage discussion as much as possible here, as this leads on to the writing task that follows.

2 I think hats are really nice
writing

It is sometimes a good idea to set a specified number of sentences, e.g. three or four, depending on the time you have available.

Reading the sentences can be done as a group or whole-class activity.

Option

If you have access to magazines, especially fashion magazines (not necessarily in English) you can make this activity more visual by asking the learners to look through and choose some pictures of ways of enhancing or changing appearance (e.g. an ad for hair colouring, a fashion picture with a large hat, or cloak). They cut them out and write a sentence about their picture.

Organise an exhibition by putting up all the pictures and sentences. Get the learners to go round reading them. You can then ask them to tell you about the one they find most striking.

Worksheet

The worksheet for this unit, on page 170, can be used to revise requests.

The learners can do the first matching exercise on their own. As people usually work at different speeds, instead of having a general class confirmation of answers, it might be a good idea to put out a sheet with the answers on your desk. The learners can then come up and check their answers as soon as they finish.

They can then join another person who has finished to continue with the dialogue writing part of the worksheet.

For feedback, you could ask the learners to act out their dialogues to the whole class. Encourage them to say their lines rather than reading them, and to deliver them with feeling.

Answer key

1. Could you iron a shirt for me, too, please? (2)
2. Could you possibly lend me some money? (3)
3. Excuse me, can we order now, please? (3)
4. Can I try on this hat? (4)
5. Can we have dinner here this evening? (1)
6. Can I look at your work? (5)
7. Could you tell me what this is made of? (4)
8. Can I see your passports? (1)
9. Can you type a letter for me, please? (5)
10. Can we stay for three nights? (1)
11. Could you get me a cup of coffee, darling? (2)
12. Excuse me, can you get me a glass of water, please? (3)
13. Can we have breakfast at eight? (1)
14. Can you tell me the price? (4)
15. Could I please leave at three this afternoon? (5)

END OF UNIT NOTES

How's the class getting on?

....

....

Language that needs more work or attention:

....

....

My learners:

....

....

8

LOVE IT OR HATE IT!

CONTENTS

Language focus: talking about what you like or don't like
structure: verb + noun or verb + -ing form

Vocabulary: good and bad features of cities, countries and jobs
pets

INTRODUCTION TO THE UNIT

The main focus of this unit is lexical, with the learners extending their vocabulary range, and functional, as they practise expressing their likes and dislikes.

A

The first lesson introduces or recycles quite a lot of words about the city. The structure is kept simple: verb + noun: *I like the people. I hate the pollution in this town.*

1 I like the energy

likes and dislikes: statements and questions; vocabulary; speaking

Warm-up

Once again, you may wish to present the main structure directly before using the book. Use pictures of some buildings in your town or city if you can get them (photos, or pictures from tourist brochures if these are available). You could also show pictures of famous buildings around the world (the Taj Mahal, the Eiffel Tower, the Sydney Opera House, the Kremlin, etc.) and elicit reactions to them. Or show pictures of very traditional buildings, followed by extremely modern buildings, to elicit a range of reactions.

Ask individual learners for their reactions. Write up answers on a continuum line going from *I love it* to *I hate it*. Encourage the class to use qualifiers, e.g. *I quite like it, It's not too bad*, etc.

Suggested steps

For the purpose of comparing opinions, it is best if the class focuses on the town where they are now studying. First, they are asked to think about the things they like; then about the things they don't like about it.

Get each person to make a choice amongst the options listed, or add their own. They can use their dictionary or consult you if they need to. Circulate and suggest other things in the town if the learners can't decide.

Put the learners in pairs, draw their attention to the example, and ask them to compare their opinions. Circulate and monitor, noting any difficulties for later feedback. They can then keep on working in pairs as they think about the things they don't like in the town.

Contrast the two questions, positive and negative: *What do you like about …?* and *What don't you like about …?* Reinforce the meaning by facial expression. When the pairs have decided what they don't like about the town, they change partners, and explain their dislikes to each other.

If you have time, establish a class 'profile' of likes and dislikes, either orally or in writing.

Either ask: *How many like the markets in the town?* (count the number of votes) *How many like the shops?* etc. or ask each pair in turn to write what they like on the board. If another pair has already written what they like, they simply add a tick. Count up and establish the things the class really likes.

Personal Study Workbook

2: vocabulary of cities and their facilities and problems
5: pronunciation of 'h'

2 A sense of history? ▭

speaking and listening

Suggested steps

Set the scene by working with the illustrations. Ask the learners to guess the four countries. (1 Egypt, 2 the United States (America), 3 Australia and 4 Greece). When they suggest a correct name, write it on the board. Brainstorm: get the learners to say everything they know about the four countries and write key words on the board, under the names of the countries.

Get the learners to guess what people like about these countries. They can write their answers in the table – or you can write them on the board. Introduce and explain the expression *a sense of history* which means that history is there, present: you can feel it, you can touch it. The recording is an unscripted one, and it does contain some words that the learners may not have come across. If your learners find listening tasks difficult, give them some help with this one. Write on the board a few things that they are going to hear, in random order: *fast cars   sunshine   a sense of history   power   the Sphinx   a museum   sunshine and sea   love of children   money   an outdoor life*

Ask them to guess which expression goes with which country. Get them to write down the expressions, with their guesses. Then let them listen for confirmation. Remind them that they do not have to understand everything, just try to catch which expressions are used for which country.

Answer key

For the answers, please refer to the tapescript on page 224.

Have a feedback session to discuss the recordings. Were the learners surprised? What do they think about the 'sense of history'? Do they like countries with a sense of history? Or countries with no sense of history? Do they like museums? Or fast cars? Do they like an outdoor life? Are people in their country relaxed, like the Australians? Do people like children in their country? If the learners come from one of the countries mentioned, ask them whether the impressions are correct, or interesting.

Personal Study Workbook

9, 10: reading and writing about cities

3 What do you especially admire about the English?
reading and discussion

In classes that have some experience of England and the English, the questions will usually provoke quite strong opinions. Some visitors will have been met with warm hospitality, others, unfortunately, may have had quite different experiences as foreigners in England. (*Note*: the article the learners are about to read is specifically about the English, not the Scots, the Welsh or the Irish, who would be the first to say that they are quite different!)

In classes that haven't visited England very much, you can still elicit a few stereotypes: what do you imagine a typical English person is like? (Many people will have images of bowler hats, tweeds, a rolled umbrella, a stiff upper lip, fish and chips, and so on. They often think of the English as cold, class-conscious, great animal lovers, rather formal and polite, etc.) Accept all suggestions, negative or positive.

Sense of humour (what people think is funny) may have to be explained. (Many English people believe that their quirky sense of humour is well-known universally, though people abroad very often have not heard of it.) If your class is familiar with any examples of English

comedy programmes on television, use those as an example.

Encourage the learners to read the article for gist. They can talk about difficulties that they encounter and enlist the help of others in the class. The text is slightly adapted from a newspaper article, which was in a series of weekly interviews with people from other countries now living in England.

> ### Language Point:
> The learners may be puzzled about the difference between *to like* and *to admire*. You can say that *to like* is about feelings, emotions, 'the heart'. *To admire* is about thinking, opinion, 'the head' – *to admire* is to think, or consider, that something is good, beautiful, wonderful, or useful.

If the learners turn to you for help, encourage them to try to work out the meaning from the context, or from words they know, e.g. they know *repair* from the previous unit, so what can the phrase *quick service from repair people* mean? They know *queue* from Unit 5, so what is good about the English if they are *patient* when they queue? Recycling words from previous units is a useful way of ensuring that they become active knowledge. You can, for example, discuss the answer to the second question (the way they talk to poor people): *What does Lisa think about the English? They're not kind … they're selfish* (words from Unit 6).

Get the learners to start making the two lists as soon as they have finished their first reading. Making the lists is a way of extending their understanding of the text (and for you a means of checking their comprehension). Encourage comparison and discussion of the results as the learners are making the lists, since this also gets them discussing the contents of the article.

For the follow-up, decide whether the class is to give scores, similar to the ones in the article, either 1. for their own country, if they are studying elsewhere, or 2. for the country in which the class is now.

1. Ask the learners to compare and talk about their scores with a partner or in small groups, then ask for them to report some of their scores to the class, e.g. *Which countries got high scores for service from repair people? Which got low scores for politeness of car drivers?* To extend their communication, express surprise or agreement and ask for reasons for their views.
2. Circulate and reinforce modifiers by translating their scores into the expressions introduced in Exercise 1, e.g. *What have you got for that? 10? Oh, you really admire (you really love) the service from repair people. What about you, Keno, what have you got for that? 7? Oh, you quite like it. And what have you got for public transport? 1? You think it's terrible! Really? Do you agree, Mala?*

In many situations, different people have quite different
opinions about their own country. If so, get them to
compare and to give reasons for their opinions. If they
have similar scores, propose a different view if you
possibly can, e.g. *What? 7 for public transport? Goodness, I
don't think it's very good at all. I wait for the bus every
morning. It's always late, it's always very crowded. There aren't
enough buses at all. I hate public transport!* or *What? Only 3
for public transport? I don't agree. I think it's quite good in this
town, really. I don't wait very long for my bus in the morning.
I quite like the buses; they're clean,* etc.

Option – Follow-up

Here is a quick revision of like or dislike expressions to
round off the lesson, if you have a few minutes spare.

Prepare a list of about 10–15 very short sentences using a
random selection of the expressions you want to revise.
For example:

I love the markets.
I quite like the shops.
I hate the parks.
The restaurants are not bad.
The tourists are terrible.
I really hate the heat.
The bridges are OK.
There are not enough cinemas.
I don't like the noise.
There are too many cars.
I really love my flat.
I admire the lifestyle.
The repair people are really terrible.
Car drivers are very polite.
I really hate the prices.
I like the street life.

Say or read out the sentences as quickly as possible.
Individually, the learners react to show whether the
sentence expresses like or dislike. For like, they clap
once. For dislike, they clap twice. Or, for like, they put
their hands on their head. For dislike, they put their
hands together in front of their chest. (Demonstrate,
using two examples.)

The essence of this exercise is speed. The learners have
to react instantly. It gives good practice in rapid
identification of the mood of a sentence heard.

Personal Study Workbook

7: reading about people living in other countries, and
   what they like or dislike
8: listening to people who live in other countries

> QUICK NOTES
>
> This went well:
> ....
> ....
>
> This didn't quite work:
> ....
> ....
>
> Things to think about:
> ....
> ....

B

In this second lesson, the learners are asked to practise
two forms: verb + noun, or verb + *-ing* form. There is
also vocabulary extension: the form is now used with
different lexical areas.

1   I like the open spaces

I like + noun; *I like* + *-ing* form; writing questions; listening

Suggested steps

The first part of this activity acts as a warm-up, and
introduces some of the words the learners will hear on
the recording. Try to get the learners to do it fairly
quickly: you can set a time limit, if this is a help, then
have a quick whole-class confirmation of the four
questions.

Answer key

1. What do you like about your city? (Accept *this city,
   the city, a city, this town,* etc. – they are all possible
   answers.)
2. What do you like about (having) a birthday? (Other
   possible answers are: a wedding, Bayram, Christmas,
   etc.)
3. What do you like about your bedroom?
4. What do you like about your job?

Play the recording. You can pause after each question to
let the learners make ticks or write down notes. Or you
can play it once through, asking the learners to listen
without writing; then once again in parts, allowing time
for notes. This is a dual listening. The second unscripted
version is prepared for partly by the answers to the
questions above.

The tapescript is on page 224.

Compare answers in pairs, then as a whole class.

Answer key

For the answers, please see the tapescript on page 224.

> **Language Point:**
>
> If you are using the second version, you may notice that the speaker uses a form not taught in this unit: *I really, really like to have a party* (*like* + the infinitive, rather than *like* + *-ing* form). Native speakers who are just chatting and not thinking about the language normally use quite a variety of forms, sometimes in ways that are not what grammar books suggest! If the learners ask about it, explain that it is a variant (often used more extensively by American speakers rather than British speakers).

Personal Study Workbook

1: *like* + *-ing* form, and contrast with simple present

2 I really like having a party 🔲
speaking

In this second activity, the form verb + *-ing* form is presented more overtly. This and the *like* + noun form are taught as possible options.

Suggested steps

Go over the examples with the class. Make sure everyone understands the two forms demonstrated. Ask for other possible examples. List the four options on the board:

1. *like* + noun
2. *don't like* + noun
3. *like* + *-ing* form
4. *don't like* + *-ing* form

Point to one category and ask an individual to give you an example sentence. Point to another category, and continue until the learners have each given an example (or until boredom sets in!).

The recording gives the four questions from Exercise 1, which you can use to let the class practise pronunciation, intonation and stress. The last question offers an alternative for people who don't have jobs (e.g. university students, housewives or househusbands): *What do you like about your life?*

Get the class to repeat the questions chorally. Then put them in pairs. They each ask the four questions, and note down answers. Circulate, and encourage the pairs to use both forms: nouns and *-ing* forms. Monitor, and jot down any difficulties that need to be addressed later. It may be a good idea to set a time limit for this first part of the exercise, so that there is time left for the second part.

Get the learners to change partners and report their first conversation. Circulate and help, especially with the shift from *I like* to *he/she likes*.

As a general feedback, ask a few of the learners to report to the class. This is also the time to deal with problems you might have heard as you listened to their pairwork. Write correct forms on the board, and have a quick drill of them with the whole class.

Personal Study Workbook

6: listening to people's likes and dislikes

3 They hate pushing trolleys
practice with verb + *-ing* form; writing and guessing

This writing exercise now focuses exclusively on the verb + *-ing* form.

Work with the illustrations, getting the learners to match descriptions and pictures by themselves, with a partner, or the whole class together.

Answer key

1. B (nurses)
2. C (sales assistants)
3. A (flight attendants)

Get the learners to write a few sentences about a particular job. You can encourage them to choose one not on the list, to make the guessing more challenging. Help them with any difficulties.

Set a time limit, then ask the learners to read their sentences out. In small classes, or if there is time left, they can write sentences about two jobs for more guessing.

A quick comparison with their own jobs is suggested at the end of this exercise. You may feel that your class has explored this topic sufficiently when they worked with the fourth question in the previous exercise. If so, omit this final section.

If time is running short, set the task as homework. Start the next lesson with the guessing activity.

Quick Check answer key

B: What don't you like about it?
A: I don't like working at night.
I like working with people, but in this job I work with machines.
I hate working with machines all the time!

```
┌─────────────────────────────────────┐
│           QUICK NOTES                │
│  This went well:                     │
│  ..............................      │
│  ..............................      │
│  This didn't quite work:             │
│  ..............................      │
│  ..............................      │
│  Things to think about:              │
│  ..............................      │
│  ..............................      │
└─────────────────────────────────────┘
```

The vocabulary area shifts here to animals and pets, with the learners expressing their reactions to them. The unit is rounded off with fluency practice, when the learners can choose the topic they wish to speak about.

1 I really hate spiders!
vocabulary and speaking

Suggested steps

Follow the steps as directed in the book. The names of the animals and insects do not of course all have to be memorised. Many of them will form part of the passive vocabulary that the learners gradually acquire. But it is useful for the learners to be exposed to a variety of creatures here, so that they can have more choice in expressing their reactions of love or hate.

Choosing a pet for different people simply adds an element of fantasy or fun to the conversation. You can set the scene by asking the class whether they think it's true that people are like their pets.

Ask the learners to choose pets with a partner, for more conversation practice. They can think of appropriate pets for all the people listed or for, say, three that they choose from the list. Get the learners to express reasons for their choices, e.g. an elephant for X because she's got a good memory; a canary for Y because he loves singing during the coffee break.

Add other people to the list if you wish, e.g. the president or prime minister of your country, a famous pop star, etc. Encourage an element of gentle mockery by encouraging ironic choices, e.g. a peacock for a pop star, because she likes to show herself off; a monkey for the leader of a political party, because he's just like one himself.

Put the learners into small groups (e.g. two pairs together) to compare and talk about their choices.

Personal Study Workbook

3: the vocabulary of pets and animals
4: the vocabulary and pronunciation of animals

2 I like listening to pop music
speaking: fluency practice

The lesson is rounded off with an opportunity for the learners to choose a topic and use their newly learnt expressions of likes and dislikes to talk about it. Help with any queries, but allow mistakes to go by unchecked at this point (make notes for later correction). Your learners will probably need to consult the dictionary or ask you for some words in order to talk about the topics suggested. The vocabulary lists can be built up as they go, and then written up in a more formal way at the end of the lesson.

In small classes, the learners can simply be asked to tell the class one or two interesting things about the conversation they had. In larger classes, it might be a good idea to have a feedback in groups, then get representatives of the groups to say one or two things that they found interesting in the feedback.

Option

Get the learners to write their vocabulary lists in an attractive way, with some drawings or illustrations (they can perhaps do this for homework). You can then have an exhibition of vocabulary sets.

Quick Check answer key

(i)
flies; my dog; playing; going; waiting

(ii)
1. When you were a child, did you have a pet?
2. What was its name?
3. What did it eat?
4. Where did it sleep?
5. Did your mother like it?
6. Why not? / Why didn't she like it? / Was it friendly?

QUICK NOTES

This went well:

....

....

This didn't quite work:

....

....

Things to think about:

....

....

D REVIEW AND DEVELOPMENT

REVIEW OF UNIT 6

1 My kitchen's too small
too and *not enough*; writing a short description

Suggested steps

The learners have worked with both the vocabulary and the structure before, and they can simply be asked to do the task as directed. Make sure the instructions are understood and help with any difficulties they may have.

It may help to set a minimum number of sentences, e.g. two or three, to be written. Set a time limit – fast workers can be encouraged to write more sentences.

Get the learners working in small groups. Draw their attention to the example. Make sure they understand that they each read one sentence in turn, and see whether others in the group have similar problems.

2 My bathroom's too dark 🔊
listening

Suggested steps

Ask the class to look at the list of items before they listen. Explain *living room* as a variant of *sitting room*.

The recording is quite short, and can be played without a pause.

The tapescript is on page 225.

Get the learners to check their answers with each other, then confirm.

Answer key

the bathroom's too small: Speaker 1 and 2
not enough bedrooms: Speaker 1
too many stairs: Speaker 1
not much light: Speaker 1 and 2
the garden: Speaker 2
the living room: Speaker 1.

REVIEW OF UNIT 7

1 Can you come and feed the cat?
reading and writing requests

This activity is a light-hearted look at the difference between what people think and what they say, leading to the writing of a short role play in pairs.

Work with the illustrations to set the scene. Make sure the class understands the difference between the thought bubbles and the speech bubbles. Go over the example with the class. Mime the parent's feelings, and read his speech bubble aloud: *Feed the cat this minute or it's goodbye pussy!* Make sure you use a very angry intonation for that sentence. Then show the parent actually speaking: read out the speech bubble in a milder, more cajoling way (or, if you prefer, with restrained anger).

Get the learners working by themselves with the other situations. Make sure they understand that they are supposed to rephrase the thought bubble as a polite (or fairly polite) request, using a *can* or *could* type of request.

> ### Language Point:
> The form presented in the thought bubbles, which is more peremptory, is the imperative for commands. This tense has not been presented yet, but we felt that since it is formally the same as the present simple, it could be presented passively, without attention being drawn to it at this point. The learners are asked to work actively with the *can* or *could* forms, which are being revised.

Put the learners in pairs, get them to read out their speech bubbles to each other and compare them. If you like, you can have a quick class feedback by asking one or two people to read their request sentences to the class. Ensure that examples of both *can* and *could* are given (the teacher is more likely to use *could*, as he is speaking in a slightly more formal situation).

The learners stay in their pairs to choose one of the situations and prepare a short dialogue between the characters. Depending on the time available and the level of the class, you could ask them to write the dialogue and then read it out (with feeling!) to the class. Alternatively, they can simply prepare it, rehearse it a bit between themselves, then improvise and act it out in front of the others.

Worksheets

The worksheet for this unit (on page 171) gives the learners the opportunity of practising the vocabulary of towns and their facilities.

Suggested steps

Distribute one worksheet to each learner. Get them to choose 10 items from the list (or add their own) and place them anywhere on plan 1 of the city. Make sure they understand the instructions. They can use their dictionaries if there are any problems, though most of the words have been presented (or can be deduced, e.g. *sports centre*). Circulate while they are doing the activity to monitor.

Put the learners in pairs. Tell them not to show their worksheet to their partner. (They can be placed with a divider between them, or work back to back.) Each of them in turn describes where they have placed the items they have chosen. The listener completes plan 2 to show their partner's city.

When they have both filled in plan 2, they compare with each other's original, to check that they got it right.

Option

Before the learners do the second part of the activity, in pairs, you can play a form of Bingo by calling out the items in the list in random order. The first learner to have all their items called out is the winner. This reinforces the pronunciation of the vocabulary items in preparation for the pairwork.

> ### END OF UNIT NOTES
>
> How's the class getting on?
>
> ....
> ....
>
> Language that needs more work or attention:
>
> ....
> ....
>
> My learners:
>
> ....
> ....

9

THOSE WERE THE DAYS

CONTENTS

Language focus: past simple tense: consolidation of *be, have, go*
regular verbs
object pronouns

Vocabulary: memories of schooldays and the past

INTRODUCTION TO THE UNIT

This unit focuses straightforwardly on the past simple tense. The three irregular verbs already presented (*to be, to have,* and *to go*) are revised and consolidated in Lesson A. Lessons B and C introduce a new focus on regular verbs, and how the past simple is formed for many verbs by adding *-d* or *-ed* to the present simple form. There is special attention paid to the pronunciation of *-ed* past tenses.

In accordance with our principle of starting from the learner's own experience, the learners encounter many of the new forms through actually using them to speak about their own past memories, or through listening to speakers using them on the recordings. There are suggestions in the notes for optional activities to make the grammar more overt, or get the learners to deduce the rules for forming the past. Use these if you feel they are appropriate for your particular class. The supplementary worksheet for this unit on page 172 also provides more overt examination of the grammar.

A

1 What can you remember?
practising simple past forms: *was/were, had*; reading

The unit starts by going over the verbs the learners have already learnt, to consolidate them. The use of past questions (*What did ...? What was ...? Who was ...?*) is introduced in the opening set of questions.

Suggested steps

If your class enjoys working things out by themselves, let them read and answer the questions quietly on their own before they go on to compare their answers. Alternatively, you can read each question out loud, giving them a few minutes to remember and jot down answers. This lets them hear the questions once before they listen to them on the recording later on. With the

past tense questions, you can signal the time frame by using your PAST gesture.

Ask the learners to compare their memories in pairs. The questions are structured so that they can use the verbs *to be* and *to have* to speak about their memories. Listen to the various pairs, help if necessary and take notes of difficulties.

Personal Study Workbook

1: past tense question forms

2 The smell of fresh grass
listening

This is a dual listening task, to be exploited in the usual way. It reinforces the question forms by giving the class the opportunity to hear the questions again. The recording is quite long, but it should not be too difficult, because the learners have worked with all the questions in the previous exercise, and they are given some of the answers in the table.

Suggested steps

Pause the recording after each set of answers, to let the learners write them in the diagram. The tapescript is on page 225.

Get the learners to compare their answers, then confirm them. Let them listen to the whole conversation again, for listening practice.

Answer key
The missing answers are:
1. Yes.
2. I can't remember.
3. A brown and white dress.
4. Yes.
5. I can't remember (I didn't have a lot of toys).
6. My grandfather.
8. A hospital smell.

3 Close your eyes ... imagine you are ... 📖
speaking; listening for instructions

Revision of the past forms of *to be* continues in this third activity, with extension of the question forms: *Where was ...? What was ...?* and *What were ...?*

This is a 'guided fantasy', which invites people to walk back along the road of their life, in their minds and memories, until they come to their secondary school. The exercise can be a powerful trigger for memory – adults are quite often surprised at the details they remember (which they thought had gone forever) when they actually go back mentally to a particular place or moment in their lives.

People sometimes have an initial resistance to doing the activity. It is usually best not to force them. Occasionally, adults listen with some scepticism at the beginning, then get drawn into the fantasy as they do start to remember. But if anyone in the class really doesn't want to take part in the exercise, let them act as observers: they listen, then sit in as listeners and recorders on the group comparisons and discussions. Ask them to give a report to the class on what they heard at the end of the activity.

Warm-up

It is often good to set the scene for the class before they start to listen, especially if they are a bit nervous about understanding recordings. Draw a road on the board and explain that it is the road of life. You can write *birth* at one end, or draw a baby (a stick baby, if you like). Say: *This is the road of my life. Here I am as a baby* (make baby sounds). *I'm at home.* (Draw a small box to signify home.) *Now here I am at six* (slightly bigger stick child). *I'm at primary school.* (slightly bigger box = school). *Here I am at secondary school* (bigger child; bigger box = secondary school). *And here I am now, today, here with you* (stick adult, class of stick learners). Work with the diagram, if you like, asking the learners a few questions about their own life roads: *How about you, Rhea? Here you are as a baby. Did you have any brothers or sisters? Did you go to primary school, Alexei? How old were you then? Were you six years old?* etc.

Then establish that the class is now going back in their minds to secondary school. Show the stick adult walking backwards – in the mind or memory (indicate your head), until it reaches the secondary school. (*Walk back along the road of your life.*) It then turns off the road. (*Turn off the road.*) It goes into the secondary school 'box'. (If you have a flannel board or an OHP, the movement of the stick adult can be shown vividly.)

The scene is now set for the recording. You can give the learners the beginning words: *Close your eyes and relax. Imagine your life is a road.*

Suggested steps

Play the recording. There are pauses between the parts, but you can prolong them if you wish, with the pause button. Play the recording up to *Open your eyes.* If you like, you can stop the recording here and let the learners give their first reactions to the exercise, before they go on to the questions.

The tapescript is on page 225.

Let the class listen to the questions on the recording and then ask them to complete the answers, as in the book. Remind them of the expression *I can't remember*, if they need it.

Put the learners into small groups of three or four to compare and talk about their memories. Circulate, encouraging them to ask each other questions after their turn, e.g. *How about you, where was your school?* Occasionally, people dominate the conversation, eager to give a lot of their memories. Move the group gently along by asking others for their contribution.

Class management: In monolingual groups, the learners are understandably very eager to talk about their memories, and they often revert to their first language to do so more quickly. This is not a disaster, as they are thereby associating their new language (in which they have written the answers) with their own thoughts and experiences in the L1. Circulate among the groups, listen and monitor. Bring them gently back to English by asking an English question when there is a break in the conversation.

If in large classes you find most groups using the L1 almost constantly, try this technique. Interrupt the conversation, tell them that it's English only for five minutes now (show them your watch). After that, they can go back to their L1 to finish their conversation. The time limit often helps them to remain in English for that time, at least.

Have a quick round-up by asking one person from each group one of the questions. If you used observers, get them to give their reports.

4 She was always good at sports
writing

This is a writing task to provide a quiet ending to an interactive lesson. If the previous activity has gone on for longer than expected (it often does!) you can set the paragraphs for homework, and get them to read to each other at the beginning of your next class period.

Option – Grammar Focus

The learners have now had a lot of practice with the past tenses they have learnt. If you want them to focus on the forms of these verbs before they go on to regular *-ed* endings in the next lesson, ask them to create a poster for the class showing all the forms learnt so far, and contrasting them with present simple forms.

Divide the class into three groups, A, B and C. Group A concentrates on *to be*, B on *to have* and C on *to go*. They comb the unit, and Lesson C in the two previous units, to extract all the examples they've had. On a sheet of paper, they list the forms in two columns, e.g.

NOW	PAST
I am	I was
You are	You were
etc.	
Questions:	
Are you …?	Were you …?
Are you and your brother …?	Were you and your brother …?
Is he/she …?	Was she/he …?
What is …? What was…?	
What are …?	What were …?
Where was …?	
etc.	

Encourage the groups to make their columns as colourful and attractive as possible. You can use consistent colour coding of past and present. (Colour helps memorisation. Many learners use colour in their notebooks for this purpose.)

Combine the three sheets (on coloured cardboard, if you have access to it) to make a class poster which can be put up and used during class time to remind people of the forms.

The learners might like to make their own lists of verb forms, for quick revision. To facilitate memorisation, encourage them to use the same colour coding as the class lists.

Personal Study Workbook

3: past tenses

Quick Check answer key

1. had   2. was   3. was   4. wasn't; was   5. had

QUICK NOTES

This went well:

....

....

This didn't quite work:

....

....

Things to think about:

....

....

B

1 Time lines

past tenses; speaking and listening

This activity acts as a warm-up for the listening task which follows in Exercise 2.

Suggested steps

Draw the learners' attention to two language points, before they start guessing:

1. *was born*: This is of course a very useful expression to know. We think it is best to teach it as a set expression (treating *born* as an adjective), rather than go into the complexities of its form at this point. Doing this can help to avoid the very common mistakes learners make, in over regularising the past form (~~I was borned~~ or ~~I borned~~). Reinforce the expression quickly by saying: *I was born in … . What about you, Jem? Where were you born? Ah, you were born in … .* To the class: *He was born in … . How about you, Sylvia?* etc.

2. the first example of a 'regular' past tense: *She lived in …* Use the past gesture. If you wish, you can highlight the form by showing on the board the contrast between NOW: *I live in … .* PAST: *I lived in …*

Get the learners working in pairs or small groups to make guesses – or do the guessing as a whole-class activity, if your class is small.

2 After that, I moved to Japan ▭

listening

Suggested steps

Ask the class to look at the multiple choices. They can now extend their predictions by seeing whether they can guess the answers to any of them before listening. You can go over the choices with them if you feel they need more help.

Play the recording once through. The tapescript is on page 225.

The learners make their choices and check them with others. You can play the recording again for confirmation, or simply listening practice.

Answer key

1. In England.
2. In a small village.
3. To an American camp for children.
4. She went to university.
5. In the south of Japan.
6. She trained as a teacher.
7. She worked in a bank and in publishing.
8. She travelled a lot.
9. Mexico.

Language Point:

The speaker on the recording uses *came*, the irregular past tense of *come*, and *got*, the irregular past of *get*, neither of them introduced overtly. There is no need to teach the forms actively, since in feedback people are more likely to say: *She went back …* But in classes which enjoy getting a lot of vocabulary, and where this is not likely to cause confusion with the regular tenses being highlighted, you can signal the two verbs as additional examples of irregular past forms.

---

3 Your time line
speaking; writing

Option – Grammar Focus

If you wish to, you can highlight the past tenses introduced so far, before getting the learners to use them in their conversation. Write up the verbs they have heard in the recording, using two columns, NOW and PAST. (Colour code the two columns if you can.)

NOW	PAST
I live	I lived
I finish	I finished
I return	I returned
I move	I moved
I enjoy	I enjoyed
I work	I worked

Get the learners to deduce the rule. (If a regular verb ends with an *e*, add *d* to the 1st person form. If a verb ends with another letter, add *ed*.)

Now ask them to provide past forms for the following verbs (write them under the NOW column: *miss change decide stay (missed changed decided stayed)*. These are verbs in the resource bank of expressions, which they can use for talking about their time lines.

You may also wish to point out that the past simple form is the same for all subject persons, unlike the present simple. Add third person examples to the above list:

NOW: *I live, she lives; I finish, she finishes*, etc.
PAST: *I lived, she lived; I finished, she finished*, etc.

This point is later revised in the Quick Check.

The learners can start a new list of verbs, regular verbs, to add to their previous list of irregular past tenses – with the same colour coding.

Suggested steps

Follow the guidelines in the book. Ask the learners to fill in their time lines by themselves (if they can't remember precise addresses, they can still write down the names of areas or districts, or even just the town in which they lived).

Make sure they understand the word *miss* (mime, or use dictionary work). Then get them working in pairs or small groups. Circulate, encouraging extension of the conversations by asking additional questions.

If you started with a grammar focus, time may be getting short, and the written task can be set as homework. It is also possible that the learners will have had enough of comparing their memories, in this and the previous lesson. Instead of asking for oral comparison, display the various descriptions and ask the class to read them. If the writing is set as homework, you could encourage people to bring in any photos they have of previous homes, or to make a drawing (if they enjoy that) to accompany their description. This may then stimulate further discussion.

Quick Check answer key
(i)
1. missed   2. stayed   3. changed   4. moved   5. lived
(ii)
1. Where was your school?
2. What colour was your home?
3. What were the names of your friends?
4. What annoyed you about your school?
5. What did you like at school?
6. Where did you live as a child?

```
QUICK NOTES

This went well:
..............................................................
..............................................................

This didn't quite work:
..............................................................
..............................................................

Things to think about:
..............................................................
..............................................................
```

C

The third lesson has a skills focus: reading and writing. But it also focuses overtly on what the past -ed ending sounds like in different verbs.

1 I telephoned Mia yesterday ...
reading and discussion

Suggested steps

The first matching exercise simply pre-teaches some of the vocabulary needed to understand the text. The class can do this together or in groups.

Answer key

1. a hairstyle	3. a broken ankle in plaster
2. an ankle	4. a screen
	5. bad handwriting

When confirming the answers, take the opportunity of using some of the other words the learners will need for the text. For example, express concern about the broken ankle: *The plaster's very heavy* (mime heaviness, write *heavy* on the board). Comment: *The hairstyle looks great, doesn't it? No? You don't think so? The handwriting's very bad – it's impossible to see all the words, isn't it? Can you see all the words? No, it's impossible ...* etc.

If there are other words which you think might prove difficult for your class, you can pre-teach them quickly before they read, e.g. *tired, enormous, nervous* (all relatively easy to mime!).

Work with the illustration to establish the concept of a diary, if this is likely to be an unknown. Show them an example of your own, if you've got one, e.g. a desk diary, a pocket diary, a year diary.

Ask the class to read the text silently (they will hear it later on the recording), concentrating on understanding the gist and seeing whether they think anything seems strange (the writer uses a telephone with a screen, which may not yet be very common everywhere).

As soon as the learners have finished reading, get them choosing the right answers from the multiple choices. These questions extend understanding of the way text referencing works. Get the learners to check their answers with each other first. When you confirm the answers, ask for reasons, e.g. 1. Mia is not the writer's mother, since Mia shows him a letter from his parents. 2. Janine is a daughter, because the writer says 'the kids' (his children seemed fine, except for Janine's broken ankle, so Janine must be one of his children). And so on.

Answer key

1. Mia is the writer's wife.
2. Janine is the writer's daughter.
3. The writer has more than one child.
4. The writer lives far away from Hong Kong.
5. The writer's parents live far away from him.
6. The writer works for a company.
7. The call was very expensive.
8. He looked at Mia.
9. He tried to read a letter from his parents.

One of the grammar points that is being indirectly brought out by this exercise is the use of object pronouns. The last two questions get the learners to think specifically about the referencing effect of pronouns. Object pronouns are revised in the Quick Check (i). If you wish to, you can use this in class to make sure that all the pronouns are presented.

You can get the learners speculating about why Mia seemed nervous. There is no answer in the text, so imaginative people can think of any possible reasons. (Is there someone else with Mia in the home? Did she break something? Did she buy something expensive for the home? etc.)

Because of time constraints, you may wish to do the last part of this exercise simply as a whole-class conversation, rather than groupwork. Elicit good points or bad points about phones with screens for the various combinations of people, e.g. it's nice for a boyfriend and girlfriend to see each other when they talk – but what if they are in old clothes, or their hairstyle's messy, or what if they are with somebody else? What if the boss sees an employee playing cards instead of working? etc.

Personal Study Workbook

2: object pronouns
6: reading (past tenses)

2 I noticed that she looked nervous about something 🎧
pronunciation of past tenses; listening

Suggested steps

Give the learners an example of the distinction they are going to listen for in the first part of the recording. They have to decide whether they hear /t/, as in *looked*, or /d/, as in *telephoned*.

Play the first part of the recording. Pause after each verb, to give the learners time to write it down under the appropriate column. If they can't decide, ask them to write it down in a third column, *Can't decide*. The tapescript is on page 226.

Get the learners to compare answers. If they couldn't decide which column was appropriate for some of the verbs, you can let them listen to the list again.

Answer key

the verb ending = /t/	the verb ending = /d/
looked	telephoned
wasn't	seemed
finished	arrived
noticed	showed
	tried

In the second part, the learners hear the text from Exercise 1, with gaps, during which time they have to supply the missing verb. You might like to get them to underline the verbs in their text so that they know exactly when they have to speak.

Doing the exercise chorally can be fun, and it takes the strain off individuals.

Finally, the learners hear the whole extract once more. Direct their attention particularly to the verbs they have said, so that they can see whether they got the pronunciation right.

3 It was a great day!
negatives with *didn't*; writing a diary with past tenses

This activity introduces the negative *didn't* (*did not*). The learners are encouraged to extend their bank of descriptive adjectives by using some new ones to talk about the day they had yesterday.

Suggested steps

Follow the steps outlined in the book. The learners make notes about yesterday, using the prompt questions, which don't introduce any new concepts or words. You can set a time limit for this first part, so that the learners move on to the next at about the same time.

Direct the attention of the class to the resource box of descriptive words. Ask them to choose one or two to describe yesterday. They will know some of them already. Others can be presented through mime, or by using dictionaries.

Put the learners into pairs, draw their attention to the examples, and get them talking about the day before. Circulate, help (e.g. with the pronunciation of *received*, which can cause problems), monitor and make notes of difficulties which you can attend to in the feedback session.

You can have a quick feedback afterwards by asking one or two people to tell you what their partner did or didn't do the previous day. (In this way, the learners see that *didn't* is the same for different persons: *I didn't, she didn't*, etc. Highlight this point on the board if you think it's necessary.)

Option

If time is short, set the diary writing exercise as homework.

Feedback can be oral, in groups, with people reading out and talking about their diaries, and a follow-up discussion on whether people really do write diaries. Alternatively, you can put the diaries up on the wall and get the learners milling round to read them. Encourage them to ask each other questions to find out more about the things mentioned in the diaries.

Personal Study Workbook

7: negatives in the past tense

Quick Check answer key

(i)
1. her   2. it   3. him   4. them
(ii)
1. Yes, she did.
2. No, he didn't.
3. Yes, she did.
4. No, he didn't.
5. No, he didn't.

QUICK NOTES

This went well:

....

....

This didn't quite work:

....

....

Things to think about:

....

....

D REVIEW AND DEVELOPMENT

REVIEW OF UNIT 7

1 Living in a new country
reading

Suggested steps

The first part of this exercise asks for expression of opinions, to set the topic of the reading passage to follow. Elicit problems from the class and write them on the board. Get the class to think about problems with language, problems between parents and children, problems of homesickness – use the word *lonely* to pre-teach it.

Get the class to read the statements and mark whether they think parents or children are the speakers in each case. The learners can do this on their own, or discuss options with a partner.

Option

Divide the class into three groups. Assign the first dialogue (A and B) to group 1, the second (C and D) to group 2, and the third (E and F) to group 3. Ask them to decide together which speaker is a parent, and which is a child or young person.

Form new groups, consisting of three people: one from group 1, one from group 2, and one from group 3. (It's more complicated to describe this than actually to do it! But it's done very easily if you 'colour code' the groups. Give each member of group 1 a red slip of paper, or badge, or a small sticky circle to put on their hands. Group 2 get a blue badge, group 3 a green one. When you form the new groups, tell them to get into groups with one blue, one red, and one green person.)

Get the new groups to compare their dialogues and the decisions they came to in their first conversations.

Answer key

1. A: Y; B: P
2. C: P; D: Y
3. E: P; F: Y

Get the groups working on the list of problems that came up as they discussed their dialogues. Put the two headings on the board, and encourage different people to come and write one problem up as soon as they have listed it in their group

The final suggesting of solutions can be done first in groups, then simply as a general class conversation.

REVIEW OF UNIT 8

1 I like salmon pâté sandwiches 🔲
pronunciation practice: final 's' sound

This is another light-hearted rhythm 'rap' to help the learners with their intonation and pronunciation. The surprise element in this one is the unexpected last line of each stanza, which breaks the pattern both of the rhythm and of the rhyme.

Suggested steps

If you like, you can go quickly over any vocabulary items that might pose problems – Ted, Fred, Ann, Dan and Jose are all names of people. Get them guessing any other unknown items (e.g. *rocks, hikes*) which might be known by somebody in the class – demonstrate, mime, or get them to use their dictionaries.

Let the learners listen to the first stanza, to set the idea of the very rhythmic first two lines, followed by the quite different final line. You can get them to repeat the rap chorally. *Holidays in the Mediterranean* is of course quite a mouthful, and usually provokes merriment at the first attempt to say it all at one go. Model the pattern by using gestures (e.g. like an orchestra conductor's baton) which point to the two stresses, on *holidays* and on *Mediterranean*.

Play the next two stanzas.

Get the learners to complete the last line of stanza 4 with something they *really* like (no special rhythm or rhyme needed). Then, when they hear it, they can all add their last line, softly, in a voice just above a whisper.

If you have recording facilities (e.g. in a language lab), you can get the learners recording themselves individually, then comparing their own rap with the one on the recording.

The tapescript is on page 226.

2 She likes trains
writing and practising rhymes

This is a simple writing task which extends the work done in the previous exercise.

Suggested steps

Get the learners to write a three-line stanza, using the pattern given, or creating their own. Here it is necessary to provide a rhyme in lines 1 and 2, but not of course in line 3.

tea: can rhyme with *me, a tree, the sea, brie* (the cheese),
  ghee, a knee, a pea …
trains: can rhyme with *brains, Danes, planes, plains, grains,*
  canes, cranes, manes, drains (a quirky thing to like?) …

Listeners say their raps in turn. If you can, record this session. It usually amuses the learners to hear the whole set of raps again on the recording.

Worksheets

The worksheet for this unit, on page 172, gives more practice with the past simple tense of the three irregular verbs learnt so far, and of regular verbs. You can use it in class, or set it as homework. (Get the learners working in pairs to guess reasons at the beginning of the next class, when they bring their homework in.)

The first two parts provide revision of many of the verbs learnt so far, and show the formation of their past tense forms. The task is an easy one, and the learners can be encouraged to do it quickly by themselves. If you are using the worksheet in class, encourage them to check whether they remember the meaning of each one of the verbs – get them to ask three other learners before they consult their dictionaries. To avoid confusion, remind the learners that Part 2 is concerned with the spelling of the past tenses, not their pronunciation.

Part 3 gives eight examples of reasons for things that were done, or not done. The learners might enjoy doing this in pairs or small groups.

Part 4 is an individual writing task, followed by a pairwork guessing exercise.

Option
You may wish to follow this up by asking the class to mention one very good reason they heard, one reason they think was a bad reason, one very silly reason, one amusing reason, etc.

Answer key
Part 1: he/she/it was; he/she/it had;
       I/you/we/they went.

Part 2:

Column 1 (live/lived)	Column 2 (talk/talked)	Column 3 (try/tried)
smoked	(stay/stayed)	tidied
used	washed	studied
moved	started	cried
typed	listened	
voted	worked	
liked	watched	
loved	kissed	
hated	asked	
admired	showed	
changed	returned	
telephoned	cleaned	
decided	repaired	
received	cooked	
	painted	
	opened	
	looked	
	finished	
	enjoyed	
	missed	
	played	

Part 3:

1. I didn't listen to the radio because the programmes didn't seem interesting.
2. Marla arrived late at work this morning because she missed the bus.
3. Gino didn't wash the car because he didn't have time.
4. We didn't watch TV last night because some friends arrived from America.
5. They didn't have any food because they didn't go shopping.
6. My parents didn't miss their village because they loved the city.
7. Our class studied a new language because we enjoyed it.
8. The crowd hated the game because their favourite team didn't play.

END OF UNIT NOTES

How's the class getting on?

....

....

Language that needs more work or attention:

....

....

My learners:

....

....

10

ONCE UPON A TIME

CONTENTS

Language focus: past simple: irregular verbs

Vocabulary: stories and storytelling
books, films, TV programmes

INTRODUCTION TO THE UNIT

The title of the unit is the traditional way of starting to tell a story in English. It sets events in a time period that is not specified but is clearly finished and in the past. Narration thus provides a natural framework for this second presentation of the past simple.

The focus here is on irregular verbs, which form their past tenses in weird and wonderful ways. Because there is such a variety of them, and so many are important, if not indeed essential, they present quite a challenge to the learners. Our strategy in trying to make the various forms more memorable has been to get the learners working with them in imaginative, contextualised situations from the very beginning. In the first section, they are given a lot of support as they write their own stories using the irregular pasts. The second lesson is structured around a central listening task, while the third recycles some of the verbs learnt by inviting the class to talk about books or films they have seen and liked.

A

1   Suddenly, a shot rang out
past simple irregular verbs; writing

Suggested steps

Because this first activity gets the learners creating their own story, we suggest that you start directly with the book this time. As a warm-up, explore the illustration with your class. Give your own feelings about the lonely railway platform at night and elicit theirs. Look at the reaction sentences with the class and talk about each. Teach *frightening* if the learners are puzzled by the word. Suggest reasons for fear, using *maybe – Maybe there are robbers*. Emphasise (recycle) *lonely*. Encourage the learners to think of a reaction sentence of their own, and either write it, or say it to a partner for comparison.

Tell the learners that the illustration is from the first page of a novel. Ask them if they are ready to start writing the novel. Some people prefer to do this on their own,

while others like working with a partner, discussing possibilities, etc. Depending on your class, you can either give them directions on this, or leave it up to them.

Go over the three possible first sentences with the class, where possible miming the drama of the situations: *It was a dark and stormy night.* (Show *dark* – screw your eyes up, you can't see anything – and *stormy*, make storm sounds). *Suddenly a shot rang out.* (Mime pistol or shotgun and make a gun shot sound.) Mime the child's long wait, sad loneliness; the two people meeting but not talking as they wait, then getting onto the train.

Make sure the learners understand that they can either choose one of the three possibilities, or create their own. While they are writing, you might like to pull out the irregular verbs encountered so far and write them up on the board, in the usual way under NOW and PAST: *ring/rang*; *sit/sat*; *eat/ate*; *think/thought*; *meet/met*; *catch/caught*.

When everyone has written their sentences, they continue the narration, either with one of the sentences given, or with a sentence of their own.

New verb possibilities to add to the list on the board are: *say/said*; and *come/came*.

Finally, the learners add at least one more sentence to conclude their little story. Circulate and help with vocabulary and past tense verbs that they might need. It's usually helpful to set a time limit here, e.g. 5–10 more minutes.

As soon as two people finish, they can pair up and read their stories to each other. They can then change partners and compare again, as others finish.

Ask if anyone heard a particularly interesting story, and if so ask the learners to read that one to the class. Or nominate one or two people to read. After the next listening activity, put the stories up as an exhibition for the class to see and compare.

Personal Study Workbook

2: irregular past tenses

2 She lit a match 🔳

listening

A group of native English speakers were asked to do the task in Exercise 1. Two of the simpler versions produced were then recorded by them for this exercise.

Suggested steps

Get the class working in pairs or small groups to read and understand the continuations, and match them to Speaker A or B. Get them to consult other learners if there are any difficulties, e.g. *doorway, cottage, match* – although the context of lighting a cigarette with a match should help – *panicked, the oven.* You can impose the usual rule – ask three other people before you ask the teacher or consult a dictionary.

Play the recording once, and let them confirm their guesses. There is a final part to each story that is not in the sentences.

One more verb can be added to the list on the board: *light/lit.*

The tapescript is on page 226.

Answer key

Sentences 1 and 6 are a continuation of Speaker A's story.

Sentences 3, 5, 2 and 4 are a continuation of Speaker B's story.

For the final part of each story, please see the tapescript on page 226.

Play the recording again, if you or the learners wish. Then ask them to put away all their notes. Put them in pairs and ask each to tell one of the stories to the other, if at all possible without consulting their book or notes. The listener can help with details. Re-telling a story they have heard is an excellent way to get the learners to use the past tenses, because of the support it gives them while they are speaking.

Option

If there is time, have a quick revision of the past tenses learnt so far in the unit, which you have written on the board. Use flash cards, or the 'ball-throwing' technique. Say a past sentence using one of the verbs on the board. Throw a ball, or an eraser or any small object, to Learner A. Learner A says a past sentence using another verb on the board, then throws to Learner B, etc. A different verb has to be used in a sentence each time.

Personal Study Workbook

5: past tenses: listening
6: past tenses: listening, reading, writing

3 I was born in South America

practice with irregular verbs

Suggested steps

Go over the present and past examples with the class, showing them that the first noun needed, *a birth*, has been put in for them. Then get them doing the matching exercise, possibly with a partner. Encourage them to do the easier nouns first (*loss* and *meeting* are close enough to the verbs to be recognisable). They can then get help with the more difficult nouns through using their dictionaries.

Add to the past tense list on the board: *leave/left; find/found; lose/lost; forget/forgot.*

Make sure that the class understands that they are to think of a true story that really happened to them. Inevitably, in some large classes especially, one or two will prefer to tell a fictional story. This doesn't matter, and can even provide matter for further amusing practice, if others try to spot whether a story is really true or not. But it is worth while insisting at the beginning that they try to think of a true story. Adults usually have a wealth of extremely rich and often moving stories from their own lives, and the task of having to incorporate one of the items in the list sometimes acts as a spur to their memories.

Set a time limit for the preparation of stories. Some learners like to write their stories. Encourage them to put down notes only to help them in their re-telling (otherwise the preparation can take too long). It will make management of the activity easier if they all start telling the stories at the same time – if they haven't finished, they can improvise the ending as they go.

Get the learners telling each other their stories, first to one person, then to a new partner. If they have used a written prompt, you could make the second re-telling more challenging by saying that this time they have to do it without their notes.

Option

It is a good idea to get the learners to copy the verbs you have written on the board, so that they start to create their own lists. If you have created a poster of verb forms for the class (the *Option* at the end of Unit 9, Lesson A) now is the time to extend it, or create a new one, to show the irregular verb forms.

One way of categorising them is through either the spelling or the sound of the endings. You can suggest that the learners make headings with the new verbs, e.g. *rang   sat   thought   met*, etc. and add new verbs in the same columns as they come across them. (For example, if the learners are concentrating on the sounds of the endings rather than the spellings, they write *thought* and *caught* in one column, and so on.)

Personal Study Workbook

3: past tenses
4: pronunciation of irregular past tenses

Quick Check answer key

Last night, there was a frightening sound at my door. I sat in my chair and didn't open the door. Then I went out of the room and I telephoned my friend. Five minutes later, the doorbell rang. My friend came in and said, 'It's only a cat!'

QUICK NOTES

This went well:

....

....

This didn't quite work:

....

....

Things to think about:

....

....

B

1 I was born in Elorin ⊂⊃
listening

Warm-up

Get the class to speculate about the illustration. It is a picture of the 'tools' of a professional storyteller from Nigeria. Get the learners to talk about storytelling in their past experiences. Did their parents tell them stories when they were children? Was there any special time for stories? (In many countries parents tell children stories at bedtime.) Were there any special stories that most children were told, for example fairy tales, legends, and so on? Can they remember any stories from their childhood? If they themselves have children, do they tell them stories?

Suggested steps

The Class Book asks the learners to work in pairs, but depending on the level of the class, you may wish to get them working by themselves to complete the answers.

Put the class into pairs. One partner focuses on A, the other focuses on B. They then work together to complete their notes. Finally, they join another pair to check and confirm their answers.

The tapescript is on page 226.

Answer key

A
He was born in Nigeria.
He is an artist and storyteller.
1. He tells stories
3. he sings

B
He learnt his job from his mother and the rest of his family.
They told stories when the sun went down.
They sat underneath the trees.
He tells stories in schools.

Use the final set of questions as a whole-class discussion, following on from the warm-up above. In multinational classes, someone may come from a country where there are professional storytellers. Ask them to talk about them to the class. What kind of stories do they tell – legends, traditional tales, new stories that they create themselves?

In classes from one country, ask whether they think there were storytellers in the past. For example, in some countries people a few generations ago told stories (as well as playing music, singing or dancing) when they gathered together in the evenings. Ask them whether there are modern types of storytellers, e.g. on the radio or television.

2 Ojumbala the rain god, and the seven children ⊂⊃
listening; reading

In the main part of this lesson, the learners are going to listen to one of Adesose Wallace's African stories. The story is told in four parts, each one accompanied by tasks in the book so that the learners can listen interactively.

Suggested steps

Ensure that the learners understand that what they are going to work with is a traditional African story. Check understanding of the concept of a 'rain god' (important in dry countries!). The scene is set by getting the learners to match the pictures with some sentences that give the gist of the first part of the story. They can do this by themselves, then check with others. Let the learners listen to Part 1, and then confirm their answers with them by going over the illustrations and the sentences.

The tapescript is on page 226.

Answer key

The order is:
Sentence 2: Long ago there lived an old man and his wife.
Sentence 4: They had seven children.
Sentence 3: The mother found that there was no food in the house for the children.
Sentence 1: She ran to tell the old man the problem.

The story continues. Here, the learners read a summary of Part 2, then listen to it. You can let the class read silently, or go over it with them before they hear it on the recording.

After they have heard Part 2, ask the learners to predict the continuation of the story, using the past tense: *Did the children stay inside? What happened next?*

Then get them to read the sentences, or read them out with the class. Give a demonstration to show *the wind started blowing* and *the children were not scared*.

Play the next part.

Get the class to confirm the two wrong sentences, and suggest correct statements.

Answer key

2. The children went outside.
4. The children were scared.

Try to get the class to predict the rest of the story. Ask: *What happened next?* to stimulate speculations in the past tense, e.g. *I think the rain god ate the children. Maybe the rain god broke the window and came in.*

When the class has finished predicting, decide whether to let them read it first, or listen to it (depending on how difficult your class finds listening). It is longer than the other sections, but very dramatic.

Play the recording.

Ask for reactions from the class. Did they enjoy the story? Did they like the singing and the drums? If they are keen, you can play the whole story to them again and let them listen to it without interruptions.

Ask them about similar stories and if there is time, let them tell the stories in groups, or to the class.

Option

Once again, re-telling the story can be beneficial in getting the learners to use the past tenses they have heard. You can do this as a chain activity. Learner A starts, giving one sentence from the beginning of the story, Learner B continues, then Learner C, and so on.

An alternative is to ask people to try to slip in an incorrect detail in their narration, making it as unobtrusive as possible. The rest of the class listens to spot the incorrect items.

Personal Study Workbook

7: listening and filling in an accident report form

Quick Check answer key

1. They were farmers.
2. He was a storyteller.
3. He tells them a story. Did he tell them a story?
4. She found the food. Did she find the food?
5. They left the house. Did they leave the house?
6. She runs to him. Did she run to him?

This final section encourages the learners to use their new knowledge for fluency practice. This unit as a whole concentrates on listening and speaking. If you would like your learners to have more practice with reading, you could use either of the two substantial reading texts in the Personal Study Workbook (Exercises 5 and 6) as class activities. Exercise 9 in the Personal Study Workbook asks the learners to think of ways of remembering all the past tenses that they are learning in the unit. This could also be used as a classroom activity, to heighten awareness of different learning styles and help the learners address the problems posed for many adults by the large amount of memorisation needed in learning the irregular past tenses.

1 It was a wonderful film
listening; asking questions using the simple past tense

Suggested steps

This is a warm-up activity for the learners' own speaking exercise, which comes in Exercise 2.

Start off by giving the class the title of the book or film (or a TV programme or video):

I saw a wonderful film last year. Its title was …. Ask me about it. (If there is no response, prompt softly: *Ask me about the stars.*) Tell the story in parts. Elicit: *What happened next?* (If you need to prompt: *Ask me what happened next. What happened after that?*)

For a film, elicit: *Who were the stars? Were they good? Who directed it? Was there any music? What was it about? Where did the action happen? (In a city? In the countryside? In what country?) What happened next? What happened in the end? Where did you see it? Did you see it with anybody? What did they think of it? What did you like about it?* etc.

For a book, elicit: *Who wrote it? What did you like about it? What characters (people) did it have in it? What were they like? What country did they live in? What jobs did they have? What happened? What happened next? Were you surprised? Did you like the ending? Was it a sad book, or a happy book?* etc.

2 When did you see the film?
practice with past tenses; speaking

This exercise encourages the learners to use the past tenses to talk about experiences in their own lives.

Suggested steps

The first matching exercise simply ensures that the basic vocabulary is known. It can be done and checked fairly quickly.

Answer key

1. a book
2. a film
3. a television set
4. a radio

Get the learners to work by themselves at first, to choose two subjects of conversation. Set a time limit, so that pairwork can start at about the same time for everyone.

Get the learners working in pairs. Draw their attention to the example. Then ask them to work through the questions in turn. They should have two items to talk about, from the list they just made. Go round the pairs listening. Jot down any problems, so that you can discuss them afterwards. Help the learners to extend their conversation by asking further questions about the books, programmes or films that they are discussing.

In a general feedback, ask the class if anyone heard about a particularly interesting book, film or programme. Let them describe it briefly to the class. Mention any interesting items that you heard as you were going round the groups and ask people to add more details. Go over any special problems and do a quick drill to correct them.

3 I just watch the news, that's all
discussion

The third activity leads on to a freer, less controlled discussion that explores opinions and differences of opinion.

Suggested steps

Get the learners categorising the different types of programmes individually. You can then have a class discussion, comparing what they have put and the reasons, before going on to the pairwork.

The learners, in pairs, choose two from the list of people (e.g. ten-year-old children and elderly people). What programmes do they think are popular with those people? They can choose some of the programmes in the illustration, or think about programmes in the country where they are. Ask them to think about their own favourite programmes and compare them with the programmes they have chosen for their two categories.

Get the learners working in small groups to talk about suitable programmes for their categories, and to discuss their own favourites. Listen and monitor.

Quick Check answer key

sits; sat; sat
thinks; thought; thought
meets; met; met
does; did; did
catches; caught; caught
hears; heard; heard
runs; ran; ran
comes; came; came
says; said; said
goes; went; went
writes; wrote; wrote

```
QUICK NOTES

This went well:
......................................................
......................................................

This didn't quite work:
......................................................
......................................................

Things to think about:
......................................................
......................................................
```

D REVIEW AND DEVELOPMENT

REVIEW OF UNIT 8

1 I really hate standing in queues
-ing forms; writing

This directed writing activity gets the learners to review the structure: verb + -ing form.

Suggested steps

Ask the learners to complete the sentences on their own. Can they find someone in the class who has written two similar sentences?

The milling exercise is designed so that the learners will form new partnerships, who work together for the next writing task. As soon as any two people discover two similar choices, they get together and start writing their paragraphs. If some people in the class are left, they then look for someone who has made one choice that is the same as one of theirs. (Anyone remaining can simply be paired off. Their paragraphs will contain more contrasts than comparisons!)

REVIEW OF UNIT 9

1 A hundred years ago, our town was very small
simple past tense; speaking

This activity and the following one recycle and reinforce the past tense of *to be* and regular verbs.

Option – Warm-up
Bring in nineteenth-century prints of another town or city (not one that the learners are going to talk about in the activity). Explore the prints with the class, describing what the prints show, setting the scene for the activity and using some of the expressions in the box.

Suggested steps

It is often more productive to put the learners into small groups to consider the four questions and think about the past.

In multinational classes, get the learners thinking about their own home towns, or perhaps places where their grandparents lived. (It doesn't have to be exactly one hundred years ago – just a long time ago.)

In classes from one country, decide whether you wish the class to talk about one particular city (for example, instead of talking about their own town, they could think about the capital city). Alternatively, they could think about the places where their grandparents lived, what they were told about them, and what the changes have been since their grandparents' childhoods.

For the feedback, encourage as many individuals as possible to give their ideas, or their grandparents' memories. Encourage the listeners to ask questions.

2 Our town was a small village then 〇〇
listening

Suggested steps

If you like, you can put the learners in pairs and ask each one to be responsible for taking notes on one of the two speakers.

Play the recording, pausing after Speaker 1 to let the class take notes. Then play Speaker 2.

Answer key
For the answers, see the tapescript on page 227.

Compare the recording with the learners' own ideas or memories to stimulate further recycling of the past tenses.

Worksheets

The worksheets for this unit are on pages 173 and 174.

In this activity, the learners work in pairs. Each is given a set of facts about a couple, in the form of documents from their past. They are asked to compare their documents so that they get all the facts about each

person, then write a 'newspaper article' about the couple's life.

Put the learners in pairs, give one of them Worksheet 10A, the other Worksheet 10B. They read and compare their 'documents' and together establish the facts of the couple's life. Circulate and help them with any difficulties.

They can write the article together or separately. Try to ensure that they use as many of the available facts as possible. Encourage them to add any other information about the couple that they can imagine to make their article full of concrete and vivid details, and to make comparison of the finished articles more interesting.

Have an exhibition of the completed newspaper articles.

Answer key
Here is an example of a possible article:
The two children of Paul and Simonetta Douglas had a party at the Grand Hotel on Saturday to celebrate their parents' Silver Wedding. Paul and Simonetta came to live in Ilkley just after their marriage. Paul was born in Cornwall, where he went to school. He liked maths, but wasn't a very good student. (His teachers said he didn't work hard enough.) Simonetta was born in Ontario, in Canada. She went to school there. Her teachers said she was a quiet but friendly child. She wasn't very good at writing at school, but she later became a writer. (There's hope for everybody!) Paul studied dentistry at Trinity College Dublin. Simonetta did her first degree at the University of Toronto, then came to London for a post graduate course in journalism. That's where she met Paul. They got married in Ontario, then they came to live in Ilkley, where Paul worked as a dentist. They had two children, first a son Jonathan, then (two years later) a daughter, Margaret. Over the years, Paul went all over the world, to Brazil, to Japan and to Australia, to give talks on dentistry. Simonetta stayed at home and wrote thrillers (detective stories, novels, etc.). Two of her well-known books are ...... and ...... She published them under the name of Simon Douglas, because, she says, more people buy books if they think the authors are men.

END OF UNIT NOTES

How's the class getting on?

....

....

Language that needs more work or attention:

....

....

My learners:

....

....

11

WHAT'S GOING ON?

CONTENTS

Language focus: present continuous for things happening now,
temporary situations and developing situations
contrast present simple and present continuous

Vocabulary: daily routines and happenings
the quality of life

INTRODUCTION TO THE UNIT

With the present simple and the past simple now well established, it is time to turn to the present continuous. This can be quite a difficult or confusing area for many learners whose language either doesn't have a continuous tense, or doesn't use it in the same way as English.

One of the problems of dealing with the present continuous tense in class is that it is easy to be led into using 'inauthentic' language for the sake of practising the form. Teachers sometimes ask the learners to say: *I'm watching television* when in fact they are doing nothing of the sort: they are sitting there practising the present continuous! The activities in this unit try to get classes using the language authentically right from the start, by getting them to think about things that are actually happening now, either at the moment of speaking, or more generally (for example, what they are learning). The examples used in the texts and the recordings also set the language in situations which would normally call for the continuous tense.

A

1 What's happening? 🔲
present continuous: things happening now

The presentation of the tense is through a listening 'game'. The class hears different sounds on the recording, and has to match a sound with one of the pictures, in other words, to decide what is happening to produce the sound. There are a number of other activities which you can use to present the continuous tense in authentic situations. These can be used either as a warm-up before the first listening activity, after it, or elsewhere as quick revision.

Warm-ups

Option 1

Stand at the window of the class. Look out and tell the class what is happening. Write on the board: *What is happening outside?* Write one thing that you see, e.g. *A car is going down the road.* Ask Learner A to go up to the window and report one other thing that is happening. Learner A: *There's a lady … there's a lady in the street, with a dog.* Supply and write up: *A lady is walking her dog* or *A lady is walking with a dog.* Learner B then goes up and reports another thing happening, etc.

This obviously works best when the window overlooks a busy city street!

Option 2

Set the scene by talking about what the class is doing now. *What am I doing?* Write up: *I'm teaching English / the present continuous. What are you doing? I'm/we're sitting, listening, writing, learning,* etc.

Then ask members of the class about their friends and families. *What about your wife, Hamdi? What's she doing now? You don't know? Can you guess? Oh, maybe she's at the market?* Write up: *She's shopping.*

Write up guesses on the board.

In a workplace situation, ask what other people in the company are doing now. In a university or other class situation, ask what others classes are doing now.

Option 3

Give Learner A a slip of paper which asks them to go to the back of the class and do something continuously, e.g. wave their arms.

Others in the class sit at the front and, without looking round, try to guess what the learner is doing. The person who guesses gets another slip and goes to the back to carry out the instructions. Instructions can include: touch your head/your toes (until I tell you to stop); read a newspaper; rub out a page of pencilled writing; nod your head; sharpen a pencil; tear a piece of paper into small bits; eat an apple; peel something, e.g.

an orange; wrap a parcel; unwrap a parcel; put the books that are there in a pile; walk back and forth; jump up and down; play with a ball, etc.

Option 4

Use pictures or photographs. This is a standard way of presenting the tense, and it does represent the way people often talk about what is 'happening' in pictures. Show pictures or flash cards, either with a lot of activity going on, or designed to elicit one particular example of a verb. Or show the learners some of your own photos, showing some activity, and ask them to describe what they think is going on.

Option 5

This is a variant of the previous activity. Use magazine pictures or other illustrations which you can cut in half. The learners first describe what they see, e.g. *It's a café. A man is sitting at a table. He's drinking a cup of coffee, espresso, maybe. Two women are sitting at another table. They're chatting.*

Then they try to guess what's in the other half, e.g. *I think a waiter is bringing the women some drinks.*

Option 6

This is another variant with pictures. Present pictures that are mysterious in some way, e.g. show just a small corner of a picture; or show a picture that has been badly photocopied and is almost indistinguishable; or copy the outline only of an activity onto a large sheet of paper or an OHP transparency.

Ask: *What's happening here, do you think? It's someone playing football, do you think?* Write: *He's playing football* on the board.

Suggested steps

The learners can do the activity by themselves, but it is usually fun for them to work with a partner or two, so that they can discuss the options.

Play the recording, pausing after number 1 to indicate that the choice for this one has already been made. This acts as an example of what is supposed to be done. Continue with the other sounds, pausing after each one to let the class speculate and make their choices.

Get them to check with others before confirming the answers.

Answer key

1. She's calling a taxi.
2. He's having a shower.
3. They're having a party.
4. They're building a new house.
5. She's walking down the street.
6. They're flying to Sydney.
7. He's making a cup of coffee.
8. She's using the computer
9. They're repairing the road.

Personal Study Workbook

2: the forms of the present continuous
3: the present continuous for describing
4: present continuous verbs and collocations

2 I'm standing in front of Government House ▭

present continuous; listening; speaking

The context here is that of reporting news events as they are actually happening, a situation in which the present continuous is very natural.

Suggested steps

The opening questions set the scene for news reporting. Get the learners to discuss the occasions on which they would expect a radio or TV reporter to be on the spot, reporting an unfolding news event. (You can elicit the two situations they are going to hear, if these do not come up: a mass demonstration and a state visit.)

To get the learners into the situation before they listen, let them read the three options for each news report. Once again, pairs can be assigned one of the two reports each.

Play the recording, pausing after the first report. The tapescript is on page 227.

Get the learners to check their answers with each other.

Answer key

1. b   2. c

Play the whole recording again, asking the learners to notice as many additional details as possible.

Get them re-telling the news reports in pairs. Alternatively, put the learners into groups of three. Learner A and Learner B each re-tell one of the news reports. Learner C listens and jots down any inaccuracies or omissions, which they then report to the other two.

Option

If your class enjoys drama activities, they can use the examples they have heard to build up a similar news report, in pairs or small groups. They then read out (or act out) their news report to the class. Others guess what the situation is.

Personal Study Workbook

5: listening to news reports from the past

3 I'm learning, but slowly

present continuous; conversation

This is a simple activity to demonstrate another context in which the present continuous is appropriate. Here the context is that of activities that are happening more generally, perhaps not specifically at the moment of speaking, but more generally, at the present time, and in an on-going way.

Suggested steps

Draw the attention of the learners to the two different structures: *I'm learning* + noun, e.g. *I'm learning English/football* or *I'm learning* + infinitive verb, e.g. *I'm learning to cook / to swim.* Ask them to complete the two sentences in as many ways as possible. Go round and encourage them to think of other possibilities as they are writing.

Chain feedback: Get Learner A to read one of their sentence completions to the class, and ask if anyone else is learning the same thing, e.g. *I'm learning to cook. Is anyone else in the class learning to cook?* Learner B then reads out a different sentence completion, and so on.

4 In the evenings, I usually watch TV
present simple / present continuous; writing

The final activity asks the learners to study examples that show the difference between the present simple used for permanent activities or states, and the present continuous used for temporary activities or states. They then practise the distinction in writing sentences about themselves.

Suggested steps

Let the learners study the sentences on their own (or simply go over them with the class, pointing out the main distinction that is being made).

Draw their attention to the bank of verbs in the box, which illustrates the way the present continuous is formed. Then ask them to write two sentences about themselves, or their families or friends, using the pattern given.

Oral feedback may be a good idea here because it allows you to monitor any pronunciation problems associated with the new tense.

The Quick Check for this lesson asks the learners to deduce the rules for using the present continuous and the present simple. If there is time, you may wish to use this exercise in class as a formal consolidation of the lesson.

Personal Study Workbook

1: contrasting the present simple and the present continuous

Quick Check answer key

(i)
usually; all the time
now; developing
(ii)
1. 's having
2. 're having
3. 's talking
4. 're writing

B

1 I'm having a wonderful time
present continuous: temporary/developing situations; listening

Here the context is one of temporary situations that are still on-going or developing.

This is a dual listening – use it as before, either deciding to play one of the levels only, or following the easier version by the harder one.

Suggested steps

Let the class read the notes and use their dictionaries for any unfamiliar terms, or go over them together, discussing any problems. Explain that there are four speakers on the recording.

Play the recording, pausing after each speaker. The tapescript is on page 227.

Get the class to compare answers, then confirm them.

Answer key

a waiter (2)
a housewife (4)
a teacher (3)
a secretary (1)
enjoying a holiday (3)
doing a temporary job (2)
doing a first job (1)
spending time on the beach (3)
working until late at night (2)
working for a big company (1)
seeing interesting things (3)
learning a language for a holiday (4)
living on a boat (1)

2 I'm studying English and really enjoying it!
reading and writing postcards

This activity builds on the previous one. The learners now read postcards from the four speakers, then use the models to write postcards of their own.

Suggested steps

Let the learners read the cards by themselves. They can use their dictionaries or ask others if they have any problems. Much of the vocabulary duplicates that in the previous exercise, so the class should really be able to read for gist without too much difficulty.

If your learners have difficulty with handwritten texts, it might be better for you to read the postcards out to them to give them some help.

Ask them to decide the answers to the four questions. Hint that there may be more than one answer in some cases. Get them to check with others before confirming.

Answer key

Dinu and Edi are doing a temporary job.
Kath's having a holiday.
Mia's at home.
Mia and Dinu are learning new things.

Establish the alternative postcard writing tasks. In the first one, the learners write from the situation in which they are working, the classroom. In the second, they imagine they are somewhere else, and write as if they were in that other place.

Draw the attention of the learners to the expressions in the box, so that they know that they can make use of them if they like.

Circulate while they are writing, and encourage them to extend their use of the present continuous. Alternatively, the postcards can be set for homework, with the feedback being organised at the beginning of the next class.

Get individuals to read out their postcards, or put them up on the wall for everybody in the class to read.

Quick Check answer key

1. I'm working
2. He's studying
3. she's learning
4. they're living
5. I'm watching

C

1 Is the cost of living going up?
present continuous: developing situations; discussion

More abstract concepts, to do with the general state of things in a country, are worked with in this activity, which acts as a warm-up for the reading and listening tasks to follow.

Suggested steps

Try to find articles in recent newspapers that mention the issues the learners will be discussing: the cost of living, unemployment, the number of years in education, water pollution, the popularity of sports. Bring in any relevant articles (in the learners' L1, if you are teaching in a non-English speaking country). For example, you can show the financial page and the sports page of a local newspaper. These are issues which are often topical and extensively discussed by people in many communities.

Establish the concepts by discussing them, or through dictionary work.

Get the learners to indicate their opinions by choosing one of the options in the survey. They then compare their views in small groups, or with the whole class.

Take a 'majority poll' of the class's opinions by tabulating the number of a, b, or c choices in each of the five questions.

Elicit opinions about the other items mentioned: the number of people (population), cars, tourists, etc. Draw the attention of the learners to the example, and ask them to give reasons for their opinions.

2 The cost of living is certainly going up!
reading; listening

Let the learners read the texts by themselves. The vocabulary has largely been introduced, and the topic as well, so they should be able to read for gist without too many problems. Set a time limit for the first reading, say 5–10 minutes.

Get the learners working in pairs to try to guess the missing words (whether the items are going up or down in each speaker's country).

Language Point: connectors

This is a good opportunity to get the learners working actively with connecting expressions, which provide clues to the missing words in the text. For example, in the first paragraph, the speaker says the cost of living is going up. The number of years in education is <u>also</u> going … . Draw the attention of the learners to the fact that *also*, *as well* and *so is / so are* are all connectors which reinforce a previous statement, whereas *but*, as they know, usually introduces a contrast, a different idea. The other major clue lies in the use of either *fortunately* to indicate that the speaker thinks it's a good idea, or *unfortunately*, to indicate a bad trend.

Have a class feedback on the guesses made. Ask the learners to try to say why they've made the choices they have. Sometimes there is no clue in the text (e.g. paragraph 1: The popularity of sports is going …). But quite often there is some internal indication as to whether the answer is up or down. For example in both paragraphs 2 and 3, the two ideas of unemployment going up and people staying in education are linked, so that it is likely that the speaker is saying that they are both rising.

When you have gone over the text with the learners, let them listen to the recording to confirm their guesses.

The tapescript is on page 228.

Answer key

1. up   up   up
2. up   up   up   down   staying the same
3. up   up   up   up   staying the same

In feedback, go back to the surveys in the previous exercises and get the class to compare their own views and those they've just heard expressed.

Option

Chain feedback: Learner A starts by comparing or contrasting items in any two countries (France, Germany, the United States, and their own country, if this is different). The comparison or contrast has to contain a linking expression: *also*, *as well*, *so is / so are*, *but*. Learner B continues, giving another comparison or contrast, and starting this time with the second country mentioned by Learner A. Again, a linking expression is obligatory. Learner C starts with the second country mentioned by Learner B, and so on.

Personal Study Workbook

6: reading texts containing the present continuous

3 Who is spending money on us?
writing

Suggested steps

If the concept of 'letters to the editor' is not a familiar one, try to show an example of this kind of page from an English-language newspaper. Explain that this is quite a popular feature in many such newspapers, and that people often write to express their opinions about a subject that was featured in a recent article in the newspaper.

Let the class read the two letters, using their dictionaries or asking for help.

Option 1

If you have copying facilities, you can use the two letters for interactive communication practice. Put the learners in pairs and give each of them one of the letters. They read them, and then, without showing them, tell their partner the substance of the letter.

The learners should establish through their reading and discussion that the two letters are about the same phenomenon, judged from opposing points of view.

Decide whether you want all the class to write about one topic (you could ask them to suggest appropriate topics) or whether you are going to allow them to choose their own. The second option allows a more personal task, but the first one often makes for a more interesting exchange of letters at the end.

Each person then writes a similar letter to an editor. The resource box gives some support for the vocabulary and format to be used.

Language Point:

As this is a formal letter to an unnamed editor, and using the greeting *Dear Sir*, the end formula in Britain is usually: *Yours faithfully*.

Feedback: The learners read their letters aloud. Alternatively, put them all up on the wall and let the learners read them. If you have easy access to word processing facilities, you might like to create a mock up of a 'letters to the editor' page in a newspaper, and display it in the class.

Option 2

As a class activity, get the learners to guess what the article that prompted the original letters was about. Can they imagine the headline? For example: *Government spending more money on sports facilities* or *Government building a new Presidential Palace* or *New government building programme: good news or bad news?* As headlines are usually short and punchy, the learners quite often enjoy making them up.

Personal Study Workbook

7: the present continuous; writing

Quick Check answer key

(i)
1. Unemployment is going up in our country.
2. The popularity of sports is staying the same.
3. Fortunately, water pollution is going down.
(ii)
1. as well   2. so is   3. so   4. also

```
┌─────────────────────────────────────────┐
│              QUICK NOTES                  │
│                                           │
│   This went well:                         │
│                                           │
│   ...................................     │
│                                           │
│   ...................................     │
│                                           │
│   This didn't quite work:                 │
│                                           │
│   ...................................     │
│                                           │
│   ...................................     │
│                                           │
│   Things to think about:                  │
│                                           │
│   ...................................     │
│                                           │
│   ...................................     │
└─────────────────────────────────────────┘
```

D REVIEW AND DEVELOPMENT

REVIEW OF UNIT 9

1 I opened the door, then you closed it
vocabulary building: opposites; past tenses: regular verbs

This is a standard vocabulary building exercise which leads on to story writing, then a miming exercise.

Suggested steps

Get the learners filling in the opposites. Set a time limit so that this first activity does not stretch on too long.

Option

Have a race, if your class enjoys competitions. Divide the class into two teams. As soon as a group finds an opposite, a member of the team writes it up at one end of the board. The other team uses the other end. Only one member of the team is allowed to be up and writing on the board at a time.

Answer key

opened – closed	stopped – started
departed – arrived	packed – unpacked
locked – unlocked	asked – answered
hated – loved	played – worked

Get the learners to start writing their story. Make sure they understand that it has to feature one pair of opposites, plus one of the items in the picture. This second requirement often acts as a spur to the writer's imagination. Give the learners the option of writing by themselves or collectively. In many classes, the learners

enjoy working with a partner to produce this kind of story, which they can discuss as they write. If the story has more than one character, the mime which follows it is facilitated by having more than one person miming. Go round, offering help and encouragement. Mistakes are best noted and corrected at a later point.

Ask the learners to mime their story to the class. Encourage the class to guess and ask questions. The person who guesses the most (or who guesses correctly) can be asked to re-tell the story at the end. The mimer listens and then corrects any misunderstood points.

2 Broke, spoke, woke ▭
pronunciation: past tenses – irregular verbs

Suggested steps

Get the learners working with their dictionaries.

If you like, set a time limit (e.g. 10 minutes) and see how many past tenses the learners can find and write in that time.

Individuals can check their guesses as to the 'odd verb out' with others, before listening to the recording for confirmation.

Play the recording once through.

The tapescript is on page 228.

Answer key

The verbs that don't rhyme are in italics.
1. broke, spoke, woke, *made*
2. rang, sang, *brought*
3. sent, *mended*, went
4. hid, did, *rode*
5. *watched*, caught, bought
6. *thought*, drank, stank
7. sold, told, *spelled*
8. *grinned*, began, ran

Let the class listen again and repeat the groups of verbs chorally to reinforce their pronunciation.

REVIEW OF UNIT 10

1 The Iceman ▭
reading; listening

The main focus is reading. The first part of the activity pre-teaches some of the vocabulary the learners will need in order to understand the text, and sets the topic at the same time.

Suggested steps

Get the learners to match the words and their definitions. Decide whether to get them working individually or in pairs, and whether they can use their dictionary or simply guess.

Get them to check with others before you confirm the answers for the whole class.

to survive – to stay alive in hard conditions
to rescue someone – to find and save a person in trouble
to search for someone – to look for a lost person
a miracle – an extraordinary event
frostbite – damage to the body caused by extreme cold

Get groups to discuss the question and decide together on a number of days, which they then write down. Or discuss it with the whole class and let each person write a number.

Having worked with some of the vocabulary, and with the theme, the learners now read the article through for gist. This is a slightly adapted version of an article that first appeared in an Australian newspaper. Encourage the learners to continue reading even if they encounter difficulty. This is once again valuable training in reading in the second language.

When most of the class have finished, discuss the article with them. Get them to re-tell the main points of the story (this acts as a help to anyone who might not have understood everything). Ask them to give reasons for the number of days they think James survived.

Play the recording once through. The tapescript is on page 228.

Ask the class to re-tell what they understood of the conversation. Play the recording again, if they wish. Then get them working together to discuss answers to the three questions.

Answer key

1. 43 days.
2. He kept moving around; he ate two chocolate bars; he drank snow; maybe he found other things to eat under the snow; he had a strong personality.
3. One speaker seems to think the story is probably true; the other thinks it's probably not true: James made up the story to sell newspapers and chocolate bars.

Elicit reactions to the story. Did they enjoy it? Did they believe it? If they think it is untrue, what do they think about this kind of joke or trick? Ask them to give reasons.

Worksheets

The worksheet for this unit, on page 175, gets the learners practising the present continuous form. Distribute it to the whole class.

In the first part, they simply write the form. This is a fairly easy warm-up, and the learners can do it by themselves and check their answers with others. Monitor that they notice the verbs ending in *y*: *fly/flies/flying* and the doubled *p* in *stop/stops/stopping*.

Answer key

2. you're walking, he's walking
3. we're having, she's having
4. they're repairing, he's repairing
5. the birds are flying, the plane is flying
6. children are using, a child is using
7. women are making, a man is making
8. we are standing, the class is standing
9. teachers are trying, the learner is trying
10. you are staying, Juan is staying
11. they are studying, Maria is studying
12. the trains are stopping, the car is stopping
13. I'm living, the kitten is living
14. we're phoning, my friend is phoning

In the second part, there are clues in the text which indicate whether the present simple (for routines, things that happen regularly, every day) or the present continuous (for things that are temporary, or on-going and developing) is to be preferred.

Let the learners do the exercise on their own, then join a partner for checking. Go round while they are checking and monitor that they are identifying reasons for the tenses. Write at one end of the board: *routine, things that happen regularly*. At the other end, write: *temporary, developing*.

Go quickly over the various choices with the class, writing up the verbs under one of the two headings on the board.

Answer key

Well, here I am in Tashkent at last. My flat's not ready, so *I'm staying* (temporary) at a big hotel in the centre of town for the first month. *I'm working* (temporary) by myself in my office at the moment, because it's still the holidays, and most people are away. It's a good introduction to the work. As you can imagine, everything here is quite different.

Thank goodness I can speak a little bit of Russian at least. Do you remember our Russian classes at school? We read Pushkin but we didn't learn how to ask for a sandwich. *I'm learning* (developing) all that kind of language very fast now that I'm here! But Russian isn't enough, so *I am taking* (temporary, developing) a two-month course in Uzbek at a language school. *I'm studying* (developing) hard, *I'm trying* (developing) to learn as quickly as I can. But I'm finding it hard. It's a very different kind of language for me. Every morning *I take* (routine) a tram to the school and *work* (routine) there for two hours. Then *I go* (routine) to my office. In the afternoons, my friend Dora *takes* (routine) me round the city to show me everything. It's a wonderful city, there's so much to see! Come and visit! Lots of love, Andy

The learners can choose to continue working with their partner or find a new partner for the writing task. Ask them first to choose the person whose letter they are going to write: either someone on holiday or in a new job. If they prefer, they can write a letter from themselves.

Make sure they understand that they don't write the verb in its correct tense, but as in the example they have just worked through, they leave a blank to be filled in, followed by the verb in brackets.

Set a time limit for ease of class management. Go round helping. Encourage them to write legibly, as their letter is going to be read by another pair!

Encourage pairs to join together as soon as they are ready, and work out the right tenses in each other's letters.

Get the pairs to read out their letters to the class, or put them up on the wall for the class to read.

END OF UNIT NOTES

How's the class getting on?

....

....

Language that needs more work or attention:

....

....

My learners:

....

....

12

MAKING PLANS

CONTENTS

Language focus: present continuous: future events, already arranged
going to + infinitive: future events,
already arranged / things you intend to do

Vocabulary: weekend activities, business activities, language
learning activities

INTRODUCTION TO THE UNIT

The focus here is on the present continuous used to talk about future events: either the simple tense for planned events (We're meeting him at 10 tomorrow morning) or the *going to* future for intentions (I'm going to write to you as soon as I get there). In everyday speech, many native speakers often use these two forms interchangeably, as was evident in the recordings of conversations made for this unit. The two have, therefore, been presented in the same unit. The emphasis is very much on learning to talk about the future, rather than on distinguishing between the two forms which do so.

A

1 My weekend's always too short
vocabulary; discussion

This acts as a conversational warm-up, establishing the topic of weekend activities. Because the conversations are about weekends generally, and what people usually do, the tense used is the present simple. The present continuous to talk about a specific weekend in the near future is introduced in the following activity.

Suggested steps

The first question can be done as a whole class activity, recycling *free time* from an earlier unit, and establishing the topic of the weekend.

Then get the learners working in pairs to complete the sets of opposites (again revising previously presented vocabulary) and ask each other questions about their weekends generally.

A quick chain activity is an appropriate rounding off. Learner A asks Learner B a question; Learner B answers, then asks Learner C, and so on.

Answer key

busy – quiet
boring – interesting
relaxing – tiring or exhausting

Personal Study Workbook

4: the pronunciation of the present continuous

2 What are you doing this weekend?
listening

The present continuous used for talking about the coming weekend is introduced in a recording of two conversations between people comparing their plans for the weekend.

Suggested steps

This is a dual listening exercise, to be exploited in the usual way. The tapescript is on page 228.

Play the first conversation, then pause to let the learners take down notes. Get them to check with each other now or after the second conversation.

When you confirm answers, you can write the verb tense on the board (*Gill's/She's going on holiday*). Make sure that the auxiliary is not omitted (many learners tend to say: *Gill going on holiday*).

Answer key

Gill's going on holiday to Cornwall with her husband, for a week. John's going to a hotel with his family.
James isn't doing much. His friend's coming on Saturday, they're having a meal and they're going to the cinema (to see a film).
Irene's working on Saturday. On Sunday she's making lunch for her mother.

Personal Study Workbook

1: the present continuous with future meaning

---

3 What are you doing on Saturday?

present continuous: future events, already arranged

The learners now use the forms they were introduced to in the listening task to talk about their own plans.

Suggested steps

Draw the attention of the class to the boxed list of possible weekend activities. Let them ask or check with others about any unknown items.

Go over the pronunciation and sentence intonation of the questions, if you feel your class needs it.

Get the class milling to ask three other people the three questions. Tell them to take some paper and a pencil to write down notes of the answers they hear.

As soon as they have got notes on three sets of answers, encourage the learners to sit down again and start preparing their reports. They can write them if they like, or simply plan. They are to report two things that are true, and one that is false. Ask them to look at the example. You can encourage them to think of very unusual or even outrageous things for the 'false' activity, so that they make the class laugh.

Unless the class is very large (when it can be done in two groups), it is usually more enjoyable to have the learners reporting to the whole class. The others have to spot the false statement.

Personal Study Workbook

3: vocabulary building
2: time expressions for talking about the future

Quick Check answer key

(i)
1. a   2. b   3. b
(ii)
1. She's going to Luxembourg this summer.
2. They are meeting their friends at the cinema.
3. On Sunday, I'm going to a party.
4. He isn't eating meat these days. / He's not eating meat these days.
5. What are they doing on Saturday?

```
┌─────────────────────────────────────────┐
│             QUICK NOTES                   │
│                                           │
│   This went well:                         │
│   .....................................   │
│   .....................................   │
│                                           │
│   This didn't quite work:                 │
│   .....................................   │
│   .....................................   │
│                                           │
│   Things to think about:                  │
│   .....................................   │
│   .....................................   │
└─────────────────────────────────────────┘
```

B

Warm-up

This lesson uses the particular context of an office. Some of the vocabulary used is specific to that context: *secretary, meeting, client, director, marketing, Sales Manager, appointment, trade centre,* and names of companies like ACE Co, HERRO and Sons, Virna Ltd, etc. If none of your learners works in this kind of situation, you may wish to set the scene by exploring an illustration of an office with them, asking the class to describe what they see, and supplying needed words.

If any of your learners work in a company, you can ask them to write the company's structure as a diagram on the board: *What is the person at the top called? Managing Director. And is there a Marketing Director?* (He or she is above the Sales Manager.) *Is there an Office Manager who looks after the staff in the office?* and so on. (These terms vary quite a bit from company to company and from one country to another in English-speaking contexts.)

1 I write down all my meetings in my diary

conversation

This exercise gives a conversational start, to associate the vocabulary of planning, meetings and appointments with the learners' own lives.

Suggested steps

Work as a whole class or put the learners into groups to discuss the questions. These have been formulated to suit as many different situations as possible. You may, however, wish to adapt them to your particular class, or omit some of them. The main thing is to set the topic, planning a week's work in advance, and to make sure that the learners know the words *planning, appointment* and *meeting* before the next activity.

2 I'm sorry she can't see you ⌑

present continuous; reading; answering questions

Suggested steps

The first part of this activity is really a reading exercise. Ask the class to study the office planner for a few minutes. You can go over the company logo at the top of the planner with the class, discussing what the main jobs are, what people do in them, and the importance for a company of having a record of all plans for the coming week.

Then get the learners working in pairs or small groups to discuss the appointments and other scheduled activities of the company, helping each other with difficulties.

Have a class feedback to ensure that they have picked up most of the details, and to give some practice with the present continuous. (*What's Petra doing at 9:30 on Monday morning? She's meeting the new secretary.*) This can be done as a chain of questions around the class.

In the second part of the activity, the class will hear some questions (incoming phone calls to the company) and will be asked to reply to them as if they were the receptionist. Set the scene by demonstrating the job of the receptionist: *Good morning, Prime Associates, can I help you?* Work with the example given, and with the expressions in the help section.

Get the class working in pairs or small groups to prepare answers to the seven questions they are going to hear. They look at the planner and decide whether they can answer *yes* or *no*. Circulate as they work and encourage them to prepare full polite answers, using the expressions in the help section.

Play the recording. Pause after each question to allow answers. There are several ways of organising the responses to the seven questions. Here are some options for you to consider.

- Have a choral response from the class to start with. (Ask them to speak softly.) It doesn't matter if they don't all say the same thing. The advantage of this kind of first response is that it takes the pressure off individual learners while allowing them all to have a go at answering.
- Play the recording again. Nominate individuals in turn to provide an answer (especially appropriate for small classes).
- Alternatively, the second set of responses can be done in groups (especially appropriate for large classes). Groups listen to the recorded questions, then answer them in turn.
- Nominate two learners to give responses to each question. Learner A answers, then Learner B gives an answer that adds one detail. Example:
  A: No, I'm sorry, she can't. She's going to Bucharest.
  B: Just a moment, please, let me check. Oh, no, I'm terribly sorry, Mrs Roman can't see you then. She's going to Bucharest.

Answer key

Examples of possible answers:
1. CALLER: Can Mrs Roman go to a meeting at 3 pm on Wednesday?
   RECEPTIONIST: I'm sorry, she can't. She's going to Bucharest. (I'm afraid she's going to be away that afternoon.)
2. CALLER: Hello, this is Mr Brown's secretary. Can either Petra or Marion see Mr Brown at 10 am on Tuesday?
   RECEPTIONIST: Let me check. I'm sorry, Petra can't. She's seeing a German client (Herr Göninge from Hamburg). But Marion's free then. She can see Mr Brown.
3. CALLER: This is John Peters speaking. I'm coming to the city on Friday and I'd like to meet Marion Dorkas at 9:30 in the morning. Is she free at that time?
   RECEPTIONIST: Let me check. Yes, she seems to be free then. (Yes, that seems fine.)

4. CALLER: Hello Penny, Guy here. Can you tell me: are Marion and Jon free for lunch on Monday?
   RECEPTIONIST: I'm terribly sorry, they're not free. They're having lunch with Petra.
5. CALLER: Hello, Herr Göninge's office here. Herr Göninge's having some trouble with his travel plans. Could he change his meeting with Mrs Roman from Tuesday morning to Monday morning, at the same time?
   RECEPTIONIST: I'm terribly sorry, but she has a meeting at that time on Monday morning. (Can I check with her and call you back about that?)
6. CALLER: Hello, it's Keith here. Is Jon busy on Friday morning?
   RECEPTIONIST: Yes, he is, I'm afraid. He's seeing Mr Stalti, from VIRNA Ltd at 10:45.
7. CALLER: Can Marion come to a meeting on Thursday afternoon?
   RECEPTIONIST: I'm sorry, she can't. She's meeting some clients at the Trade Centre. (She's got a meeting at the Trade Centre. She's meeting the Sales Manager of RGG Computers.)

Option – Follow-up

If there is time and the learners are not thoroughly fed up with Prime Associates, get them working in pairs to create two more questions of the kind they have just heard. They ask the class (or another pair) their two questions. The others reply.

3 Next Thursday, I'm meeting the new students
asking questions about plans

The previous exercise focused on answering questions in a fictional situation. This one brings the learners back to their class and puts *them* in the position of asking the questions.

Suggested steps

Get the learners to create a diary in their notebooks. Or draw an empty weekly planner on the board, and ask one of the class to fill it in as you answer questions. Write your name at the top. Add next week's dates.

Draw the attention of the class to the example. If necessary, elicit the first few questions, e.g. *Ask me what I'm doing on Monday morning … Monday evening.*

Option

You can practise the 3rd person form by asking for a report on your week from the class, perhaps as a chain of statements: *(Your name) is meeting the Director at 10 am on Thursday. She's/He's going to the cinema on Wednesday evening,* etc. This also practises time expressions.

Quick Check answer key

1. you doing
2. answering
3. is seeing
4. Is; office
5. Where are they meeting?

C

1 I'm going to read a newspaper ...
going to + infinitive; reading

The reading text introduces the *going to* future for intentions.

The text of the letter presents very few new items of vocabulary, and so no pre-reading tasks have been given. If you think there are any words which would cause problems for your learners, quickly go over them before they start reading. You can also make sure that everyone understands the context. Olga, who was part of an English class, left to go and live in Canada. This is the letter she writes to the class.

Suggested steps

Ask the learners to read the letter by themselves. They can simply make a note of any difficulties they encounter at this point.

After the first reading, ask the learners to bring up any of their difficulties, and explain them.

You may wish to read the letter out to the learners at this point, to get them to associate sound and sense. Alternatively, ask them to do the memory work first, then read the letter out loud as confirmation.

Get the learners to shut their books. They then try to remember the things Olga's going to do to improve her English.

Answer key

She's going to try to take an evening course at the
   university.
She's going to read a newspaper every day.
She's going to try to get a part-time job.
She's going to get some cassettes and books.
She's going to write a diary in English.

Get the class to check their answers with each other.

Personal Study Workbook

5: future plans; reading

2 She's going to get a part-time job ▭
listening

The class now hears the text of the letter in Exercise 1, but with four variations. Point out to them that the letter is being read by the teacher of the English class that Olga wrote to.

If your class usually finds listening very difficult, let them follow the text as they hear it. If they enjoy listening and picking up clues, get them to keep their books shut and try to pick out the four differences from listening only.

Play the recording once. The tapescript is on page 229.

Answer key

1. In the text she says she's going to visit the university, but on the recording she isn't going to visit the university.
2. In the text she says she's going to read a newspaper every day, but on the recording she's going to read magazines every day.
3. In the text she says she's going to spend a lot on cassettes, but on the recording she's going to spend a lot on courses.
4. In the text she says she's going to write a diary in English, but on the recording she's going to find a Canadian boyfriend.

3 My learning resolutions
present simple and *going to* + infinitive; writing;
conversation

At the end of Unit 12, the learners will have completed half this elementary level of study. It is, therefore, an appropriate time to take stock of what their learning habits actually are, and what 'resolutions' or intentions they have to help them continue improving their English from now on.

Suggested steps

In the first part of this exercise, the learners use the present simple to indicate what they do regularly, or sometimes, etc.

Get the class to read the lists and tick the frequency expressions. You can then have a quick comparison of the results before going on to the next part. Go through the list, asking how many of them read their English books at home. Write the number on the board, to give a profile of the work habits in the class.

Then get the learners to make two lists: one of things which they intend to do, and one of other things which they don't intend to do. If you feel it is necessary, draw their attention to the different form they are using now. In the first activity they said: *I read (sometimes, often, every day)*, but now they are listing things they are *going to* do.

The learners then compare their intentions with a partner, or in small groups. Draw their attention to the example. Go round the groups, monitoring and making notes of any problems that need later attention.

Personal Study Workbook

6: writing about future plans

Quick Check answer key

(i)
1. to; I'm not going to get a job.
2. 's; She isn't going to use a dictionary.
3. 're going; They aren't going to read the newspaper every day.

(ii)
1. Are; Yes, I am.
2. What; I'm going to use my dictionary.
3. Why; Because it's interesting.
4. Is; Yes, Martin is.

QUICK NOTES

This went well:

....

....

This didn't quite work:

....

....

Things to think about:

....

....

D REVIEW AND DEVELOPMENT

REVIEW OF UNIT 10

1 They found both alligators in bed
reading; past tenses

These are two articles, slightly adapted from an English-language paper that is published in Japan, which revise past tenses while getting the class to express some reaction: amusement, disgust, disbelief, etc.

Suggested steps

Explore the illustrations with the class, to make sure they understand *alligators* and *worms*. Ask them to describe what is happening in each illustration. What's their reaction to it? Express some strong reaction yourself to model the marked intonation patterns used to express emotions.

Divide the class into two. Each group works through one of the texts.

Get the learners to join a partner from the other group. They show each other their work, and go through it together.

Answer key

No alligators in bed!

John M Butler had two 1.2-metre alligators as pets. For 23 months, he *asked* for official permission to keep them in his motorhome. He applied in November 1989 for a permit. The officers finally went to his motorhome in Miami, Florida in October 1991 to make sure it was big enough for alligators.

When the officers *arrived*, they *found* both alligators in Mr Butler's bed. Mr Butler *was* at the hospital getting treatment for alligator bites. The officers *took* away the alligators, and *refused* to give him official permission to keep them. Mr Butler later complained. He *said* it was wrong to take away his property without his permission.

No live worms for lunch!

On Friday, a group of animal lovers *said* that eating live worms was terrible. David Diamond, 53, *ate* the worms, in a pub, to get money for a new hospital. The worms *came* from his own garden.

'Worms are not as bad as people think,' Diamond said. 'They *were* just like spaghetti. A quick bite, and they soon *stopped* wriggling,' he *told* the local newspaper. He said that eating worms was not so terrible and that officers of the British Army also ate them.

Ask two people to read the completed texts for confirmation. Get the class to express their reaction.

2 The police caught him
writing a short news article

Asking the learners to discuss possible news events in groups is often a good way to get the writing activity going. Explore the illustrations with the class, or let groups speculate about them. What do they think happened before the pictures? What happened afterwards? Can they think of other interesting or intriguing events?

If your learners enjoy writing collaboratively, they can create their news reports in pairs or even small groups.

Circulate and help with structures and vocabulary. Make sure the stories are being written in the past tense.

If time is short, the stories can be written as homework. Organise a reading out loud session or a display of articles on the wall at the beginning of the next class.

Option – Follow-up

For oral practice, ask each learner to read someone else's news report. They are then to re-tell it to the class, as if they were news reporters on radio or TV.

REVIEW OF UNIT 11

1 A special memory
vocabulary and discussion

This conversational activity sets the scene for the listening to follow. Encourage your class to talk about as many different ways of saving special memories as they can.

If you like, you can prepare for this activity in the previous lesson. Ask the class to bring in any examples of special memories that they would like to show. Have they got any scrapbooks or photograph albums, for example? Have they got any special collections of photos, e.g. wedding photos? Have they got any other collections that remind them of the past, e.g. postcard collections, ticket collections, etc.

Bring in some items of yours to show and talk about, e.g. a set of newspaper clippings, or a scrapbook.

2 What are you doing? □□
listening, writing down notes; speaking

Like the exercise in Unit 9, this is a guided fantasy to help people remember a particular event from their own past experiences. In this activity people are invited to 'save' a special moment from the past. The recording asks questions and directs the listeners to jot down notes about their memories.

Suggested steps

Make sure the learners have some paper and pen or pencil to jot down notes.

Give them a few minutes to decide on the 'special moment' that they are going to think about. Emphasise that it should be something they are happy to talk about in class (not a very intimate memory, for example). Ask them to tell their partner what particular moment they have chosen.

Tell them that they are going to go back in their minds to the time. Mime walking backwards in your mind, as you did in Unit 9. They are going to imagine that they really are back in that special moment.

Play the recording in parts, pausing it at appropriate spots to let the learners jot down their memories. Numbers have been added to the tapescript on page 229 to suggest appropriate pauses. Places to pause are before the numbers.

After the end of the recording, get the learners to work with a partner. They show each other their notes, and talk about them. Encourage them to remain in the special moment by using the present continuous. You can give them an example by talking about your special moment, or demonstrate by being a partner to one of the learners, and asking questions about their notes. (*Well, my special moment is my wedding day. I'm sitting at the table in the restaurant. There are lots of friends around me. They're all wearing colourful clothes. There's a lot of food on the table. We're eating …*)

Worksheets

The worksheets for this unit, on pages 176 and 177, offer communicative practice with the present continuous.

Put the learners in pairs. Give Worksheet 12A to one partner and Worksheet 12B to the other. Arrange their seating so that they don't see each other's worksheets.

Make sure they understand the instructions on their worksheets. Go over them with the whole class if necessary. They are to ask questions about their partner's weekly planner and use the details heard to fill in their empty planner.

Go round while the learners are carrying out the task to help if necessary, monitor and take notes about problems to be discussed later.

Abbreviations: appt = appointment, sales rep = sales representative (= salesperson), re = about

At the end, the learners can compare their completed planners to confirm that they got all the details.

Have a general feedback with the class to find out how much they can say about the two people whose planners they have been working with. They should have picked up quite quickly that the two are a married couple, Dana and Adrian; Dana works in an office, Adrian is a teacher; they have two children, Susan and Jimmy; Dana's mother is called Lena.

```
┌─────────────────────────────────────────────┐
│            END OF UNIT NOTES                  │
│                                               │
│   How's the class getting on?                 │
│   .........................................   │
│   .........................................   │
│                                               │
│   Language that needs more work or attention: │
│   .........................................   │
│   .........................................   │
│                                               │
│   My learners:                                │
│   .........................................   │
│   .........................................   │
└─────────────────────────────────────────────┘
```

13

BETTER AND BETTER

CONTENTS

Language focus: comparative and superlative adjectives
modifiers *a bit, a lot*

Vocabulary: features of countries and cities

INTRODUCTION TO THE UNIT

The unit introduces the comparative and superlative (regular and irregular) forms of adjectives in the context of comparing countries, cities, and facilities. The learners are given the opportunity to use their general knowledge and to talk about the type of environments that they live in or prefer. The modifiers and negative forms are provided to build up greater precision in the learner's repertoire.

A

This lesson provides a general knowledge quiz context for initial work with comparison. It is worth reviewing the activities with adult learners to find out what they enjoyed and to help them to define and take responsibility for their preferred styles of learning.

1 Is Greenland bigger than Australia?

comparative adjectives; listening

Warm-up

Write the name of one of the world's large cities on the board. Ask the learners the name of the country in which the city is located. Ask someone to write the name of another well-known city next to yours. Ask the learners to say the name of its country. Then ask: *Which city is bigger? Is … bigger, or is … bigger?* Check the concept by asking: Which city is smaller? Repeat with the names of two countries.

Use the different map projections (the Peters projection (bottom) and the standard projection (top)) to show how views differ about the accurate representation of the size of countries. Ask the learners to say what differences they can see between the two projections.

Suggested steps

Ask the learners if they were good at geography at school. What do they remember from studying geography? Establish the idea of a geography quiz. Put

the learners into pairs. The pairs ask each other the first quiz question. Model pronunciation for them, especially the weak form of *than* /ðən/. Ask for feedback and encourage dispute, but don't reveal the answer.

Ask the learners to ask each other the remaining questions alternately and to record their agreed answers to all ten questions on one sheet of paper for their pair. If you want to extend the amount of time the learners spend speaking English, ask a pair to join another pair and to come to one agreed set of answers for the ten questions.

Note that answers 1–8 are either *yes* or *no*, but 9 and 10 need the names of the countries.

When the learners listen to the recording of people doing the same quiz, ask them to write the correct answers they hear on the recording next to their own answers. Let them check in pairs.

Note that on the recording the word *larger* is used sometimes and means the same as *bigger*. It may be a good idea to present *large/larger* before listening, to increase confidence while listening.

The tapescript is on page 229.

Encourage pairs to check answers with other pairs if your classroom and class size make that practicable.

Ask for quiz scores from the pairs and encourage discussion. In case of dispute, you can quote actual areas in square kilometres from the key.

Answer key

1. No   2. Yes   3. No   4. No   5. No   6. Yes   7. Yes
8. No   9. Chile   10. New Zealand

Comparative areas in sq. km are:

1. Greenland	2,175,600	Australia	7,682,300
2. China	9,561,000	Brazil	8,511,968
3. India	3,287,693	Canada	9,976,147
4. Italy	301,245	Japan	371,000
5. Mexico	1,967,180	Indonesia	1,919,263
6. France	551,000	Spain	504,000
7. Iceland	102,828	Cuba	114, 524
8. Turkey	780,576	Egypt	1,000,250
9. Chile	756,943	Kenya	582,644
10. Thailand	513,517	New Zealand	268,675

1, 2: comparative adjectives

2 It's a bit smaller than ... ⬭⬭⬭
comparative adjectives and modifiers

Suggested steps

This is a dual listening task. The previous listening task will have introduced passively modifiers like *a bit*, *much*, *a lot*. Reproduce the diagram from the book on the board to elicit and establish meanings of the various modifiers. Use concrete items in the classroom to practise meaning, e.g. books, watches of different sizes.

Return to the topic of countries. Ask the learners for examples of countries that are *a bit bigger*, *much bigger*, *a bit smaller*, *a lot smaller* than your country or the one in which the class is studying.

Assign a letter to each learner (A, B or C). Learner As listen to the first recording and make notes, Learner Bs listen and take notes on the second recording, and so on. The tapescript is on page 230.

In threes (a Learner A, a Learner B and a Learner C) the learners read out their notes and the group tries to guess the identity of the three countries.

As a class, elicit feedback and compare answers.

Answer key

Country 1 – Australia
Country 2 – Italy
Country 3 – China

3 It's much, much bigger than Belgium
writing and guessing

Suggested steps

This is a written consolidation of Exercise 2. Tell the group to use the note-taking frameworks from the listening task in Exercise 2 as a guide for their own paragraph construction. Alternatively, use one of the country descriptions in the previous listening activity as a dictation.

The learners could do the writing for homework if that is more convenient, and the next lesson could start with the guessing game.

Option – Follow-up

This practises other comparative adjectives, and comparative forms using *more ...* and *less ...*

Prepare a worksheet by drawing a flag in the centre of a page with 'Our country' written on it. Radiating outwards, add headings as follows:

flatter than	hillier than
cheaper than	more industrialised than
a bit poorer than	less industrialised than
a bit richer than	more popular with tourists than
prettier than	less popular with tourists than

Ask the learners in pairs to add countries to complete the comparisons. Elicit an example to clarify the task.

Tell the learners to change partners and compare lists.

If there is time, a whole-class feedback might be a useful way of encouraging accurate pronunciation of completed sentences as well as discussion of completions.

Language Point:

The rules for forming comparative adjectives are a little complex. Try to elicit that adjectives with three or more syllables usually take *more* + adjective and that some adjectives ending in *g* or *t* usually double the letter before adding *-er*; adjectives ending in *-e* add only *-r*. It's worth telling the learners that in spoken English people don't always apply the rules strictly and *more* + adjective is sometimes preferred to adjective + *-er* with some single syllable adjectives.

Personal Study Workbook

4: vocabulary extension – adjectives and comparatives
5: comparative forms

Quick Check answer key

(i)
greener; later; wetter; prettier;
richer; finer; flatter; hillier;
poorer; simpler; bigger; noisier;
cheaper; freer; thinner; lovelier

more popular; less popular
more interesting; less interesting
more expensive; less expensive
more modern; less modern
more industrialised; less industrialised
more polluted; less polluted
more crowded; less crowded

(ii)
1. much   2. a lot; than   3. much   4. bit

```
QUICK NOTES

This went well:
.................................................................
.................................................................

This didn't quite work:
.................................................................
.................................................................

Things to think about:
.................................................................
.................................................................
```

B ░░░░░░░░░░░░░░░░░░░░░░░░░

This lesson moves from vocabulary consolidation to reading. There is a further development of comparative forms. Again, ask the learners about activities that they find useful, or enjoyable.

1 I like living in the city centre
vocabulary and speaking; comparatives using *more* and *less*

Suggested steps

Use the illustration to practise the zone descriptions (countryside, city, coast, etc.). Get the learners to ask you about members of your family and where they live.

The learners could talk about their families in groups, then carry out the adjective assignment task individually before resuming the same groups for comparison and explanation. The example exchange is not a drill, just an example of the sort of language that might be used. It can act as a guide for weaker learners.

Encourage a whole-class feedback to exploit differences of viewpoint.

Note that use of *because* is possible when the learners compare choices, if the learners already know it; otherwise it may be better not to overload them.

2 Tales of two cities
reading; speaking

Warm-up

Use the photos in the book to elicit the learners' knowledge of the two cities. The past tense can usefully be recycled if any students have actually visited the two cities.

Suggested steps

The learners can work with the sentence list in groups but should each record guesses. The list pre-teaches some of the vocabulary in the reading texts about Istanbul and Brasilia.

Remember to tell the learners to read the texts silently and on their own to check their answers. This is the initial reading task. A further check on answers can be carried out in groups.

Answer key

1. It's very polluted. (Istanbul)
2. It's very tidy. (Brasilia)
3. Hotels are all together in one part of the city, banks in another part and schools in another. (Brasilia)
4. There are many people shouting as they sell things in the streets. (Istanbul)
5. You can't see shops because they are inside large buildings. (Brasilia)
6. It is a place full of contrasts. (Istanbul)
7. There is an exciting underground cathedral. (Brasilia)
8. There is a lot of space around the buildings. (Brasilia)

9. There is a lot of noise inside the covered bazaar. (Istanbul)
10. At busy times of the day, the traffic is terrifying. (Istanbul)

The introduction of *both* may need a quick teacher presentation to establish what it means. Questions 1-8 could be asked and answered alternately in pairs with a whole-class example to clarify the task.

Answer key

1. Are both cities planned? No, they aren't. Brasilia is planned, but Istanbul isn't.
2. Are there interesting buildings in both cities? Yes, there are.
3. Are both cities impersonal? No, they aren't. Brasilia is impersonal, but Istanbul isn't.
4. Are both cities tidy? No, they aren't. Brasilia is tidy, but Istanbul isn't.
5. Are both cities quiet? No, they aren't. Brasilia is quiet, but Istanbul isn't.
6. Is traffic a problem in both cities? No, it isn't. It's only a problem in Istanbul.
7. Are both cities great fun? No. Istanbul is great fun, but Brasilia isn't.
8. Are both cities extraordinary? Yes, they are, in their different ways.

The practice with *more/less* + adjective could be a whole-class activity and extended via a comparison of two other towns or cities in the country where you are teaching. Encourage sharing of different views since the learners then have to use English to explain their viewpoint.

Personal Study Workbook

6: more practice with comparatives

3 My city's not as old as Istanbul ▢▢
comparison with negative form; listening; writing

This activity is designed to highlight the negative form *not as ...* (+ adjective) *... as*. It is designed to allow the learners to write answers to the recorded questions as if someone was asking about *their* town or city. Thus the learners have some freedom to choose their answers.

Suggested steps

It may be a good idea to pre-present the forms and use the examples to model the writing-while-listening task.

The tapescript is on page 230.

With weaker learners, give sentences with gaps; others can write the full sentences. Remind them of vocabulary offered in the unit so far.

When the learners compare their answers, ask them to underline any errors they find in their partner's work for the original writer to correct.

Before pair practice with new sentences, remind the learners of variants to simple *Yes/No* + short form answers, for example *No, I don't think it's as nice as ...,*

No, not really, Yes, of course it's nicer.

More practice with comparatives is given in the worksheet for this unit on page 178.

Quick Check answer key

(i)
1. Lisbon is not as big as London.
2. The suburbs are not as dirty as the city centre.
3. Department stores are not as lively as bazaars.

(ii)
1. Are both cities beautiful?
2. Are both countries popular?
3. Are both buildings impressive?
4. Are both men lively? / Are both boys lively?

QUICK NOTES

This went well:

....

....

This didn't quite work:

....

....

Things to think about:

....

....

Lesson C introduces the superlative form in a controlled and manageable context and then extends into some irregular superlative forms.

1 The nicest and most interesting cafés ...
superlatives

Warm-up

As a warm-up, ask for three or four personal items from the learners (a watch, bag, ring, glasses, for example). Ask the learners to guess how much each cost. Check with the owners and write up the prices on the board with the most expensive price at the top and the lowest price at the bottom of the list. Ask the learners which one was the cheapest. Elicit that *cheapest* means the item at the bottom of the list on the board. Ask someone to say which is the *most expensive* thing on the list.

Suggested steps

The advertisements are a simple presentation device for superlatives. Ask the learners to look at the ads first. All the ads say *cheapest* but which café in the group really has the cheapest coffee?

The true/false exercise can be done in pairs and then checked with other pairs.

Answer key
1. Dino's is cheaper than the Coffee Corner. (T)
2. The Expresso Bar is more expensive than the Coffee Corner. (T)
3. The Coffee Corner is cheaper than the Expresso Bar. (T)
4. The Expresso Bar has the cheapest coffee. (F)
5. The Coffee Corner has the most expensive coffee and cake. (F)
6. Dino's has the cheapest coffee. (T)

Before starting the next activity, check that concepts and differences of formation of the comparative and superlative are understood. Go through an example with the adjective table.

Ask the learners to complete the adjective table and then ask them to explain to you some of the rules for formation of comparative and superlative adjectives. Encourage discussion.

Answer key

Coffee cups   i – cheaper   ii – cheapest

Adjective	Comparative adjective	Superlative adjective
cheap	cheaper	cheapest
nice	nicer	nicest
quick	quicker	quickest
fine	finer	finest
expensive	more expensive	most expensive
relaxing	more relaxing	most relaxing
good	better	best
bad	worse	worst

Personal Study Workbook

3, 7: superlatives

2 The best place for a cup of coffee
writing with superlatives

Suggested steps

Ask a learner which restaurant they think is the best in town for local food. Promote discussion by asking: *Do you agree, Luca?* or *What do you think, Sandra?*

Use the tourist list to explain the task. Suggest to the learners that they complete the list in pairs.

Good oral practice can be encouraged by asking pairs to report on their choices.

Tell the learners that the final lists will be typed up as a handout for new students or displayed. Don't produce a final class list if pairs want to retain their choices.

If the activity proves fruitful, you could build up more sections to the list as homework or as part of the production of a more ambitious leaflet, e.g. 'the best things that are free in this city', 'the most beautiful places for a walk'.

Personal Study Workbook

8, 9, 10 superlatives; reading and writing

3 Host families
comparatives and superlatives

Suggested steps

Use the photo and the text to draw from the learners the purpose of the advert. Ask the learners to ask each other if they have ever had students staying in their house, or get them to talk about their homestay experiences. (Avoid embarrassing questions.)

Let interviewing take place in pairs. The learners can change pairs to report responses and have discussion. Have a whole-class round up to pick up answers to the more amusing questions, e.g. 'the best word to describe your family', 'the worst thing about life in your home for a visitor'. Elicit responses from individuals frequently to ensure maximum participation and the development of faster comprehension and conversational exchange, e.g. *How about you, Pia? Is it the same in your house, Sacha? Do you agree, Paolo? Why? Why not?*

As a grammar follow-up, ask the learners to find how many comparative forms and how many superlative forms they can find in the questionnaire.

Brainstorm for ideas for the paragraph and write the ideas on the board as a resource. Encourage the use of *because …* so that the learners give reasons to support their statements about families.

For weaker learners, prepare a framework of sentences for the target paragraph, e.g. *The best host families are*

....
because they have .... *They probably also have* ....
The best host families try to ....
.... *and* ....
Finally, they ....

Encourage the learners to exchange paragraphs and to check each other's work for accuracy. Talk to individual learners about the types of mistake they typically make. This will help them to take more responsibility for correction and checking of written work.

Quick Check answer key

(i)
They are the best family on our list.
This is the worst coffee in town.
This is the best place to eat.
Coffee at Dino's is cheaper than coffee at the Coffee Corner.

(ii)
largest; biggest; most beautiful; poorest; most varied; most popular; best; worst

---
| QUICK NOTES |

This went well:

....

This didn't quite work:

....
....

Things to think about:

....
....

D REVIEW AND DEVELOPMENT

REVIEW OF UNIT 11

1 Away from home
role play

This activity revises the present continuous form using the theme of being away from home.

Suggested steps

Assign roles, either parent (Group A) or young person (Group B). Put weaker learners in the young person's role since answering is easier than asking questions.

Read through the paragraphs with the class and establish the situation by asking questions, e.g. *How does the parent feel? What does she worry about, do you think? How does her daughter or son feel, do you think? Is she/he having a good time? Is she/he busy?* Ask the 'parents' to make a list of at least five questions to ask their son or daughter. Ask the learners to use some of the verbs from the box in the questions.

Model one question, e.g. *Are you eating enough food?* so that the present continuous form is used when the learners construct their own questions.

Tell the learners in the 'young person' role to make a list of at least five things to say to their parents. They should use some of the verbs from the box.

Give gentle support as questions are built by individuals.

When pairing a parent and son/daughter tell the learners to imagine they are on the phone. Put them back to back if possible to simulate a phone conversation. Practise the start of a phone conversation, e.g.

YOUNG PERSON: *Hello.*
PARENT: *Oh, hello, is that you, (name)?*
YOUNG PERSON: *Oh, hello, Mum, how are you?*

It is a good idea to record conversations if this is possible. Then work can be done on particular aspects of pronunciation and discourse and it gives you, the teacher, a record of what the learners could achieve in a role play at this stage in the course. The learners might also be interested to listen to the role plays again at the end of the course together with later recordings or a later recorded repeat of the same role play situation.

Ask for feedback from pairs about their conversations. Was the parent a worrier? Was the student trying to make the parent feel easier? Lead from there to discuss feelings the learners have when they are away from home. Do they phone or write? How often? Which is worse – being away from home or being left at home when one of the family is away?

2 Short or long sound? ⊂⊃
pronunciation /ɪ/ and /iː/; dictation

This exercise requires discrimination of short from long vowel sounds.

Suggested steps

Demonstrate by example first what students are to do to show successful discrimination.

Answer key

1. /iː/   2. /ɪ/   3. /iː/   4. /iː/   5. /ɪ/   6. /iː/   7. /ɪ/
8. /iː/   9. /iː/   10. /ɪ/

Check answers then play 1, 4, 5, 6, 9 again for dictation. Remember to pause after each sentence during dictation to give time for writing. Let five learners write one each of the five sentences on the board after pair checking. For the text of the sentences please refer to the tapescript on page 230.

REVIEW OF UNIT 12

1 What are you doing this evening? ⊂⊃
present continuous; pronunciation

Suggested steps

Review the present continuous for future meaning to check that the learners understand the concept. Ask the learners: *What are you doing this evening?* Ask: *Is the question asking about 'now' or 'the future'?*
Remind the pairs that there may be several ways of completing the conversation.

Ask selected pairs to read out their conversations in full. Discuss any differences. For example, some learners may use full form questions; others may use the more authentic elliptical forms (*Who are you going with?* versus *Who with?*)

Finally, let the learners listen to the recorded version of the conversation and compare it with their own. Remind the learners that these are not right or wrong answers in any absolute sense, and are possibly different from their own.

Answer key

For the answers, please refer to the tapescript on page 230.

The learners could repeat the questions as a self-access exercise or as homework. If you do this part as a class exercise, practise question intonation and then let the learners practise the dialogue in pairs, while you monitor.

2 What are you doing after class?
conversation

Suggested steps

This is a reasonably free conversation phase. Get the learners relaxed first, perhaps by getting them to stand up and move around while asking the questions. Join in yourself, as your participation helps to validate the activity and cements the bonds between you and your learners.

Reporting can be done in a more formal arrangement.

Worksheets

The worksheet for this unit, on page 178, offers communicative practice with comparative and superlative adjectives.

Put the learners into pairs, and make sure the instructions are clear to all before starting the pairwork. Illustrate and label the items *line*, *circle* and *square* on the board. Give one learner in each pair Card 1 and the other Card 2.

On Cards 1 and 2 there are some grouped shapes labelled A–E. The shapes are either lines, squares or circles. There are some differences in the relative sizes of the groups of shapes on Card 1 and Card 2. Pairs have to describe the shapes on their cards accurately until they find four of the differences.

For example: *On my card, line B is longer than line C.*

Each time they find a difference they have to write down what it is.

For example: *On Card 2 line B is longer than line C, but on Card 1 the lines B and C are the same.*

Learners cannot look at each other's cards. They have to sit back to back or hold their card so that their partner cannot see it.

When everyone has finished, the cards are placed next to each other and the sentences assessed for accuracy in describing the differences.

Teachers can easily make up similar worksheets for a large class, or for learners who complete the task quickly.

END OF UNIT NOTES

How's the class getting on?

....

....

Language that needs more work or attention:

....

....

My learners:

....

....

14

A SPIRIT OF ADVENTURE

CONTENTS

Language focus: present perfect: with *ever* and *never* for unfinished time
                  with *this week/month/year*
                  contrast present perfect with simple past

Vocabulary: sporting activities
              illness
              stress and relaxation
              learning English

INTRODUCTION TO THE UNIT

This unit introduces the present perfect, one of a number of challenging tenses in English. The learners meet the present perfect here only when used with *ever, never, this week, this month* and *this year*. The use of these adverbials should give a comforting signal to the learner of a general need for the present perfect.

Contrast between the present perfect and simple past is included as a writing exercise but teachers can also derive spoken practice from the same activity to develop in learners the ability to use the two forms flexibly and appropriately, and to understand one or two conceptual differences in how the tenses reflect actions in time.

This lesson uses 'dangerous' sports to contextualise the use of the present perfect with *ever* and *never*.

1 The first time was really fantastic
vocabulary and listening

Warm-up

Using the pictures in the book, ask the learners to rank the activities from least to most dangerous and from least to most exciting. Ask for reasons and establish the vocabulary (names of sports and items of equipment such as *balloon, parachute, air tank, skis*) at the same time.

The listening activity is designed to draw the learners into the themes of sport and excitement. The use of the simple past and present perfect is for passive understanding only at this stage.

Suggested steps

Ask the learners to write down which picture they think is associated with the description in the recording, so that weaker learners can listen to the second part of the recording for extra help without feeling defeated. The tapescript is on page 230.

Answer key

The speaker is talking about skydiving, bottom, right picture.

The second part of the recording adds more helpful, specialised vocabulary (*plane, cord, parachute*), but essentially relates the same experience as the first part. An option here with weaker groups is to use the second part only, but to play it in two parts (first part up to *I felt like a little bird*).

Answer key

The person in the recording felt *terrified, free, happy, fantastic*.

Personal Study Workbook

1, 2: present perfect: grammar focus

2 I love excitement
present perfect with *ever/never*; listening

Suggested steps

Work with the diagram to establish the idea that the question *Have you tried ...?* refers to any time in a person's life up to and including the present (now). Ask the learners to tick the grid individually for each sporting activity. Do the grid yourself.

Model the exchanges with the present perfect as this is the first presentation of it. Build up a rhythm for the question form *Have you ever tried ...?* as you ask different learners.

Ask one or two learners to ask you the same questions and then you can model stress and pronunciation in the answer forms *No, never* and *Yes, I've tried it*, or *Yes, I've done it*. These answer forms are a little less conversational than *Yes, I have* or *Yes, once* but are used here to aid awareness of the form.

The learners can ask or answer all the questions with a partner, but if your classroom and group size allow more flexibility, get them to move around asking several learners one or two different questions each. Move round and monitor that the learners are not using the simple past. If they are, stop them and carry out a little repair work on pronunciation of the /v/ sound in *I've …*

Ask the learners to report on which people in the class seem to like excitement. Encourage discussion of the reasons why they like excitement.

The listening task offers useful reinforcement of the names of sports and the question forms with the present perfect. It also models additional variations of answer forms *Yes, I have* and *No, I haven't* and shows contrast between the present perfect and the simple past. You might like to use it to build language awareness of these other appropriate short answer forms after checking the answers to the set task.

The tapescript is on page 231.

Answer key

Speaker 1 (woman) has tried karate and horse riding. She hasn't tried scuba diving.
Speaker 2 (man) has tried water skiing. He hasn't tried sky diving or motor racing.

Personal Study Workbook

3, 4: present perfect: question forms and short answers

3 Once was enough!
contrasting the past simple and the present perfect; writing

Suggested steps

The diagram in Exercise 2 can be used once again for initial language awareness work on the present perfect and simple past. Use an example of a 'once only' completed experience from your own life then ask the learners for examples. Try to elicit the difference in concept between simple past answers for completed actions/events which happened at one specific time in the past (*I went sailing once, in 1994*) and present perfect questions with *ever* (*Have you ever tried sailing?*) which enquire about whether or not something happened at some time within the whole duration of one's life up to the time the question is asked.

Option

Photocopy the following gapped sentences and distribute them to your learners. Or write the sentences on an OHP transparency. This sentence completion exercise will consolidate tense contrast and prepare for the later paragraph writing activity.

Complete the answers, using the right tenses.
1. Have you ever tried sky diving? Yes, I .... I .... it when I was in the Bahamas.
2. Have you ever tried karate? No, I ...., but my brother .... it once, when he was fifteen.
3. Have you ever watched motor racing? Oh, I .... it many times. But the first time I .... it was the most fantastic.

Answer key

1. Have you ever tried sky diving? Yes, I *have*. I *tried* it when I was in the Bahamas.
2. Have you ever tried karate? No, I *haven't*, but my brother *tried* it once, when he was fifteen.
3. Have you ever watched motor racing? Oh, I *'ve watched* it many times. But the first time I *watched* it was the most fantastic.

To compose a simple paragraph for the sports magazine, the learners answer the listed questions (preferably from actual experience) and then adapt and join the sentences of their answers together to form a paragraph.

To offer a semi-authentic visual framework for the writing, the paragraph could be written inside a speech bubble with the learner's name and country alongside or underneath.

Here is an example which might be used as a model.

Yes, I have tried a sport only once. I tried karate when I was at school. I was 14. I hated it because it was boring and my feet got cold. I've never wanted to try it again. Once was enough!

The learners can read their paragraphs to each other in pairs before a selection is read to the class. Displaying paragraphs or producing them as a 'mini magazine' would be a good way of sharing the learners' own work.

Personal Study Workbook

5, 8: sports
6: pronunciation of the present perfect

Quick Check answer key

(i)
I have tried
You've done
She has watched; She's watched
(ii)
1. Yes, I have, several times.
2. No, she hasn't.
3. No, I didn't.
4. Yes, they did, twice.
5. Yes, they have.
6. No, I don't.

B

1 Fit for life?
vocabulary

Suggested steps

Elicit the meaning of *fit* by miming actions which suggest 'strong', 'healthy', 'running without getting tired' and contrast it with mimes of *unfit* (running for two seconds and being out of breath). Ask the learners *Are you fit or unfit?* Check their understanding by asking the follow-up question: *How do you know?*

The first vocabulary sorting exercise is fairly easy, so you might give pairs a time limit as a challenge.

Answer key

Sport	Health problems
volleyball	stressed
skiing	a cold
soccer	a cough
golf	a stomachache
swimming	tired
sailing	sore feet
riding	a sore throat
tennis	a broken arm
	a headache
	a bad back
	a broken leg

Check the pronunciation of new vocabulary as a whole class. (Remember that the primary stress is on the first syllable in *a headache*, *volleyball* and *stomachache*, but on the final syllable in *sore feet*, *a broken arm*, *a broken leg*, *a sore throat*, *a bad back*.)

Answer key

to have ...

a sore throat	a headache
a cold	a broken leg
a cough	a broken arm
a stomachache	a bad back
sore feet	

to feel ...
tired   stressed

to play ...
tennis   soccer
volleyball   golf

to go ...
swimming   sailing
skiing   riding

The learners can practise the new vocabulary if you give prompts to enable them to formulate simple questions in pairs, e.g. you/ever/stressed? (*Do you ever feel stressed?*) tennis/sometimes? (*Do you play tennis sometimes?*) like/swimming? (*Do you like swimming?*) know anyone/broken leg? (*Do you know anyone with a broken leg?*)

2 Have you had a sore throat this year?
present perfect with *this week/month/year*

Suggested steps

Build up time lines on the board or on an overhead transparency. Ask the learners for today's date, and the date of the first day of the month and the week. Ask several learners: *Have you played tennis this year / this week / this month?* Point to the appropriate time line to show it means from the beginning of the week/month until now. Elicit a variety of short answer forms: *Yes, I have / No, I haven't / Yes, once / Yes, lots of times / No, not once / No, not at all.*

Prepare the learners for the interviewing. Elicit the sort of vocabulary from Exercise 1 that might be appropriate for five health questions (*headache*, *stressed*, etc.). Elicit possible questions (*Have you had a sore throat this year?*) and ask the learners to practise questions on you. Check pronunciation, stress, rhythm and form.

Give the learners time to prepare their ten questions if this will help the flow of the activity. Show the scoring system.

Option

If it is possible, for variety, this activity could be done as a street interview or as an interview in the school, rather than in pairs.

During the feedback, ask the learners to explain the scores they have given. The question about health and activity could be a whole-class discussion. There will probably be enough disagreement to get the learners talking. Encourage the learners to look at mental health, and to talk about friends who don't exercise but still seem to be in good condition. Elicit contributions from as many learners as possible by asking questions like *Do you agree, Yuri? What do you think, Stella? Why do you say that?* Use names frequently to make discussion more personal.

Language Point: recently

Although *recently* is not introduced in this lesson, you might like to add it to the repertoire to show a non-specific time expression that is commonly used with the present perfect.

Personal Study Workbook

7: the vocabulary of health and sickness; listening

3 Reflexology

reading; discussion

Suggested steps

Let the learners study the illustrations and talk about them in pairs for a limited time (e.g. five minutes). After pairs have talked about the illustrations, elicit feedback. Ask: *What is happening in the pictures? Why are there body words on the feet?* Establish the notion of massage as something that many people believe is good for health.

Explain that the notes were written by someone after reading the text in the book. Let pairs read out their completed, guessed questions before reading the text. Check any problems with meaning, but don't challenge sentences at this stage.

Answer key

Possible questions:
What is reflexology?
When did it (first) start?
What do reflexologists believe?
How does it work?

Encourage reading as a scanning activity to help verify the questions the learners wrote; try not to let the learners read intensively and slowly with dictionaries. After pairs have revised their questions, check the questions with them.

If you anticipate that discussion about the benefits of reflexology may be too challenging for your class, give a more structured task by giving groups specific statements to assess together. Here are some possible statements. Ask the learners if they agree, disagree or are not sure.

Reflexology has no effect.
Reflexology is an important art.
Reflexology is psychological not medical.
A hot bath is more effective than reflexology.

Give the groups a time limit for discussion. Circulate and listen not only to the content of the discussion but also for language problems for follow-up work. Show interest and encourage the groups as this reinforces the importance of groupwork in the language learning process. Don't correct language obtrusively as this may reduce confidence to contribute. Have a short whole-class feedback.

Quick Check answer key

1. Yes, I've played quite a lot.
2. Yes, I've worked very late every evening this week.
3. No, I've had some problems with my boat.
4. No, I haven't had time to be ill.
5. No, I've felt fine, really relaxed.

QUICK NOTES

This went well:

....

....

This didn't quite work:

....

....

Things to think about:

....

....

This lesson is one of several which encourage self assessment by adult learners. It might be incorporated into a regular self review or review of syllabus, if you have chosen to involve the learners in decisions about the learning process.

1 Is your English in good shape?

present perfect; negative forms

Suggested steps

Draw a line on the board with the number 1 at one end and 10 at the other. Ask individual learners to say what score they think they have achieved on their learning of English up till now. Ask for reasons. Then move on to the list of statements. Encourage the learners to add new sentences using the present perfect. This might be a good time just to show the negative form of the present perfect by providing an example.

After the learners have compared ticks and new sentences, you might ask individuals to report what their partner has ticked as this will yield some *she/he hasn't +* past participle forms.

2 Personal progress

writing

Suggested steps

Reassure the learners that this is an activity to help them to think more about their own progress. The scores are for their own use.

This activity could be done as homework to give students a little more reflection time or if your group is not confident enough, or too embarrassed, to share self assessment.

Encourage sharing of self assessment and be sensitive to any signs of vulnerability. The activity is partly a device to encourage the learners to take more responsibility for their own learning.

Personal Study Workbook

9, 10: reading and writing a progress report

3 A journal entry
reading; writing

Suggested steps

Establish the nature of a journal. Ask if anyone has kept a journal and why (when travelling perhaps, or on a course). Make a distinction between a *journal* and a *diary* as the expressions may be confusing. A diary is a daily record of events and can be very brief. A journal is like a diary but a bit more detailed. It usually records some kind of progress, as in travelling or learning.

Give a reading task, for example: What have been the good things and what have been the problems for the learner in the journal?

The writing activity could be done as homework or as part of a regular journal writing process for self assessment, thus enabling you to have written input from your learners to refer to when you discuss progress with individuals. Remember not to over-correct personal writing as this can devalue the sensitive process of self appraisal.

Quick Check answer key

1. b   2. a   3. b   4. a   5. a

```
QUICK NOTES

This went well:
.............................................................
.............................................................

This didn't quite work:
.............................................................
.............................................................

Things to think about:
.............................................................
.............................................................
```

REVIEW OF UNIT 12

1 Guessing game
going to for things you intend to do; writing; discussion

Suggested steps

Write a list for yourself first and say: *I'm going to do three interesting things this week. What are they?* Ask the learners to try to guess the three things. This will model the activity and the *I think you're going to ...* form of the guesses.

Before forming their small groups, the learners can each take a bit of time to prepare if they are not sure of some of the words needed to describe the things they are going to do during the week.

Make sure that the example is studied carefully so that the learners put 'X' and not the name of the person, and so that they see the *going to* form again.

REVIEW OF UNIT 13

1 The easiest pet to keep is a fish
practice with superlatives

Suggested steps

Establish again that *most* and *least* are opposites, and that *to keep* means *to look after* or *to take care of* (to feed, keep healthy and happy).

Do one or two of the questions with the class as examples.

A class feedback after pair comparisons will add interest and allow reporting in the third person forms, e.g. *Carlos thinks that a snake is the quietest pet.*

2 They're pretty independent ⊂⊃
listening

Suggested steps

Go through the gapped table of notes and ask for guesses before listening to the recording. This will also consolidate vocabulary items like *bark* and *brain*.

The tapescript is on page 231.

Answer key

1. easiest to keep?	cat	only needs a bit of food each day, independent
2. most intelligent?	pig	large brain
3. longest life?	parrot	eats the right things (fruit and nuts)
4. noisiest?	my dog	barks a lot

Encourage the learners to complete their notes by discussing the answers with each other after one listening. A second listening can be played as a final check if necessary.

Encourage some free discussion of pets to round off.
Horror stories about pets could be fun and provide extra
practice at narrative telling.

Worksheets

The worksheet for this unit, on page 179, can be
photocopied and cut into four different workcards, each
with slightly different combinations of ticks and crosses
in answer to the questions. This is a milling activity.
Each learner has a card and moves around asking the
other learners questions until they find their partner
(someone with the same ticks and crosses as them). For a
class of eight, you will need to photocopy the four cards
twice (making eight cards in all) in order to have
duplicates (partner cards) for each of the four
combinations of ticks and crosses. For larger classes,
make extra photocopies. Circulate and check that they
are formulating the questions correctly.

END OF UNIT NOTES

How's the class getting on?

....

....

Language that needs more work or attention:

....

....

My learners:

....

....

15

DOES BEING TIDY SAVE TIME?

```
CONTENTS

Language focus:    -ing forms

Vocabulary:        everyday activities
                   offices, managing information, computers
```

INTRODUCTION TO THE UNIT

The -ing forms are introduced here in a number of ways:
- with the verb to keep, as in I keep forgetting, meaning something that a person does regularly but often not intentionally
- following before and after, as in after opening my letters
- with for as in pencils are useful for writing notes
- as the subject of a sentence as in sending a fax message is easy

To continue developing a sense of the differences between forms, the -ing form is contrasted with the present perfect and present simple tenses. The activity contexts allow for active participation on the part of the learners. If your learners don't have jobs, ask them to consider the questions about desks and computers in terms of their situation at home or in terms of their general knowledge and viewpoints.

1 I'm very absent-minded
vocabulary and speaking

Suggested steps

The learners will need to know the meaning of absent-minded. Demonstrate its meaning by putting a few items (pen, paper, book) down in different parts of the room and then asking the learners Where did I put my pen/book? Establish the meaning of the concept, i.e. being absent-minded means forgetting things like appointments, forgetting or losing small items; it often happens when someone is very busy or has too much on their mind.

Ask the learners to explain well-organised (this may elicit tidy, good planning).

Ask the learners to put a cross on the line to indicate how absent-minded or well-organised they are. If they put it half-way on the line, encourage them to express that in English, e.g. Sometimes I'm ...., other times I'm .... or I'm both .... and ....; it depends on the situation; or I'm a bit of both.

Option

To give the learners more practice with I keep ...ing you can do this activity with them on the board or you can draw it on paper and give it out as a worksheet.

Draw one central oval. Write in it the words: I keep ...

Around it, draw four circular clouds.

Under the first cloud write: at home

Under the second cloud, write: cinemas/restaurants, etc.

Under the third cloud, write: at work

The fourth cloud is left completely blank for the learners to put in what they like.

Draw a box and write in these vocabulary items:

forgetting keys
forgetting to take my coat/jacket/sweater
losing papers
putting on different coloured shoes
forgetting my money
leaving my umbrella behind
locking my car keys inside the car

Ask the learners to think about the things they keep forgetting in their everyday life. Ask them to put the expressions from the box into an appropriate cloud and to add other expressions to the cloud with no heading.

Then each learner joins a partner and they compare their diagrams to see if there are similarities.

Emphasise that the target expression is I keep forgetting/losing/leaving ... Encourage the learners to use the whole phrase and remind them of the final -ing sound (to prevent the error I keep forget).

After the learners have compared their diagrams, encourage class feedback in order to elicit third person forms (Carlos keeps forgetting ...; She keeps losing ...).

Personal Study Workbook
1: -ing forms
2: keep + -ing

2 Ever? Sometimes? All the time?

contrast of verb forms; writing questions

This is a language awareness activity to remind the learners of differences between present simple and present perfect verb forms and the -ing form.

Suggested steps

Put one missing verb in as a class and then let the learners complete the table individually.

Encourage the learners to come up with interesting questions. Give one or two interesting examples, e.g. *Have you ever lost a lot of money? Do you keep forgetting names?* When the learners have completed their six questions, ask them to exchange them with a partner and check each other's questions for errors.

The questions can then be used for pair or group oral practice if you feel your learners can benefit from controlled spoken practice, either to develop fluency or to improve pronunciation, stress and question intonation.

3 No, I've never forgotten anyone's birthday! ▭

answering questions; listening

Suggested steps

The statements for ticking are there to check awareness of appropriate answers before the learners circulate asking the six questions they wrote in Exercise 2.

Answer key

Numbers 1, 4 and 6 are correct.

Remember to put the learners in new pairs so that the six questions are not familiar to the partner.

Option

If you want the learners to move around the class asking several people rather than restricting the practice to pairs, you can give each person in the class a number between 1 and 6, and ask each learner to ask only the one question in their list of six that corresponds to the number they were given.

When you play the recording, remember to use the pause control after each recorded answer to give the learners time to write down the questions.
The tapescript is on page 231.

Answer key

a. Have you ever lost your passport?
b. Do you sometimes watch TV in the evenings?
c. Do you keep losing addresses and phone numbers?
d. Do you keep breaking things?
e. Do you sometimes lock your car keys in the car?
f. Have you ever forgotten your wife's birthday?

The second listening, complete with questions, can be used as an overall check. Let the learners have a little time to compare questions with each other and to check for any little errors.

Quick Check answer key

(i)
1. a   2. b   3. b
(ii)
1. birthdays; my passport; my keys
2. windows; my leg; cups
3. the garden; the living room; my son's desk

```
┌─────────────────────────────────────┐
│             QUICK NOTES              │
│                                      │
│  This went well:                     │
│  ..................................  │
│  ..................................  │
│  This didn't quite work:             │
│  ..................................  │
│  ..................................  │
│  Things to think about:              │
│  ..................................  │
│  ..................................  │
│  ..................................  │
└─────────────────────────────────────┘
```

B

1 Before going home ...

before and *after* + -ing form; speaking

Warm-up

Use the illustration in the book to explore the learners' different views on tidiness. There may be some interesting differences in multilingual groups.

Suggested steps

If your class members do not have jobs, rewrite the questions for a different context, e.g. a room, their bedroom, or flat.

Let your learners decide how to get individual reactions in their groups, perhaps by discussing options, e.g. one person could read the questions, or questioning could rotate, or each individual might read all the questions and then they all discuss them together. The aim is to give initial familiarity with the *before/after* + -ing form. Circulate, monitoring the language used and giving encouragement rather than correction.

To practise the language further, assign a number to each member in each different group (e.g. for five-member groups, 1–5). Then ask all the 1s to form a new group, all the 2s and so on. This enables reporting of the original group's reactions to the tidiness questions and extends the use of forms. This time, monitor and ask the learners to self-correct if they are making the common error of not pronouncing the -ing sound, for example if they are saying 'After go' instead of 'After *going*'.

Have a brief whole-class feedback, perhaps asking for reports from people who didn't say much in the groups.

Personal Study Workbook

3: *before/after + -ing*

2 It's time to tackle the memo mountain
reading

Suggested steps

The number guessing might best be done as a whole-class activity to save time and to keep the class in settled places for reading individually. Maximise the learners' oral contributions by asking *What do you think, Pedro? How about you, Cara? Do you agree, Hans?*

Spend a little more time orienting the group to the text before they read. Help the learners to guess the meaning of the title 'Time to tackle the memo mountain'. Start by establishing the meaning of *memo* by encouraging guesses: *It's in an office. Is it made of paper or plastic, do you think? Yes, paper. It's a note from the manager to other workers. What does it say: 'Please do this' or 'Hello, darling'?* Then establish the meaning of *memo mountain*. Is a mountain big or small? Ask them what they think 'International Clear your Desk Day' might be.

The initial reading task is to find the numbers and compare them with the learners' guesses, so remind the learners of this initial scanning purpose. They should be asked to work quickly and not to worry about individual words that are not familiar.

Answer key

1. The average office worker looks for things on or around the desk for 45 minutes a day.
2. Office workers look at each piece of paper up to 5 times a day.
3. Worldwide, computer printers print out 2.5 million pieces of paper every minute.
4. Worldwide, photocopiers copy 60 million sheets of paper an hour.

The follow-up questions demand a more intensive reading. This might be done collaboratively, if your group likes working in that way with texts.

Answer key

1. Untidy desks, says Mr Treacy, lead to lost information …
2. Mr Treacy says two hours is enough to clear a desk.
3. … the best thing to do, after looking at each piece of paper, is to act on it.
4. Untidy desks, says Mr Treacy, lead to (lost information and) high stress.

Have a class discussion about what people do with mountains of paper (either in the office or in the home).

Personal Study Workbook

5: the vocabulary of office work

3 Other useful purposes
-ing forms after *for*; writing

Suggested steps

The writing activity could be done for homework or as a quiet, individual activity.

For more practice with the expressions *useful for + -ing* and *handy for + -ing*, bring in a small bag with a number of small items in it, e.g. a comb, a rubber band, a wine cork, an empty match box. Ask the learners to take out one item and to suggest an interesting and unusual use: *It's handy for…* . Tell them to mime the use for others to guess if they don't know the English word for the *-ing* expression.

They then pass the bag on to another person who takes out another item. Again, check correct pronunciation of the *-ing* forms.

Option

An extension activity would be to ask the learners to design an office poster entitled 'Tired of all that paper?' and get them to add suggestions, e.g. *Old memos are useful for …, Old letters are good for …*

Quick Check answer key

(i)
1. Before leaving their desks, they tidy them up.
2. Before writing to customers, they find their addresses.
3. After reading a letter, they put it in the bin.
4. After using the books, they put them away.

(ii)
1. for putting
2. for making
3. for killing

```
QUICK NOTES

This went well:
..........................................................
..........................................................

This didn't quite work:
..........................................................
..........................................................

Things to think about:
..........................................................
..........................................................
```

1 Managing information is useful

-ing form as subject

Suggested steps

Explain *managing information* by showing an area phone book and a computer disk and asking the learners what they are for. Do they have each item at home? What are the differences between them? Encourage answers that enable revision of the comparative and *can* forms as in, for example:

Disks can hold more information.
Disks are smaller and lighter.
You can use a telephone book with no electricity, but you can't use a disk without a machine.

The table completion could be done in pairs.

If you want oral practice of *-ing* forms as the subject of sentences, ask the learners to report their table in this way: *Tell me about your table, Ana. What was important in the past? What is important today?*

Remembering things was important in the past.
Storing information on disk is important today.

Have a discussion to see which of the things from the past are still important today. The continuing importance (and difficulty) of remembering things will probably be a key topic here, as people seem to have more and more to remember.

Personal Study Workbook

4: *-ing* forms as subjects

2 Writing things is not very useful

writing with *-ing* forms

Suggested steps

Go through the examples carefully so that the learners understand the task and realise that there are a variety of ways of completing the sentences successfully. Encourage the learners to write something that they really believe, not just anything that completes the sentences.

In pairs, the learners should discuss their sentences freely. Circulate and help this process of discussion and reaction. Move into the topic of computers and their advantages and disadvantages, in preparation for the next exercise.

Personal Study Workbook

8: *-ing* forms; writing

3 Using computers 🔲🔳

speaking; listening

Suggested steps

Write the questions up on the board during the previous activity and elicit guesses about the meaning of *disadvantages*. Use questions like: *Do you think it means 'good' things about computers or 'bad' things?*

Ask each learner to consider the three questions first and to make notes in answer to them.

Then form small groups so that the learners can talk to others about their notes.

In preparation for listening, have a whole-class feedback from the small group activity and discuss good things / bad things about computers.

If you have the facilities and space, you might let stronger members of the group listen to the more challenging version of the listening and the less able listeners tackle the shorter version. Otherwise, start with the shorter version and use the more challenging one as a follow-up instead of repeating the first one.

The tapescript is on page 232.

Answer key

Information in brackets is heard only on the second version.

Good things about computers
They are good for keeping lists of names and addresses.
They are useful for storing names and figures.
(They are good for writing letters.)

Bad things about computers
When the computer goes down, everything is lost.
For children, using computers a lot is bad. They play games (and don't do any work).
It's not very good for your eyes.
You can get a bad back.

Encourage discussion of language learning by computer, but keep your questions and language within the capabilities of the group.

Option

For optional topic extension and discussion:

Ask the learners to study these three sentences comparing human brains and computers:

Brains are smaller and more powerful than computers.
Computers store more information than brains.
Computers and brains both work very fast.

Ask the learners to discuss whether they agree or disagree with the sentences and then to write two more sentences of comparison about brains and computers.

With a strong group of adults, the topic could become the basis for a piece of writing, or a short oral presentation about computers and their effect on our lives. For example, computers make revising a text easier, but on the other hand, do they replace part of our memory, making us less imaginative and less individual?

Personal Study Workbook

6: listening
7: reading

Quick Check answer key

1. Writing
2. Putting
3. Learning
4. Storing

```
┌─────────────────────────────────────────┐
│            QUICK NOTES                    │
│                                           │
│   This went well:                         │
│   .....................................   │
│   .....................................   │
│                                           │
│   This didn't quite work:                 │
│   .....................................   │
│   .....................................   │
│                                           │
│   Things to think about:                  │
│   .....................................   │
│   .....................................   │
│                                           │
└─────────────────────────────────────────┘
```

D REVIEW AND DEVELOPMENT

REVIEW OF UNIT 13

1 The best shops are in the market
role play

Suggested steps

Decide where to situate the role play. If the learners are all very new to the place in which they are studying, get them to imagine their home town.

Any activity that tries to control the use of particular language flies in the face of spontaneous discourse, so don't insist on *The best place …* formulation for things in the town that don't fit. It is better to say *There aren't any jobs in this town* than *The best place is …* if there isn't a best place.

Encourage pairs to use appropriate language to start off the conversation. For example, provide them with a setting (a café, the street, a train station) then relate the openers to the setting, e.g.

A: *Nice coffee, isn't it?*
B: *Mm.*
A: *Do you live here in* .... *or are you visiting? Oh, only visiting?*
B: *Perhaps you can help me …*

Practise some of the target forms before the role play is planned.

Use other examples, e.g. *Where can I get really cheap shoes in* ....*?*

(The learners give suggestions.) *So the best place to get shoes is* .... *Ask the 'Where …' question again, Jose. Answer him, Maria. Start with 'The best …' With a partner ask and answer one question about cheap T-shirts and nice cakes.*

Encourage the pairs to perform their role plays for the class. You can add a dimension by introducing a third person who disagrees and has alternative suggestions for the best places: *No, that's rubbish, the best place …* or *No,* .... *is much better than* ....

2 Large or larger? ▭
pronunciation: final sound /ə/ in comparative adjectives

Suggested steps

Before listening, get the learners to practise saying some of the adjectives and their comparatives. Ask the learners about any differences in sound. (Comparatives are longer, often have a slightly stronger stress and have a final schwa /ə/ sound.)

The tapescript is on page 232.

Answer key

1. larger
2. high
3. bigger
4. wet
5. small
6. large
7. nice
8. safer
9. bigger

1. Newcastle is larger.
2. Last year was wetter.
3. The shopping centre is smaller.
4. Your house is nicer.
5. It's safer to live here.
6. The crime problem is bigger.

Option

A variation for the listening activity is to allocate the sentences to different learners, e.g. Learner A listens to odd numbered sentences (first speaker), Learner B listens to even numbers (second speaker on the recording). Then odds and evens are paired to check answers to their sentences. The answers are written up on board, the whole class listens to all the sentences and the 'evens' judge the accuracy of the 'odds' and vice versa.

REVIEW OF UNIT 14

1 I haven't broken anything this week
speaking

This exercise offers practice of present perfect question forms.

Suggested steps

Ask the learners to ask you questions first to model the forms and build stress, rhythm and fluency.

For learners who have not broken anything recently, suggest adding the question form *Have you ever broken anything big / anything small / a bone in your body?*

Option

The following activity gives practice of the present perfect and simple past using the topic of winning and losing things.

Ask the learners: *Have you ever won anything? What did you win? When was that?*

The learners interview each other, complete the information in the table, then report their findings. (If someone says they have never won anything, their partner can ask similar questions about losing.)

I won ...	*What?*	*When?*
at school?		
at sport?		
a competition?		
a lottery?		
a ....?		

I lost ...	*When?*	*Where?*
a wallet?		
a bag?		
money?		
a cat/dog?		
a watch?		
a ....?		

2 How did it happen?
the past simple and the present perfect

This activity revises the contrast between the present perfect and past simple forms.

Suggested steps

Study the example to establish the different tenses and to note that the time marker *this month* signals the use of the present perfect.

The dialogue completion could be done in pairs, and then followed immediately by individual stories from each partner. Remind each learner to ask: *Have you broken anything this year?* before the storyteller begins the narrative with the past tense forms.

Monitor the stories and ask for one or two to be told to the class. Repeat *Have you ...?* question forms before each story: *What about you, Ismail, have you broken anything this year? (Yes.) OK, can you tell us about it?*

Answer key

1. *Have you broken* anything this week, Michael?
   Yes, I *was* at home in the bathroom and I *dropped* my watch on the floor. The glass *broke*. So the next day, I *bought* a cheap one.
2. Well, I've never *broken* an arm, but I *broke* my leg on a skiing holiday this winter. It *was* my first time skiing, and at the end of the first day my teacher *said* I *was* very good. But when I *went* back to the hotel, I *fell* down the steps and *broke* my leg. So that *was* the end of my skiing holiday!

Worksheets

As well as giving useful practice in the *-ing* form as subject, the worksheets for this unit, on page 180, give the learners the opportunity to reflect together on what they find easy or difficult about different aspects of learning English. This should help them take control of their learning and may point to areas where they need to put in more effort.

The learners work in pairs, one with Worksheet 15A and one with Worksheet 15B. Circulate while they are discussing and make a note of any points they raise that you may be able to help them with in class.

Have a whole-class feedback session and see if there is general agreement about what the learners find easy or difficult. Were there any interesting new things that were added to the lists?

END OF UNIT NOTES

How's the class getting on?

....

....

Language that needs more work or attention:

....

....

My learners:

....

....

16

OUR NEIGHBOURHOOD

```
                        CONTENTS

    Language focus:    relative pronouns
                       present perfect with just and yet
                       giving directions: imperatives
    Vocabulary:        neighbourhoods
```

INTRODUCTION TO THE UNIT

This unit offers a variety of new forms and functions. The learners extend their understanding of the present perfect tense by encountering its use with *just* and *yet*. They are also introduced to relative pronouns as part of a reading text. Direction expressions are also presented with follow-up oral practice drawing on the locality in which the learners are situated. There is a good variety of skills development.

A

1 This is my newsagent's, on the corner
speaking

Warm-up

In the centre of the board draw a simple outline of your house or apartment block. Ask: *Whose home is this, do you think?* Start to draw other buildings and roads. Ask questions about each to stimulate guessing. Give clues. (*What's this building? Think of money. Yes, it's a bank.*) Label each building as you build up a simple map. Involve your learners as much as possible, giving encouragement for each guess and using their names frequently to personalise the interaction. When your drawing is complete, introduce the expression *neighbourhood* as a description of the area around where a person lives.

Suggested steps

Give the learners an A4-sized piece of paper and ask them to put their home in the middle, and then continue drawing some of the buildings and places around where they live. Ask them to label the places they draw.

For added interest with international groups, ask the learners to draw their home in their own country rather than draw their accommodation/neighbourhood in the country where they are temporarily living and learning English.

If necessary, give guidance to the learners before they compare their drawings with a partner, perhaps by writing cue words on the board to stimulate ideas for questions, e.g. *buildings / How far is .... from your home? / like – dislike? / big – small? / old – new? / busy – quiet?*

2 There are a lot of markets
vocabulary and speaking

Suggested steps

Let the learners check through the items on the vocabulary list first and then consider the discussion questions.

Pin all (or a selection) of the maps on the board or on one wall. Ask the learners to come and look at the maps to check what things are included and to see similarities and differences.

Develop the discussion questions either in groups or as a whole-class discussion. Ask the learners to imagine they are from another society and to comment on what they would learn from the maps if this helps to promote better analysis.

This activity might easily lead on to an oral or written presentation on 'ways of life', perhaps prepared as homework but shaped in class.

Personal Study Workbook

5: vocabulary of the neighbourhood

3 What does the word neighbourhood mean to you?
reading; relative pronouns

Suggested steps

To prepare the learners for the reading, ask them what differences they think they would generally find between neighbourhood maps drawn in England and those drawn in Canada. Ask them to read the text not only to complete the two lists but also to check if anything they said is mentioned in it.

Connect back to the earlier activity by asking for comparisons between things mentioned in the reading text and things that appeared on the learners' own neighbourhood maps.

The activity after the reading introduces the learners to relative pronouns and clauses. Go through the examples carefully to build understanding of the concept of adding information by use of *who/that/where* clauses to extend sentences.

The learners select clauses from the box to extend the four sentences. They should also refer back to the reading text to see in context how the clauses give additional information.

Answer key

1. Two scientists who are doing research in psychology have just completed a study.
2. People drew maps of all the places that were important to them personally.
3. The study shows a society where families live far apart.
4. An important building in England is the pub where people get together to chat or play darts.

Personal Study Workbook

1: present perfect forms
4: relative pronouns in definitions
8, 9: reading and writing using the present perfect

Quick Check answer key

1. where   2. who   3. that   4. where   5. who

```
QUICK NOTES

This went well:
.............................................................
.............................................................

This didn't quite work:
.............................................................
.............................................................

Things to think about:
.............................................................
.............................................................
```

B

1 Our neighbours have just moved ⬜⬜ ⬜⬜
listening; present perfect with *just*; speaking

Suggested steps

You could use the picture of the workmen on the left to introduce the concept of *has/have just* + past participle. Use a question sequence like this one: *What has happened in the picture? (They have finished the road.) Have they*

finished it a short time before the picture or a long time? (A short time.) Yes, they've just finished the road.

Pretend that another person has suddenly come into this room. Tell that person what you have just finished or started. (*We've just finished an exercise. We've just started to look at a picture of some workmen. We've just listened to our teacher explaining something.*)

Study the tapescript (on page 232) before class to understand the task and the answers.

The second version of the dual listening offers a more elaborate unscripted version with additional vocabulary and detail. Use it for a greater challenge if you want your learners to practise extracting particular aspects of meaning from more complex input. Alternatively, use both recordings to compare differences in the structure of scripted and unscripted spoken discourse.

Let the learners compare their choices of pictures that match the listening. They can justify their choices if they are different.

Answer key

1. top left picture
2. centre left picture
3. centre right picture
4. bottom right picture

The following list of possibilities may help remind the learners of things that typically may have just happened which they can tell the class about:

– someone has just moved into/out of my flat, building, street
– someone has just returned after a holiday
– they have just started to build something in my street
– a new shop, office has just opened/closed
– someone has just bought something (new car, dog, alarm system)
– nothing has happened in my street at all!
– I never notice anything in my street …

The list also helps to illustrate that *just* is quite flexible in terms of time reference. It may mean a few minutes ago or a few weeks.

Give examples from your own street if that helps to start the conversation off. Practise pronunciation, especially with learners who have difficulty with 'j' sounds or who fail to voice the final consonant sound of the past participle (for example, who say *have just start* instead of *have just started*).

The learners might talk in small groups, perhaps in an informal setting. Monitor the groups for language use.

2 Oh, have you met them yet?
present perfect with *yet*

Suggested steps

This activity is used to introduce the concept of *yet* so the exchanges are controlled examples of its use. Use the example to elicit the time frame that *yet* embodies, e.g. *Have you met your new neighbours **yet**? Yet* refers to the time between when the event occurred, (i.e. the actual day your new neighbours moved to your street), and when the speaker asks whether you have met them (now, the time of speaking).

In dialogue 2, check that the learners know that the contracted form *my television set's* stands for *my television set **has*** …

You could use the dialogues for controlled speaking practice, or ask the learners to improvise extensions to the mini conversations for fluency practice.

Finally, the learners write their own short conversation with B's part missing. They ask another person to write in B's question.

Personal Study Workbook

2, 3, 7: *just* and *yet*

3 There have been a lot of changes recently
writing a description; discussion

Suggested steps

This activity could be set as homework, with lesson time being used to generate ideas and vocabulary in terms of the paragraph frameworks. Note that option 1 offers practice in three tense forms (past simple, present perfect and present simple).

Displaying the learners' writing, perhaps as an interesting montage on a noticeboard or in a magazine, is a good way of evolving a collaborative spirit. This is as important with adults as it is with younger learners.

Quick Check answer key

(i)
1. I don't know, I haven't met her yet.
2. Sorry, I haven't finished with it yet.
3. No, I haven't even started it yet.
4. Well, it hasn't arrived yet.
5. No, not yet. / Not yet.

(ii)
1. started	4. He's; fallen
2. met	5. They've; bought
3. seen	6. We've; come

```
┌─────────────────────────────────────┐
│             QUICK NOTES               │
│                                       │
│  This went well:                      │
│  ...................................  │
│  ...................................  │
│                                       │
│  This didn't quite work:              │
│  ...................................  │
│  ...................................  │
│                                       │
│  Things to think about:               │
│  ...................................  │
│  ...................................  │
└─────────────────────────────────────┘
```

1 It's the second street on the right
vocabulary and listening

Suggested steps

Use the illustrations in the Class Book, the vocabulary of directions and words such as *traffic lights*, *roundabout*, *bridge*. Elicit reasonable pronunciation and stress (e.g. primary stress on the first syllable of the first two expressions listed here).

After studying the direction instructions, draw a simple map on the board. Put a cross to indicate 'You are here'. Call a learner to the board and ask the other learners to call out directions for that learner to draw a line to indicate understanding.

Option

For further practice, create a simple maze in the classroom using tables and chairs. Blindfold one person. A partner gives the blindfolded person instructions (one at a time) for getting through the maze without colliding with any furniture. Remind the instruction-giver to say 'Stop' as appropriate since the person cannot see when to stop in order to turn. Change the maze for each person. Alternatively, put a piece of chocolate at the end of the maze and guide the learner to the chocolate.

The listening activity will consolidate understanding of the direction expressions. When the correct drawing has been chosen, ask the learners to write the instructions down, using the map as a guide.

The tapescript is on page 000.

Answer key

The correct diagram is B.

2 The building is on your right
practice with directions

This is a task-based activity with a guessing element, but the learners need to know the area around the school fairly well. If the learners are new to the area, use clear town or city street maps with several labelled buildings for the learners to work from.

Suggested steps

Encourage the learners to draw simple maps with their place of study in the centre. If they are not confident of their drawing ability, show them the example in the unit or model a map on the board.

Go through the example with the learners to clarify the sort of language they might use for the guessing task with their new partners.

If some learners finish more quickly than others, ask them to do the exercise again with new partners.

3 From the bus stop, you just cross the road, and you're there
writing directions

Use the sample notes to clarify what 'notes' are.

Option

If this activity is done as homework, it could be extended as revision by asking the learners in pairs to phone each other up, make an arrangement to meet and give the directions to their respective homes.

Personal Study Workbook

6: directions

Quick Check answer key

1. Take the first street on the right. Then, go down the street, take the second street on the left. Cross at the traffic lights, then take the first street on the left, and you are there.
2. Go down the street. Turn left and cross the bridge. Take the second street on the right. Turn right at the traffic lights. Go down to the roundabout and take the first street. The house is on the left.
3. Go down the street and turn left. Take the first street on the right, then take the second street on the right. Go down the street and take the second street on the right again, and you are there.

QUICK NOTES

This went well:

....

....

This didn't quite work:

....

....

Things to think about:

....

....

REVIEW OF UNIT 14

1 Guess the name of the sport ▭
vocabulary game

Suggested steps

You will need to organise this guessing game. On the recording there are five clues for each sport. Tell your learners that they can write down their guess after any of the clues. This means they may make a guess after clue

1, change it after clue 2 and then change again after the other clues.

Pause after each clue to give time for the learners to write, but don't replay any clues.

When going through the answers, start first by asking the learners what they wrote down after clue 1, then after clue 2 and so on to the point where they were sure of their guess. After clue 5, give them the answer.

Keep a list of the learners' names and write down numbers 1, 2, 3, 4, or 5 according to when they wrote down each of their correct guesses (i.e. after clue 1, 2, 3 and so on).

The winner is the learner with the most points (i.e. with the most correct guesses made with the least number of clues).

The tapescript is on page 233.

Answer key

1. skydiving
2. horse riding
3. motor racing
4. scuba diving
5. hot air ballooning
6. golf

2 In my life up to now
present perfect

This activity suits the end of the lesson and would probably benefit from an informal atmosphere.

Suggested steps

Prepare the learners for this activity by using changes in your own life to complete the sentences for you. Ask the learners to guess what you are going to put before writing things in, as this will promote involvement.

After they have completed their own sentences, put the learners in small groups to discuss the changes they have noted.

Ask the learners for feedback by asking them to report anything interesting or unusual about other learners' changes and reasons. This enables additional oral practice of third person forms *She/He …*

REVIEW OF UNIT 15

1 *Untidy* is the opposite of *tidy*
word-building: prefixes

Suggested steps

Explain that the columns are to help the memory to recall the prefixes *un-*, *in-*, and *im-*.

As completing the table is relatively straightforward, spend a little time on word stress, to show that the prefix is pronounced with some prominence but is not generally the main stressed syllable, for example in words like *unimpŏrtant*.

Option

A memory game. The learners study the completed table of opposites for a few minutes, then shut their books. Divide the class into two teams. Call out an adjective from the list to each team in turn. A team member gives the opposite of the adjective, and makes an appropriate sentence with it.

Example:

TEACHER: *tidy*

TEAM A MEMBER: *untidy*: *My daughter's room is always untidy.*

TEACHER: *efficient*

TEAM B MEMBER: *inefficient*: *Some companies are very inefficient, but my company isn't.*

You can make the game more challenging by forbidding the use of these words in the sentence: *it, person, thing,* or a person's name.

Give one point for the opposite and one point for a correct sentence.

An alternative is to let one of the learners be the caller and judge of the sentences so that the game is run entirely by the learners.

2 Giving up the piano was a big regret ☐☐
listening

Suggested steps

Use the example, *not studying hard enough*, to remind the learners of *-ing* forms as subject phrase and to show that a negative *not* followed by an *-ing* form can be used as an answer to a question, as in: *What's been the biggest regret in your life? Not studying hard enough (has been the biggest regret).*

Tell the learners that on the recording there are three voices – a male interviewer, Kate (a woman) and Chris (a man). The interviewer asks Chris first and the handwritten example represents his answer. The tapescript is on page 233.

Answer key

Chris

Biggest regret	not studying hard enough
	not learning sciences properly
	not learning languages
Happiest moment	happy most of the time

Kate

Biggest regret	giving up the piano
Happiest moment	seeing her little boy in a school concert

If you are teaching in an English-speaking country, the learners could ask the two questions as a street interview or they could interview other people in the school as a change from each other. Remember that the learners can put in adjectives other than 'biggest regret' and 'happiest moment' (for example, *most dangerous moment, most embarrassing moment*) and can alter the time frame from *in your life, up to now* to *this year, this month*.

Worksheets

The worksheet for this unit is on page 181.

Stage 1

Photocopy the worksheet and cut it into strips, so that there is just one question on each strip. Give each learner one question strip and ask them to go around the class, ask every other learner their one question and add up the total number of *Yes* and *No* answers. The learners have to answer *Yes* or *No* to each question they are asked.

With creative learners you could build a list of questions instead of using the one supplied here.

Stage 2

Give everyone a copy of the complete list of questions, or put them up on an OHP transparency or on the board. Put one or two of the individual *Yes* and *No* totals on the board. See if the learners can guess which question fits which *Yes/No* total score.

(Adapted from Classroom Dynamics by Jill Hadfield OUP 1992.)

END OF UNIT NOTES

How's the class getting on?

....

....

Language that needs more work or attention:

....

....

My learners:

....

....

17

IT'S WORTH DOING WELL

```
                         CONTENTS

Language focus:   adverbs ending in -ly
                  contrasting adjectives/adverbs
                  connecting words of sequence
                  imperatives

   Vocabulary:    how people do things
                  hobbies and crafts
                  rude/polite actions
```

INTRODUCTION TO THE UNIT

This unit again offers variety. It introduces adverbs gently but overtly so that the learners understand the way they function and how they are formed. There is also a review of imperatives and the extended use of connecting expressions like *first, next, then* which describe steps in a sequence or process. The topic of politeness gives plenty of scope for cross-cultural comparison.

A

1 I can do this quickly!
problem solving and discussion; adverbs

Suggested steps

Establish the notion of *a puzzle* by putting two simple puzzles (one a word puzzle, the other a number puzzle but not ones from this unit) on the board. Ask the learners to solve them and establish *quickly* and *slowly*.

Make sure everyone opens the book and starts the puzzles in this unit at the same time.

Answer key

A. I am 24.

B.
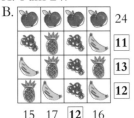

```
         24
         11
         13
         12
15  17  12  16
```

C. orange, yellow, blue, red, green, brown
D. tomatoes, cheese, lettuce

After doing the puzzles and the group interviews you could move into a general discussion of who was good at maths/language at school.

You could also ask the learners to contribute puzzles of their own to extend this part of the lesson.

Personal Study Workbook

2: adverbs

2 Special skills 🎧
listening and discussion; adverbs

Suggested steps

Ask the learners to find out from a partner something they can do *quickly, easily* and *confidently* before moving into the list in this activity. The thing they say can then be added to the list.

The list of abilities could be completed in pairs by reformulating them as questions, e.g. **Can you** *add up the cost of your shopping* **quickly, easily and confidently?** Tell the learners to record yes if they can do each thing in the manner of only two of the three adverbs.

> ### *Language Point:*
> Some learners may want to say something like: *I can add up quickly and easily but **not** confidently.* Teach the use of this short negative form at the end of a list.

The listening task is short and gives a simple interpretation of answering *yes* to particular questions. Put or keep the learners in pairs for this so that they can react and discuss immediately without disruption.

The profiles are in the tapescript on page 233.

The follow-up activity gives an additional task framework in which to use adverbs and apply the learners' own ideas. Put the learners into different letter pairs after they have chosen A, B or C and have thought of at least one of the two new things.

Encourage further use of adverbs by getting pairs to ask other pairs questions about the new things they have listed. For task B, for example: *Can you make clothes quickly and easily?*

3 A good waiter works quickly
adjectives and adverbs contrasted

Suggested steps

Before referring to the book, ease into this activity by eliciting information about the learners' dentists: *What's the name of your dentist? Is she/he careful? Is she/he quick? How about yours, Marco?*

Then ask: *How does a good dentist work?* If the learners come up with adjectives (*quick, gentle*) say: *In what way does a dentist work?* and suggest adverbs like *carefully, gently.* Ask them to choose one or two others from the book. Then ask the learners to complete sentences for politicians and drivers before comparing their answers. Ask the learners to give reasons for any unusual choices, e.g. *Why do you think a good politician speaks slowly?*

You might do the second part of Exercise 3 first if you want to change pace and allow the learners some individual thinking time to help language awareness. Alternatively, the whole activity could be done as homework and followed up at the start of the next lesson.

Make sure the learners study the examples of adjectives and adverbs. Ask them to describe to you the rules of adverb formation that the examples suggest. It might also be a good idea to practise pronunciation to show how the schwa (ə) is the sound that is used when saying most adverbs with an *-ally* ending.

Answer key

interesting – interestingly	sad – sadly
nice – nicely	cheap – cheaply
safe – safely	expensive – expensively
practical – practically	beautiful – beautifully
natural – naturally	usual – usually
special – specially	useful – usefully
noisy – noisily	easy – easily
happy – happily	busy – busily
pretty – prettily	untidy – untidily

The adverb form *well* from the adjective *good* may be known to the learners. Give them a chance to guess by supplying clues, e.g. *Are you good at English? Yes, I speak English very .... What is the missing word, Pedro? Tell me something you do well, Isabel. How about you, Toshi?*

Personal Study Workbook

1, 3: contrasting adjectives and adverbs
4: adjectives and adverbs: vocabulary extension

Quick Check answer key

1. well   2. skilfully   3. easily   4. confidently

┌─────────────────────────────────────┐
│   QUICK NOTES   │
│   │
│ This went well: │
│ ....   │
│ ....   │
│   │
│ This didn't quite work: │
│ ....   │
│ ....   │
│   │
│ Things to think about: │
│ ....   │
│ ....   │
│   │
└─────────────────────────────────────┘

1 My favourite hobby is ...
vocabulary; speaking

Suggested steps

You could mime to establish the name of a hobby or craft and to begin the process of sharing the concept of hobbies as spare time interests. This will also help with the task of guessing that sort of activity. Then the learners can study the illustrations in small groups and work together on the hobby vocabulary.

Use a quick feedback to check understanding of vocabulary and to establish further any cultural differences in terms of the concept of a hobby, or particular national traditions in terms of crafts. This will bring the material closer to the learners' own experience and understanding. Talk about your own hobbies and craft skills and bring in materials, tools etc. associated with them. This will lead naturally into the question and answer practice about hobbies. The pair practice also recycles the present perfect tense. Encourage the learners to ask supplementary questions for a better conversational style, e.g. *Have you ever tried cooking? Yes, I have. I love cooking. What sort of cooking do you like? How often do you cook?*

Option 1

Ask the learners to write the names of hobbies under these headings:

I've tried these hobbies once or twice
I've never tried these hobbies and don't want to
I'd like to try these hobbies
My favourite hobbies are ...

With a partner, the learners ask about hobbies under the different headings. Examples:

Which hobbies have you tried once or twice?
Which hobbies don't you want to try? Why not?
Which hobbies would you like to try? Origami? Why?
What are your favourite hobbies?

Option 2

Ask one person to mime their favourite hobby. The others ask questions about the mime.

Example:

A: *(miming) Can you guess my favourite hobby?*
B: *Do you do it regularly? (Every day? Every month?)*
C: *Did you learn it easily/quickly?*
B: *Is it expensive?*

For the miming activity, note also the use of another adverb *regularly* in the example questions about the mime. Try to encourage its use (and reasonable pronunciation) and try to build in other adverbs (e.g. *carefully*, *firmly*) as naturally as you can. This will help prepare for the reading text in Exercise 2.

2 Use a small linoleum block

imperatives; adverbs

Suggested steps

Use the illustrations to establish the hobby (printing). Talk about the different effects created by, for example, hand printing and machine or electronic printing. Make sure that the task is clear by establishing the difference between imperatives (instruction words) and adverbs (words indicating how something is done).

The learners could work in pairs if that arrangement works well with this type of activity.

The learners could check answers with each other. Monitor and help out as necessary.

You could ask particular learners to read the instructions aloud since reading out instructions is an authentic reading aloud activity. This will also give you an opportunity to draw attention to the sequence-marking time expressions to be used in Exercise 3 (*first, then, next, after that, finally*).

Answer key

3. First, *draw* the shape on the lino block as clearly as you can.
4. Use a special knife. Cut away all the parts around the shape very *carefully*.
5. Next, put printing ink onto the lino block.
6. Press the shape *firmly* onto the paper.
7. After that, *remove* the shape carefully.
8. Repeat this *regularly* to build up a pattern.

Option

Any fast finishers could try this additional text which may be photocopied; alternatively it could be used as reinforcement or as a homework task.

Complete these instructions using expressions in the box.

> easily   firmly   roll   slowly   build

Starting pottery – the first steps

Pottery is a great art. But with one traditional method, beginners can make pots more .... This is called 'coiling'. Coiling is a way of building up a pot by using long strings of clay. This is how you do it.

1. First,  the clay out gradually into long strings.

clay   strings

2. Then, make the base of the pot: press a ball of clay down 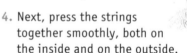 to form a flat circle.

base

3. After that,

....

up the walls of the pot. Put the strings gently around the base, one on top of the other, in coils.

4. Next, press the strings together smoothly, both on the inside and on the outside.

5. Add the strings ...., then there is time for the bottom part to get harder before you add another string.

6. You can now decorate your pot.

TRUE TO LIFE ELEMENTARY   © Cambridge University Press 1995

Answer key

Pottery is a great art. But with one traditional method, beginners can make pots more *easily*. This is called 'coiling'. Coiling is a way of building up a pot by using long strings of clay. This is how you do it.

1. First, *roll* the clay out gradually into long strings.
2. Then, make the base of the pot: press a ball of clay down *firmly* to form a flat circle.
3. After that, *build* up the walls of the pot. Put the strings gently around the base, one on top of the other, in coils.
4. Next, press the strings together smoothly, both on the inside and on the outside.
5. Add the strings *slowly*, then there is time for the bottom part to get harder before you add another string.

Personal Study Workbook

6: imperatives

3 First you ...
writing

Suggested steps

For a change of pace, the learners could do this activity individually. Emphasise that the instructions they write must be simple by telling the learners to imagine that they are writing instructions for children who are interested in the hobby they choose.

Explain to the learners that if their instructions have five or more steps it is OK to repeat link expressions like *after that*, *then* and *next*.

If you have limited time, this would make a good homework task and the learners could read their instructions as a revision guessing activity at the start of the next lesson.

Personal Study Workbook

7: adjectives and adverbs; writing

Quick Check answer key

1. Walk slowly down the stairs.
2. Drive patiently in the car park, and park tidily.
3. Behave well when there are visitors.
4. Chat quietly in the corridors.
5. Dress formally for work.

QUICK NOTES

This went well:

....

....

This didn't quite work:

....

....

Things to think about:

....

....

C

This lesson aims to build awareness of cross-cultural influences on language learning, particularly different notions of politeness. Clearly, there are individual interpretations of 'norms' of politeness within societies and groups, so teachers should avoid hard and fast notions of 'right' or 'wrong'. Raising awareness of differences and encouraging sensitivity to social and cultural context is the intended outcome.

1 Is it important to say *please* ...
discussion

Suggested steps

If you are teaching a monolingual group, ease into the activity by choosing a context in which *please* or *thank you* are usually said. Focus on intonation in the first language and how that can change what is communicated, since actual words may be too well known to arouse interest. Alternatively, focus on a situation in which different learners might have different views on the necessity for politeness in their L1, for example with family members at home, with teachers, at work.

The list of situations in the book will no doubt give rise to *It depends ...* type statements, e.g. *It depends on how well you know the person*, *It depends who it is*, *It depends on the country you are in*. Encourage the learners to explore these differences rather than to come up with firm answers. Draw on your own experiences or those of any learners who have visited English-speaking countries.

When the learners are talking in groups, build their confidence to talk in English by not over-correcting and not breaking the momentum of their discussion. Keep a note of common areas of weakness in speaking for follow-up repair work.

2 Politeness is one of the most important things ⬜⬜ ⬜⬜
listening; writing; discussion

Suggested steps

The speakers on the recording live in Britain but are not all of English origin. The easier, first listening is quite short and well supported by the handwritten notes. You may, therefore, prefer the slightly more challenging, second version. The tapescript is on page 233.

You might provide your own example of a completed sentence to show the learners one way of expressing a viewpoint after *because...*, e.g. *I agree with Speaker 3 because politeness is a sign of respect for other people. I believe that people are happier when others are polite to them.* With weaker groups give complete sentences of opinion and ask the learners to copy the one they agree with most.

Answer key

For the answers, please refer to the tapescript on page 233.

Personal Study Workbook

5: listening

3 Doing things politely ...
reading; rewriting

Suggested steps

Establish the meaning of *etiquette* by eliciting guesses: *Is 'etiquette' about being polite or rude, do you think? Is it about doing things in a very unusual way or in a usual way that people accept?* Alternatively, show pictures as examples, e.g. the placing and use of knives, forks and spoons for a formal dinner, formal wedding conventions. Ask the learners if they think etiquette is important to them or old-fashioned these days.

The text introduces a few new adverbs. Do a second sentence rewriting as an example if the learners are still in doubt about how to complete the task successfully.

Again, this activity might make a suitable homework task. The learners could check their answers with one another and discuss them at the start of the next lesson.

Answer key

1. Being polite is important because it makes life less stressful.
2. Being polite makes the quality of life better.
3. Politeness really means thinking about other people.
4. Polite families live happy lives.
5. Young people are more informal (less formal) than older people.
6. It is not very hard to learn to be polite.

Quick Check answer key

1. Is it very important to be polite? / Do you think it's very important to be polite?
2. Why is it/politeness important?
3. Are young people less formal than their parents?
4. What is the main rule (for politeness)?

QUICK NOTES

This went well:

....

....

This didn't quite work:

....

....

Things to think about:

....

....

REVIEW OF UNIT 15

1 Working late is a problem ⟐
the *-ing* sound in sentences; dictation; discussion

Suggested steps

You might like to model two sentences that are similar to ones on the recording, so that the learners can try to pick up the phonological difference between, say, *be* and *being* or *work* and *working*. Obviously, the faster a speaker speaks, the more difficult it is to discriminate, so there is some risk of frustration. The learners can use the grammatical construction of each sentence as a guide to their answers.

Answer key

1. (✓) I like *being* early for work.
2. (✓) I like *working* with tidy people.
3. (✗) I like work which gives me regular hours.
4. (✗) Work practices in the modern office are very important.
5. (✓) *Being* a manager is a hard job today.
6. (✗) Be a good worker so your manager can see how important you are.
7. (✗) I want to be in a top position in the company.
8. (✓) *Working* late is a problem for parents with young children.
9. (✓) I hate *leaving* work early when the traffic is terrible.
10. (✗) Leave work early and start late – that's what I think.

The second part of the activity is a dictation, so pause the recording after each of the three sentences to allow time for writing.

After checking the accuracy of their dictations, the learners can discuss their views on the issues raised in each of the three sentences. Start the learners off by asking them to ask you questions based on the sentences, e.g. *Do you like being early for work? Why?/Why not? Do you like work which gives you regular hours?* Then they can ask each other the same questions in pairs. Allow for a few minutes of general feedback, as this gives important reporting practice in the third person forms (*Maria says she likes being early for work because she …*).

The tapescript is on page 233.

2 Before leaving the building ...
writing with *before* or *after* + *-ing*

Suggested steps

You can devise other contexts if you prefer a less predictable and more amusing set of instructions, e.g. *Before getting married …, After watching a sad film at the cinema …, After using my car …*

Let the learners complete the sentences on their own, then ask them to get into small groups to compare what they have written.

Ask for feedback from the groups so that everyone can see the different sorts of instructions that have been produced for the same sentence beginnings. The use of *please* with the instruction is not obligatory; it depends on the context and how much you want a favourable response from the person or people to whom you are communicating the instruction.

Writing instructions for a language class might produce sentences like: *Before starting (to learn) English, be sure you have a lot of free time. After coming to classes, write down new words in your word book. Before coming to class, do your homework. After coming to class, do some exercises in the Personal Study Workbook.* Use one of these or similar to start the learners off.

REVIEW OF UNIT 16

1 I haven't had time yet
writing; discussion

Suggested steps

Before asking the learners to write their own lists, it may be helpful if you generate one or two other examples first, perhaps about yourself, using one or two of the words in the box.

If your learners need it, carry out a concept check of the meaning and use of *yet* after the groupwork. Concept check questions for *I haven't finished my homework yet* might include: *Did you start your homework before now?* (Answer: *Yes.*) *Is your homework finished now?* (Answer: *No.*) *Are you going to finish your homework in the future?* (Answer: *Yes.*)

2 I like teachers who have lots of ideas
vocabulary; relative pronouns

Suggested steps

Make sure that your learners remember the range of relative pronouns available for use: *who/where/that*.

After the initial matching activity, make sure that the learners understand the follow-up task by going through an example or two. Remember that verbs other than the verb *to be* can be used and that after *where* there is usually a pronoun or noun.

Answer key

1. c. I like teachers *who* have lots of ideas.
2. d. I like restaurants *where* the waiters are friendly.
3. f. I like shopkeepers *who* chat with people.
4. a. I like children *who* put their toys away.
5. b. I like books *that* are interesting to read.
6. e. I like cars *that* are very quiet.

For the group activity it may be easier to tell the learners in Group A to use just *who* or *that* and for the learners in Group B to write endings that start with a verb (as in the example). This will lead to a larger number of possible matches of beginnings and endings between the two halves of your class.

Have a brief feedback to listen to the most interesting or amusing sentences.

If the activity is successful, a similar follow-up activity using only *where* sentences could be tried.

Worksheets

The worksheet for this unit is on page 181. This can be carried out as a milling activity, where the learners walk round the class and talk to other learners individually, or as a whole-class activity, with each learner performing in front of the other class members.

Cut the worksheet up so that each adverb is on a separate piece of paper. (It would be better still if these could be pasted on card.) Put all 15 cards in a box. (You can add other word cards for bigger classes or duplicate the more difficult adverbs.)

Write all the adverb words on the board.

The learners take one adverb card each from the box, look at the adverb, check its meaning and then put it in their pocket.

The learners should try to talk to others in the class in the manner of the adverb they have chosen. The aim is for another learner to guess their adverb from the way they speak, without seeing the word. Remind them to look at the complete list on the board to help their guesses.

If you are doing this as a milling activity, the learners could take another adverb card from the box when the first has been guessed correctly.

END OF UNIT NOTES

How's the class getting on?

....

....

Language that needs more work or attention:

....

....

My learners:

....

....

18

ON YOUR TRAVELS

<table>
<tr><td colspan="2" align="center">CONTENTS</td></tr>
<tr><td>Language focus:</td><td>recommendation/advice: should, shouldn't
obligation: has to, have to
lack of obligation: doesn't/don't have to</td></tr>
<tr><td>Vocabulary:</td><td>travel, tourism</td></tr>
</table>

INTRODUCTION TO THE UNIT

This lesson proceeds via the theme of travelling to introduce the learners to the use of *should* for recommendation. It then offers a reading text to tackle the more complex concept of obligation through the use of *have to / don't have to*. The *must* construction is deliberately avoided at this level. The learners are helped to recognise the difference between expressions used for recommendations, obligation or lack of obligation. Relative pronouns are recycled in Lesson C, which uses listening and writing activities to explore opinions on the related theme of tourism.

A

1 Travels and trips
conversation

Warm-up

Before opening the book write the following on the board: BA010 – 49C. Ask the learners where they might see these letters and numbers. (They are a British Airways flight and seat number.)

Suggested steps

Use the illustration to establish the topic of travelling by plane, train or boat. Ask the learners whether they like flying, or whether they prefer other forms of travel.

For the listing of countries, restrict the learners to listing countries they have travelled to unless they are unlikely to have travelled beyond their own national frontiers. In the latter case, use places in their own country. If you know your learners are frequent travellers, ask them to list their favourite travel locations from the past ten years.

Help the learners to establish the language needed to guess places on their partner's list, e.g. *I think you've been to / visited* .... or *Have you been to* ....? or *I think* .... *is on your list. Am I right?*

Remind the learners that after the guessing activity, they are to talk about only one trip. The guiding questions will enable them both to question a partner and to prepare answers to questions about their own recent trip. Encourage a change in order of the questions or the addition of others, to prevent a mechanical quality to the interaction.

There is no need to change partners if the questioning is taking a long time, but try to have a brief feedback session so that the learners can report interesting things they have found out.

2 You should raise your ankles ▭▭
should/shouldn't; writing lists; discussion

Suggested steps

Sit with your ankles raised and ask the learners why it can be a good idea to do this when travelling on a long flight. (It is good for the circulation and stops your ankles from swelling up.) Establish the meaning of *You should ...* as *It's a good idea to ...*

Form groups for the sentence writing. Provide each group with a large sheet of paper, perhaps with a drawing of a plane at the top, and the title 'How to be a good long distance air traveller'. Provide marker pens (if possible) to make the wall displays more striking. Ask the learners for an example of a long distance air trip to establish an agreed meaning of 'long distance'.

Elicit from the learners that the long form of *shouldn't* is *should not* and check their understanding of its meaning by asking: *When someone says 'You shouldn't drink something ...', do they mean it's a good idea or a bad idea to drink it?*

Encourage groups to choose one person in their group to do the writing.

Display the lists and let the learners move around reading them and chatting. Regroup as a whole class to report any interesting or controversial ideas.

The listening is unscripted and quite challenging, so spend some time looking at the notes already in the table and discussing the task. The learners have to take notes as they listen to two pairs of people doing the same task the learners themselves have just done. The learners then decide whether the answers they hear are broadly similar to or different from their own.

Remember to finish the activity by eliciting a few reactions to what the speakers on the recording have said. Try to encourage your less confident members to contribute by asking manageable questions, e.g. *Do you think it's a good idea to take a good book on a long flight, Hong?* Encourage the learners to ask each other the same questions you asked to maintain their confidence to ask, not just answer, questions.

Answer key

For the answers, please see the tapescript on page 233.

Personal Study Workbook

1: should/shouldn't

3 Visitors to my country
writing

Suggested steps

Find out how many people have had visitors from other countries and what their visitors liked or didn't like about their country.

If your class all come from the same country, build up vocabulary for the four missing sections of the letter together (that is, food, things to see, things to bring, things to be careful about). With a multilingual group, ask the learners to make lists for each category individually.

Introduce the learners to letter conventions (place of address, date, appropriate ways of ending). Encourage the learners to use a new paragraph for each section of new information that they put in their letter.

You could ask the learners to read out their letters in groups and to help each other to improve them or correct any mistakes. Discuss any interesting differences of content and lead into actual situations in which the learners have had visitors and advised them (or wished they had).

Option

I went to Bolivia with my briefcase ... (a vocabulary game)

Get together pictures of common travel items, e.g. *suitcase, passport, tickets, first-aid kit, bottled water, travel iron, travel plug, ear-plugs, book, magazine, walkman.*

The learners are in teams. Each person completes the sentence *I went to ... .* Use as many words as you can which start with the same letter as the country you went to. You get a point for each word that starts with the letter.

Example: *I went to Peru by plane but I forgot my passport.* (You get 3 points!)

It is a good idea to give an example first so that the learners know exactly what to do. An additional rule is to allow only one country with the same first letter, as

this will prevent unfair repetition of items used by previous players.

Personal Study Workbook

4: pronunciation practice
5: the vocabulary of travel

Quick Check answer key

1. You shouldn't eat salads. / I don't think you should eat salads.
2. You shouldn't sleep on a long flight. / I don't think you should sleep on a long flight.
3. You shouldn't eat too much. / I don't think you should eat too much.
4. You shouldn't put your bag under the seat. / I don't think you should put your bag under the seat.
5. You shouldn't stand up before the aircraft has come to a complete stop. / I don't think you should stand up before the aircraft has come to a complete stop.

QUICK NOTES

This went well:

....

....

This didn't quite work:

....

....

Things to think about:

....

....

B

1 You have to buy a visa at the airport
have to, should and *don't have to*; reading

Suggested steps

If possible, bring in your passport and a camera. Ask the learners to identify each item and then use them to establish the concept of obligation: *Which is more important when you travel? (A passport.) Why? Yes, you have to have a passport when you go from one country to another. Can you choose? No, you can't. You have to have it.*

Open the Class Book and ask the learners to read the information under the illustrations of the passport and camera. Ask them: *Why is the passport more important?* to elicit *Because you have to have one to go from one country to another.* Ask: *Why is the camera less important?* to elicit *Because you don't have to have one to go from one country to another.*

Prior to group reading ask the learners to tell you (or tell their group, if they are in groups) one interesting thing about either Kashmir, Turkey or Japan.

To avoid confusion, set up several groups, each consisting of three learners and assign a different letter (A, B or C) to individual members of each group. Each learner then reads the text assigned to them.

As a task to take into their first reading, ask the learners to check what travellers have to do and don't have to do when visiting that country. The learners complete the true/false task after first reading.

Remind the learners to use the true/false sentences to guide their report to the others in the group, not just to read the sentences out like a list.

Spend time on vocabulary clarification at the end of the group information exchange.

Answer key

A. Travelling to Kashmir
1. Most travellers don't have to have a visa to enter India. (F)
2. Travellers have to go to an Indian embassy to get a visa. (T)
3. Tourists don't have to have any photos for their visa. (F)
4. Travellers with Indian visas don't have to have special permission to visit Kashmir. (T)
5. It's not a good idea to take any local currency. (F)

B. Travelling to Turkey
1. Visitors from most countries have to get a visa before travelling to Turkey. (F)
2. When you arrive in Turkey, you have to buy a visa. (T)
3. Tourists with a visa have to leave after 30 days. (F)
4. It's a good idea to get local currency when you arrive. (T)
5. It isn't a good idea to travel with cash for emergencies. (F)

C. Travelling to Japan
1. Tourists from many countries don't have to have a visa for the first 90 days of their stay. (T)
2. English tourists don't have to have a visa for the first year. (F)
3. Americans don't have to have a visa for the first 3 months. (T)
4. Australians have to have photos and a return ticket to get a visa for Japan. (T)
5. It isn't a good idea to carry cash. (F)

Personal Study Workbook

2: *should* and *have to*
7, 8: reading

2 You don't have to have a passport
have to / don't have to; speaking

Suggested steps

Ask the learners to complete the sentences individually, then compare their ideas with others.

Option

If the learners all come from one country you may prefer to see if any learners have had experiences of obligations (visas, stated maximum stay, contact address) when they have visited other countries. If you choose this option, the sentence completions can still be carried out as printed and the speaking in pairs will also feel more genuine.

For the final discussion, try to arrange the learners in a circle or round a table. The learners should be encouraged to give opinions and counter opinions about changes in international travel. Let them talk openly. Try not to overdirect the exchanges but offer stimulus questions if the learners need help, e.g. ask them about the effects of the increasing availability of air travel, the enlarging of the European Economic Community, political changes in countries that have previously been 'closed'. Encourage anecdotes about crossing borders, customs, visas or immigration.

Personal Study Workbook

3: *should / have to*: question forms

3 Travellers should take a hat
obligation, lack of obligation and recommendation; writing sentences

Suggested steps

This would make a good consolidation homework task or a quiet activity to change the pace after the discussion. Note that *required* is used as a synonym for *obligation* for the purposes of this activity.

If it is done for homework, the learners could be asked to write the three extra sentences themselves and could exchange them with a partner at the beginning of the next lesson, as a quick revision activity.

Answer key

(G)	1.	Travellers to hot countries should take a hat.
(R)	2.	Passengers have to check in on time.
(G)	3.	On business trips, you should take business cards.
(G)	4.	Tourists should carry travellers' cheques.
(NR)	5.	You don't have to pay airport departure tax.
(R)	6.	Australians have to get visas to travel to Japan.
(NR)	7.	The Dutch don't have to have a passport to go to France.
(G)	8.	Travellers in hotels should be quiet at night.
(R)	9.	You have to have two photos for passports.
(G)	10.	Air travellers should drink lots of water.

Quick Check answer key

1. should   2. have to   3. has to   4. don't have to
5. shouldn't

C

1 What is a good tourist?
reading; writing; discussion

This activity prepares learners for the vocabulary and contexts in the listening task in Exercise 2.

Suggested steps

Take the first sentence (*A good tourist is someone who doesn't eat the local food*) as an example to make the task clear. Ask the learners to think of their own country, town or city when they consider the example. Do they agree with it? Ask a learner who doesn't agree to complete the sentence differently, e.g. *A good tourist is someone who eats the local food and learns about its importance to the people.*

When pairs have rewritten one or two sentences, ask them to meet up with other pairs and discuss their changes. In the group discussion let the learners talk freely. The idea is not to drill the written sentence forms as a conversational form, but to exchange their views on tourists using the sentences as a springboard.

If the activity is going well, ask the learners who finish quickly to write one or two of their own sentences starting *A good tourist is someone who* … or *A bad tourist is someone who* …

2 A good tourist is somebody who respects the traditions ▭▭ ▭▭
listening; speaking

Suggested steps

It is useful here to spend a little time exploring the meaning of the title of the activity as the learners will hear it on the recording. *Some**body*** means the same as *some**one***. Ask the learners to try to explain *respects* and *traditions* in simple language if they can. If they can't, explain *traditions* by giving examples of traditions to clarify the meaning, then ask the learners to guess possible meanings of *respect*.

The dual listening gives you an opportunity to show the learners that the same gist can come from different versions. The first recording is a scripted version of the second one, which was not scripted.

Instead of playing the shorter recording (version 1) twice, you could try playing the longer recording (version 2) if the learners want to listen again. Some expressions will be different, but the substance is the same and as each person's contribution is longer it may give more time for note-taking (assuming your learners can now sample incoming speech for information and don't try to follow every word).

The tapescript is on page 234.

Telling an anecdote yourself should encourage the learners to share their anecdotes and at the same time help them to understand how to structure a simple authentic story.

Personal Study Workbook
6: listening

3 Is tourism good for countries? ▭▭
listening and discussion; writing

Suggested steps

Ask the learners to read the gapped texts before they actually listen. This will make the listening task easier by familiarising the learners with the content. This type of heavily supported listening activity, though somewhat artificial, should help the learners to stop trying to catch every word they hear and develop the more natural sampling of incoming messages.

Answer key

For the answers please refer to the tapescript on page 234.

You could use the group discussions as preparation for the paragraph writing for homework. Ask groups to report on their discussions about tourism. Put up helpful vocabulary or opinions on the board as a resource for the writing. Make sure that the learners are clear about how to express opinions (*I think* …) and reasons (… *because* …). With weaker learners, create a framework for the paragraph writing to reduce the level of error. The summaries from the previous listening task illustrate possible frameworks.

If you want to give the writing task a more realistic context, you might produce a simple magazine series called '*Viewpoints*' (this one would be *Viewpoints on tourism*) in which different paragraphs are reproduced in simple magazine form for the class, and other people, to read. Simple illustrations, cartoons, tourist ads, etc. could be added to make the magazine a more substantial project.

Personal Study Workbook
9: writing

Quick Check answer key

1. Souvenirs: a postcard; a pot; a carpet; a doll; a book
2. Customs and traditions: singing; a national holiday; a queue; a dance
3. Things that are useful for travelling: a toothbrush; a suitcase; a credit card; a book; a first-aid kit; bottled water

```
QUICK NOTES

This went well:
....................................................
....................................................

This didn't quite work:
....................................................
....................................................

Things to think about:
....................................................
....................................................
```

D   REVIEW AND DEVELOPMENT

REVIEW OF UNIT 16

1   I've bought something that's orange
revision of *just* with present perfect

Suggested steps

It's generally a good idea to go through one example with your learners so that they know how to play guessing games, so think of something before you present this activity and let your learners try to guess it.

Tell the learners to write down their item's colour, size, material and use before they say their sentences to a partner. Remind them to read the complete sentences (*I've just bought something ...*) since these practise the grammatical form that is being revised.

Rotate pairs after the first round so that there are always new items to guess and the learners become more fluent by repeating their own sentences several times to different people.

Think of a difficult one yourself and challenge the whole class to guess it to round the activity off.

Option

For further practice of *have just* + past participle use this activity, which is quite controlled, but provides a frame for guided conversation.

The learners complete each of these two sentence beginnings with appropriate expressions from the box (or they use their own), then compare answers.

I've just had … I've just made …

```
a new hat   holiday   a cold   a letter   a phone call
a good friend   a good decision   an accident
a daughter
```

Then they choose two people from this second box and tell a partner what each person has just had or just made.

```
aunt   uncle   friend   manager   sister   colleague
mother   father   I   brother   cousin
```

The partner asks additional questions as in this sample exchange.

Example:
PARTNER A: *My cousin has just had a baby daughter.*
PARTNER B: *When? Is she pleased?*
PARTNER A: *Last week. Yes, she's very pleased, because she already has two boys.*

The resource box of words is there as a prompt for learners who can't easily think of anything themselves. Encourage the learners to use their own real examples with … *just had* … and … *just made* …

REVIEW OF UNIT 17

1   Read these carefully
adverbs and instructions

Suggested steps

The learners might work in pairs while reading the instructions, helping each other with vocabulary. A dictionary might also be useful as the learners will probably not know the English words for the missing nouns.

With an ambitious group, ask them for homework to write instructions for something else. Classmates can try to guess during the next lesson.

Answer key

1. Place your paper on to the glass *carefully*.
   These instructions are for making a *photocopy*.
2. Be careful not to tie the bandage too *tightly*.
   These instructions are for treating someone with a *burn*.

2   We have reprimanded him severely ⊏⊐
listening for adverbs

Suggested steps

Encourage guessing of difficult vocabulary by asking the learners to let easier parts of particular sentences (and the letter as a whole) help them to guess the difficult words.

Before listening, remind the learners that the task is one of listening for four specific items of difference (two different words and three additional adverbs). They should read the letter while listening.

Encourage checking in groups. The tapescript is on page 234.

Answer key

Dear Mr Johns,

Thank you for your letter. We are always very happy to get letters from our customers. However, we were sorry to hear about your *bad* experience with our shop assistant. He behaved very *rudely*. I can only say that this is not what we *usually* teach the staff in our company, and we have reprimanded him *severely*.

We are enclosing a free voucher. Please use it when you are next in one of our shops.

Yours *sincerely*,

J Bean
Customer Services Manager
Trading Post Stores

Worksheets

The worksheets for this unit are on page 182.

Put the learners into pairs. Each learner has eight questions on either Worksheet 18A or Worksheet 18B. Each learner asks their partner one question at a time and keeps a record of their answers.

At the end of eight questions each learner tells their partner the correct answers and their final score.

The winner is the partner with the highest score at the end of the eight questions.

END OF UNIT NOTES

How's the class getting on?

....

....

Language that needs more work or attention:

....

....

My learners:

....

....

19

A LOOK AT LIFE!

```
                          CONTENTS

   Language focus:   expressing wishes with would like: positive, negative,
                         question forms
                     would with other verbs

      Vocabulary:    views on life
                     how people spend time
                     beauty
```

INTRODUCTION TO THE UNIT

The use of *would like* when ordering food or in other immediate request situations has already been featured in Unit 3. This unit extends the use of *would like* for less immediate wishes or dreams (the wish for more time to do certain things, for example) touched on in Unit 6. The learners are asked to reflect on and talk about their current life situation. A good variety of activities is employed to extend form and meaning and to build vocabulary. Writing ability is developed through the presentation of new linking expressions (*On the one hand … on the other hand …*). The topic of beauty provides the basis for further development of reading, listening and oral skills in the final lesson.

A

1 Life is just a bowl of cherries
speaking

This activity is really a warm-up, drawing the learners into the theme of the lesson.

Suggested steps

Write *Life is …* on the board. Explain what the expression *life* means by relating it to *to live* and *living* and *the things you do and the things that happen in the years you are alive*. Invite the learners to write a completion to the sentence *Life is …*

With multilingual groups, ask the learners if in their country there are any well-known expressions used to summarise what 'life' is. Ask them to write down other completions for *Life is …* and then to explain them to a partner. They can write them in their own language, if necessary.

In monolingual groups, ask the learners to tell their partners which of the sayings about life in the Class Book they like best and why. Pairs can discuss any others that they know before a general feedback.

2 Is your life in balance?
vocabulary; speaking

Suggested steps

Use the picture of scales to elicit the meaning of *balance* and *life in balance*.

It may be easier to redraw the scales as a worksheet if you don't want the learners to write in the book.

Go through an example or two for yourself with the scales so that the learners understand what to do with the expressions. Model the uses of *would* at the same time, e.g. *I don't have enough time with my friends, so I'd like to have more time with my friends. Did I say **I like** … or **I'd like** …? Yes, **I'd like**. Would you like to have more time with your friends, Igor? How about you, Jaime? Would you like …?*

When each learner has assigned the expressions into the appropriate scales, form pairs for comparison of the scales. Before pairs commence, model target uses of *would* again. Try to elicit that *I'd like* means *I wish* and is not really the same as *I'd like a cup of coffee, please*.

After comparisons have been made in pairs, review the use and meaning of *would* questions and answers with one or two learners since this is the first time the form has been presented. The example exchanges could be practised as a reinforcement dialogue if that is the sort of controlled practice your class finds beneficial.

Language Point:

Establish that *Would you like …?* means *Do you wish you could have something that is perhaps difficult to have?* here; it's not quite the same as offering someone something simple in everyday situations (as in *Would you like a cup of coffee?*).

Note also that *I'd like …* can be followed by a noun as in *I'd like **more time*** or by an infinitive form as in *I'd like **to see** my parents more often*.

Personal Study Workbook
1: *Would you like …?* + answers

3 What would grandparents like?
writing

Suggested steps

This exercise is a controlled written practice of the form
I think (pronoun)'d like … . Write two examples for the
learners to start them off. One example should be …
would like (+ noun) *because …*; the other … *would like* (+
infinitive + noun) *because …*

To make the practice more realistic, you could choose
real people from the culture of the learners (if
monolingual) or from the culture in which the learners
are learning or from popular international culture
(internationally well-known people).

Encourage the learners not to read their sentences word
for word but to maintain eye contact in the group
feedback and to try to develop fluency.

Personal Study Workbook
2: *I'd like* + noun
3: *I'd like* + infinitive

4 I'd like to have a long holiday ⊂⊃
listening

Suggested steps

This listening activity would make an excellent 'two
piece' jigsaw activity. Divide the class into two halves.
One half listens to one person on the recording; the
other half listens to the other person on the recording.

Then put the learners in pairs so that each pair has
learners who listened to different people on the
recording. Each re-tells what their recording contains
and the partner tries to guess what that person does for a
living.

Pairs can talk to other pairs to compare guesses before
you give the answers. The tapescript is on page 234.

Answer key
Speaker 1 is a parent.
Speaker 2 is a flight attendant.

Personal Study Workbook
4: long and short forms of *would*

Quick Check answer key
(i)
She'd like = She would like
We'd like = We would like
He wouldn't like = He would not like
Why would you like to be a pilot?
Why wouldn't you like to live in Paris?
(ii)
1. b   2. c   3. b

QUICK NOTES

This went well:
....
....

This didn't quite work:
....
....

Things to think about:
....
....

B

1 I'd like to live in a world that's clean
writing; reading aloud

Suggested steps

Make sure the learners understand the mood of the topic
(dreams of a better world for all) before they complete
their own sentences.

You can decide the size of group to create an
appropriate length of poem. A group size of five is
probably a good option.

If you prefer, you could listen to the sample poems on
the recording first (Exercise 2) so that the learners have a
clearer idea of the task and creative outcomes that are
possible.

For the group reading, encourage group members to
read one line each (not necessarily their own) in the
order which the group has decided for its poem. This
ensures that everyone participates.

2 A world that's kind to children ⊂⊃
listening

Suggested steps

The idea here is listening for pleasure; there is no
specific task. You might help the learners' understanding
by supplying the written tapescripts of the poems from
the recordings, if preferred. The tapescript is on page
234.

Alternatively, photocopy gapped text versions of the
scripts and do a conventional listening task.

Round off this two-part creative activity by encouraging
a bit of discussion about the current state of the world
and whether your learners are optimists or pessimists.
You might passively introduce *on the one hand … and on
the other hand …* here in preparation for Lesson B,
Exercise 3. Steer the learners to further use of *would like*
by asking questions such as: *Would you like to see more
computers/universities/televisions/novels/psychologists in the*

world? Why? / Why not? What would you like your government to do? Spend a little time working on the short answer forms *Yes, I would / No, I wouldn't*, reminding the learners that in short answers they cannot use *I'd*.

3 Would you like to live to be 100 years old?
would ('d) with other verbs; writing

Suggested steps

As a warm-up, elicit from the learners information about the oldest person in their family, or the oldest person they have ever met. Alternatively, use photos of anyone very old in your own family or the pictures in the book.

As the groups make lists of advantages and disadvantages, encourage them to note down verbs, e.g. *get tired / know a lot / see great grandchildren*, as this will add variety to their paragraph writing. Check that the learners understand that the use of *on the one hand … on the other hand …* enables contrasting information to be presented (advantages/disadvantages).

The study of the examples and the paragraph writing could be given as homework. Again, this unit offers an opportunity for a class magazine project (perhaps called *Life is …*) with sayings about life, paragraphs about being a hundred, poems and other interesting material, e.g. cartoons, pictures and photos.

There are several good songs about age and experience, e.g. *When I'm 64* (Beatles), *Both sides now* (Judy Collins), *Old friends* (Simon and Garfunkel), *My way* (Frank Sinatra). One of these might make a useful additional activity, especially if you can find a karaoke version.

Personal Study Workbook

6, 8: *would*

Quick Check answer key

1. I wouldn't like to be a teenager again.
2. Would you keep forgetting things?
3. Why would your father like to have more money?
4. I'd like to live in a world that's green.
5. Perhaps someone would listen to me.

QUICK NOTES

This went well:

....

....

This didn't quite work:

....

....

Things to think about:

....

....

 C

This lesson changes topic to consider the nature of 'beautiful faces' and concentrates on skills development. There is, of course, an indirect link to the previous topic of old age.

1 A question of beauty
discussion

Suggested steps

The topic under discussion is the adult, female face. It is of course necessary to be sensitive to gender issues here, and encourage discussion of perceptions by both men and women of what is beauty in a female face.

You might raise interest in the topic by asking the learners: *When someone says 'She's got a beautiful face' what do they mean? Can everyone agree that it's beautiful or is a beautiful face very different for each person, or different for men and women, or for different cultures?*

Then ask the learners to look at the faces in the book, choose and give reasons for their choice in groups of three.

Have a quick general feedback and encourage reasons which specify the physical characteristics of a beautiful face, e.g. shape and size of face and of features like eyes, nose, lips, as these will link to the findings from the text.

2 The perfect look?
reading; discussion

Suggested steps

Read the article first yourself to gain a sense of the content. Use probing questions to steer the guesses about the title towards some of the content, e.g. *Can a computer draw a face? How can it draw a perfect face? How is it possible to know that the face is perfect, do you think? What do you think the perfect look is like?*

The preparatory questioning makes rapid reading more possible because the learners take more known material into the reading, but remind the learners of the task for the first reading, that is, to remember two things from the text. Try to impose a time limit so that the learners try to gist read and don't try to read too intensively.

The two things remembered from the text can be written down as notes to save time. Let pairs circulate among other pairs to widen the scope of comparisons.

The second reading can be completed more carefully, hence building up awareness that the same text can be read in different ways for different purposes. This slower reading should help the learners to have a guess at the missing part of the last paragraph. Encourage the learners to share their views.

Before the listening activity it might be good to write some of the learners' guesses for the missing final sentence on the board. This should build motivation to listen.

Language Point: similar to / the same as

The learners need to be aware that ... *is similar to* ... (in the last sentence of the text) is not identical in meaning to ... *is the same as* ... . You might illustrate this by showing a gradation from similarity to difference, as follows: *is exactly the same as / is the same as / is similar to / is different from / is completely different from*. Use question examples to check the learners' understanding of differences, e.g. *Is 3 x 4 the same as 4 x 3? Is hockey similar to ice hockey? Are they the same? Are you similar to your brother or completely different?*

Personal Study Workbook

7: reading

3 So what did they discover? ▭▭ ▭▭

listening; discussion

Suggested steps

The listening activity is linked to Exercises 1 and 2 and is in two parts: the first part is a dual listening with two people trying to guess the missing part of the sentence just as your learners have just done; the second part of the recording tells you the actual missing sentence from the text.

After the first listening, let the learners compare notes to check understanding. Discourage multiple listening as this is often not available in real-life situations.

After the second listening (the recorded reading of the missing part of the text) check sentence completions before grouping the learners for discussion. The tapescript is on page 235.

Answer key

The woman thinks the most beautiful face is a balanced face (a very symmetrical face).
The man thinks the most beautiful face is similar to the face of a top model, or a traditional beauty like the Mona Lisa.

Missing part of the text:
Scientists discovered that the most beautiful face is similar to the face of a young child.

Broaden the topic if your group is interested in doing so, e.g. cultural differences, the influence of TV and other visual media on ideas of beauty, the power of the face as an icon in advertising, global culture, the way you look versus the way you live / the way you are.

Personal Study Workbook

5: *would like*; listening

Quick Check answer key

1. pretty   3. best
2. picture   4. difficult

QUICK NOTES

This went well:

....

....

This didn't quite work:

....

....

Things to think about:

....

....

D REVIEW AND DEVELOPMENT

REVIEW OF UNIT 17

1 I speak more quickly than my brother

adverbs; comparative forms of adverbs

Suggested steps

This activity introduces comparative adverb forms at the same time as reviewing adverbs. After the missing adverbs have been completed, spend a little time presenting a few examples of the comparative forms using yourself as the context, e.g. *I speak more clearly than my brother and I eat more carefully than my daughter.*

Answer key

easy – easily
gentle – gently
good – well
careful – carefully
peaceful – peacefully

Encourage one or two examples from your learners before they build up sentences for the conversational practice. If your class has problems with stress and rhythm, you might spend some time practising delivery of certain sentences to build fluency.

This activity is straightforward, but note that the example encourages the learners to add comments to their initial practice of comparative adverbial forms to prevent their mini-conversations from being too mechanical. Practise this a little before they start their groupwork.

> **Language Point: good, well, better**
>
> The adverb form of *good* (*well*) does not take the comparative form '*more well*'. The word *better* is used for comparative forms of both adjective (*good*) and adverb (*well*), as in:
>
> *I can sing better than you can.* (comparative adverb)
> *I had a better holiday than my friend.* (comparative adjective)
>
> The superlative form for both adjective and adverb is *best*.

2 Adverb mime
revision of adverbs

Suggested steps

Perform a mime example yourself first for the learners to guess.

Give the learner pairs a starter list of instruction sentences if they are going to find it difficult to instruct other pairs unassisted, e.g.

Sit like this.
Drive like this.
Sing like this.
Telephone like this.
Eat like this.
Walk like this.
Smile like this.
Drink like this.

Alternatively, get pairs to build their own lists before they start.

During the game, give encouragement and note down any language problems for later repair work.

REVIEW OF UNIT 18

1 The shoe shops were shut ▭
pronunciation /ʃ/ and question intonation

Suggested steps

Make sure you model the target sound /ʃ/ first so that the learners are clear about it.

The target sound /ʃ/ occurs 16 times in Sheila's part (and twice in the other person's part), but several of those 16 sounds are found in repeated instances of the same word (*shoes*).

The learners can practise asking the questions as a self access activity in the language laboratory, or you might practise question intonation in class using the questions in the dialogue, with the learners then practising in pairs while you monitor performance.

If the learner pairs are sufficiently engaged, let them rotate the parts of the conversation so that each learner has a chance to practise the other part of the conversation with its plentiful supply of /ʃ/ sounds.

Answer key

Did you have a good weekend, <u>Sh</u>eila?
No, terrible … <u>sh</u>ocking.
Yes, but I hadn't got any good <u>sh</u>oes.
Couldn't you buy <u>sh</u>oes?
Yes, I got some ca<u>sh</u> and went <u>sh</u>opping. But the <u>sh</u>oe <u>sh</u>ops were <u>sh</u>ut.
I packed my old <u>sh</u>oes.
Well … I had a reserva<u>ti</u>on for the 4 o'clock train.
I asked permi<u>ssi</u>on to leave work early.
He said <u>sh</u>ort days are not effi<u>ci</u>ent.
We got into a long discu<u>ssi</u>on.
I got to the sta<u>ti</u>on late.

2 I got a cheap charter flight ▭
pronunciation /tʃ/ and question intonation

Suggested steps

Proceed as for Exercise 1 above. The featured sound /tʃ/ occurs 15 times in Charles' part, and once in the other person's part.

Again, practise question intonation chorally if the learners respond to that sort of practice.

Use the recording for final question practice, when the learners can ask the questions with reasonable speed and fluency.

Again rotate pair practice so that each learner practises the answer portion of the dialogue.

Answer key

<u>Ch</u>arles, hello!
I got a <u>ch</u>eap <u>ch</u>arter to Chicago.
Yes, I had time to <u>ch</u>eck in, and <u>ch</u>ange some travellers' <u>ch</u>eques.
Wonderful. The flight attendants were <u>ch</u>eerful. There was a great choice for lun<u>ch</u> – <u>ch</u>icken or <u>ch</u>eese omelette and some delicious <u>ch</u>ocolates.
No, but I had a nice <u>ch</u>at with the person next to me - <u>ch</u>arming man.
I wat<u>ch</u>ed a film about <u>ch</u>ildren. It gave me a headache.

3 I lost all my cheques! ▭
pronunciation /ʃ/ and /tʃ/

Suggested steps

Write the rule on the board (one hand /ʃ/, two hands /tʃ/) so that the learners can see it easily while they listen to the recording.

Model the task by saying a sentence with either /ʃ/ or /tʃ/ and asking the learners whether they should raise one or two hands.

The tapescript is on page 235.

Worksheets

The worksheets for this unit are on page 183. The learners each receive both Worksheet 19A and Worksheet 19B and have two tasks:

Task 1: To complete the description of the sort of companion they would like. (Worksheet 19A)

Task 2: To make up descriptions for two people who want to become companions. They can be imagined people or real people such as friends of the learner. (Worksheet 19B)

When the learners have finished the tasks, they circulate and talk to other learners to see if they can find a companion from someone else's Worksheet 19B who matches the description of the sort of person they are looking for.

END OF UNIT NOTES

How's the class getting on?

....

....

Language that needs more work or attention:

....

....

My learners:

....

....

20

I'M SO SORRY!

```
                    CONTENTS

Language focus:    apologising
                   complaining

    Vocabulary:    shops and shopping situations
                   hotel situations
```

INTRODUCTION TO THE UNIT

This unit explores two related functions, apologising and complaining. The first lesson looks systematically at some of the language that can be used when shopping or returning something to a shop. The next two lessons move on to more general complaints and apologies, getting the learners to consider questions of register, politeness and cross-cultural differences.

A

1 I bought my watch at the duty-free shop
conversation

Warm-up

Take off your wrist watch, hold it up and ask the learners to ask you questions about it. If necessary, prompt the learners with: *Ask me: Where? / How long? / Cost? / Any problems?* Make sure that the questions asked are appropriately constructed and use the new expression duty-free shop in your answers. Ask the learners if they often go shopping in a duty-free shop when they travel.

Suggested steps

Ask the learners to choose one thing they have with them and to ask each other similar questions.

Monitor and encourage the pairs.

Have a quick, whole-class reporting session of the pair conversations.

2 You can pay with a credit card
vocabulary and speaking

Suggested steps

Draw three boxes quickly on the board arranged vertically. In the first box write *Wake up*. Ask the learners what to put in the next box. Mime an action

(*get out of bed* or *turn off the alarm clock*). Ask for suggestions for the third box. Then move into the flow diagram in the book.

Option

Draw three boxes. Ask three learners each to do one of three simple mimes (waking up / getting dressed / eating breakfast). Ask the learners which mime goes in box 1, 2 and 3. Draw a fourth box and ask what the next step is (go to work / read the paper, perhaps).

Ask the learners to look at the flow chart and to tell you what they think it is about. (A step by step guide to shopping.) Ask them not to worry about difficult words at this stage.

The flow chart can be completed in pairs, with a dictionary if necessary.

Answer key

1. Ask the shop for information.
2. Decide not to buy.
3. Ask for the item.
4. Decide not to buy.
5. Pay with a credit card *or* Pay by cheque.
6. Pay by cheque *or* Pay with a credit card.
7. Get a receipt.
8. Ask to see another item.

It may be useful to focus answers to the discussion questions using an example of a particular item, e.g. a television, a kettle, a hairdrier, especially if your learners are from one country and are studying English in their own country.

Ask the learners to prepare their answers to the questions, but not to write them down.

It may be appropriate to introduce the useful form *It depends ...*, as in *It depends where you go* or *It depends on the shop*.

Encourage anecdotes of particular shopping experiences which focus on the target vocabulary (*refund/guarantee/ receipt/exchange/credit card/cheque*).

3 Can I try it on, please?
vocabulary; writing a dialogue

Suggested steps

To save time, allocate one dialogue to one half of the class and the second dialogue to the other half.

You may like to practise stress, rhythm and intonation in the dialogues chorally before the learners practise in pairs. (Be careful especially of the noun *refund* which has main stress on the first syllable *re*.)

Try to add variety to the dialogue reading, using the following options:

Options

Read the shopping dialogue round the class, one exchange per person.

Ask pairs to act out the dialogue.

Ask pairs to mouth the dialogue without sound, concentrating instead on facial expressions, gestures and other body language.

Then repeat with dialogue voices supplied by two other learners as the mime is repeated.

Ask pairs to change one word in the dialogue and then to read it out. Others try to spot the word change.

Ask the learners to improvise a contrasting disaster dialogue (one in which there is an argument, or the customer or shop assistant behaves badly).

> ### Language Point:
> Remind the learners that these are not real conversations but prototypical ones. It may be useful to ask the learners in what ways real shop conversations might be different (more distractions, hesitations, less language, perhaps) and whether in their own language customers and assistants interact in that way.

Answer key

(Using the sentences from the box)

1.

CUSTOMER: Can I try it on, please?
SHOP ASSISTANT: Yes, madam, please come this way.
CUSTOMER: Have you got a bigger size?
SHOP ASSISTANT: Yes, we've got a size 20.
CUSTOMER: Is there a cheaper one?
SHOP ASSISTANT: Well, there is, but it's not the same quality, of course.
CUSTOMER: I'd like a different colour.
SHOP ASSISTANT: Oh, but the blue looks so nice on you!
    or I'm afraid that's the only colour we've got.

2.
Various alternatives are possible.

4 I'm terribly sorry ▭
listening and speaking

Suggested steps

Politeness is not just conveyed in the actual words but in the way in which they are spoken, and in the accompanying body language. You might demonstrate this to your learners by saying *Can I see your receipt?* in several different ways and asking the learners which ones seem more polite and why (softer voice, rising intonation, smiling and eye contact versus over-strong stress, flat intonation, no eye contact, grim face). Also, politeness is culturally defined, so your learners may not find it easy to pass judgement on politeness in an English-speaking country. This is not a major issue at this level since the main aim here is to sensitise the learners to these factors, not to try to provide 'right' answers.

Play the recording. The tapescript is on page 235.

The final discussion in this activity should take place informally with pairs or small groups feeling free to converse naturally in a less controlled way.

Answer key

The first shop assistant says sentence 1.
The second shop assistant says sentence 3.

Personal Study Workbook

3: using polite forms when apologising

Options – Follow-up

As the lesson raises cultural issues of politeness as well as useful shopping language and shop assistant/customer encounters, you might like to follow up in any of these ways:

Build up and display a range of authentic materials from shops in English-speaking countries (receipts, guarantees, consumer magazines, adverts for goods, duty-free information, tourist guides to shopping).

Develop cross-cultural awareness by building up charts of dos and don'ts, 'things to look out for' when shopping in a particular country and shopping stories. If the learners visit English-speaking countries or build up experiences within one, these lists can be extended, discussed and modified.

Quick Check answer key

(i)
I'm sorry
please
excuse me
1. please
2. Excuse me
3. I'm sorry
The long form is: It has stopped.
(ii)
Excuse; isn't; refund
terribly; receipt

This went well:

....

....

This didn't quite work:

....

....

Things to think about:

....

....

B

1 My room's too cold
vocabulary

Warm-up

Start the lesson by complaining about one or two things, e.g. *It's too hot/cold in here*, *This pen's no good*. Elicit basic dimensions of meaning of this type of utterance by asking: *Am I saying it's OK or it's not OK? How do I feel at the moment, happy or a bit annoyed?* Ask the learners for similar examples using objects as prompts.

Option

Mime shivering and elicit *It's cold* by asking *What's the problem?* Ask the learners what the difference is between saying *It's cold* to the class and saying *It's cold* to the school heating engineer or the principal. What change in the strength of the utterance is made by adding *too* as in *It's too cold*? (This implies that the temperature in the room is below a known, acceptable temperature.)

Suggested steps

Revise *too* before dealing with its use when complaining. Put some very small writing on the board and ask the learners to read it. Elicit *I can't*, then ask them *Why not?* to elicit *It's too small*. Repeat with a very tight knot in a piece of string: *Could you untie this, please? Why not?* (*It's too tight*) and a ball and tiny bag: *Could you put the ball in the bag, please? Why not?* (*The ball's too big.*)

This vocabulary matching exercise presents complaints in a very abbreviated form, but they are suitable when talking to friends or strangers about matters for which neither party feels personally responsible.

Language Point:
Remind the learners of the importance in English-speaking countries of 'dressing up' most complaints within softer, polite language when complaining to strangers and holding them responsible, as for example in shops, at stations, on planes and trains (unless there are very good reasons for a more direct approach!).

Answer key

1. This doesn't fit. – fashion shop, garage, jewellers
2. There's a button missing. – fashion shop
3. The lights don't work. – hotel, plane, garage
4. The soup is cold. – restaurant, hotel, plane
5. The room's too cold. – hotel, restaurant
6. The air conditioning doesn't work. – hotel, plane, restaurant, college, garage
7. This the worst service I've ever had on any flight. – plane
8. Look at this necklace I bought – the diamonds are not real. – jewellers
9. The cookery course wasn't long enough. – college

Personal Study Workbook

1: using polite forms when complaining

2 This cappuccino's cold!
writing and guessing

Suggested steps

Practise one or two examples to model the use of polite forms around the basic complaint in the shop context, e.g. *Excuse me …*; *Can I exchange this* ...., *please, it's too* ....

Make sure the learners use items from the shops that are not too obvious, e.g. *Excuse me, there's a page missing* is a better challenge than *This is the wrong book* if trying to guess *bookshop*.

You could supply a few examples on slips of paper for new or weaker learners. You could also write the extended list of shops on the board for the learners to choose from and to refer to when guessing.

3 I never complain ▢▢ ▢▢
listening and discussion

Suggested steps

You could ask the learners to stand on an imaginary line in the classroom in order to express their view of their complaining behaviour in shops and hotels. Then they could talk to someone at a further point on the line, since their declared behaviour is different.

Encourage the learners to ask each other for reasons for their behaviour. This phase can also be use to introduce passively some of the vocabulary from the listening activity, e.g. *calm, it works, it's the only way*. This can be done by asking the learners questions like *Do you think it works when you complain a lot, or do you think it doesn't help? Do you stay calm when you complain, or do you get angry?*

Before listening the learners should look at the questions for the two conversations. You might ask them to give possible reasons why people complain or don't complain. Note: this is a dual listening, so decide if you are going to use the first, simpler scripted version or the second, unscripted version.

For the checking in pairs, ask the learners to ask the questions alternately so that each gets a chance to ask and answer.

With an ambitious group the second listening can be used to develop vocabulary. Ask the learners to spot vocabulary that isn't in the first listening, e.g. *sarcastic, rational, articulately.*

Answer key

For the answers, please refer to the tapescript on page 235.

4 Is there a problem with the light?
mime

Suggested steps

The best way to communicate the activity is to mime a problem yourself first, e.g. *The bed in room 231 has a broken leg*, and ask the learners to guess what the problem is. Explain that you are in a hotel and are trying to communicate a problem to the hotel receptionist.

If the learners are still shy about performing in front of the class, put them in pairs first with one sentence each. Then have one or two whole-class mimes.

Some situations to mime:
I can't open the window in my room.
The phone doesn't work.
The person in the next room is playing loud music.
There is a plate of rotten food under the bed.
I've lost my key.
Someone has stolen my passport.
There is no hot water for a shower.
Another person is sleeping in the bed in my room.
I'd like some clean towels, please
I've lost my sunglasses / contact lenses in the hotel
    swimming pool.

Quick Check answer key

1. a watch; a skirt; a diamond necklace; a jacket;
   a T-shirt
2. a watch; a travel iron; a Walkman
3. a cake; fish; bread
4. a diamond necklace
5. a bowl of soup; fish; a hotel room

QUICK NOTES
This went well:
....
....
This didn't quite work:
....
....
Things to think about:
....
....

This lesson builds on the cultural comparisons and cross-cultural awareness raising of the earlier lessons and looks at apologies in the context of written language and situations.

1 Cultural confusions
discussion; reading

Warm-up

If you can, find a picture or a film clip that illustrates 'unusual' but common social behaviour, e.g. a Western TV dinner with a family eating dinner on individual trays while watching TV. Ask the learners for their reactions.

Suggested steps

Form small groups of three learners.

When assigning groups to Question 1 or Question 2, make sure that the learners try to think of everyday behaviour rather than the more obvious festivals or national customs. Prompt their thinking with topics on the board – food and eating, husbands and wives, visiting homes, young people and freedom, boyfriends/girlfriends, getting married, inside the home, shopping, housework. Ask them to use their own experiences or any gleaned from films, books or from people they know.

When the Question 1 and Question 2 groups come together, circulate and note down a few interesting examples. Write them on the board.

Ask the learners to talk briefly about their examples to the whole class.

Re-form the original groups of three for the reading task. Assign letters A, B and C within each group so that individual learners know which text to read. Explain that they must tell the story in their text to the others after the reading and identify the main cultural problem within it.

Walk around the class quietly to help particular individuals who have difficulties with their reading.

To assess the three problems you might have a whole-class discussion. Help the learners by asking them to think about the consequences of the situations and the strength of the attitudes of people in the host culture.

Ask the learners to think again about their own examples from the beginning of the activity and to assess how serious each behaviour might be in other cultures.

2 Mr and Mrs Smith regret
reading; apologies

Suggested steps

Write the word *sorry* on the board in tiny letters and then stand in front of it. Ask a learner directly in front of you to read the word on the board. When she/he says they can't, say *I'm very sorry* and move to one side. Ask the learners when and why they say *sorry*. Establish the meaning of *apologise* and an *apology*.

Ask the learners to read the apologies and to try to decide whether they are written or spoken and in what situation they were used.

Then ask the learners to match the situations and the apologies either in pairs or individually. Let them check their answers in pairs.

Option

Copy each apology and each situation on separate pieces of paper. Give one piece of paper to each learner (18 pieces in all). Ask the learners to find their partner. Then ask each pair to read out their apology and situation.

Try to elicit from the learners the broad differences between an informal and a formal apology. (The words *apologise* and *regret* are generally more formal than *sorry*; written apologies are likely to be formal, as are apologies by organisations.)

When comparing ways of apologising in the same situations in the learners' own language(s), with a monolingual group you could ask the learners to write up equivalents in their own language. With multilingual groups, choose one or two of the situations only and ask different learners to write the equivalent apologies in their own language and to try to translate. Elicit simple differences between languages or cultures, e.g. the length of the utterance, whether the apology is direct or indirect, the degree of formality, the effect of the apology on the receiver, the importance of the relationship between the giver and receiver of an apology.

Answer key
1. h   2. i   3. c   4. g   5. e   6. f   7. a   8. b   9. d

3 I'm sorry, I completely forgot
writing short notes of apology

Suggested steps

Ask the learners about the degree of formality needed in the note. (You will have to decide what is appropriate for the note from learner to teacher.) Notes to friends in English-speaking countries like New Zealand would generally be informal, using *sorry* in preference to *apologise*. Remind the learners that notes are usually short and at this stage of learning it might be less confusing to use complete sentences.

With weaker learners prepare a skeleton note and ask them to complete the gaps, or offer them a jumbled note to rewrite in the appropriate order.

Possible other situations: notes of apology to a friend who is staying with you:

1. telling your friend you are going to be late back because …
2. saying sorry that you didn't have time to go to the shops for food because …
3. saying sorry, but you have had to go to another city for two days because …

Personal Study Workbook
6: writing notes of apology

Quick Check answer key
(i)
informal
formal
formal
speaking
writing
(ii)
1. we can't come
2. the service has been delayed
3. the delay to the 8.05 service to Reading
4. put you to so much trouble

QUICK NOTES

This went well:

....

....

This didn't quite work:

....

....

Things to think about:

....

....

D REVIEW AND DEVELOPMENT

REVIEW OF UNIT 18

1 You shouldn't swim in the rivers
reading and vocabulary

Suggested steps

The sentences are all about health, so you might spend a little time establishing some key vocabulary before the learners tackle the sentences.

If the learners are from many countries and are learning outside of their own country, go through the list answering for the country in which are learning, then ask them to answer for their own country and compare answers with others.

With learners from the same country learning in their country, form small groups so that each statement can be discussed before a group answer is agreed. It may be helpful to have an 'exceptions' category if the sentences are mostly true or false but have one or two exceptions, e.g. in some countries where people generally pay for dental treatment, school children may not have to pay for the school dentist.

Elicit the difference between *have to* and *should* at the end of the activity to check that the learners remember the distinction between something that is obligatory (*have to*) and something that is a good idea (*should*).

2 You have to work hard
writing

Suggested steps

It is always a good idea to model the activity rather than just explain it, so take 'Learning English' and ask the learners to suggest sentence completions for the four sentence beginnings, e.g. *You have to remember the different tenses of verbs.*

After the groups have chosen their topic, written their completed sentences and compared them with those of other groups, ask for one or two examples for a whole-class oral feedback. Check sentence stress when listening to the examples.

REVIEW OF UNIT 19

1 I wouldn't like to be an actor
writing with *wouldn't like*; reading

Suggested steps

Go through the expressions in the box first to check understanding. Ask questions like: *Which expressions in the box are near water?* (the seaside; the bottom of the sea); *Which expression is painful?* (a toothache).

Remember that the learners don't have to use expressions in the box. Supply the pieces of paper for them to write on if you can, so that they are all the same colour and size.

Options

To make the guessing more active, you could divide the class into several groups and give each group a few pieces of paper each to guess. Tell the class that when his or her own sentences are read out the writer mustn't say 'me' to the question *Who wrote these sentences do you think?*

This activity can be extended by asking each learner to add a '*because …*' clause to each of the sentences for homework, e.g. *I wouldn't like to have a dog because I don't like noisy animals.*

Worksheets

The worksheet for this unit is on page 184. Prepare the workcards by pasting the worksheet onto card, if possible, and cutting it up so that each picture and word is on a separate card.

Put the learners in groups of three.

Two of the learners each have a pile of cards. One pile comprises a pile of pictures for the customer (who is complaining); the other pile is a pile of cue words for the shop assistant (who is apologising). The third learner is an observer.

The customer turns up the top picture card in her/his pile and has to think of a complaint for it, and explain the complaint to the shop assistant in a polite way.

The shop assistant turns up the first card in her/his pile and has to apologise politely, using the expression on the card.

The third, observing learner listens and holds up the card with 'not polite enough' on it if she or he thinks that either the customer or the shop assistant has not been polite enough during each round. The mini conversation then has to be repeated in a more polite way.

When the teacher claps hands or blows a whistle each learner rotates their role so, for example, the observer becomes the customer, the customer becomes the shop assistant, and so on.

Circulate and monitor the exchanges for later repair work.

```
END OF UNIT NOTES

How's the class getting on?
...................................................
...................................................

Language that needs more work or attention:
...................................................
...................................................

My learners:
...................................................
...................................................
```

21

ALL YOU NEED IS LOVE ... OR MONEY

CONTENTS

Language focus: *need/want* + noun or infinitive
                  don't need / don't want + noun or infinitive

Vocabulary: money, needs, success in life

INTRODUCTION TO THE UNIT

Two important themes for personal discussion in most adults' lives, money and success, are explored in this unit. The language focuses on structures using *need* or *want* + a noun or an infinitive verb. These are not particularly difficult in themselves, and the unit therefore encourages considerable recycling and consolidation of vocabulary, as well as practice of skills, especially listening and writing.

A

1 A good start in life
need + noun; *need* + *to*; speaking and writing

This exercise serves as a warm-up for the general theme of the unit: things that are needed or desired in life. The language structure *need* + *to* is introduced indirectly in the model for the note that the learners write. Encourage the learners to deduce the meaning from the context, or consult a dictionary.

Suggested steps

The beginning of this exercise asks people to think about their own priorities. You can start by working with the illustration, asking the learners to imagine what it's like to be starting out in life, full of hope. Go over the possibilities, discussing them with the learners if they wish to do so. Then ask them to make their own choices individually.

It's not necessary to have comparison or feedback at this point because this will follow the writing task. Draw the learners' attention to the model note given. Ask them to use the same format and complete the greeting and the sentences. Go around helping if necessary.

If some learners finish before others, get them reading each other's notes, and commenting on them.
In small classes, all the learners can be asked to read their short note. One member of the class could keep a record of the 'gifts' chosen. Do most people have similar ideas,

or are they very different? The writing task does sometimes spur discussion on these matters.

In large classes, it will probably be more convenient to pin all the short notes up, allowing the learners to move around and read them. They can be asked to show graphically the choices made by their class. For example, a 'bar graph' is easy to put up on the board. The horizontal axis lists the 'gifts' chosen, the vertical axis shows the number of people who chose each 'gift'.

Personal Study Workbook
2: *need / need to*

2 Money can't buy you love
discussion

This is another activity which is not very threatening and allows further exploration of the personal associations that money has for each learner.

Suggested steps

Ask the learners to do the matching task individually.

Answer key
1. b   2. d   3. a   4. c

The discussion questions can be done in groups or as a whole-class activity. Encourage the learners to express opinions on the views, or to compare them with the opinions the class has just been expressing about what is important in life.

3 I don't need much money
need / don't need + noun or infinitive; discussion; listening

Need and *don't need* have been presented in context so far, with the meaning emerging from the context. You may wish to pull the meaning out more clearly before proceeding with this activity.

Suggested steps

The use of the expression *enough* in the first statement is a way of expressing the meaning of need. Write on the board:

I need money = I haven't got enough money.
I don't need money = I've got enough.

Then let the class tick the possibilities by themselves. Or you can read out each statement, explaining when necessary, and allowing some quiet time for them to decide and tick to show their views.

Ask them to add one more opinion about money. Offer help if it is needed.

As the learners finish the task, get them organised in small groups to compare their statements. Ask them to find out who has a great difference of opinion between when they were younger and now on each question. They can then report this to the class later.

Ask one spokesperson from each group to tell the class about their discussion. Was there a majority opinion in their group?

Do most people in their group worry about money, or are they carefree? etc.

4 I think about money all the time ⬚⬚ ⬚⬚
listening

The listening activity has been prepared by the previous exercise. It is a dual listening. Decide as usual whether to use only one of the recordings, or both in sequence.

Ask the class to read the beginnings and endings of the statements. Can they guess some possible endings? Encourage them to discuss possibilities with others.

Play the recording once through. Ask the class to check their answers with others and see whether they can agree.

Confirm the answers with the class. It is always useful for them to listen to the whole recording again. The tapescript is on page 236.

Answer key

1. f   2. c   3. g   4. a   5. d   6. e   7. b

Encourage comparison of the speakers' views with the learners' own opinions. Which speaker did they prefer or think most convincing?

Personal Study Workbook
5: *need* and *don't need*

Quick Check answer key

1. doesn't need
2. needs
3. need
4. need
5. don't need
6. needs

B

1 A stock exchange is a busy place
vocabulary; discussion

This activity is a warm-up to the theme of the reading passage which follows. The idea is to pre-teach the expressions *stock exchange* and *stockbroker* and allow the learners to compare their reactions to the life style of someone who works in a financial institution, has a good standard of living but a lot of stress with it. There are obviously no right or wrong answers to the activity.

Suggested steps

Go over the photos with the class. In single nationality classes, you might like to elicit the learners' ideas about stock exchanges in their own country. Are they similar to the ones in the photos? Have they ever been in one? Do they know anyone who works in one?

In multinational classes, ask the learners, in groups, to compare their ideas about the life of a stockbroker in their own countries, with those of others. They can then tell the class about the most significant points of difference in their views.

Personal Study Workbook

3, 4: the vocabulary of money, currency, financial institutions

2 We are what we earn
reading; discussion

The first activity is a pre-reading task, to make the learners familiar with the vocabulary they will need to read the article.

Suggested steps

Encourage the learners to work in pairs or consult each other. They can use the dictionary if the group fails to come up with an answer.

Go over the expressions and their meanings with the class. To extend the vocabulary work, you could ask them to notice how the words fall into lexical groups. Ask them how many words in either column are related in meaning to money (*secure financially, salary, to earn*). How many express emotions? (*fear, anxiety, afraid of, worried about, possibly secure*)

Answer key

greatest fear – what a person is most afraid of
strongest anxiety – what a person is most worried about
is secure financially – has enough money
a salary – the money people get for their work
valuable to society – useful for the community
to earn – to receive money for work

Ask the class to read the article by themselves. The main difficulties of vocabulary have been dealt with. Encourage them to read without stopping. Once they have read through the article, get them in pairs or small groups discussing any difficulties they may have with the meaning. Circulate, and offer help.

Still in their small groups, the learners extract from the article what they think is good or bad about Bob's way of life. Write up two headings on the board, and ask the groups to fill in the details under each. There may be differences of opinion, so the same item could possibly appear in two lists.

The third activity asks the learners to extract an overall, gist meaning to the second paragraph, and to respond to it. The second paragraph is a more abstract speculation about people's attitudes to money and to their society, drawing conclusions from the specific 'case study' explored in the first paragraph. In small classes, you may wish to go over each statement with the learners, eliciting their opinion. Ensure that they are given scope to write their own opinion, if they prefer. In larger classes, groupwork can lead to reporting to the class and choosing the most popular statements. New statements can be put on the board, which will also help with the following exercise.

Personal Study Workbook

6: reading

3 A letter to the editor
writing a short letter

Letters to the editor have been used before in the book, so this type of activity should be familiar to the class. In addition, the previous two activities have acted as warm-ups for this writing task.

Suggested steps

If you feel your learners need more support for the writing task, put a few possible sentence beginnings on the board. For example:

Bob Hainemann is happy and …
Bob Hainemann is happy but …
People now are worried because …
Money does say a lot about us but …

People with high salaries are (not) more valuable to society because …
I agree (do not agree) that we are what we earn. In fact … or On the contrary …

If time is short, the activity can be started in class and finished for homework. Ask the learners to bring their first draft back to class with them.

Option

Pairwork can often be extremely fruitful at this point. The exercise helps the learners to realise that writing is an exercise in communication. When people write, it is usually for a specific reader. A reader's comments can help writers improve their first drafts.

Ask the learners to work in pairs. They exchange their drafts. Each person is given the task of reading their partner's draft and saying:

– What is the one thing that is most interesting in the letter?
– Is there anything which you as a reader would like to know more about?
– Is there anything which is not clear?
– Is there anything which could be cut or changed to improve the letter?

The partners discuss the letters with each other. Circulate and contribute comments and advice. Each learner is then asked to edit their draft according to the comments they received, and to produce a rewritten, fair copy.

Personal Study Workbook

7: writing

Quick Check answer key

1. in   2. to/towards   3. about   4. in   5. in   6. of
7. to

QUICK NOTES

This went well:

....

....

This didn't quite work:

....

....

Things to think about:

....

....

C

1 I don't need to go to university 🔲
listening

Suggested steps

To aid listening comprehension, it is always useful to go over as much of the material as possible beforehand. It is likely to help the learners if they read the three gapped paragraphs before they listen to the recording. Can they guess what could possibly fill any of the blanks? Encourage them to compare their guesses.

Play the recording once, right through. The learners fill the gaps, or check their guesses. You can then play the recording again, in three sections, for confirmation of the answers. The tapescript is on page 236.

Draw the attention of the class to the difference in meaning between *need* and *want* – this prepares for the next activity.

Answer key

1. Janina *wants* to study Spanish but she *doesn't* really *need* it for her job. She *wants* to go on a holiday in Mexico.
2. Olga *wants* a child but she *doesn't want* to give up her job and she *needs* the money.
3. Jim *doesn't need* to go to university because he's 75 years old but he *wants* to be a student again and he certainly *doesn't want* to sit at home in front of the TV for the rest of his life.

Personal Study Workbook

1: *need*, *want* and *would like*

2 You don't need to do that
grammar practice; discussion

The focus in this exercise is the semantic difference between *need* and *want*.

Suggested steps

The learners are invited to study the examples to become familiar with the difference between the two verbs. Let them read the examples individually, then go over them with the whole class. In monolingual groups, a quick translation is often an easy way to ensure that the meaning of both verbs has been understood. In multilingual groups, the examples have to convey the difference, so make sure the class understands by eliciting more examples. What do they need, for example, to learn English? They need to practise, read a lot, etc. They probably want to speak to native speakers, watch English video, etc., but they may not *need* to do these things.

Get the learners choosing and completing their three sentences. Circulate and offer help. As soon as they have finished, pair them off to read each other's sentences and talk about them.

3 To be a success, you need...
writing; reading; discussion

Suggested steps

Make sure the concept of *success* is understood. The learners can consult their dictionaries and help each other with the meaning.

Because they have just completed sentences individually, it might be more enjoyable for the learners to work in pairs this time. Encourage the pairs to discuss their sentence and try to come to a common view on the best ending.

After reading out the sentences and making a list of things mentioned, the learners can read the answers given by seven people in a magazine survey. Encourage them to consult each other over difficulties.

The comparison of views which rounds off the reading exercise can be done in pairs or as a whole-class activity.

Quick Check answer key
(i)
1. need   2. need to   3. need to   4. need
(ii)
1. want to   2. want   3. want to   4. want

QUICK NOTES

This went well:

....

....

This didn't quite work:

....

....

Things to think about:

....

....

D   **REVIEW AND DEVELOPMENT**

REVIEW OF UNIT 19

1 Key or keep? 🔲
pronunciation: final consonants

Here the class is invited to discriminate between minimal pairs of sounds which alter the meaning of a whole sentence.

Play the recording in sections, pausing after each. Get the learners to compare their answers. If there is disagreement, let them listen a second time.

If the class wishes, they can listen to the recording one more time before the pairwork. The tapescript is on page 236.

Answer key

1. a   2. b   3. a   4. b   5. b   6. a

2 Some of my friends are psychologists 🔲

pronunciation of consonant clusters

Suggested steps

Get the learners working in pairs or small groups. They can use their dictionaries if they like, in order to build up as many jobs ending in -sts as they can.

Have a class feedback before listening to the recording. How many jobs have the various groups been able to find? Let them have an initial practice of the final clusters by using the back chaining technique, repeating in turn: *artists … dentists and artists … psychologists, dentists and artists … Some of my friends are psychologists, dentists and artists.*

The class can repeat chorally to start with, then work individually, or in pairs.

The recording acts as further modelling for the final clusters. Pair the learners before playing the recording. Tell them they are going to hear a list of job words and they have to listen carefully and identify the job that doesn't end in -sts.

Play the recording once. The tapescript is on page 236.

Get the learners to check the answer with each other. Then play the recording again for confirmation.

Answer key

Poets does not end in -sts.

REVIEW OF UNIT 20

1 I'm sorry, it was an accident 🔲

vocabulary: nouns; adjectives

The first part of this exercise builds vocabulary by emphasising the relation between adjectives and some nouns.

Suggested steps

Get the learners working singly or in pairs to find the adjectives. Set a time limit, e.g. five minutes, and encourage them to consult each other as well as the dictionary. Ask them to check the meanings, as they will need these for the next part of the exercise.

Answer key

Noun	Adjective
possibility	possible
confidence	confident
tidiness	tidy
patience	patient
accident	accidental
danger	dangerous
stupidity	stupid
importance	important

Have a quick feedback to ensure that the adjectives are familiar. Then ask the class to continue the activity.

Use the recording for confirmation of the answers, and also to give a model of the appropriate intonation patterns. You can ask the class to repeat the apologies if they find choral repetition a useful support before doing the role play themselves. The tapescript is on page 236.

Answer key

1. I'm sorry, that was totally accidental!
2. I'm very sorry. I'm sure she didn't realise it was dangerous.
3. Oh dear, I'm sorry. They've never been very tidy, I'm afraid.
4. I'm so sorry. I should be more patient.
5. Sorry. I guess that was rather stupid.
6. It says: The editor regrets that it wasn't possible to include your article in the January magazine.
7. Oh, I'm terribly sorry. I just didn't think it was very important.
8. Well, I'm sorry, but I can't. I'm not very confident.

Pair the learners and ask them to read each one of the mini dialogues, with plenty of feeling. It may be useful to model one or two of them with the whole class before they begin. Circulate while they are reading, and encourage them to make a noticeable difference between the anger or annoyance expressed by the complainer, and the apologetic tone of the reply.

2 Oh dear, I'm sorry 🔲

apologies

Suggested steps

This is an extension of the previous activity. Instead of simply reading apologies, the learners now have to listen and respond spontaneously in an appropriate manner. The tapescript is on page 237.

If you like, you can start off with a choral apology, for example: *I'm very sorry*, which can be appropriate for all the complaints. Then play the recording again. This time, individual learners should apologise, using a slightly different form each time, e.g. *Oh, I'm so sorry …* or *I'm terribly sorry. It won't happen again*, etc.

Worksheets

The worksheets for this unit are on pages 184 and 185. This is a mingling exercise, for classes of three or over. For classes of over three, photocopy multiples of Worksheets 21A, B and C.

Each learner is given one worksheet, with three questions and three answers. The idea is that they find a partner, and ask each other the questions in turn. If the partner has a suitable answer, they write it down. They then ask others until they have found suitable answers for their questions, and suitable questions for their answers.

Make sure the class understands the instructions. They are to work with one other learner at a time. Insist that they are not allowed to show each other their worksheet. They must read out their questions, in turn – the partner decides whether any of their answers is suitable, and reads it out if so.

When everyone has finished, have a general feedback to see whether everyone found the same 'appropriate' answers. There are some answers which could possibly suit more than one question!

Answer key

Possible combinations of questions and answers are:

Worksheet A
Question 1 – Ba (Worksheet B, answer a.)
Question 2 – Ca
Question 3 – Cc

Worksheet B
Question 1 – Cb
Question 2 – Ab
Question 3 – Aa

Worksheet C
Question 1 – Ac
Question 2 – Bb
Question 3 – Bc

END OF UNIT NOTES

How's the class getting on?

....

....

Language that needs more work or attention:

....

....

My learners:

....

....

22

THE RIGHT CLIMATE?

CONTENTS

Language focus: *what's it like?* questions
if clauses + imperatives or present simple
when clauses + imperatives or present simple

Vocabulary: weather, climate
protection against the weather

INTRODUCTION TO THE UNIT

A strong vocabulary-building element is integrated in this unit with work on two related structures: *if* or *when* clauses, coupled with either imperatives or present simple verbs in the main clauses. *What's it like?* questions are introduced and practised in context, and with a lot of exemplification.

A

1 Average temperatures in January
discussion; guessing; listening

The first part of this activity serves as an introduction to the thematic area of talking about the weather. *What's it like?* questions are then modelled in the listening.

> **Language Point:**
>
> *What's it like?* questions can be confusing for speakers of many other languages. The function of *like* is not immediately apparent, and there is a temptation to use it in the answer. There is also the risk of confusion with other similar structures, such as *What I like* or *What I'd like.*
>
> In this unit it is treated as a crystallised expression. It may be useful to explain to the class that *What's it like?* is a question about the state or condition of a place or thing – for example, *What's Lisbon like?* invites a description of Lisbon, e.g. *Lisbon's very beautiful. What's January like?* invites a description of the weather in January, e.g. *It's very cold.* It can also be used of people: *What's Jan like?* invites a description of Jan, e.g. *Jan's cheerful, and very friendly.* In many languages, the equivalent question would involve using *how*. Though it may be useful to translate *What's it like?* questions to make sure a monolingual class understands its scope, care must then be taken to ensure that they do use the structure *What's summer like?* and not *How's summer?*

Warm-up

The first part of the activity concentrates on weather. If you feel your learners need more overt presentation of *What's it like?* questions before going on to the listening exercise, you can write two types of *What's it like?* questions and answers on the board:

What's it like in January? It's cold.
What's (your town) like in June? It's hot.

Explain the meaning of the questions (as in the language point above).

This can be followed, if you like, by either of these two exercises. (Alternatively, they can be used as a follow-up to the lesson if you begin directly with the book.)

Option 1

Prepare slips of paper with either a question or an answer. For example, for a class of ten, use five question slips:

What's Lisbon (or another city) like?
What's London like in January?
What's Sydney like in January?
What's the city centre like?
What's the country like?
Prepare five answer slips:
It's rainy.
It's crowded.
It's very beautiful.
It's hot.
It's not very crowded.

Distribute the slips at random. People with questions then find their partners, either by milling and asking the questions, or by asking them out loud, and asking the learner with an appropriate answer to respond.

Option 2

Divide the class into two. Get half the class to write *What's it like?* questions about any topic. Help with suggestions if necessary. The other half of the class write three completions with an adjective: *It's ...* The first half then ask their questions and see if they can find a partner with a suitable answer from the other half of the class.

With groups which are familiar and friendly with each other, you can ask them to write questions of the type: *What's X like?* (naming someone in the class). The second half complete either *He's …* or *She's …* with an adjective describing physical appearance (*tall, short,* etc.) or personality (*friendly, amusing,* etc.) The question writers then see whether they can find a suitable reply.

You can then go on to the first activity in the book.

Suggested steps

Make sure that the concept of 'average temperature' is understood, and the expression *weather forecaster.* An illustration from the local paper showing weather charts can be a help.

If the class doesn't know the average temperature for the town or city, ask them to guess. Then get them to guess the other missing temperatures, discussing and comparing their ideas with a partner.

Divide the board into two parts: NORTHERN HEMISPHERE and SOUTHERN HEMISPHERE, and explain the meaning with the use of the illustration in the book. Ask for some guesses to be put on the board, in the right section. Under NORTHERN HEMISPHERE, guesses should be written up for Anchorage, Rome and Istanbul; under SOUTHERN HEMISPHERE, Johannesburg, Buenos Aires and Mawson. Putting guesses on the board helps with the listening, because it pre-sorts the cities into two groups. In addition, the names of the cities are displayed and worked with before the learners hear them on the recording.

The aim is to help the learners practise extracting specific information from a text they listen to. Emphasise that they don't need to understand everything in the interview. They should simply try to pick out the temperatures mentioned for each of the cities.

Play the recording, pausing after the meteorologist's first speech, to let the learners take down notes and consult each other on their answers.

Get them to check with others before either confirming the answers or playing the recording a second time. The tapescript is on page 237.

Personal Study Workbook

1: *What's it like?* questions and answers

2 What's it like in your town?
vocabulary; conversation

This activity offers a change of pace between two listening exercises. It expands and consolidates vocabulary about weather.

Suggested steps

Go over the illustrations with the learners, emphasising the gradation in the first. Get them working by themselves or in pairs to fill in the missing words.

Answer key

freezing cold chilly cool warm hot boiling hot
1. changeable
2. windy
3. stormy
4. snowy
5. wet
6. humid

After checking their answers with others, then with you, the learners complete the sentences about the seasons. They can use dictionaries if the words are not familiar, or ask others.

The learners show their sentences to each other and discuss them in small groups.

Option

In small classes, you can play a form of Snap as feedback to this part of the activity. Learner A reads out a question and sentence completion. If anyone else has a similar answer, they say *Snap!* and that gives Learner A one point for each similar answer. Learner B then reads out one of their questions and answers, and so on.

3 Winter? What winter? ▭▭ ▩▩
listening; discussion

The learners are exposed to more weather vocabulary in this listening exercise.

Suggested steps

Work with the illustrations. Ask the learners to make guesses based on the temperatures given in Exercise 1. You can ask a few questions to help their guessing, e.g. *What's winter like in Alaska? Is it cold? Is the winter short or long? Is there snow or ice? Is there a little bit of snow or a lot?* etc.

Play the recording in segments. This is a dual listening – as usual, decide whether to use one of the recordings only, or both.

Pause the tape after the first section (on Anchorage) to let the learners take down notes. The tapescript is on page 237.

When the three sections of the recording have been played, get the learners to check their answers with others in the class. You can also invite them to write on the board, when they are sure they've got the right answer.

Answer key

For the answers, see the tapescript on page 237.

Personal Study Workbook

3: weather vocabulary
5: listening

4 In Scotland, the weather's changeable
writing

This is a writing task to round off an interactive lesson.

Suggested steps

Work with the short description of weather in Scotland. Elicit or explain the meaning of *sometimes* and *at other times*. In monolingual classes it may be useful to elicit a translation of the expressions.

The writing can be started in class, and finished for homework if time is short. Arrange a reading or exhibition of the descriptions at the beginning of the next class.

Quick Check answer key

What's Moscow like in winter?
It's freezing cold.
What's summer like in Vancouver?
It's dry and pretty warm. / It's warm and pretty dry.
What's it like in Cairo in January?
It's a bit similar to San Francisco in June.

```
QUICK NOTES

This went well:
...........................................................
...........................................................

This didn't quite work:
...........................................................
...........................................................

Things to think about:
...........................................................
...........................................................
```

B

1 My ideal day
vocabulary and conversation

The first activity acts as a warm-up to the lesson.

Suggested steps

Make sure the concept 'ideal' is understood. Go over each one of the days with the class, asking the learners to jot down details about their ideal weather. Ask them to work singly or in pairs.

Encourage the learners to use at least two adjectives each time, e.g. *dry and warm*.

To compare their choices, let the learners mingle and compare their ideal days with as many people as possible. Ask them to note differences down. This can then lead to a general feedback: Who found the greatest difference for 'an ideal day on a winter holiday?'

Alternatively, the learners can mill, trying to find someone whose choices are exactly like theirs, or with only one major difference.

2 What do you do when it's very hot?
question forms with *when*; speaking

This activity can form the basis of pairwork, as suggested in the book, or in small classes, a chain of questions and answers might be successful.

Suggested steps

If you use pairwork, circulate while they're engaged in the activity, making sure they take turns and helping with the additional question. Ask some of the learners to write their additional question on the board, so that gradually a bank of new questions is built up. If you use a chain, make sure that the questions come alternately from Section A and Section B. One learner can be delegated to take down additional questions, as a dictation exercise, on the board.

Ask for general feedback, e.g. *Who has heard an interesting answer? A funny answer? An incredible or unbelievable answer?*

Personal Study Workbook

4: pronunciation

3 Don't forget the sunscreen!
reading

The preceding exercises have served to set the scene for this reading passage. The first activity, therefore, simply ensures that any possible remaining vocabulary problems are dealt with before reading.

Suggested steps

Get the learners to underline unknown expressions, and ask help from other learners before confirming the answers. You can use the illustration to help with understanding.

Ask the class to read the three incomplete sentences of advice before they read the text. This gives them a focus as they read through.

Let the learners read the text silently. If there are any difficulties, they should be encouraged once again to consult others, then the dictionary, then ask you for help.

Depending on your learners' preferences, you can get them completing the sentences singly or in pairs. Ensure that they compare their sentences with those that others have written. Ask for a few sentences to be read out loud.

The role play that follows can be a very enjoyable way to complete the lesson. If time is short, preparation for it can be set as homework, then the actual role play done in pairs next class.

If there is time, get the class preparing their role plays in pairs. You can give an example by improvising one of the role plays with one of the pairs. Ask them to work together first, then get one or more pairs to perform for the class. Encourage the learners to express a lot of feeling in Partner B's role, especially. The learner should sound worried!

Personal Study Workbook

6: reading

Quick Check answer key

1. put
2. Put
3. sure
4. Remember / Don't forget
5. Remember / Don't forget
6. forget
7. forget

```
┌─────────────────────────────────────────────┐
│                QUICK NOTES                    │
│                                               │
│   This went well:                             │
│   .........................................   │
│   .........................................   │
│                                               │
│   This didn't quite work:                     │
│   .........................................   │
│   .........................................   │
│                                               │
│   Things to think about:                      │
│   .........................................   │
│   .........................................   │
│                                               │
└─────────────────────────────────────────────┘
```

C

1 Natural disasters

listening; discussion

This exercise provides a brief warm-up to the theme of natural disasters.

Suggested steps

Encourage the learners to work in pairs or small groups with the illustrations first. Then ask them to guess the countries.

Answer key

A Mexico City
B USA (Florida)
C India
D Australia

2 We quite often get earthquakes

vocabulary

Suggested steps

In multinational classes, ask the learners to complete the answers for their own country. They then find a partner from another country, compare their ticks, and discuss the differences between the two.

In single nationality classes, ask the learners to work in pairs to complete the table. If there are any disagreements between them, ask them to write their two perceptions on the board.

When everyone has completed the table, have a general feedback. Go over the disagreements noted on the board to start with, and see if people can give reasons for their views. Then see whether there are disagreements over any of the other disasters.

Ask the class for personal anecdotes relating to being involved in a natural disaster. If you have such an anecdote yourself, use it for listening practice. Tell the class about it simply, then get them to reconstruct the story in pairs.

3 What do you do if there's a storm?

If constructions with present simple

This offers fairly controlled speaking practice, with a drill element, but it also allows the learners to talk about their own feelings and emotions in times of stress.

Suggested steps

Tell the learners that they are to ask two other people in the class (including yourself) the two questions, and take notes on the answers.

In small classes, each person can report on the answers they got. They can reinforce an answer someone else has already given, e.g. *I asked Timo too, and he said the same to me: he's frightened and stays in.* Or they can point to differences, e.g. *I asked Timo, and he said to me he loves storms! Timo, what do you really feel?*

In larger classes, one person reports on one answer they received. Another person then reports an answer from a different person, and so on.

The two final questions in this exercise simply give more scope for working with the structures, and recycling imperatives, which are going to be used in the writing activity that comes next. It does not really matter if the learners don't know, or if they come up with contradictory advice. Many people think that in an earthquake, it is best to stand inside the frame of an open door for protection. In floods, standard advice is to climb to the top floor, or even onto the roof if necessary, and await rescue. If there is time, and if these things are to hand, people are often advised to take supplies, warm clothing or blankets and, most importantly, water with them.

4 If you hear a fire bell
writing with if clauses

Get the learners discussing the situation in pairs or small groups. They should prepare a sentence for each one of the contingencies.

You could get different groups to write one of their sentences of advice on the board, then ask the class to order them, delete if necessary, and fashion them into a notice to be placed in a hotel room.

If time is short, the sentences can be written as homework, then put on the board in the following class.

Personal Study Workbook

7, 8: writing

Quick Check answer key

1. If there's a storm, I feel nervous.
2. If it's very windy, I'm worried / I get worried about possible damage.
3. If there are floods, the best thing to do is to go to the top floor.
4. If you're on the tenth floor, don't use the lift.

```
┌─────────────────────────────────────────┐
│              QUICK NOTES                  │
│                                           │
│   This went well:                         │
│   ...................................     │
│   ...................................     │
│                                           │
│   This didn't quite work:                 │
│   ...................................     │
│   ...................................     │
│                                           │
│   Things to think about:                  │
│   ...................................     │
│   ...................................     │
└─────────────────────────────────────────┘
```

D REVIEW AND DEVELOPMENT

REVIEW OF UNIT 20

1 I often apologise
vocabulary; conversation

This first activity personalises the theme of apologies, and allows a revision of the various polite forms. It can be done as pairwork followed by a general feedback, or, in small classes, as a whole-class activity.

2 I'm sorry I'm late ⊂⊃
making apologies

Suggested steps

The learners prepare their apologies with a partner. In classes which enjoy drama, encourage them to think of implausible reasons to add to the apologies.

Ask each person to find a new partner, and try out their apologies.

The tapescript is on page 237.

Optional Follow-up

Ask each pair to choose one of the apologies and prepare a short improvised role play of the situation. Each pair performs for the class. Which was least plausible? Which was funniest?

REVIEW OF UNIT 21

1 People don't really need cars
need / don't need + noun

Suggested steps

In this first activity, the learners practise their persuasive skills. It may help if you demonstrate with one or two members of the class first.

As soon as the learners have made their choices, pair them off and let them try to persuade each other. Encourage them to use the structures *need this for …* and *need this because …*

Circulate, monitor and offer help where needed.

2 Children need to feel secure
need / don't need + infinitive; discussion

This continues the discussion started in the previous exercise, extending it now to the question of whether children's needs are the same as those of adults.

Suggested steps

Allow the learners to make their own choices first. Then put them into small groups for discussion.

Ask the groups to prepare a short summary of their discussion. Did they add anything to the list? Did they agree on the main needs for adults and for children? You can ask the groups to try to agree on the three main needs, and report them to the class.

Worksheets

The worksheet for this unit, on page 186, is a board game which practises the structure: *when* clause + imperative.

What you will need:
1. Some dice – one for each group of players.
2. Twelve small cards for each player (big enough for them to write one sentence on each) or paper cut up into small squares. This can be done by the learners in step 1.
3. Something to act as a marker for each student's position on the board. This can be any small object: a small button, a small piece of coloured card or paper, different coloured pins or tacks, etc.

The game can best be played in groups of four or five. Photocopy enough boards and group your class around them.

Before the game starts:
It is important that the learners should make up their 'cards' before they see the board. Distribute 12 cards to each player (or ask the learners to divide up sheets of paper so that they have 12 pieces each). On each card, the learners are to write one instruction, command or sentence of advice.

Give some examples:
Sit down and have a cup of tea.
Count to ten.
Relax.
Go to see the doctor.
Go to bed.
Put on some soothing music.
Get up earlier in the morning.
etc.

The game:
Group the players around the board. The first player throws the dice and moves their marker the number of spaces shown on the dice. If they fall on a blank space, they remain there until next turn. If they fall on a space with an instruction, e.g. *Go back three spaces*, they obey it. If they fall on a space with a *when* clause, they have to try to complete the sentence with one of their ten cards. The object is to try to find a plausible whole sentence, e.g. *When it's too hot outside, go to bed.* Amusing sentences can be accepted by the rest of the group even if they are not wholly plausible!

The first person to reach home is the winner.

END OF UNIT NOTES

How's the class getting on?

....

....

Language that needs more work or attention:

....

....

My learners:

....

....

23

CELEBRATIONS

CONTENTS

Language focus: offering, inviting; accepting, declining
shall for offers

Vocabulary: national festivals, family celebrations

INTRODUCTION TO THE UNIT

This unit has a dual structure: on the one hand, it is based on functions: offering or inviting, and either accepting or declining the offers or invitations; on the other hand, it has a strong theme running through it, in which cross-cultural perceptions of celebrations are explored. *Shall* is introduced for offers. In form, this is a future simple, so the learners are familiarised with the tense, a lead-in to the more intensive study of it in the following unit. A reading text on a new festival is the central focus for Lesson A, while Lessons B and C provide the learners with plenty of interactive practice with either giving invitations or replying to them.

A

1 National festivals
vocabulary; discussion

The whole of Lesson A focuses on the thematic area of the unit. Its main aim is to expand the learners' awareness of the variety and richness of practices in different parts of the world, as well as to expand their vocabulary and increase their confidence in talking about festivals and celebrations. The first activity, particularly, offers an opportunity for cross-cultural exploration.

Warm-up

Exploit the illustrations with the whole class as a discussion warm-up. If there are other festivals which would be more interesting or relevant to your particular class, try to use additional photos or magazine pictures to start them considering national festivals and how they vary. List the different things that are being celebrated on the board.

Answer key

Picture A shows Carnival in Rio de Janeiro.
Picture B shows a *hanami* in Japan (cherry blossom party).
Picture C shows the Day of the Dead festival in Mexico.

Picture D shows the Chinese New Year festival.
Picture E shows Hallowe'en in New York.
Picture F shows Santa Lucia festival in Sweden.

Suggested steps

Ask the class to choose the most important festivals in their country, and to rank them 1, 2 and 3. Even in single nationality groups, the perceptions that people have of the relative importance of various festivals may well differ considerably.

Get the learners working in groups of two or three to compare their answers to the questions in the book. The task involved will probably be different in single nationality or multinational classes.

In multinational groups, people from one country could work together and prepare a report for the class about their festivals. Single nationality groups will probably have to check first if they have chosen different orders for their three festivals. If that is so, encourage them to give as many reasons as they can, and to see if they can arrive at the same order within their group. They could then prepare a report comparing their three festivals to one other one from another country.

Make sure that the concept of a 'commercialised' festival is understood. Explain that it involves using a festival to stimulate sales of various items in shops – including food, drink, greeting cards and all kinds of gifts. Many people feel that the Western festival of Christmas has been very highly commercialised in recent years, and that its purpose now is to make people spend money rather than to be with their families. The groups should consider whether any of the festivals that they are talking about have been commercialised in this way.

For feedback, one member from each group can report to the class. Otherwise, re-form groups so that they contain one member from each of the original groups, and get them to compare their previous work.

Personal Study Workbook

4: vocabulary of special occasions

2 Kwanzaa

reading; vocabulary

Suggested steps

The pre-reading questions can be done as a whole-class exercise, or in pairs who then get together with others to compare their conjectures.

Use the illustrations to get the learners to speculate about Kwanzaa. They should try to guess the answers to the five questions, adding as many details as they can manage.

Ask the learners to read through the article, trying to find the five answers. If at all possible, they should try to do this without using their dictionary at first. Encourage them to keep on reading, even if they don't understand everything in the article. This encourages confidence in reading for gist, which is one of the reading subskills that the learners need to develop to be able to cope with the longer passages of reading they will meet as they become more proficient in the language.

Option

For classes which enjoy competitions, this kind of rapid first reading for gist can be encouraged by getting the learners to work in pairs and see which pair can find the five answers first.

In pairs or groups, get the learners to discuss which of the suggested titles is best for each paragraph. They should check their answers with others. They could also suggest other answers as titles if they are not satisfied with the choices.

Answer key

1. c   2. b   3. b

Option

If you would like your learners to work on the text in more detail, get half the class, working in pairs, to extract details from it that show positive aspects of Kwanzaa. The other half, also working in pairs, should pull out details which could be interpreted as negative. Individuals then find a partner from the other half of the class and compare notes. This can provide a focus that leads on to the last part of the exercise, comparing responses to the idea of Kwanzaa.

The three questions at the end of the exercise provide an opportunity to draw out the response of the learners to the text. The discussion can be a whole-class exercise.

Personal Study Workbook

6: reading about a special festival

3 In the old days, people sang

writing

Suggested steps

This activity provides a calm end to the lesson, but, if time is short, it can be assigned as homework. An

exhibition of writing produced can then be scheduled for the next class period.

Go over the two examples with the class. The paragraph offers a lot of support for the learners, and they should then be able to continue on their own. The poem is designed to make the idea of producing a poem a bit less daunting for the learners. The first letter of each line, reading downwards, gives the word FIESTA. Other words can also be used to start lines in this way. If the learners need a bit of help, you could suggest alternatives: PARTY, for example, or HAPPY DAY or FUN or FEAST.

Allow the learners some quiet time so that they can do their writing task without disturbance. You can go round and offer help or make suggestions in a quiet way.

Organise an exhibition to display the results. Since this is creative writing, expressing an idea is what matters. Language mistakes which do not hinder communication are not really as important as communication in this type of exercise.

Quick Check answer key

1. traditional   2. modern   3. gifts; candles   4. feasts
5. commercialised

QUICK NOTES

This went well:

....

....

This didn't quite work:

....

....

Things to think about:

....

....

B

1 Would you like to come?

vocabulary; discussion; inviting

From national festivals, the learners move on to talking about their own celebrations.

Warm-up

In this first part of the activity, the scene is set for inviting friends to a party. The learners first work in pairs, comparing their experiences on celebrations. In small classes, you might like to do this first discussion exercise with all the learners together. You can start by telling them about your own special day, e.g. birthday, name day, or anniversary, and what you usually do for it.

Suggested steps

When they have established a purpose for celebrating, and selected a place in town for it, get the learners working in pairs to complete the telephone conversation. Circulate and offer any help needed. Encourage them to read their dialogue with each other. Help with pronunciation and intonation patterns. One or two can be invited to read their dialogue to the class.

The class is now ready to listen to the beginning of the dialogue. Explain that they are going to hear a telephone call like the one they've just written. Their task is to listen for gist, and to notice the invitation question, and write it down. The tapescript is on page 237.

Get the learners to check the invitation questions they wrote down, and to compare them with the ones they used in their dialogue.

Answer key

Would you like to come?

Personal Study Workbook

2: listening to dialogues (inviting, accepting or declining)
5: listening

2 Saying yes □□
accepting invitations; listening

Suggested steps

The activity continues, with the telephone caller receiving a positive acceptance to the invitation.

Play the recording and ask the learners to take the words used to accept as dictation. The tapescript is on page 237.

Get the learners to check their answer with each other before you confirm it.

Answer key

Yes, I'd love to come.

In pairs, the learners then reconstruct the whole telephone conversation, taking it in turns to invite, and to accept. Invite one or two pairs to perform their role play for the class. Encourage creative extension of the telephone call.

3 Saying no □□
declining invitations

Suggested steps

As a warm-up to the next telephone call, the class now examines what happens when an invitation is unwelcome or impossible. Ask them to consider this question: How important is it to give a reason for declining, in their country? Would it be considered rude (as it often is in most English-speaking situations) *not* to give a reason?

Get the class to look through the list of possible excuses for declining. Ask them to imagine other excuses, in pairs if they like, and write them down.

The choices made are then used as a springboard for talking about declining invitations. This short discussion is really a means of setting the scene for the next listening task, while bridging possible cultural differences.

Let the learners listen to the next conversation, and write down the reason given for declining the invitation. The tapescript is on page 237.

Get the learners to check their answers with each other.

Answer key

I've got to work at the restaurant on that night.

A milling exercise provides an interactive close to the lesson. Explain to the class that they should try to role play the dialogue with as many other people in the class as they can, in the time given. A short time is usually best – set the limit of about five minutes or so. With each other person, they should play both roles, in turn – the inviter, and the invited.

Join the milling activity and help if there are any difficulties. Remind the learners that they should add a reason when they decline an invitation.

Options

The milling role play can be done in two parts. In the first part, for three to five minutes, the learners try to work with as many others as they can, but all invitations are accepted. During the second half, all invitations are to be declined, with reasons.

This alternative telephone activity, which is a variant of the well-known party game 'Pass the parcel', is usually enjoyed by groups of adults. Ask the class to sit in a circle. Play a cassette of lively music and give the participants a telephone (a toy telephone or some representation of one) to pass around while the music is playing. When the music stops, the person holding the telephone has to dial it, then improvise a conversation inviting someone to a celebration. Although the replies are not heard, the object is to make it clear through the caller's responses whether the invitation is accepted or not. Encourage players to think of outrageous or amusing reasons to which they react. You can start off by giving an example: *What! You mean you can't come to my party because you've got a hippo in your bath! That's ridiculous! I don't believe you!*

Personal Study Workbook

1, 7: writing invitations, accepting and declining

Quick Check answer key

(i)
1. b   2. b
(ii)
1. Would   2. sorry/afraid   3. would; like to   4. I'd

C

1 Shall I do the washing up?

shall for offers

The warm-up in this activity is a matching exercise, which shows the learners situations in which *shall* is used for making offers.

Suggested steps

Read the five offers out loud, to model the intonation pattern for the class.

Ask them to work singly or in pairs to match each one with a picture. They should check their answers with others before the next part of the exercise.

Play the recording, pausing it after each exchange. Number one is given in the book as an example. The tapescript is on page 238.

Get the learners to check their answers with others.

Answer key

Conversation 1 Offer B. Yes.
Conversation 2 Offer E. Yes.
Conversation 3 Offer D. The person says *no* at first, then accepts help with the drying.
Conversation 4 Offer C. Yes.
Conversation 5 Offer A. Yes.

The next activity will ask the learners to improvise a situation in which they make various offers. If you feel that they need more supported practice before moving into improvisation, use the illustrations, and get the pairs to reconstruct the mini conversations they've just heard. You can refresh their memories by playing the tape again just before this practice, if it's helpful. They should then be confident enough to tackle the freer production in the next exercise.

Personal Study Workbook

3: *shall* used for offers

2 Yes, that would be wonderful!

accepting or declining offers

Here, the learners are given situations to choose from, but they have to supply the conversation. If the class has worked through the conversations in the previous exercise, they should be able to manage this task. If you feel they still need a bit of support, choose one of the situations and improvise a conversation with one of the students as an example before the beginning of pairwork.

Get the learners working in pairs. They choose two situations, so that they can take it in turns to play the role of the host, and the role of the guest.

While they are improvising, circulate and offer help with structures or vocabulary, if needed.

You may like to invite one or two pairs to perform their roles in front of the class. Be supportive and helpful. Mistakes can be noted mentally or jotted down quickly, to be dealt with later. It is usually best not to interrupt an improvisation for language correction. If there are recurring mistakes, they can be highlighted in a non-threatening way at the end of the class.

3 Anyone who comes to your home is a guest

listening and discussion

Warm-up

As the listening in this activity focuses upon cross-cultural patterns of hospitality, it would be good to raise the learners' awareness of the topic by eliciting their own views about it and encouraging them to talk about their own experiences. This can be done either in a whole-class discussion or in groups which then feed back to the others.

In multinational classes, organise mixed nationality groups, to consider these questions:
– How important is hospitality in your countries? Compare this with others in the group.
– What do you usually do when guests come to your home?
– What does 'being a good host' (or good hostess) mean?
– Is there a difference in hospitality patterns between the older and the younger generations?

Ask one representative from each group to report the group's discussions and findings.

In single nationality classes, organise small groups to try to summarise the hospitality patterns in the country.
– Would they all agree on the importance of being hospitable to guests in their country?
– Do they all do the same kinds of things when guests come to their homes?
– What, typically, would 'being a good host' (or a good hostess) mean?
– Do they think that the older generation and the younger generation have the same hospitality patterns?

One representative can report the group's discussions, or write down a summary on the board.

Suggested steps

The next step is to see how much your class knows about hospitality patterns in other countries. They are going to listen to two speakers, one from St Lucia, one from India. Ask them to find the two places in an atlas or on a map of the world. Can they guess what the two speakers are going to speak about? Ask them to brainstorm ideas, and make a list of them on the board.

Before listening to the recordings, ask the learners to read the gapped notes. Are they similar to the ideas they have brainstormed? Can they guess what expressions will be used to fill the gaps?

This is a dual listening. As usual, decide whether to use one of the two versions, or both. Play the recording, pausing after the first speaker. The tapescript is on page 238.

Get the learners to compare their notes, and see whether they can get a complete set, before moving on to the second speaker.

If the class wishes, play them the recording again. Ask them to check their completed notes with others.

Answer key

For the answers, please see the tapescript on page 238.

The writing activity has been well prepared by the previous exercise. It can be assigned as homework if time is short. You can collect the paragraphs to read and comment on them. In the next class, ask for volunteers to read their paragraphs – or pin them up on the wall for the class to read.

Quick Check answer key

1. Shall I
2. Shall I; I'll
3. Shall I; newspaper/paper
4. Shall I; I'll do
5. Shall I; be wonderful/great/nice/lovely

```
                    QUICK NOTES

    This went well:
    ...........................................................
    ...........................................................
    This didn't quite work:
    ...........................................................
    ...........................................................
    Things to think about:
    ...........................................................
    ...........................................................
```

D REVIEW AND DEVELOPMENT

REVIEW OF UNIT 21

1 I want to spend, spend, spend ▭
pronunciation: initial consonant clusters

The focus in this pronunciation exercise is the combinations of consonants that give so many learners problems at the beginning of words. The exercise is in three parts.

Suggested steps

In the first part, the learners are simply asked to listen and repeat. There is a gap on the recording for the repetition. Ensure that the learners repeat with pace and rhythm as close to the original as possible, so that their repetition fits into the gap.

It is often useful to have the class repeat the phrases chorally in the first instance. This is less threatening for any individual who is having difficulties. You can then see how people are getting on by repeating this part of the recording, and asking particular learners to repeat.

Different nationalities find different combinations difficult. In single nationality classes, emphasise the ones that are particularly troublesome for your learners. In multinational classes, get the learners to help each other with their difficulties. The tapescript is on page 238.

In the second part, the learners hear four complete sentences. They have to identify the sound that is at the beginning of the last word in each sentence. Go over the possibilities with the class: /bl/, /br/, /pl/ and /pr/. Make sure they understand the instructions.

Play the recording, pausing it between numbers.

Get the learners to check their choices with others.

Answer key

1. /br/   2. /pl/   3. /pr/   4. /bl/

The third part of the exercise allows more practice in complete sentences, this time with a rhythmical beat to help pronunciation.

Make sure the learners understand the instructions. They hear one word on the recording, for example *spend*. They say: *I want to spend, spend, spend.* There is a gap after the initial word for them to insert their sentence. They will then hear the complete sentence spoken.

Play the recording. Ask the class to say the sentences chorally in the first instance. You can then repeat this part of the tape, asking individuals to have a go.

2 I really want to play 🔲
consonant clusters and sentence rhythm

Pronunciation work on initial clusters continues with this 'rhythm rap'.

Suggested steps

Get the learners working in pairs to fill in the gaps if they can. They can consult others if they are stuck.

Play the recording once, right through. The tapescript is on page 238.

Get the learners to check their answers together. Then play the recording one more time, so that the class can practise saying the lines in rhythm.

Pairs can then read the rap together. Encourage them to emphasise the rhythm and try to keep to the pace of the recording.

REVIEW OF UNIT 22

1 What was your first holiday like?
speaking: *was like*

It may be helpful to remind the class of the particular structure that is being practised in this exercise: what something was like in the past. Go over the two examples and point out that the phrase is used in the questions, but not in the answers. Give a few more examples to help, e.g. *What was summer like this year? It was hot. What was spring like? It was beautiful,* etc.

Option

If the learners need a bit of support to start the pairwork, go through the questions as a chain to begin with. Help the first person formulate question 1: *What was your first trip to another country like?* Learner 2 answers, then asks the second question: *What was your first day at work like?* and so on. The class can then divide into pairs or threesomes to go through all the questions.

2 Wise words for the fridge
writing advice

Suggested steps

Many people use magnets to affix interesting or amusing small notices onto their fridge door. Make sure that the class understands that they are being asked to write a sentence of advice, using one of the beginnings. Encourage them to make their mini-poster as colourful and striking as possible. Some learners may like to create their poster on their own, while others may prefer to work in pairs or small groups.

When everyone has finished, organise an exhibition of the mini-posters. Each person can present their own, reading out the sentence and answering questions about it from the class.

Worksheet

The worksheet for this unit, on page 187, gives the learners examples of many different types of invitations, both formal and informal. The first activity is a reading exercise. The learners then write two invitations themselves, and, in groups, practise answering them.

Distribute the worksheets. Encourage the learners to read for gist to start with. They can then work in pairs to answer the questions or on their own, comparing their answers afterwards. Circulate as they are working and help as needed.

Answer key

1. Numbers 1, 4 and 5 are formal invitations. Answers to these would be in the third person, e.g. Mr and Mrs Alvin Pedworth are pleased to accept the invitation to …
2. 1, 2, 4, 5 and 6
3. 3, 5 and 6 – and, very likely, 2.
4. 1, 3 and 6
5. 1, 2, 3 and 4
6. 2 and 6 (Valentine's Day, Hallowe'en)

You could have a feedback session for the answers before proceeding to the next part of the activity. If there are any difficulties with any of the invitations, they can be discussed at this point. Question 7 asks for preferences – ask for reasons for the learners' choices.

Encourage the learners to think of two special occasions that are happening fairly soon. They then imagine a celebration for each one – dinner, reception, dance, etc. and write an invitation for it.

The next part of the activity introduces a game element. Get the learners working in groups and help them with any difficulties.


```
┌─────────────────────────────────────────────┐
│           END OF UNIT NOTES                   │
│                                               │
│   How's the class getting on?                 │
│   .........................................   │
│   .........................................   │
│                                               │
│   Language that needs more work or attention: │
│   .........................................   │
│   .........................................   │
│                                               │
│   My learners:                                │
│   .........................................   │
│   .........................................   │
└─────────────────────────────────────────────┘
```

24

LOOKING AHEAD

CONTENTS

Language focus: the present simple for talking about the future
the future simple for future facts and predictions

Vocabulary: age and attitudes to age
personal predictions about the future
predictions about the future of the world

INTRODUCTION TO THE UNIT

This is the last unit of the book, an appropriate place to look forward to the future. The unit starts once again from the learners' own point of view. They are encouraged to use a variety of verbs in the present tense to express their own hopes and ambitions for the future. They are also given models of the future simple to start using the tense: first for their personal predictions, then for predictions about the world we live in. The unit offers a balance of practice with the verb tense, and consolidation of all four skills.

1 Thirty-five will be a good age
future simple tense for future facts

Warm-up

The presentation of the tense is through a conversational exercise with individuals writing down the age they are looking forward to for themselves in the future, and then talking about their choices. This really acts as a warm-up for the rest of the activities, so you may wish to start simply by going through the activity yourself, as a model for the class. Write an age that you'd like to be on the board, and ask your learners to write the ages they would like to be. Tell them why you chose that particular age.

Draw the attention of the class to the questions listed as examples. By eliciting, get them to ask you the questions. Answer their questions. You might like to put up a model of the future simple by writing the gist of your answers on the board. When you are sure they have got the models straight in their minds, ask them to go through the same process.

Suggested steps

The learners write down their preferred future age. Although you might think this step is not strictly speaking absolutely necessary for the conversation to work, it does give the activity a much sharper focus, and helps the learners complete their sentences later on.

Get the learners in small groups to go through the questions together and discuss their preferences. This part of the activity is a prelude to the sentence completion which comes next, so it is usually better to keep it fairly short – five to eight minutes is usually ample for small groups to get an idea of everyone's opinions on age.

Ask each learner to complete the series of questions about the age they chose. As so often, the learners will probably finish their task at different times. It's often a good idea to get three or four of them together as soon as they finish, and start them off with the comparison part of the exercise. (This has the added advantage of allowing new groups to be formed in larger classes.)

Work with each group as it starts, to make sure they understand that they are to compare their ambitions and hopes, and explain the reasons for them.

It is often satisfying for the learners to have a summary of their group discussion at the end. One person can be asked to say a few words about the discussion, or report on one of the more striking or unusual ambitions that were mentioned.

Option

Organise a chain feedback after the group discussion. Get one learner to read one of their sentence completions to the class, and ask if anyone else has a similar ambition. The next person then reads out a different sentence completion, and so on.

Personal Study Workbook

1: future time expressions
2: the future simple

2 I'll need to travel a lot

I'll need to / I'll have to

This is a reading task, which offers more practice with the future simple. As some deduction or even guesswork is required, it is usually more fun for the learners to do it in pairs.

Warm-up

Before using the book, ask the learners to imagine the following situation: They are intending to become a doctor, and practise in Tanzania. What will they need to do to achieve that ambition? Write their suggestions on the board. Do the same with a second scenario: They are now budding writers. What will they need to do to become famous best sellers? Write their suggestions on the board. Then ask them to open their books and look at the ideas written by two people who did have exactly these hopes.

Suggested steps

If you do not use the above warm-up, it will probably still be useful to set the scene by establishing that the matching exercise concerns two people, one who wishes to become a doctor and live in Tanzania, the other who has the ambition of becoming a famous writer.

Let the learners sort out the six beginnings and endings of sentences, talking it over with their partners. Ask them to check with one other pair before going over the answers with them.

Answer key

1. a   2. d   3. f   4. b   5. e   6. c

> ### Language Point: I'll need to *and* I'll have to
> *I'll need to* and *I'll have to* are presented here, as earlier, simply as interchangeable options.

The discussion about what the learners themselves will need to do in order to achieve their own ambitions can be a brief follow-up with the whole class, especially in smaller classes. In large classes, it might be better to get them working in two or three groups, and then have a spokesperson from each group report to the whole class.

Option

If there is time, you could use this activity as the basis for a slightly more extended role play. Working in pairs, the learners improvise a consultation between one of the young people they've been reading about, and a career counsellor. The young people tell the counsellor about their wishes and ambitions, the counsellor advises them on what they'll need to do to achieve them.

Personal Study Workbook

3: questions and short answers using the future simple tense

4: listening to questions and answers with the future simple

3 Is age important?

reading and discussion

This activity follows on from the discussions in the previous two exercises. The first part is a warm-up, to make the learners aware of the issues being raised by the letter they are about to read.

Suggested steps

Get the learners to decide individually when the stages in life begin and end.

Ask them to join one or two others and compare their ideas. Differences of opinion should be brought out into the open in the group, and discussed.

While the learners are still in groups, draw their attention to the question about whether people worry about getting older. Ask a representative of each group to sum up the discussion and the differences of opinion, if any.

The learners have worked with letters to the editor of a newspaper in earlier units, but it might be useful to draw their attention once again to the form of the letter. Point out the impersonal address (*Dear Sir* – a female editor would usually be addressed as *Dear Madam*) and the end formula (*Yours faithfully*) which is customarily used when a letter begins with an impersonal address, in fairly formal letters in Britain.

Ask the learners to read the letter through, trying to understand as much of the meaning as possible from a first reading. They could then discuss any problems they have with one or two others in the class.

Option

If you feel you would like your learners to re-read the text, concentrating a bit more closely on its details, try this activity before you turn to the more general questions about attitudes to age in their country.

Divide the board into two sections, one headed: *Images of young people on TV*, the other *Images of old people on TV*. Invite the learners to come up and write details from the text on the board.

Elicit and add any details that have not been noted. You can then go over the details with the class. The work on the board provides a focus for moving on to the more general questions. You can ask whether these images are the same as the ones on TV in their country, whether there is anything they would add for their own country, and so on.

You might wish to draw the attention of the class to the last sentence in the letter. Can they explain the phrase *if we're lucky*? (What are the alternatives to getting old?)

Work with the two questions that follow the letter. Elicit responses from the whole class, if it's a small one. Or get the learners talking about the two questions in small groups, then reporting to the class.

Option – Follow-up

If the class found the letter interesting and thought-provoking, they can be asked to write a similar letter to the editor about attitudes to age in their own country. They can use the letter in the book as a model, or to compare attitudes which are the same, or perhaps more favourable to older people, in their country.

Personal Study Workbook

5: comparing the future simple with the *going to* future

Quick Check answer key

(i)
1. Will; I'll   2. will; She'll   3. Will; they'll
4. Will; he'll
(ii)
1. Does; she'll   2. Would; he'll   3. Do; they'll

```
QUICK NOTES

This went well:

.............................................................

.............................................................

This didn't quite work:

.............................................................

.............................................................

Things to think about:

.............................................................

.............................................................
```

B

1 You'll never get a good job!
reading and writing predictions; discussion

This activity introduces the negative form of the future simple tense. Two forms are given: *you'll never* + verb and *you won't* + verb. It may be useful to note the stronger negation achieved by using *you'll never* (it results in a more forceful, slightly more emotional prediction).

If you wish to emphasise the language point being taught in the activity, you can write the future simple tense on the board before the learners start to read. Write positive statements on one side, negative on the other, and show the long forms, for example by using brackets:

I'll do it (I will do it) I won't do it (I will not do it)
You'll do it (You will do it) You won't do it (You will not do it)

Ask the learners if they can supply the question forms (use the long form for positive questions. The short form is normally used for negative questions): *Will you*

do it? Won't you do it? (the negative question has a more emotional, 'coaxing' tone).

Get the learners to supply the future simple tenses for one or two other verbs, especially those they will meet in the sentences: *get, have, keep, be, make.*

Suggested steps

The learners can read the predictions and underline the future tenses on their own, or working with a partner.

They should then complete one or both sentences for themselves. You can help start the activity by giving them a prediction that was made about you, when you were younger. Can they guess whether it was accurate?

As the learners finish writing their sentence, organise them into small groups to compare with one or two others. Ask them to decide on one interesting or unusual prediction that they will then report to the class.

Answer key

Future tenses underlined:
You'll never get
You'll have
You won't keep
You'll be
You (just) won't
You'll never be

Personal Study Workbook

6: pronunciation, using the future simple
8: reading about predictions

2 I read my stars in the paper
vocabulary and discussion

This is a warm-up for the listening activity which follows. It sets the scene by getting the learners to think about the various ways in which people try to predict their personal future.

Use the illustration as suggested, to start the conversation. This can be done as a whole-class discussion, unless the class is very large.

Some people have reservations about trying to predict the future. If your learners are likely to find the subject distasteful, you can simply go over the vocabulary of the different ways, and not ask them to personalise the topic by talking about their own views. If, on the other hand, your class is interested in the topic, you can encourage them to put their own points of view and give reasons for them.

3 You'll have two sons ☐☐
listening and discussion

This is a fairly long anecdote, to which the learners can be encouraged to listen for gist. Their task is to pick out the four main predictions that the fortune teller made about the speaker's father. In many classes, it will be useful to divide the anecdote into sections, using the pause button, and get the learners guessing about what they're going to hear in each section.

Suggested steps

Before listening, set the scene: a fairground; a young man with his girlfriend; a fortune teller in a little tent; the fortune teller is going to tell the young man's future. Ask the learners *What is she going to look at?* They will probably guess his hand, or the palm of his hand. Tell the class that this fortune teller did something unusual: she also studied something else. Can they guess what?

The learners listen to the first part of the anecdote, up to the end of the first prediction. They should confirm their guesses about what the fortune teller studied, and try to catch her first prediction. Ask them to write the prediction down.

Ask them: *What did the fortune teller predict next? Something about the young man's job, perhaps?* Play the next section, to the second prediction. Repeat the procedure for the third and the fourth prediction. Then tell them that in one respect, the fortune teller was wrong. Ask them to guess what that was. Then play the recording to confirm the answer. The tapescript is on page 239.

Get the learners to check their answers with others.

Option

In classes with good listening skills, you might prefer to reverse the procedure. Let the class hear the whole anecdote. They then work with a partner or in groups to reconstruct it as much as they can. You can then play the recording again in sections to confirm the story they have created.

Answer key

1. You'll marry a woman with dark hair and blue eyes.
2. You'll sell things for a large company.
3. You'll have two children – two sons.
4. You'll live to be 73 years old.

Ask for the learners' response to the story. (It is a true story, which happened to the father of one of the authors.) Do they think the future can be predicted? Or was the fortune teller simply lucky in her guesses? Unless personal anecdotes have already emerged in the previous warm-up exercise, this is a good place to ask if anyone has had any experiences themselves of this kind of prediction, or has heard stories from others.

Option – Follow-up

Classes that enjoy creative writing can be set a homework task – to create a fictional story about one of their relatives or friends, involving a fortune teller and predictions made, which later turn out to be either right or wrong.

Personal Study Workbook

7: listening to predictions

4 Your English will soon be very good

writing predictions

A game-type activity rounds off the lesson. If there is a danger that predictions might be written about some people in the class and not about others, ask the learners to write their names on two slips of paper. Collect the slips, then get each member of the class to choose two. They write predictions about these two people.

Using the second person form *you'll* increases the personalisation of the predictions, and practises that form. If you wish your learners to practise the third person, you can ask them to write *he'll* or *she'll*. This narrows the guessing range somewhat! Alternatively, model the *he'll* or *she'll* form as a response to guessing: *Oh, you think she'll marry a stranger? What do you think, Bilge?*

Quick Check answer key

(i)
1. He will   2. a; d
(ii)
1. Will he be rich in ten years from now?
2. Will she be a good teacher?

```
┌─────────────────────────────────────────┐
│              QUICK NOTES                  │
│                                           │
│  This went well:                          │
│  .......................................  │
│  .......................................  │
│                                           │
│  This didn't quite work:                  │
│  .......................................  │
│  .......................................  │
│                                           │
│  Things to think about:                   │
│  .......................................  │
│  .......................................  │
└───────────────────────────────────────────┘
```

C

1 I think children will need languages

the future simple; discussion and listening

In this lesson, we move from personal futures to the future of people in general, and of the world.

Suggested steps

Establish the concept of thinking about children's needs in the future. How is the world changing? What is life going to be like for people in twenty years' time? Will they need different skills to be successful and happy?

Ask the learners to go over the list of possible needs, consulting their dictionaries or each other if they have problems. They can then discuss the issue in small groups, choosing two expressions together.

Take a rapid poll of the class's opinions by asking the groups to report on their discussion and their choices.

This is a dual listening activity. As usual, decide to play one of the levels only, or use one after the other. Explain to the learners that there are four speakers on the recording that they are going to listen to.

Play the recording, pausing after each speaker. The tapescript is on page 239.

Get the learners to check their answers with each other.

Answer key

The speakers mention the following: to speak more languages; to read a lot; to know how to use a computer; to have lots of imagination; to be very fit; to enjoy their hobbies; to tackle the problem of pollution.

The need mentioned on the recording that is not in the box is: a lot of money

Conduct a general feedback. Find out how close the speakers' opinions were to the learners' own ideas. Did other ideas emerge that were not mentioned on the recording? Is anything being done in the learners' country or countries to help prepare children for the future?

2 What will happen to our world?
vocabulary; reading; discussion

Warm-up

You may wish to establish the idea of predictions based upon a trend visible over a certain number of years. You can do this with items that are relevant to your own town. For example, divide the board into three columns: the first is labelled *20 years ago* (or write the date 20 years ago), the second *Now* (or the date this year) and the third *20 years from now* (or the date twenty years in the future). Elicit guesses from the students to the following questions:

What was the population of the town 20 years ago? What is it now? (approximate guesses)
What do they think it will be 20 years from now? etc.

Possible items to ask about include the number of cars, schools, universities, radio stations, TV stations, traffic lights, etc.

Suggested steps

Go over the first part of the article with the class. Establish that these figures for 1972 and 1992 often indicate a trend. Ask if they think that trend will continue. They should then be able to read the four predictions and decide individually whether they think the predictions are accurate, or not.

As learners finish the task, get them working in pairs to compare their opinions. Draw their attention to the example given. Encourage the learners to give reasons for their views, in the way shown in the example.

Options for feedback

Establish a profile of the majority views by putting the options up on the board:

Population: many more people Yes .... No ....

Put the number of *yes* opinions and *no* opinions in the class for each option.

In each case, ask if there is a pair who had differing views when they compared their answers. Ask each one to explain their partner's reasons to the class.

Use the lining-up technique. One corner of the room represents *yes*, the other corner *no*. People in one corner find a partner from the other corner and try to persuade them to change their opinions by giving good reasons for their own opposing view.

Options – Follow-up

The material in the article, and the reasons for agreeing or disagreeing with its prediction, can be used by the learners to write a homework paragraph answering the article's title question: *What will happen to our world in the future?* Encourage each learner to add one more aspect to the debate. They could think, for example, of whether more people will live in flats rather than houses; whether cars will be banned from the centres of cities; whether more people will own aeroplanes, etc.

This paragraph-writing exercise would also be a good follow-up to the supplementary worksheet given below.

Another follow-up possibility, if your class enjoys illustration and creative activities, is for groups to create posters displaying the facts of the article, and drawing one conclusion from them. The conclusion can take the form of a slogan for the poster, e.g. *Save the elephants.* Illustrations can be either drawn, or cut from magazines and pasted onto cardboard. Have a poster exhibition in your class. Get each group to present their poster: their aims, their own concerns about the future, etc.

Try to draw out one pleasing thing about each poster and mention it after the group's presentation: praise the choice of colours, for example, or a striking design, or a strong, neat overall effect, or a balanced, effective slogan.

Personal Study Workbook

9: writing, using the future simple

Quick Check answer key

1. The future won't be exciting in this country. / The future will be boring in this country.
2. Children will need to learn languages.
3. The population of the world won't increase. / The population of the world will decrease.
4. There will be many more cars in the world.
5. There won't be any more *Quick Checks* in this book.

```
┌─────────────────────────────────────────┐
│              QUICK NOTES                  │
│                                           │
│  This went well:                          │
│  ......................................   │
│  ......................................   │
│                                           │
│  This didn't quite work:                  │
│  ......................................   │
│  ......................................   │
│                                           │
│  Things to think about:                   │
│  ......................................   │
│  ......................................   │
└─────────────────────────────────────────┘
```

D   REVIEW AND DEVELOPMENT

REVIEW OF UNIT 22

1 When I have a free day
writing; speaking

This exercise gives the learners quite a lot of choice and some support in writing sentences about their own lives.

Suggested steps

If you feel they need to go over the basic structure they learnt in Unit 22, write a model sentence for yourself on the board, e.g. *When I go on a long journey, I write my letters.* Talk about the example with the class to establish that they are concerned here with things that happen often, regularly, or in a routine way, not just once. (For example, you can tell them how little time you normally have for writing letters; the letters pile up on your desk. So the long journey gives you a chance to catch up with all that correspondence.)

Let each person write three sentences. As they finish, get them into groups of three or four to read their sentences with each other and talk about them.

In a feedback session, ask each person (or one person from each group in larger classes) to tell the class one interesting or amusing sentence heard in their group discussion.

Option

Collect in the sentences. Read some of them out. The person who wrote the sentence mustn't reveal it. Others have to try to remember who wrote the sentence.

REVIEW OF UNIT 23

1 Please come and see my new flat ▭
discussion; inviting and accepting or declining

Warm-up

The warm-up for the listening exercise concentrates on ways of celebrating the fact that someone has moved into a new flat or house. The discussion can be carried out by the whole class or in groups.

With multinational classes, organise a comparison of different cultural practices by getting the learners to write them on the board. For example, under the heading *gifts*, they could write: *Not in X* (their country) or *Flowers in Y*, etc.

With single nationality classes, see whether there is general agreement about practices in the country. Write up: *Gifts: We don't take any* or *We take …*

Then ask whether there are any particular variations, in individuals or families. For example, some families might always take a gift of food or drink when one of their members moves into a new house or flat.

Suggested steps

When the class is ready for the listening exercise, explain that they are going to hear three short phone calls. Draw their attention to the four possibilities listed.

Play all three phone calls. Get the learners to check their choice with others. The tapescript is on page 239.

Answer key

Number 4 is correct.

Play the recording again, pausing after each phone call. Ask the learners to identify what the phone call was, i.e. whether that particular friend can come to the party, or not.

After the first phone call, pause to let the learners write down the excuse given, as dictation.

Answer key

We're going to be away on Saturday.

Option

As a follow-up, you could ask the learners to role play the three phone calls. They can then think of a different occasion for a celebration, and role play phone calls of invitation to that. The answers should illustrate the various choices of accepting, declining or expressing uncertainty.

2 Enjoy your new flat!
reading; writing

Suggested steps

The situation has been set by the previous activity. You can use the illustration to go over some of the language that may be needed by the learners for the writing activity.

If time is short, set the writing as homework. Next lesson, have a feedback session.

In feedback, get the learners to read out their messages to the class (in larger classes, work in groups). Alternatively, the messages can be pinned up on the wall for people to read. Talk about ways that some people used to make their messages friendly, or amusing.

Worksheet

The worksheet for this unit, on page 188, allows the learners to use the future simple to write sentences about their own opinions of future possibilities. It is simple, but encourages them to ask questions and find out other people's views.

Distribute the worksheet to the class. Go over the example statements with them and explain that they are to write similar statements about their own views, under each one of the five headings. Go round and monitor as they are writing, helping with any vocabulary or structure problems.

Explain the second part of the exercise. The learners now turn their statements into questions. Go over the example questions with them.

As they are doing this second part of the exercise, go round and make sure that the learners have got the right question forms. Help with any problems encountered. If questions with *there* prove to be difficult, give a few more examples on the board: *Will there be more cars? Will there be smaller classes?* etc.

As each person finishes, get them working in pairs to ask and answer each other's questions.

For feedback, ask the class some general questions. Was there any case where pairs wrote the same question? What was the most interesting question they heard? Was there any question which was impossible to answer?

END OF UNIT NOTES

How's the class getting on?

....

....

Language that needs more work or attention:

....

....

My learners:

....

....

WORKSHEETS

WORKSHEET 1A

Do not show your plan to your partner.

Ask your partner questions to find out:

1. Where are the meeting rooms?
2. Where is the coffee shop?
3. Where is the restaurant?
4. Where are the toilets?
5. Where is the television room?

Mark them on your plan.

Answer your partner's questions about the things on your plan.

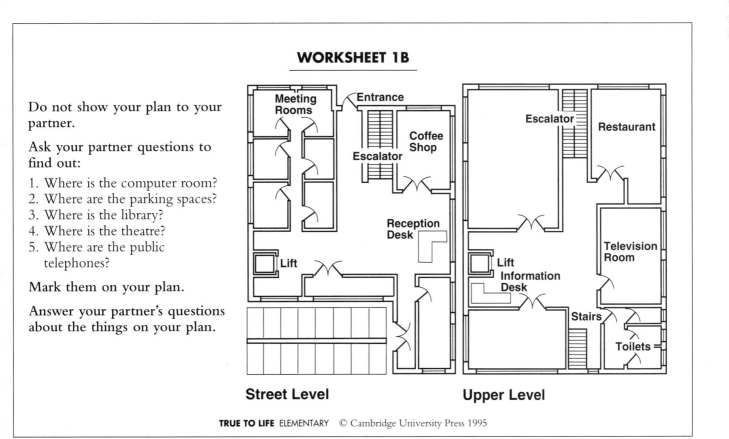

Entrance

Escalator

Reception Desk

Lift

Computer Room

Parking Spaces

Public Telephones

Street Level

Theatre

Escalator

Lift

Information Desk

Stairs

Library

Upper Level

TRUE TO LIFE ELEMENTARY   © Cambridge University Press 1995

WORKSHEET 1B

Do not show your plan to your partner.

Ask your partner questions to find out:

1. Where is the computer room?
2. Where are the parking spaces?
3. Where is the library?
4. Where is the theatre?
5. Where are the public telephones?

Mark them on your plan.

Answer your partner's questions about the things on your plan.

Meeting Rooms

Entrance

Coffee Shop

Escalator

Reception Desk

Lift

Street Level

Escalator

Restaurant

Lift

Information Desk

Television Room

Stairs

Toilets

Upper Level

TRUE TO LIFE ELEMENTARY   © Cambridge University Press 1995

WORKSHEET 2A

Look at the pictures and choose seven things to put into the house. Put each of them into any one of the rooms.

Don't show your plan to your partner.

Take it in turns to describe your plan.

Example:

A: *I've got a television set. It's in the sitting room.*

B: *Oh, I haven't got a television. But I've got a radio, in the kitchen.*

Put a tick (✓) beside the picture of the things that your partner has.

TRUE TO LIFE ELEMENTARY © Cambridge University Press 1995

WORKSHEET 2B

Look at the pictures and choose seven things to put into the house. Put each of them into any one of the rooms.

Don't show your plan to your partner.

Take it in turns to describe your plan.

Example:

A: *I've got a television set. It's in the sitting room.*

B: *Oh, I haven't got a television. But I've got a radio, in the kitchen.*

Put a tick (✓) beside the picture of the things that your partner has.

TRUE TO LIFE ELEMENTARY © Cambridge University Press 1995

WORKSHEET 3A

Imagine that you are a guest at this hotel. What would you like for breakfast? Choose something to eat, and something to drink. Telephone Room Service and order your breakfast.

1. Greet the waiter who answers the phone. What do you say? If you don't remember, look at Lesson A, Exercise 2.
2. Say what food you would like.
3. Thank the waiter and say goodbye.

The
GRAND HOTEL
&
Baby Grand Restaurant

If you wish to have our Continental or English breakfast delivered to your room, please fill in this form and leave it outside your room, or ring Room Service, Number 7 on your telephone.
Thank you.

Room No _ _ _ _ _ _ _ _   Date _ _ _ _ _ _ _ _ _

No. of people _ _ _ _ _ _ _ _ _ _ _ _ _ _ _ _ _ _

**Continental Breakfast   English Breakfast
£8.50   £10.50**

Beverages   **Monday-Friday 7-9.30**
Tea   ☐   **Saturday-Sunday 8-10**
Coffee   ☐
Chocolate   ☐

Cold Beverages
Orange juice   ☐   Scrambled eggs   ☐
Cold milk   ☐   Poached eggs   ☐
                              Fried eggs   ☐
Bread   Sausage   ☐
Croissant   ☐   Black pudding   ☐
Brown toast   ☐   Bacon   ☐
White toast   ☐   Mushrooms   ☐
Ryvita   ☐   Tomatoes   ☐
Preserves   ☐   Hashbrowns   ☐
Honey   ☐
                              Extra Items
Cereal   Hard boiled egg   ☐
Cornflakes   ☐   Ham cooked   ☐
All Bran   ☐   Cheddar cheese   ☐
Weetabix   ☐
Alpen   ☐
Rice Crispies   ☐
Coco Pops   ☐
Branflakes   ☐
Kelloggs Special
   Low fat   ☐
Frosties   ☐

WORKSHEET 3B

Imagine that you are a waiter at this hotel. A guest telephones to order breakfast.

1. Answer the phone. What do you say? If you don't remember, look at Lesson A, Exercise 2.
2. Ask what the guest would like.
3. Write down the order.
4. Ask the guest's room number.
5. Repeat the order, to make sure it's correct.
6. Thank the guest politely and say goodbye.

The
GRAND HOTEL
&
Baby Grand Restaurant

If you wish to have our Continental or English breakfast delivered to your room, please fill in this form and leave it outside your room, or ring Room Service, Number 7 on your telephone.
Thank you.

Room No _ _ _ _ _ _ _ _   Date _ _ _ _ _ _ _ _ _

No. of people _ _ _ _ _ _ _ _ _ _ _ _ _ _ _ _ _ _

**Continental Breakfast   English Breakfast
£8.50   £10.50**

Beverages   **Monday-Friday 7-9.30**
Tea   ☐   **Saturday-Sunday 8-10**
Coffee   ☐
Chocolate   ☐

Cold Beverages
Orange juice   ☐   Scrambled eggs   ☐
Cold milk   ☐   Poached eggs   ☐
                              Fried eggs   ☐
Bread   Sausage   ☐
Croissant   ☐   Black pudding   ☐
Brown toast   ☐   Bacon   ☐
White toast   ☐   Mushrooms   ☐
Ryvita   ☐   Tomatoes   ☐
Preserves   ☐   Hashbrowns   ☐
Honey   ☐
                              Extra Items
Cereal   Hard boiled egg   ☐
Cornflakes   ☐   Ham cooked   ☐
All Bran   ☐   Cheddar cheese   ☐
Weetabix   ☐
Alpen   ☐
Rice Crispies   ☐
Coco Pops   ☐
Branflakes   ☐
Kelloggs Special
   Low fat   ☐
Frosties   ☐

WORKSHEET 4

Work with one or two partners. Talk about this question:

Where can you buy things in your town?

Go to the shops or markets. Write down examples of the prices. Write answers to the questions.

1. Where can you buy good **expensive** shoes?
   Names of shops or markets:

   Example of prices:

   Comments: What are the shoes made of? Are they special? Are they durable? Are these good places to buy shoes? Why or why not?

   Where can you buy good **cheap** shoes?
   Names of shops or markets:

   Example of prices:

   Comments: What are the shoes made of? Are they special? Are they durable? Are these good places to buy shoes? Why or why not?

2. Where can you buy good, **expensive** clothes?
   Names of shops or markets:

   Example of prices:

   Comments: What are the clothes made of? Are they special? Are they durable? Are these good places to buy clothes? Why or why not?

   Where can you buy good **cheap** clothes?
   Names of shops or markets:

   Example of prices:

   Comments: What are the clothes made of? Are they special? Are they durable? Are these good places to buy clothes? Why or why not?

3. Decide on one other item to buy.
   Where is it **expensive** to buy the item?
   Names of shops or markets:

   Example of prices:

   Comments: Are these good places to buy the item? Why or why not?

   Where is it **cheap** to buy the item?
   Names of shops or markets:

   Example of prices:

   Comments: Are these good places to buy the item? Why or why not?

TRUE TO LIFE ELEMENTARY   © Cambridge University Press 1995

WORKSHEET 5A

A survey – Who does the work at home?

Ask five people these questions. Put M (man/father), W (woman/mother) and C (child) in the boxes.

In your house …	1	2	3	4	5
– who makes the meals?	☐	☐	☐	☐	☐
– who does the washing up?	☐	☐	☐	☐	☐
– who cleans the bathroom?	☐	☐	☐	☐	☐
– who tidies the sitting room?	☐	☐	☐	☐	☐
– who tidies the garden (if any)?	☐	☐	☐	☐	☐
– who buys the food ?	☐	☐	☐	☐	☐
– who feeds the pets (if any)?	☐	☐	☐	☐	☐
– who cleans the car (if any)?	☐	☐	☐	☐	☐
– who makes the beds?	☐	☐	☐	☐	☐
– who ....?	☐	☐	☐	☐	☐

WORKSHEET 5B

A survey – What do people do in their spare time?

Ask five people these questions. Put a number in the boxes, like this:

1/w = about once a week	1/m = about once a month	1/y = about once a year
2/w = about twice a week	2/m = about twice a month	2/y = about twice a year
3/w = about three times a week	3/m = about three times a month	3/y = about three times a year
etc.	etc.	etc.

How often do you …	1	2	3	4	5
– eat in a restaurant?	☐	☐	☐	☐	☐
– go to a film?	☐	☐	☐	☐	☐
– go to the theatre?	☐	☐	☐	☐	☐
– read a book?	☐	☐	☐	☐	☐
– read a newspaper?	☐	☐	☐	☐	☐
– watch television?	☐	☐	☐	☐	☐
– listen to the radio?	☐	☐	☐	☐	☐
– play sports?	☐	☐	☐	☐	☐
– watch sports?	☐	☐	☐	☐	☐
– ....?	☐	☐	☐	☐	☐

WORKSHEET 6A

(i) (ii) (iii) (iv) (v) (vi)

Work with a partner who has Worksheet 6B. You each have six short paragraphs about the people in the pictures above.

Each paragraph is one half of a description about one person. Put the two halves together, complete the last sentence with one of the expressions in the box, and match the descriptions to the pictures.

1. Amos is quite an old man now. He's got thick white hair and beautiful eyes. He's always smiling, and he's a very kind person.

2. Her eyes are brown too, just like her hair, and she's got a lovely wide mouth. She smiles a lot. She's very interested in travel and …

3. He always sings in the bathroom. He's very artistic, and he always draws funny pictures of his friends. He's interested in an outdoor life …

4. Bessie is a grandmother. She's a big woman, and she really looks very confident, very kind. She's got lovely short straight hair and grey eyes. She's a good cook and very musical.

5. He's very practical: he buys wonderful food that is not very expensive. And he's artistic too. A plate of his food …

6. Lia is a very interesting person. She's got curly hair and small artistic hands. She's lively, but sometimes she's very sad, and she doesn't know why.

> g. lots of things with his hands, and he's very good at it.
> h. looks like a painting, it's so beautiful and colourful.
> i. usually stays in and reads, or watches TV.
> j. and sings a lot of songs for them.
> k. and is looking for a job as a gardener.
> l. knows a lot about different countries.

TRUE TO LIFE ELEMENTARY   © Cambridge University Press 1995

WORKSHEETS

WORKSHEET 6B

(i)　(ii)　(iii)　(iv)　(v)　(vi)

Work with a partner who has Worksheet 6A. You each have six short paragraphs about the people in the pictures above.

Each paragraph is one half of a description about one person. Put the two halves together, complete the last sentence with one of the expressions in the box, and match the descriptions to the pictures.

A. Every Sunday she makes dinner for her three daughters and their families, and in the evening she plays the piano …

B. She looks very confident, but sometimes she's very shy with new friends. She's interested in music and parties, but at the weekends she …

C. Lee is quite a small man, with large eyes and lovely round cheeks. He's a waiter in a restaurant, and he knows all about food. At the weekend, he always makes very nice meals for his family and friends.

D. Mario's a big man, with long strong arms and large hands. His hair is dark and curly. He's a happy person – he sings a lot when he's by himself.

E. He's still very lively. People think he looks very serious because of his white hair, but he's a lot of fun. He's a very practical person, too – he makes …

F. Shirley is very small, and people sometimes think she's shy. But with her friends, she's very confident, and very kind. She's not serious at all – she's really very lively. She's got long straight brown hair.

---

g. lots of things with his hands, and he's very good at it.
h. looks like a painting, it's so beautiful and colourful.
i. usually stays in and reads, or watches TV.
j. and sings a lot of songs for them.
k. and is looking for a job as a gardener.
l. knows a lot about different countries.

TRUE TO LIFE ELEMENTARY　© Cambridge University Press 1995

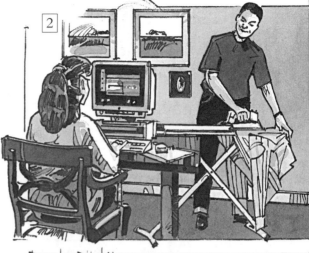

Match the questions and the pictures.

1. Could you iron a shirt for me, too, please?
2. Could you possibly lend me some money?
3. Excuse me, can we order now, please?
4. Can I try on this hat?
5. Can we have dinner here this evening?
6. Can I look at your work?
7. Could you tell me what this is made of?
8. Can I see your passports?
9. Can you type a letter for me, please?
10. Can we stay for three nights?
11. Could you get me a cup of coffee, darling?
12. Excuse me, can you get me a glass of water, please?
13. Can we have breakfast at eight?
14. Can you tell me the price?
15. Could I please leave at three this afternoon?

Work with a partner. Write a dialogue, using one of the 15 questions. Each person in the dialogue speaks at least three times.

Read your dialogue to the class.

TRUE TO LIFE ELEMENTARY   © Cambridge University Press 1995

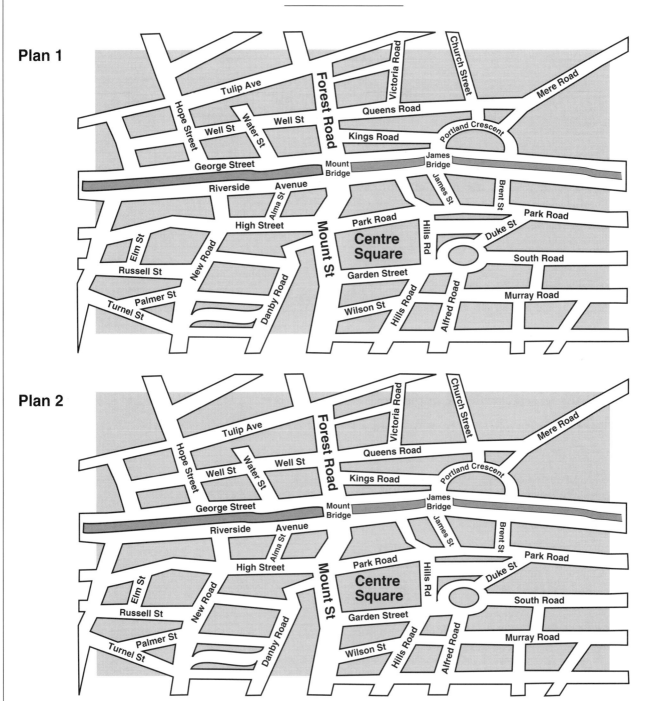

Plan 1

Plan 2

Choose ten of the following items. Choose a place for them in the city, and mark them in on Plan 1.
Don't show your plan to your partner. Take turns describing your plans. Fill in Plan 2 with details of
your partner's city.

a statue of an important person		a park	a market	a bridge	a car park	a department store

a statue of an important person   a park   a market   a bridge   a car park   a department store
a shoe shop   a clothes shop   a hat shop   a food shop (all kinds of food)   a café   a cinema
a butcher's (shop for meat)   a bakery (shop for bread)   a cake shop   a theatre   a town hall
a greengrocer's (shop for fruit and vegetables)   a flower shop   a shop for radios and TVs   a school
a video shop   a furniture shop   a restaurant   a university   a playground for children
a sports centre

TRUE TO LIFE ELEMENTARY   © Cambridge University Press 1995

WORKSHEET 9

1 Complete this table of irregular verbs.

I am	I was
you/we/they are	you/we/they were
he/she/it is	he/she/it ....
I/you/we/they have	I/you/we/they had
he/she/it has	he/she/it ....
I/you/we/they go	I/you/we/they ....
he/she/it goes	he/she/it went.

2 **Regular verbs**. *I, you, he, she, it, we* and *they* all use the same past simple form: *I live / she lives – I lived / she lived.*

Put the verbs in the box under the appropriate column. There are three other verbs that are like *try/tried.*

live liv<u>ed</u>   talk talk<u>ed</u>   try tr<u>ied</u>
      stay stay<u>ed</u>

wash	start	smoke	listen	work	watch	
use	move	kiss	ask	show	return	tidy
clean	type	repair	cook	paint	vote	
open	look	study	like	love	finish	hate
admire	enjoy	cry	change	telephone		
decide	miss	receive	play			

3 Complete each sentence with one of the expressions in the box.

1. I didn't listen to the radio because the programmes ....

2. Marla arrived late at work this morning because she ....

3. Gino didn't wash the car because he ....

4. We didn't watch TV last night because some friends ....

5. They didn't have any food because they ....

6. My parents didn't miss their village because they ....

7. Our class studied a new language because we ....

8. The crowd hated the game because their favourite team ....

didn't play	missed the bus	didn't go shopping	loved the city	didn't seem interesting
didn't have time	arrived from America	enjoyed it		

4 Write three things that you did in the last year, and three things you didn't do. Give reasons.

1. I .... because ....

2. I .... because ....

3. I .... because ....

4. I didn't .... because I ....

5. I ....

6. I ....

Work with a partner. Read the first part of the sentence. Ask your partner to guess your reason.

TRUE TO LIFE ELEMENTARY   © Cambridge University Press 1995

CERTIFIED COPY OF AN ENTRY
Pursuant to the Births and Deaths Registration Act

CAUTION—Any person who (1) falsifies any of the particulars on this certificate, or (2) uses a falsified certificate as true knowing it to be false, is liable to prosecution.

North Cornwall Registry Office

Paul Andrew Douglas   22.5.1943

Trinity College Dublin

Simonetta is a quiet child. She tries hard, but she doesn't always understand the work in class. She finds writing especially very difficult. But she's very friendly and her classmates like her a lot.

McDonald Primary School, Kingston, Ontario.

This is to certify that
Paul Andrew Douglas
has been awarded an Honours Degree
in
Dentistry
24th June 1965

Douglas
Simonetta and Paul are delighted to announce the birth of their daughter Maria Margaret, born June 29th. A little sister for Jonathan

The Last Party
by
Simon Douglas

Murder in the Old Town
is the second detective thriller by Simonetta Douglas, who writes under the name Simon Douglas.

Murder in the Old Town
by
Simon Douglas

Work with a partner who has Worksheet 10B.

There is a party to celebrate Paul and Simonetta's Silver Wedding (25 years of marriage). You are two reporters from the local newspaper.

Compare the documents you have about Paul and Simonetta, and write an article for your newspaper about their life.

You can start like this:

Paul and Simonetta Celebrate 25 Years of Happy Married Life

The two children of Paul and Simonetta Douglas had a party at the Grand Hotel on Saturday to celebrate their parents' Silver Wedding. Paul and Simonetta came to live in Ilkley just after their marriage. Paul was born in …

TRUE TO LIFE ELEMENTARY   © Cambridge University Press 1995

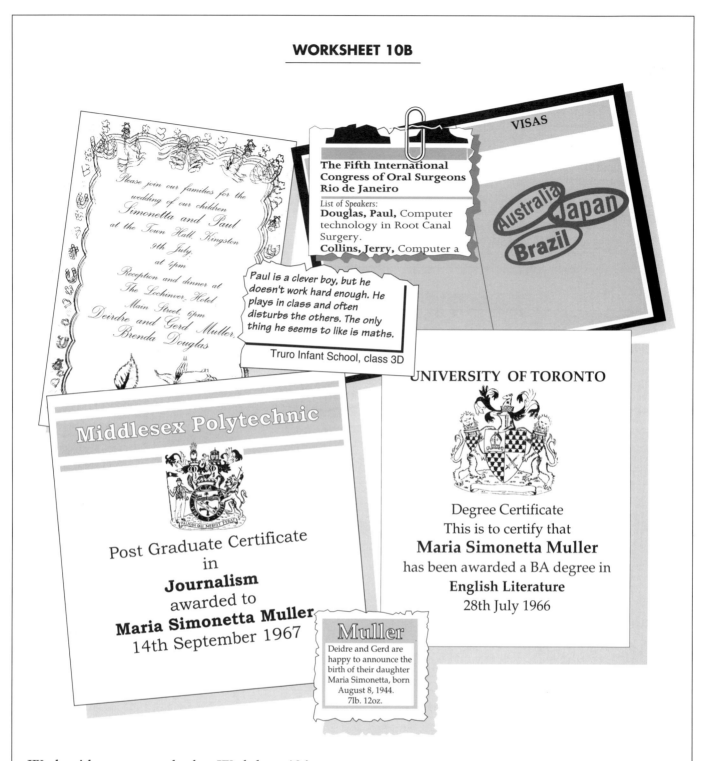

VISAS

Australia Japan Brazil

The Fifth International Congress of Oral Surgeons Rio de Janeiro

List of Speakers:
Douglas, Paul, Computer technology in Root Canal Surgery.
Collins, Jerry, Computer a

Paul is a clever boy, but he doesn't work hard enough. He plays in class and often disturbs the others. The only thing he seems to like is maths.

Truro Infant School, class 3D

Please join our families for the wedding of our children
Simonetta and Paul
at the Town Hall, Kingston
9th July
at 4pm
Reception and dinner at
The Lochinver Hotel
Main Street, 6pm
Deirdre and Gerd Muller,
Brenda Douglas

Middlesex Polytechnic

Post Graduate Certificate
in
Journalism
awarded to
Maria Simonetta Muller
14th September 1967

UNIVERSITY OF TORONTO

Degree Certificate
This is to certify that
Maria Simonetta Muller
has been awarded a BA degree in
English Literature
28th July 1966

Muller
Deidre and Gerd are happy to announce the birth of their daughter Maria Simonetta, born August 8, 1944.
7lb. 12oz.

Work with a partner who has Worksheet 10A.

There is a party to celebrate Paul and Simonetta's Silver Wedding (25 years of marriage). You are two reporters from the local newspaper.

Compare the documents you have about Paul and Simonetta, and write an article for your newspaper about their life.

You can start like this:

Paul and Simonetta Celebrate 25 Years of Happy Married Life

The two children of Paul and Simonetta Douglas had a party at the Grand Hotel on Saturday to celebrate their parents' Silver Wedding. Paul and Simonetta came to live in Ilkley just after their marriage. Paul was born in …

TRUE TO LIFE ELEMENTARY © Cambridge University Press 1995

WORKSHEET 11

1 Look at these verbs used in Unit 11. Write the present continuous form. Number 1 is an example.

1. I call	I'm calling	she calls	she's calling
2. you walk	....	he walks	....
3. we have	....	she has	....
4. they repair	....	he repairs	....
5. the birds fly	....	the plane flies	....
6. children use	....	a child uses	....
7. women make	....	a man makes	....
8. we stand	....	the class stands	....
9. teachers try	....	the learner tries	....
10. you stay	....	Juan stays	....
11. they study	....	Maria studies	....
12. the trains stop	....	the car stops	....
13. I live	....	the kitten lives	....
14. we phone	....	my friend phones	....

2 Read the following letter. Put the verbs in brackets in the right tense: the present simple, or the present continuous.

Dear Siri,

Well, here I am in Tashkent at last. My flat's not ready, so I .... (to stay) at a big hotel in the centre of town for the first month. I .... (to work) by myself in my office at the moment, because it's still the holidays, and most people are away. It's a good introduction to the work. As you can imagine, everything here is quite different.

Thank goodness I can speak a little bit of Russian at least. Do you remember our Russian classes at school? We read Pushkin but we didn't learn how to ask for a sandwich. I .... (to learn) all that kind of language very fast now that I'm here! But Russian isn't enough, so I .... (to take) a two-month course in Uzbek at a language school. I .... (to study) hard, I .... (to try) to learn as quickly as I can. But I'm finding it hard. It's a very different kind of language for me. Every morning I .... (to take) a tram to the school and .... (to work) there for two hours. Then I .... (to go) to my office. In the afternoons, my friend Dora .... (to take) me round the city to show me everything. It's a wonderful city, there's so much to see! Come and visit!

Lots of love,

Andy

Work with a partner. Compare your letters. Give reasons for your choices.

3 With a partner, write a short letter from a person on holiday, or a person with a new job. Use at least four verbs. Put the verbs in brackets, as in the letter above.

Give your letter to another pair and ask them to put the verbs in brackets in the right tense: the present simple, or the present continuous.

TRUE TO LIFE ELEMENTARY   © Cambridge University Press 1995

12 Monday	See Mr Ross 10am Dentist appt 4pm Remember to send flowers for Mum's birthday!	Interview new secretary 10.30 am Lunch with Ella and Peter 1 pm Jimmy's school play 6.30pm – remind Adrian!	15 Thursday
13 Tuesday	Tea with Jay 4.30 pm To opera with Adrian and Jay 7.30 pm Remember to arrange babysitter.	Planning meeting 11 am. Adrian's end of term. Take him to Mario's to celebrate Remember to arrange babysitter	16 Friday
14 Wednesday	11 am: see sales rep re computers. Get plants for garden 4.30 – remind Adrian!	Take Susan to music class 9am Barb's wedding 11 am. Remember – ask Mum to have children. Remind Adrian!	17 Saturday
		Get flowers for the table. Julia, Tom, Hulya, Metin for dinner.	18 Sunday

This is a woman's planner for next week.

Work with a partner who has got Worksheet 12B.

Don't show your planner to your partner. Your partner has got a weekly planner for a different person.

Find out what is on your partner's planner, by asking questions. Complete the empty diary above.

Example: *What's your person doing on Monday morning?*

What can you say about the two people? Can you guess their names? Can you guess what kind of jobs they've got? Talk about your guesses.

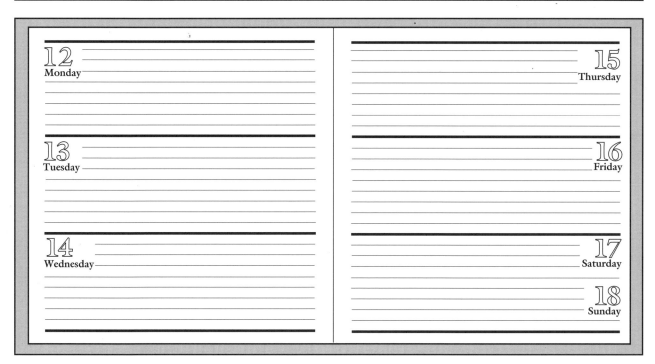

12 Monday	Class meeting 10. am
	Drive Dana to dentist's 3.30
	Buy card for Lena's birthday
	Remind Dana about her Mum's birthday!

13 Tuesday	Jay for tea 4.30 pm
	Get babysitter 6.30
	To opera with Dana and Jay 7.30

| 14 Wednesday | Remember: mark exams for 10B ! |
| | Meet Dana at garden shop 4.30 - remind Dana! |

Meeting about next year's courses 9 am	15 Thursday
Football 4 pm	
Drinks with Fred after game	

| End of classes, hurray, hurray ! | 16 Friday |
| Take Jimmy to swimming pool, 4 pm | |

Take kids to Lena's 10 am	17 Saturday
Remember to get flowers for wedding!	
Shopping for dinner party - don't forget drinks	18 Sunday
Football 3 pm	

This is a man's planner for next week.

Work with a partner who has got Worksheet 12A.

Don't show your planner to your partner. Your partner has got a weekly planner for a different person.

Find out what is on your partner's planner, by asking questions. Complete the empty diary above.

Example: *What's your person doing on Monday morning?*

What can you say about the two people? Can you guess their names? Can you guess what kind of jobs they have got? Talk about your guesses.

TRUE TO LIFE ELEMENTARY © Cambridge University Press 1995

CARD 1

DON'T LOOK AT YOUR PARTNER'S CARD

Describe the squares (A and E), the lines (B and C) and the circle (D) on your card to your partner. Find four differences between your card and your partner's and write each difference down.

<u>When you have finished</u>, look at both cards.

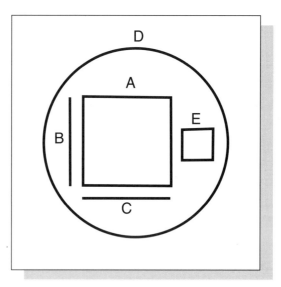

Use these words: bigger smaller longer shorter inside outside

---

CARD 2

DON'T LOOK AT YOUR PARTNER'S CARD

Describe the squares (A and E), the lines (B and C) and the circle (D) on your card to your partner. Find four differences between your card and your partner's and write each difference down.

<u>When you have finished</u>, look at both cards.

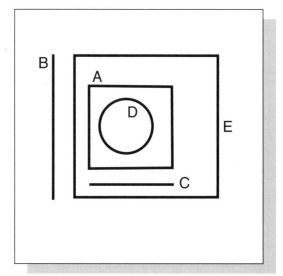

Use these words: bigger smaller longer shorter inside outside

TRUE TO LIFE ELEMENTARY   © Cambridge University Press 1995

WORKSHEET 14

INSTRUCTIONS

Find your partner (the person with exactly the same eight ticks and crosses on their card) by asking *Have you … recently?* questions for each picture on your card. Don't look at other cards until you have found your partner.

Example: *Have you eaten fish recently?*
Answer *Yes, I have* if you have a tick (✔).
Answer *No, I haven't* if you have a cross (✗).

INSTRUCTIONS

Find your partner (the person with exactly the same eight ticks and crosses on their card) by asking *Have you … recently?* questions for each picture on your card. Don't look at other cards until you have found your partner.

Example: *Have you eaten fish recently?*
Answer *Yes, I have* if you have a tick (✔).
Answer *No, I haven't* if you have a cross (✗).

INSTRUCTIONS

Find your partner (the person with exactly the same eight ticks and crosses on their card) by asking *Have you … recently?* questions for each picture on your card. Don't look at other cards until you have found your partner.

Example: *Have you eaten fish recently?*
Answer *Yes, I have* if you have a tick (✔).
Answer *No, I haven't* if you have a cross (✗).

INSTRUCTIONS

Find your partner (the person with exactly the same eight ticks and crosses on their card) by asking *Have you … recently?* questions for each picture on your card. Don't look at other cards until you have found your partner.

Example: *Have you eaten fish recently?*
Answer *Yes, I have* if you have a tick (✔).
Answer *No, I haven't* if you have a cross (✗).

WORKSHEET 15A

Which of the things on the list do you find easy or difficult? Tell a partner about some of them and find out about your partner. Add one new thing to the list.

Try to explain and give reasons.

Study these examples of *-ing* forms before you start.

Examples:

Using verb tenses is hard because ***I keep forgetting*** the 's'. How about you?
Talking in English outside the classroom is easy for me because I have a Canadian boyfriend. Is ***talking*** in English easy for you?
Listening to English is a big problem because people talk so fast.
Asking for things in shops is difficult for me because I don't know many words and sometimes I can't understand the shop assistants. Is it the same for you?

LIST

Using verb tenses is ....

Saying things in the right order is ....

Travelling in an English-speaking country is ....

Listening to English is ....

Spelling words in English is ....

Writing sentences in English is ....

Judging my progress in English is ....

Talking in English outside the classroom is ....

...........................ing .... is ....

TRUE TO LIFE ELEMENTARY   © Cambridge University Press 1995

WORKSHEET 15B

Which of the things on the list do you find easy or difficult? Tell a partner about some of them and find out about your partner. Add one new thing to the list.

Try to explain and give reasons.

Study these examples of *-ing* forms before you start.

Examples:

Using verb tenses is hard because ***I keep forgetting*** the 's'. How about you?
Talking in English outside the classroom is easy for me because I have a Canadian boyfriend. Is ***talking*** in English easy for you?
Listening to English is a big problem because people talk so fast.
Asking for things in shops is difficult for me because I don't know many words and sometimes I can't understand the shop assistants. Is it the same for you?

LIST

Using my dictionary is ....

Reading newspapers in English is ....

Receiving information about my progress is ....

Learning English at home is ....

Asking for things in shops is ....

Asking questions in the classroom is ....

Speaking English in groups in the classroom is ....

Finding time to come to class is ....

...........................ing .... is ....

TRUE TO LIFE ELEMENTARY   © Cambridge University Press 1995

WORKSHEET 16

Have you had the best days of your life yet?

Have you fallen asleep in your English class yet?

Have you had more than seven days off work yet?

Have you discovered true love yet?

Have you had a holiday this year yet?

Have you written a letter to a friend this month?

Have you paid all your bills this month yet ?

Have you shouted at someone this week?

Have you tidied your bedroom this week yet?

Have you borrowed any money this year?

Have you bought a very expensive present for someone this year?

Have you found the ideal job for you yet?

Have you made anyone laugh today?

Have you kissed anyone this week?

Have you called anyone a bad name this week?

TRUE TO LIFE ELEMENTARY   © Cambridge University Press 1995

WORKSHEET 17

dreamily	quickly	loudly
quietly	slowly	perfectly
strangely	angrily	anxiously
tiredly	happily	politely
rudely	simply	calmly

TRUE TO LIFE ELEMENTARY   © Cambridge University Press 1995

WORKSHEET 18A

What do you know about Australia? A Traveller's Quiz

Read these instructions before starting the quiz.

Read each one of the eight quiz sentences to your partner.

After each of your questions, your partner reads a different one to you.

Ask your partner to answer *True* or *False* to each sentence you read. Tell your partner to guess their answer if they don't know. Don't accept *I don't know* as an answer.

Questions

1. You have to drive on the left in Australia. True or false?
2. You have to throw away any fruit you have before leaving some states and entering others in Australia. True or false?
3. You have to pay airport tax before leaving Australia on international flights. True or false?
4. Visitors have to show a passport when they go from one state to another in Australia. True or false?
5. You have to ski in New Zealand because there is no snow in Australia. True or false?
6. You have to fly from the east to the west of Australia because there are no trains. True or false?
7. Citizens have to vote in Australia. True or false?
8. Children in Australia have to sing the Australian national song every morning at school. True or false?

Answers
1. True.
2. True (because there is a problem with fruit fly).
3. True.
4. False.
5. False. (There is good skiing in Australia in Victoria and New South Wales.)
6. False. (You can travel by train from Sydney to Perth.)
7. True. (Citizens with voting rights have to register on election day or perhaps pay a fine.)
8. False.

TRUE TO LIFE ELEMENTARY   © Cambridge University Press 1995

WORKSHEET 18B

What do you know about Australia? A Traveller's Quiz

Read these instructions before starting the quiz.

Read each one of the eight quiz sentences to your partner.

After each of your questions, your partner reads a different one to you.

Ask your partner to answer *True* or *False* to each sentence you read. Tell your partner to guess their answer if they don't know. Don't accept *I don't know* as an answer.

Questions

1. Australians have to do military service. True or false?
2. Australians don't have to change the time on their watches when they travel from one part of Australia to another. True or false?
3. Australians have to buy all their cars from other countries because they don't make cars in Australia. True or false?
4. Australians don't have to buy camels from other countries because there are wild ones in the deserts in Australia. True or false?
5. People who go to live permanently in Australia have to become Australian citizens. True or false?
6. All visitors or people returning to Australia have to declare all food and plants at customs when they enter the country. True or false?
7. Anyone who has a dog in Australia has to have a dog licence. True or false?
8. You can eat kangaroo in expensive restaurants in some parts of Australia. True or false?

Answers
1. False.
2. False. (There are several time differences between states.)
3. False. (Cars are made in Australia.)
4. True. (Camels first came to Australia in the 19th century with people from Afghanistan who helped to build the railways.)
5. False.
6. True.
7. True.
8. True. (Kangaroo fillet is popular with some people in some states, but is not allowed in other states of Australia.)

TRUE TO LIFE ELEMENTARY   © Cambridge University Press 1995

WORKSHEET 19A

Seeking a companion

You have just arrived in a new city to work. You want to meet other people who are learning English and decide to go to an organisation which keeps computer lists of possible companions. Complete the sentences to describe the sort of person you are looking for.

The sort of companion I'm looking for is learning English and is ☐ a man ☐ a woman

I'd like a companion who is about .... years old.

These are some of the activities I'd like to share with my companion:

....

I'd like a person who is ...., ..., and ....

Choose three from this list:

kind   amusing   generous   shy   exciting   active   well educated   outgoing interesting   a non smoker   a smoker   likes parties   likes restaurants   likes conversation a good listener   quiet

I'd like a companion who is a .... or a .... (name of job or profession)

WORKSHEET 19B

Think of two of your friends who would be happy to become English conversation companions. Complete these two profiles for the two people.

Profile of Companion 1

Name: .... Age: .... Job: ....

Things she/he likes doing with other people: ....

This person is ...., ..., and ....

Choose three from this list:

kind   amusing   generous   shy   exciting   active   well educated outgoing   interesting   a non smoker   a smoker   likes parties likes restaurants   likes conversation   a good listener   quiet

Profile of Companion 2

Name: .... Age: .... Job: ....

Things she/he likes doing with other people: ....

This person is ...., ..., and ....

Choose three from this list:

kind   amusing   generous   shy   exciting   active   well educated outgoing   interesting   a non smoker   a smoker   likes parties likes restaurants   likes conversation   a good listener   quiet

WORKSHEET 20

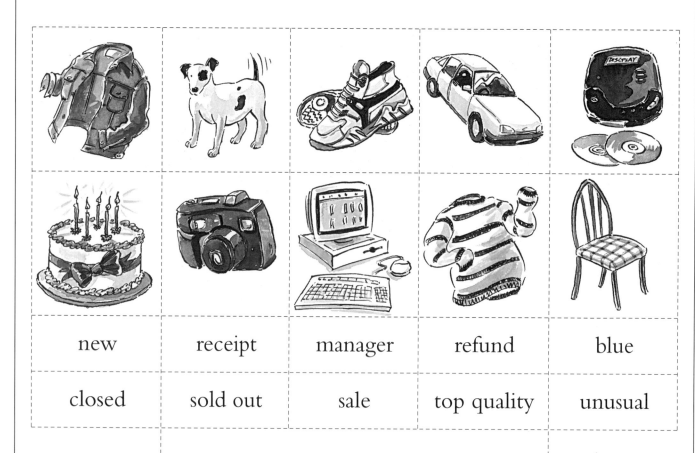

new	receipt	manager	refund	blue
closed	sold out	sale	top quality	unusual

Not polite enough

WORKSHEET 21A

Take turns to ask and answer questions. Find people who have good answers for your three questions. Find people who have the right questions for your answers.

Questions:

1. What do I need to be a success in life? ....

2. What do I need to learn English? ....

3. What do I need to do to have a healthy life? ....

Answers:

....? a. You need music and lots of good friends.

....? b. First, you need to turn off the music.

....? c. You need a lucky lottery ticket.

WORKSHEET 21B

Take turns to ask and answer questions. Find people who have good answers for your three questions. Find people who have the right questions for your answers.

Questions:

1. What do I need to do to be an airline pilot? ....

2. What do I need to do to talk to a teenager? ....

3. What do I need for a good party? ....

Answers:

....?   a. You need a lot of hard work.

....?   b. You need to listen and not talk.

....?   c. You need to stay in bed and drink a lot of liquids.

TRUE TO LIFE ELEMENTARY   © Cambridge University Press 1995

WORKSHEET 21C

Take turns to ask and answer questions. Find people who have good answers for your three questions. Find people who have the right questions for your answers.

Questions:

1. What do I need to get rich fast? ....

2. What do I need to do to be a good friend? ....

3. What do I need to do for a cold? ....

Answers:

....?   a. You need a good teacher.

....?   b. You need to practise, and pass a lot of exams.

....?   c. You need fresh air and exercise.

TRUE TO LIFE ELEMENTARY   © Cambridge University Press 1995

When you need a change in your life...		When you're hungry...		When you can't remember a word in English...	Go back four spaces.	HOME
Go back ten spaces.						
When you've got a cold...		When everything seems to be going really well for you...	Go forward two spaces.		When you haven't got enough money...	
					Go back five spaces.	
					When you feel really angry...	
When it's too hot outside...		Go forward three spaces.	When you find other people difficult...		When you feel like singing...	

START

TRUE TO LIFE ELEMENTARY © Cambridge University Press 1995

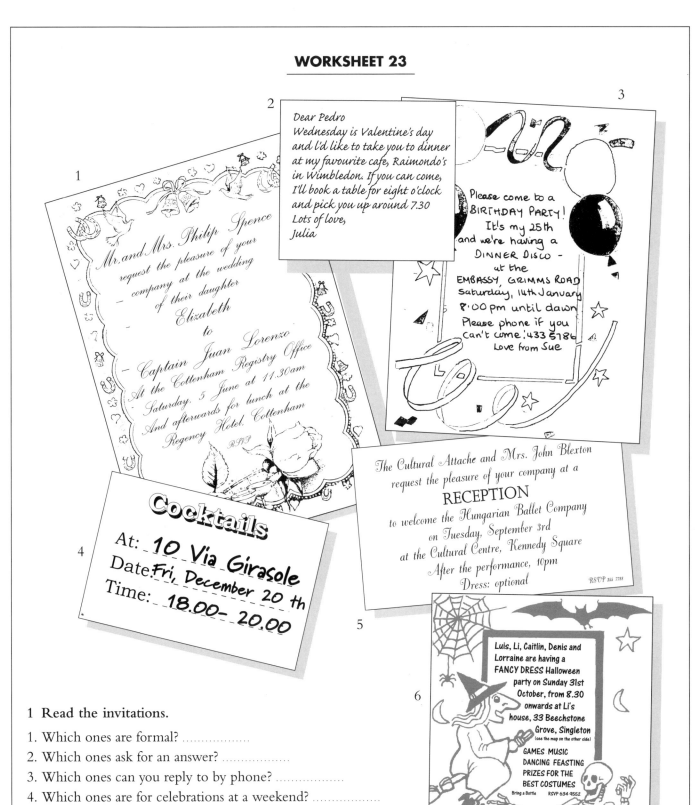

2

Dear Pedro
Wednesday is Valentine's day
and I'd like to take you to dinner
at my favourite cafe, Raimondo's
in Wimbledon. If you can come,
I'll book a table for eight o'clock
and pick you up around 7.30
Lots of love,
Julia

3

Please come to a
BIRTHDAY PARTY!
It's my 25th
and we're having a
DINNER DISCO –
at the
EMBASSY, GRIMMS ROAD
Saturday, 14th January
8.00pm until dawn
Please phone if you
can't come: 433 5786
Love from Sue

1

Mr. and Mrs. Philip Spence
request the pleasure of your
company at the wedding
of their daughter
Elizabeth
to
Captain Juan Lorenzo
At the Cottenham Registry Office
Saturday, 5 June at 11.30am
And afterwards for lunch at the
Regency Hotel, Cottenham
RSVP

4

Cocktails
At: 10 Via Girasole
Date: Fri, December 20 th
Time: 18.00 - 20.00

5

The Cultural Attaché and Mrs. John Blexton
request the pleasure of your company at a
RECEPTION
to welcome the Hungarian Ballet Company
on Tuesday, September 3rd
at the Cultural Centre, Kennedy Square
After the performance, 10pm
Dress: optional
RSVP 555 7788

6

Luis, Li, Caitlin, Denis and
Lorraine are having a
FANCY DRESS Halloween
party on Sunday 31st
October, from 8.30
onwards at Li's
house, 33 Beechstone
Grove, Singleton
(see the map on the other side)
GAMES MUSIC
DANCING FEASTING
PRIZES FOR THE
BEST COSTUMES
Bring a Bottle   RSVP 634 9552

1 Read the invitations.

1. Which ones are formal? ....
2. Which ones ask for an answer? ....
3. Which ones can you reply to by phone? ....
4. Which ones are for celebrations at a weekend? ....
5. Which ones are for personal or family celebrations? ....
6. Which ones are for national holidays or celebrations? ....
7. Which one would you most like to go to? ....

Compare your answers with others.

2 Now write two invitations, each one on a separate slip of paper. Sit with three or four others. Put your invitations face down on the table.

In turn, pick up one invitation. Read it out to the group. Give an answer to the invitation.

TRUE TO LIFE ELEMENTARY   © Cambridge University Press 1995

WORKSHEET 24

Each heading has one statement about the future, as an example. Write two more statements under each heading.

A Your plans to continue learning English

1. I'll go on to Book Two, now.

2. ....

.... ?

3. ....

.... ?

B Changes in the education of children in the future

1. There will be computers instead of teachers.

2. ....

.... ?

3. ....

.... ?

C What houses will look like, twenty years from now

1. People won't live in houses.

2. ....

.... ?

3. ....

.... ?

D What cities will look like, twenty years from now

1. There will be many parks in the city centres.

2. ....

.... ?

3. ....

.... ?

E Life in twenty years time

1. People won't go out to their jobs. They'll work at home.

2. ....

.... ?

3. ....

.... ?

Now make the statements you wrote into questions. Number 1 has been done as an example.

A 1. Will you go on to Book Two, now?

   2. ....

   .... ?

   3. ....

   .... ?

B 1. Will there be computers instead of teachers?

   2. ....

   .... ?

   3. ....

   .... ?

C 1. Will people live in houses?

   2. ....

   .... ?

   3. ....

   .... ?

D 1. Will there be many parks in the city centres?

   2. ....

   .... ?

   3. ....

   .... ?

E 1. Will people go out to jobs, or will they work at home?

   2. ....

   .... ?

   3. ....

   .... ?

Join a partner. In turn, ask each other your questions, and answer them.

TRUE TO LIFE ELEMENTARY   © Cambridge University Press 1995

TESTS

1 Numbers and times   10 marks

Write these numbers in words.

17   _seventeen_

31   ....

66   ....

20   ....

99   ....

11   ....

Write these times in words.

2.10   _ten (minutes) past two_ ....

5.00   ....

7.15   ....

11.30   ....

9.45   ....

8.05   ....

2 Question construction   10 marks

Complete the questions with one appropriate word.

Example: _What_ .... is your name?

1. Where .... you usually buy your shirts?

2. .... time is it?

3. .... do you spell that?

4. Have they .... a phone in their flat?

5. A: Where .... she live?

   B: I think she lives in Smith St.

6. A: .... they in France?

   B: No, they're in Greece.

7. A: How .... do you do the washing up?

   B: Every day.

8. A: .... your hair long?

   B: No, it's quite short.

9. .... do you do in the evenings?

10. .... you go to work on Saturdays?

3 Vocabulary – food groups   5 marks – 1 mark for each correct column

Put two words from the box under each column.

1 drink   2 salad   3 meat   4 vegetables 5 fruit

....

....

| pineapple   milk   peach   lettuce   potato |
| cucumber   chicken   carrot   fruit juice   beef |

4 Vocabulary – family and gender   5 marks

Write in the missing words.

Male   Female

1. man   and   ....

2. husband   and   ....

3. ....   and   sister

4. grandson   and   ....

5. ....   and   mother

5 A, an, any and short answer forms   10 marks

Choose either *a*, *an* or *any*. Then complete the short answers with one word.

Example: Have you got (*any*/*a*/*an*) brother?
     Yes, I _have_ .

1. Is there (*any*/*a*/*an*) rice in the kitchen?
   Yes, there ....

2. Have we got (*any*/*an*/*a*) old sweater for Maria?
   Yes, we ....

3. Do you eat (*any*/*a*/*an*) big meal in the evenings at home?   No, I ....

4. Is she (*any*/*a*/*an*) engineer?   No, she ....

5. Does the room have (*a*/*an*/*any*) bath?
   No, it ....

6 Prepositions   10 marks

Write *to*, *at*, *in*, *on* or *from* in the spaces.

I go (1)………. English classes twice a week, (2)……….
Wednesday and Friday. I always sit next (3)………. Carlos;
he's (4)………. Argentina. The class finishes (5)………. nine
and then we all go (6)………. the café (7)………. the end of
the street and talk (8)………. English.
(9)………. July there are many English tourists. They're
very noisy (10)………. the evenings.

7 Much *or* many   5 marks

Write *much* or *many* in the spaces in the conversation.

METTE: How (1)………………. money have you got?

HANS: I haven't got any.

METTE: Oh, well, there aren't (2)………………. things to
do in town on a Monday evening, so let's stay in and
watch a video.

HANS: Have you got (3)………………. videos?

METTE: Yes, lots.

HANS: Great! We can watch some horror films then.

METTE: I haven't got (4)………………. time. I start work
at the hospital at nine and there aren't (5)……………….
buses in the evening, so I usually leave here at eight.

8 Pronunciation – sentence and word stress   10 marks

Read each question. Circle the word or expression with
the main stress in each reply. Then underline the part of
that stressed word or expression with the strongest sound
Example: How old is your daughter?   She's (eleven).

Question	Reply
Can I help you?	1. Yes, I'd like some pineapples, please.
What's this behind here?	2. It's the toilet.
What does she do?	3. She's an electrician.
What time do you get up?	4. I get up at seven, usually.
Where's the radio?	5. There isn't a radio.

9 Possessive adjectives and genitive forms   5 marks

Study the sentences. Write a possessive adjective or an
apostrophe (') in the correct place.
Example: A: What does *your*………………. cousin do?
         B: He's a lawyer. My cousin's wife is an
            engineer.

1. I've got one sister and one brother. ……………….
   brother lives in Jersey.
2. The neighbours have a new car. It's Italian. They like
   ………………. car very much.
3. My parents house is in the Pyrenees.
4. You can leave ………………. bicycle in the garage.
5. My wifes boss comes from Nepal.

10 Changing sentences to negative form   5 marks

Change each sentence to its negative.
Example: I've got a brother.   **I haven't got a brother.**
                               Negative sentence

He likes coffee.   ……………………………………

There are some big trees
in our garden.   ……………………………………

She's got a new car.   ……………………………………

They're tired.   ……………………………………

I get up early on Sundays.   ……………………………………

11 Use of link words and adverbial expressions
                                              10 marks

Complete the text by putting *too*, *enough*, *both*, *or*,
because, *and* or *but* in the appropriate gaps. You will need
to use some words twice.

My new trousers are OK (1)………………. my new shoes
are (2)………………. big. Many of my clothes are brown,
black (3)………………. purple, (4)………………. dark
colours go with my dark hair. Every year I like to buy
one (5)………………. two thick sweaters made of wool. I
have two new, purple sweaters and (6)………………. of
them are very warm. It's not usually cold
(7)………………. here in winter for coats so I only wear
my old coat occasionally. I want some new jeans
(8)………………. my old jeans are (9)………………. small
for me now. I'd also like some new shirts (10)……………….
ties.

12 Identifying grammar   10 marks

Correct the mistake in each sentence.
Example: There ~~are~~ *is* some rice in the jar.

1. She like to go out a lot.
2. I like two cups of coffee, please.
3. There are some biscuit in this tin.
4. I buy shoes about three times year.
5. Where does she buy she clothes?
6. Its very easy to find a cheap restaurant here.
7. I think we're to kind to them.
8. I always make a cake big on her birthday.
9. How you spell that?
10. I drink a lot of water every days.

13 Vocabulary – head and face   5 marks
Write the correct words in the diagram.

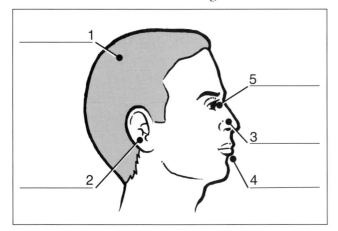

Total = 100 marks

1 Present simple and present continuous   10 marks
Fill in the gaps with the correct form of the verb in brackets.

Usually she (1)................................ (eat) anything but at the moment she (2).......................... (eat) only fruit and vegetables.

A: What (3)...................... (do)?

B: I (4)........................ (watch) TV. There's a good film on.

I (5)................................ (go) to Paris tomorrow.

Sometimes they (6)............................ (live) in Brazil, but right now they (7)........................... (travel) to the Himalayas. They (8)............................. (have) friends there.

The cost of living (9)......................... (go down) in Canada just now, but people still occasionally (10)............................ (complain) about the high price of food.

2 Vocabulary – opposites   10 marks
Write the opposites of the verbs in brackets in sentences 1–10.

Example: I like (to laugh) when I watch old films.
   to cry

1. I don't seem (to find) money very often.
   ....

2. My grandmother always wanted (to be born) at home. ....

3. It's easy (to like) my new job. ....

4. She's trying (to open) the front door. ....

5. I love (to spend) all my money. ....

6. Do you want (to ask) another question?
   ....

7. It's easy (to forget) the bad days. ....

8. They decided (to get up) at two in the morning.
   ....

9. Prices never seem (to go down) these days.
   ....

10. I want (to finish) this exercise now. ....

3 Vocabulary – compound nouns   5 marks
Draw a line from each word in list A to a word in list B to make a compound noun.

A	B
news	copier
frost	time
story	paper
hair	teller
lunch	bite
photo	style

4 Past tense forms   5 marks
Five of the underlined past tense forms in this text are wrong. Draw a circle around the wrong verbs. Write the correct forms below.

I once <u>knowed</u> a person with an old car. He <u>drove</u> it for years with no problem and then suddenly on a dark night the car <u>stoped</u>. He <u>rang</u> the only garage, 50 miles away. It <u>was</u> Sunday. The mechanic <u>was</u> not there. Then he <u>thinked</u> of an answer to his problem. He <u>shout</u> again and again in the dark, 'Is anybody there?' Finally someone <u>heared</u> him and <u>came</u> to help. It was the mechanic from the garage on his motorcycle. The mechanic <u>found</u> the problem: no petrol!

1. ....   4. ....
2. ....   5. ....
3. ....

5 Vocabulary – collocation   5 marks
Choose the correct verb in the sentences below.
Example: Please *bring*/take me a cup of coffee.

1. I'm *receiving/having* trouble with my car at the moment.

2. He never *makes/cooks* coffee for me in the morning.

3. It's a good idea to *begin/open* a bank account.

4. Please *fill in / write up* this form.

5. She *works for / works to* a company with international offices.

6 Question formation with various verb forms

10 marks

Unscramble these words to make questions and write the questions in the correct word order.

1. she Indian cook food can?

....

2. you bread the pass please could?

....

3. job like about what does his he?

....

4. did on they holiday when this go year?

....

5. to next study what we week are going?

....

6. born you were where?

....

7. party Saturday to coming you are my on?

....

8. in living like a flat you do?

....

9. summer anywhere they going are the in?

....

10. read five when could she was she?

....

7 Past tense forms and final sounds of irregular verbs

5 marks

Five of these verb pairs rhyme (have the same final sound) in their past tense forms; the others don't rhyme. Which ones rhyme?

1. hide – do
2. sing – bring
3. buy – teach
4. think – drink
5. speak – wake
6. call – crawl
7. say – read
8. leave – believe

8 Spelling and little slips   10 marks

Correct ten mistakes in this diary entry.

Tuesday September 10

Today was very unusual. Me sister Hanne arived from Norway. He was very cold and quiet ill. Perhaps she ate somthing bad on the boat.
My mother rang too say hello to Hanne. She seemed very happy. My father is in America and when he phoned yesterday from New York he had lots of news. The TV station is going to ask him to be there top news reporter. My mother think they are trying to made him do too much.

9 Use of the indefinite and definite article   6 marks

Put either *a* or *the* in each space.

I've got (1).......... dog. His name is Guy. He likes walking in parks so every day I take Guy to Green Park near my house. Sometimes there's (2).......... young woman in (3).......... park. She also has (4).......... dog. We often talk about our dogs. Her dog is very big with (5).......... long tail. She likes her dog very much because it helps her to feel safe. Her flat is in (6).......... centre of town. It can be dangerous at night there.

10 Vocabulary – membership of word groups   4 marks

In each group, find the word which is in the wrong word family.

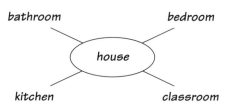

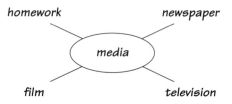

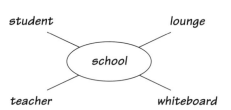

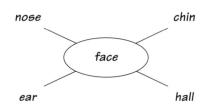

11 Use of can, could, I'd like *and* I like   10 marks

What did the other speaker say? Choose sentences from the box to complete each of these mini conversations.

1. A: ....
   B: No, I can't. I never learnt at school..

2. A: ....
   B: Me too. More fun, aren't they?

3. A: Is it OK to have one here?
   B: ....

4. A: ....
   B: Yes, of course. Here you are.

5. A: Can I get you a drink?
   B: ....

6. A: ....
   B: OK. What does it like?

7. A: ....
   B: Would you? Really? I wouldn't.

8. A: ....
   B: Can you? Which ones?

9. A: How's Jane these days?
   B: ....

10. A: ....
    B: Seventeen, I think.

She loves her new job.
One day, I'd like to have a child.
No, but you can smoke in that part of the restaurant.
I'd like a cup of coffee, please.
Could you pass the water?
At what age can you drive in your country?
I can speak three languages.
Can you swim?
Can you come and feed the cat?
I like happy people.

---

12 Connecting expressions   10 marks

Put each of these expressions in an appropriate place in the text.

---

when   but   at the moment   now   ago   because
as well   so   then   also

I was very tall (1)...................... I was young
(2)...................... my friends always called me 'Mr Big'.
Each time a ball went into a tree they asked me to get it
(3)...................... it was easy for me to reach up. I could
(4)...................... get things from the top shelves of the
cupboard in the classroom. (5)...................... I don't seem
so tall; most of my friends are tall (6)...................... .

Two years (7)...................... I broke both my legs in
car accident. I spent six weeks in hospital and
(8)...................... another two weeks at home. Last
year I broke my arm in a game of soccer. Last week I
broke my finger (9)...................... this week
everything is OK – (10)......................!

13 Short answer forms   10 marks

Complete the answers using the short form.
Example: Is he Italian? No, he *isn't*.............. .

1. Can they swim? No, they ....
2. Would you like to have white hair? No, we
   ....
3. Are you singing that new song? Yes, I
   ....
4. Do you like dancing? Yes, I ....
5. Is she going to work tomorrow? Yes, she
   ....
6. Did he miss you? No, he ....
7. Was she a lively child? Yes, she ....
8. Are they trying to get into the shop? Yes, they
   ....
9. Does she think they're interested in the house? Yes,
   she ....
10. Are you going to buy some rice for the party? No, I
    ....

Total = 100 marks

TEST 3 UNITS 13–18

1 Comparative and superlative adjectives   10 marks

Complete the table below. The first line has been done for you.

adjective	comparative adjective	superlative adjective
nice	*nicer*	nicest
quick	....	quickest
big	....	....
bad	....	worst
....	better	....
expensive	....	....
....	more exciting	....

2 Characteristics of cities – vocabulary and grammar

8 marks

Read the passage below. In each set of brackets cross out the word which does not fit.

Bangkok – the city of angels

Have you been to Bangkok, the capital of Thailand? It is a city which some people hate but which many others love. The first thing you notice is the traffic. There are so many cars and buses that things move very (*slow/slowly*). It would be faster to walk but the weather is hot and the air is (*pollution/polluted*) with exhaust fumes. In the streets you have to fight your way through hundreds of people. Everywhere is very (*crowds/crowded*).

It sounds terrible but, for many people, Bangkok is the (*lively/liveliest*) city on Earth. There is always something happening. It is also full of (*interesting/interested*) things to see. Around every corner you will find a (*beautiful/beautifully*) temple or a busy street market where things are (*cheaper/cheapest*) than in the shops.

Whether you love it or hate it – you'll always (*remembering/remember*) Bangkok!

3 Collocations   10 marks

Choose a word from the box below to fill each gap. You will have to use some words more than once.

play   have   go   feel

1. I like to .... swimming every week.
2. I can't swim today because I .... a bad cold.
3. Do you want to .... tennis? No, I .... too tired.
4. Do you .... sailing? Yes, but I .... a bad back.
5. I .... a sore throat, but I can still .... golf.
6. I .... horse riding and then I .... relaxed.

4 Short forms of **have** and **have not**   6 marks

Complete the responses using the short form. The first one has been done for you.

1. Have you tried it?   Yes, *I've* .... tried it.
2. Have they brought it?   Yes, ... brought it.
3. Has he saved it?   Yes, ... saved it.
4. Has she lost it?   Yes, ... lost it.
5. Have you tasted it?   No, ... tasted it.
6. Have they found it?   No, ... found it.
7. Has she written it?   No, ... written it.

5 Asking questions   6 marks

Write the correct forms of the verb in brackets in the gaps.

1. Do you keep .... your keys?   (lose)
2. Have you ever .... your purse?   (lose)
3. Do you sometimes .... your passport? (forget)
4. Have you ever .... where you are? (forget)
5. Have you ever .... your umbrella on the bus?   (leave)
6. Do you ever .... your computer on? (leave)

6 Prefixes   8 marks

Tick (✔) to show whether these words take *un*, *in*, or *im* to make their opposites. For example, *tidy* takes *un* to become *untidy*.

	un	in	im
tidy	✔	......	......
expensive	......	......	......
safe	......	......	......
polite	......	......	......
happy	......	......	......
formal	......	......	......
helpful	......	......	......
patient	......	......	......
convenient	......	......	......

7 –ing forms of verbs   6 marks

Complete the sentences using the correct form of the verbs given in brackets.

1. After .... out of bed, I shower and get dressed.   (get)
2. I always clean my teeth before .... to bed. (go)
3. A fax machine is great for .... urgent messages.   (send)
4. I am not very good at .... my time. (manage)
5. I don't like .... reports.   (write)
6. He is always .... things in the wrong place.   (put)

8 Relative pronouns   8 marks

Complete these sentences using the words in the box.

> when   when   who   who   that   which   where
> where

1. I saw the girl .... delivers the newspapers.
2. I remember the car .... you sold to Paul.
3. The office .... she works is in the centre of town.
4. I know the man .... works in the bank.
5. The letters .... they wrote were full of mistakes.
6. That was the week .... I was in hospital.
7. Rice grows in countries .... there is a lot of rain.
8. Was that the time .... we got lost

9 Vocabulary – the neighbourhood   6 marks

What are they talking about? Choose your answers from the box below.

> library   supermarket   bank   petrol station
> cinema   restaurant   corner shop   police station
> café

1. 'They serve beautiful food but it is very expensive.'

   ....

2. 'I need to pay in a cheque.'

   ....

3. 'You can get all your shopping in one place.'

   ....

4. 'I often drop in for a quick cup of tea and a snack.'

   ....

5. 'It's a bit more expensive than the big shops but the service is better.'

   ....

6. 'I must fill up the car and check the oil.'

   ....

10 Adverbs   6 marks

Write an adverb in each gap so that the second sentence means the same as the first sentence.

1. He makes a noise when he eats.
   He eats ....
2. She is a quick thinker.
   She thinks ....
3. He was very polite when he asked.
   He asked ....
4. She is confident on a horse.
   She rides ....

5. He is careful when he drives.
   He drives ....
6. The baby is happy when she plays.
   The baby plays ....

11 Giving directions   10 marks

Look at this map.

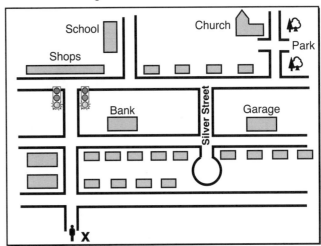

Fill in the gaps in the sentences to give directions from X to the park.

'To get to the park, go (1)..................... ahead until you reach the traffic lights. Turn (2)..................... Take the (3)..................... turning on your (4).................... and you will see it. It is (5)..................... the church.'

Fill in the gaps in the sentences to give directions from X to the garage.

'To get to the garage, take the (6)..................... turning on the (7)..................... . Go (8)..................... the bank. (9)..................... Silver Street and you will see the garage on your (10)..................... .'

12 Obligations and recommendations   6 marks

Write *should*, *shouldn't* or *have to* in each gap so that the second sentence means the same as the first sentence.

1. You can't visit China without a visa.
   You .... have a visa to visit China.
2. It is a good idea to take some cash.
   You .... take some cash.
3. It is not sensible to travel alone.
   You .... travel alone.
4. You can't travel without a passport.
   You .... have a passport to travel.
5. Shoes are not allowed indoors.
   You .... take off your shoes.
6. See the palace if you can.
   You .... see the palace.

13 Connecting words of sequence   10 marks
The diagrams show how to make soup from a packet.

Use the words in the box to complete the instructions below. Number the sentences to show the right order.

Finally   Then/Next   After   First

Number	Instruction
....	.... put the soup powder in a cup.
....	.... drink the soup.
....	.... pour on the boiling water and stir.
....	.... boil some water.
....	.... that wait for five minutes.

Total = 100 marks

TEST 4 UNITS 19–24

1 Using would and would not   6 marks
Complete the sentences using the phrases in the box.

| I'd be   I'd like   I'd like to   I would |
I wouldn't like to   I wouldn't

1. For dessert .... a piece of chocolate cake.
2. Would you like a cup of tea? Yes, please,
   ....
3. I like France but .... live there.
4. When I finish college .... be a teacher.

5. If I went on a boat .... seasick.
6. Would you like to be a traffic warden? No,
   ....

2 Vocabulary – expressions with time   8 marks
Complete these sentences using *for*, *to* or *with*.

1. I'd like to have more time .... play tennis.
2. I want to spend more time .... my family.
3. I always have time .... a friend.
4. I need more time .... finish my work.
5. We just had time .... a drink.
6. You need more time .... relax.
7. They spend a lot of time .... their children.
8. I just need time .... think.

3 Making apologies   6 marks
Match each situation with a suitable apology.

1. You didn't do your homework.
2. You don't agree with your friend.
3. You bumped into someone.
4. You're late for work.
5. You knocked over someone's tea in a café.
6. You can't go to a friend's wedding.

a. I'm sorry, I missed the bus.
b. I'm sorry, I wasn't watching where I was going.
c. I'm sorry, I just didn't have time.
d. I'm sorry but I'll be on holiday then.
e. I'm sorry, can I buy you another one?
f. I'm sorry but I think you're wrong.

4 Vocabulary – nouns and adjectives   10 marks
Read the passage below. In each set of brackets cross out the word which does not fit.

I am learning to drive but I don't have much (confident/confidence). My first instructor was (impatient/impatience). I tried to drive with (care/careful) but he made me so nervous that my driving was (dangerous/danger). We were (lucky/luck) that we didn't have an (accidental/accident)!

My new instructor is (kindness/kind) and doesn't get angry at my (stupidity/stupid). She is calm and that is very (importance/important) to me. My driving is getting better every day and I am (certain/certainty) that I will pass my test next month.

5 Complaining   9 marks

Complete the following conversation by writing one word in each gap. Then answer questions (a) and (b) underneath.

CUSTOMER: Excuse me. Can you (1) .... me? I bought this suit yesterday but when I got it home I (2) .... a small hole in the jacket.

SHOP ASSISTANT: Let me see. Oh, yes. Are you (3) .... it was like this when you bought it?

CUSTOMER: Yes, I'm certain. I saw it as (4) .... as I took it out of the bag.

SHOP ASSISTANT: Well you should have checked it more (5) .... in the shop, shouldn't you?

CUSTOMER: Perhaps, but now I'd like my (6) .... back, please.

SHOP ASSISTANT: We don't give refunds.

CUSTOMER: I'm sorry but I am not satisfied. I want to speak to the person in charge. Please call the (7) ....

a. Was the customer rude or polite? ....

b. Was the shop assistant helpful or unhelpful?

....

6 Using need and want   8 marks

Complete these sentences using the words in the box.

| need (2)   needs   needn't (2)   want (2)   wants |

1. I'm afraid you .... an operation on your wrist.
2. What sort of party does she .... for her birthday?
3. My car .... new tyres.
4. She's got plenty of dresses but she .... a new one for the dance.
5. I'll be a couple of hours so you .... wait.
6. You must have a passport and you will also .... a visa.
7. Do you .... another cup of coffee?
8. This one can be mended so you .... buy a new one.

7 Reading – attitudes to money   10 marks

Read this passage carefully. Then decide whether the statements below it are true (T) or false (F), or if you can't be sure because the passage doesn't say (?). Show your answer by ticking the right box.

My name is Tom. I am a road sweeper and I wouldn't change my job for all the money in the world. I don't get paid very much but money isn't everything. I enjoy working outside – except when it's wet. I like meeting people and I like being able to spend time with my family. Of course a little more money would be nice. We have to be careful about what we spend, but we have a comfortable home, a small car and we have a holiday every other year. We don't really need anything else.

Most of my friends work in offices. They are on high salaries but they are always stressed. They just can't relax. Me? I don't worry about anything. I also get a lot of job satisfaction. When I clean a street I do it properly. I feel really good when I look back and there's not a cigarette packet or a piece of paper to be seen.

Statement	T	F	?
1. Tom is happy in his work.	☐	☐	☐
2. Tom likes working in the rain.	☐	☐	☐
3. Tom thinks he has plenty of money.	☐	☐	☐
4. Tom would like a bigger car.	☐	☐	☐
5. Tom worries about money.	☐	☐	☐
6. Tom's friends earn more than he does.	☐	☐	☐
7. Tom is going on holiday this year.	☐	☐	☐
8. Tom would prefer to work in an office.	☐	☐	☐
9. Tom is proud of his work.	☐	☐	☐
10. Tom smokes cigarettes.	☐	☐	☐

8 Vocabulary – the weather   8 marks

What will the weather be like? Choose the most appropriate symbol and write the letter A, B, C or D. next to each statement.

A   B   C   D

1. 'There will be violent thunder storms in the east today.' ....
2. 'It's going to be boiling hot today without a cloud in the sky.' ....
3. 'Temperatures will be below freezing so watch out for ice on the roads.' ....
4. 'Remember, don't shelter under a tree if there is the possibility of lightning.' ....
5. 'We can expect heavy showers throughout the day.' ....
6. 'Good news for skiers – heavy snow will fall for the next three days.' ....
7. 'Please take care and protect yourself from harmful ultraviolet radiation.' ....
8. 'I think you'd better take your umbrella.' ....

9 Vocabulary – celebrations   10 marks

What are they talking about? Choose your answers from the box below.

> holiday   present   party   birthday   greeting   commercialism   invitation   tradition   feast   festival

1. 'At Christmas the shops just want to make as much money as possible.' ....
2. 'It's important to keep customs alive by doing things in the old ways.' ....
3. 'It was just what I wanted and so beautifully wrapped.' ....
4. 'Thanks for the card but I don't feel any older than I did yesterday!' ....
5. 'There was so much food and drink that we couldn't eat it all.' ....
6. 'I'm not religious but I'm glad to have a day off work.' ....
7. 'It goes on for days with processions in the streets and parties every night.' ....
8. 'Sometimes I send a letter, but usually I just phone my friends and ask them if they would like to come.' ....
9. 'We went round to Paolo's house. There was plenty of food and drink, and we danced to his new jazz records.' ....
10. 'The first thing he says is always "Happy Christmas".' ....

10 Accepting and declining   10 marks

These are parts of replies to an invitation to a party. Is the person accepting or declining the invitation? Put a tick (✔) or a cross (✗) to show your answer.

	Accept ✔ or Decline ✗
1. Thanks, I'd love to.	
2. Unfortunately I can't …	
3. I'm afraid I won't be able to …	
4. I am looking forward to it.	
5. I'll be away then so …	
6. I'd love to but …	
7. I'll see you then.	
8. I apologise but I've already …	
9. Shall I bring some …	
10. I'll be there!	

11 Short forms of will and will not   8 marks

Complete the responses using the short form. The first one has been done for you.

1. Will you do the washing up?   Yes, *I'll* .... do it later.
2. Will they be here soon?   Yes, ... be here at two o'clock.
3. Will he write the letter?   Yes, ... write it.
4. Will she get the job?   Yes, ... get it.
5. Will you be at the party?   No, ... be there.
6. Will they pay you?   No, ... pay me.
7. Will she say sorry?   No, ... apologise.
8. Will we see Peter today?   Yes, ... see him this evening.
9. Will you take the dog for a walk?   Yes, ... take him right now.

12 Talking about the future   7 marks

All these sentences are about the future. For each one decide whether it uses the present simple tense, the future simple tense, or the present continuous tense. The first three have been done for you.

	Present Simple	Future Simple	Present Continuous
1. I hope to have a holiday next year.	✔		
2. I will need to study hard.		✔	
3. I'm going to Japan in June.			✔
4. She will need to be very fit.			
5. I want to be a pilot when I leave college.			
6. I hope to see you at the party.			
7. I will be 40 next year.			
8. He is leaving in two weeks.			
9. You will marry a rich woman.			
10. They will be back in three years.			

Total = 100 marks

TEST ANSWER KEYS

TEST 1

1 Numbers and times

Numbers	Times
thirty-one	five o'clock
sixty-six	seven fifteen / a quarter past seven
twenty	eleven thirty / half past eleven
ninety-nine	nine forty-five / a quarter to ten
eleven	five (minutes) past eight

2 Question construction

1. do   2. What   3. How   4. got   5. does   6. Are
7. often   8. Is   9. What   10. Do

3 Vocabulary – food groups

1. drink – milk, fruit juice
2. salad – lettuce, cucumber
3. meat – beef, chicken
4. vegetables – potato, carrot
5. fruit – pineapple, peach

4 Vocabulary – family and gender

1. woman   2. wife   3. brother   4. granddaughter
5. father

5 A, an, any and short answer forms

1. any (rice)   Yes, there is.
2. an (old sweater)   Yes, we have.
3. a (big meal)   No, I don't.
4. an (engineer)   No, she isn't.
5. a (bath)   No, it doesn't.

6 Prepositions

1. to   2. on   3. to   4. from   5. at   6. to   7. at   8. in
9. In   10. in

7 Much or many

1. much   2. many   3. many   4. much   5. many

8 Pronunciation – sentence and word stress

1. Yes, I'd like some p<u>i</u>neapples, please.
2. It's the t<u>oi</u>let.
3. She's an electr<u>i</u>cian.
4. I get up at s<u>e</u>ven, usually.
5. There <u>is</u>n't a radio.

9 Possessive adjectives and genitive forms

1. My   2. their   3. parents'   4. your   5. wife's

10 Changing sentences to negative form

1. He doesn't like coffee.
2. There aren't any big trees in our garden.
3. She hasn't got a new car.
4. They aren't tired.
5. I don't get up early on Sundays.

11 Use of link words and adverbial expressions

1. but   2. too   3. and   4. because   5. or   6. both
7. enough   8. because   9. too   10. and

12 Identifying grammar

1. She like**s** to go out a lot.
2. I**'d** like two cups of coffee, please.
3. There are some biscuit**s** in this tin.
4. I buy shoes about three times **a** year.
5. Where does she buy **her** clothes?
6. It's very easy to find a cheap restaurant here.
7. I think we're to**o** kind to them.
8. I always make a **big cake** on her birthday.
9. How **do** you spell that?
10. I drink a lot of water every **day**.

13 Vocabulary – head and face

1. hair   2. ear   3. nose   4. mouth   5. eye

TEST 2

1 Present simple and present continuous

1. eats   2. 's eating / is eating   3. are you doing
4. 'm watching / am watching   5. 'm going / am going
6. live   7. are travelling   8. have   9. is going down
10. complain

2 Vocabulary – opposites

1. to lose   2. to die   3. to hate (dislike)   4. to close
5. to save   6. to answer   7. to remember   8. to go to bed
9. to go up   10. to start

3 Vocabulary – compound nouns

frostbite   storyteller   hairstyle   lunchtime   photocopier

4 Past tense forms

1. knew   2. stopped   3. thought   4. shouted   5. heard

5 Vocabulary – collocation

1. having (trouble)   2. makes (coffee)
3. open (a bank account)   4. fill in (this form)
5. works for (a company)

6 Question formation with various verb forms

1. Can she cook Indian food?
2. Could you pass the bread, please?
3. What does he like about his job?
4. When did they go on holiday this year?
5. What are we going to study next week?
6. Where were you born?
7. Are you coming to my party on Saturday?
8. Do you like living in a flat?
9. Are you going anywhere in the summer?
10. Could she read when she was five?

7 Past tense forms and final sounds of irregular verbs

1. hide (hid) / do (did)
3. buy (bought) / teach (taught)
5. speak (spoke) / wake (woke)
6. call (called) / crawl (crawled)
7. say (said) / read (read)

8 Spelling and little slips

Today was very unusual. **My** sister Hanne ar**r**ived from Norway. **She** was very cold and **quite** ill. Perhap**s** she ate som**e**thing bad on the boat.
My mother rang **to** say hello to Hanne. She seemed very happy. My father is in America and when he phoned yesterday from New York he had lots of news. The TV station is going to ask him to be **their** top news reporter. My mother think**s** they are trying to ma**k**e him do too much.

9 Use of the indefinite and definite article

1. a   2. a   3. the   4. a   5. a   6. the

10 Vocabulary – membership of word groups

house – classroom
media – homework
school – lounge
face – hall

11 Ability, wish, ordering, liking, permission

1. Can you swim?
2. I like happy people
3. No, but you can smoke in that part of the restaurant.
4. Could you pass the water?
5. I'd like a cup of coffee, please.
6. Can you come and feed the cat?
7. One day, I'd like to have a child.
8. I can speak three languages.
9. She loves her new job.
10. At what age can you drive in your country?

12 Connecting expressions

1. when   2. so   3. because   4. also   5. Now   6. as well
7. ago   8. then   9. but   10. at the moment

13 Short answer forms

1. can't   2. wouldn't   3. am   4. do   5. is   6. didn't
7. was   8. are   9. does   10. (I)'m not

TEST 3

1 Comparative and superlative adjectives

quicker
bigger; biggest
worse
good; best
more expensive; most expensive
exciting; most exciting

2 Characteristics of cities – vocabulary and grammar

slow/slowly; pollution/polluted; crowds/crowded;
lively/liveliest; interesting/interested; beautiful/beautifully;
cheaper/cheapest; remembering/remember

3 Collocations

1. go   2. have   3. play; feel   4. go; have   5. have; play
6. go; feel

4 Short forms of **have** and **have not**

2. they've   3. he's   4. she's   5. I haven't / I've not
6. they haven't / they've not   7. she hasn't / she's not

5 Asking questions

1. losing   2. lost   3. forget   4. forgotten   5. left
6. leave

6 Prefixes

	un	in	im
expensive		✓	
safe	✓		
polite			✓
happy	✓		
formal		✓	
helpful	✓		
patient			✓
convenient		✓	

7 -ing forms of verbs

1. getting   2. going   3. sending   4. managing
5. writing   6. putting

8 Relative pronouns

1. who/that   2. that/which   3. where   4. who/that
5. which/that   6. when   7. where   8. when

9 Vocabulary – the neighbourhood

1. restaurant   2. bank   3. supermarket   4. café
5. corner shop   6. petrol station

10 Adverbs

1. noisily   2. quickly   3. politely   4. confidently
5. carefully   6. happily

11 Giving directions

1. straight   2. right   3. second   4. left   5. opposite
6. second   7. right   8. past   9. Cross   10. left

12 Obligations and recommendationss

1. You have to have a visa to visit China.
2. You should take some cash.
3. You shouldn't travel alone.
4. You have to have a passport to travel.
5. You have to take off your shoes.
6. You should see the palace.

13 Connecting words of sequence

Number	Instruction
2	Then/Next put the soup powder in a cup.
5	Finally drink the soup.
3	Next/Then pour on the boiling water and stir.
1	First boil some water.
4	After that wait for five minutes.

1 *Using* would *and* would not
1. I'd like   2. I would   3. I wouldn't like to   4. I'd like to
5. I'd be   6. I wouldn't

2 *Vocabulary – expressions with time*
1. to   2. with   3. for   4. to   5. for   6. to   7. with
8. to

3 *Making apologies*
1. c   2. f   3. b   4. a   5. e   6. d

4 *Vocabulary – nouns and adjectives*
~~confident~~/confidence; impatient/~~impatience~~; care/~~careful~~;
dangerous/~~danger~~; lucky/~~luck~~; ~~accidental~~/accident;
~~kindness~~/kind; stupidity/~~stupid~~; ~~importance~~/important;
certain/~~certainty~~

5 *Complaining*
1. help   2. found/saw/discovered   3. sure/certain
4. soon   5. carefully/thoroughly   6. money   7. manager
a. polite   b. unhelpful

6 *Using* need *and* want
1. need   2. want   3. needs   4. wants   5. needn't
6. need   7. want   8. needn't

7 *Reading – attitudes to money*
1. true   2. false   3. false   4. doesn't say   5. false   6. true
7. doesn't say   8. false   9. true   10. doesn't say

8 *Vocabulary – the weather*
1. C   2. A   3. D   4. C   5. B   6. D   7. A   8. B

9 *Vocabulary – celebrations*
1. commercialism   2. tradition   3. present   4. birthday
5. feast   6. holiday   7. festival   8. invitation   9. party
10. greeting

10 *Accepting and declining*
1. ✓   2. ✗   3. ✗   4. ✓   5. ✗   6. ✗   7. ✓   8. ✗   9. ✓
10. ✓

11 *Short forms of* will *and* will not
2. they'll   3. he'll   4. she'll   5. I won't   6. they won't
7. she won't   8. we'll   9. I'll

13 *Talking about the future*
4. future simple   5. present simple   6. present simple
7. future simple   8. present continuous   9. future simple
10. future simple

QUICK CHECK EXERCISES

Unit 1 Lesson A QUICK CHECK

(i) Put the words in the right column.

a .... an ....
a .... an ....
a .... an ....

> accountant   secretary   doctor
> engineer   parent   optician

(ii) Complete the sentences.

Short forms
What...... your name?
I'm a waitress.
He...... a mechanic.
She's a nurse.

Long forms
What is your name?
I .... a waitress.
He is a mechanic.
She .... a nurse.

Is your name Lee? Yes, it ....
Is she a teacher? Yes, she ....

A: What's .... name?
B: Juanita. And is your name Paul?
A: Yes, it .... 's your address?
B: It' .... 34 South Parade.
A: What do you do?
B: .... a dentist. What do you .... ?
A: Oh, I'm .... electrician.

Unit 1 Lesson B QUICK CHECK

(i) Write the short forms.

Long forms
There is a light.
There is not a light.

Short forms
.... a light.
There .... a light.

(ii) Complete the sentences.

A: Is .... a computer in the building?
B: Yes, there ....
A: .... there an information desk?
B: No, there ....
A: Are there .... parking spaces?
B: Yes, there ....
A: Are .... public telephones?
B: No, ...

Unit 1 Lesson C QUICK CHECK

(i) Put the words in the box into the right column.

Adjective	Noun
....	....
....	....
....	....
....	....
....	....
....	....
....	....

> `chair   good   comfortable   main
> free   thing   people   new   time
> job   interesting   important

(ii) Complete the sentences, using a word from the box.

1. The .... thing in my life is my family.
2. A comfortable .... is important in an office.
3. A lot of .... time is important to my happiness.
4. What about my job? It's ....

(iii) Look at the sentences. Complete them.

1. Petra is a nurse.
2. People work for money.
3. An interesting job is important for Ben.

The subject in sentence 1 is Petra.
The subject in sentence 2 is ....
The subject in sentence 3 is ....
Find two verbs: ....
Which sentence has two adjectives? ....

TRUE TO LIFE ELEMENTARY   © Cambridge University Press 1995

QUICK CHECK EXERCISES

(i) Look at the examples and the rules below. Use the words in the box to complete the gaps.

Example: We've got .... friends in the U.S.A.
Use *some* with plural nouns, in .... sentences.
Example: Have you got .... friends in Mexico?
We haven't got .... friends in Mexico.
Use *any* with plural nouns, in negative sentences and in ....

any	some	positive	questions	any

(ii) Complete the sentences.

1. Have you got .... sister in another country? Yes, I ....
2. .... you .... any cousins in another country? No, I ....
3. This is my friend John. ....'s got a brother in Rio.
4. This is my friend Mary. ....'s got a sister in Italy.
5. We'................ a friend in Brazil. We .... got any friends in Africa.
6. They've got .... friends in America. They haven't got .... cousins in Europe.

(iii) Complete the sentences with *and* or *but*.

1. She's got some friends in Canada .... a pen friend in Edinburgh.
2. He hasn't got any daughters .... he's got two sons.
3. They've got cousins in America .... in New Zealand.
4. They've got a lot of friends .... they haven't got any cousins.

(i) Study the example, then complete the rule.

Example: She's got a television set, some plants and some money.
Use *a* with a singular ....
Use .... with plural nouns – and with the noun money.

(ii) Put the words in the box into the right column.

Singular noun   *Plural noun*

child	sisters	country	radio
knives	family	woman	sons
sister	men	computer	families
man	radios	women	knife
countries	son	children	computers

(ii) Complete the sentences.

W............ have you got in your bag? I've got .... pen and .... money.
How many phones .... you ....? I .... got any.
How many plants .... he got? .... got three.
H............ .... books has she got? She's got lots.
I *have got* is the long form. .... is the short form.
She .... got is the long form. .... is the short form.
They have .... is the long form. .... is the short form.

Put the words in the right order.

1. your got What motorhome has?
2. and little a bed big It's four got beds.
3. is kitchen My room the favourite.
4. over some sink We've the plants got.

Complete the sentences.

A: What .... you have for breakfast?
B: Just some coffee .... some toast. What .... you?
A: I .... tea and some cereal.

C: What .... would you like breakfast?
D: .... eight, please.
C: .... would you like?
D: .... like .... coffee and toast, please.

What are the missing words?

Example: *What's your favourite* .....*drink*.......... *? Tea.*

1. What's your favourite .... ? Carrots.
2. What's your favourite .... ? Peaches.
3. What's your favourite .... ? Salmon.
4. What's your favourite .... ? Lamb.

Unit 3   Lesson C   QUICK CHECK

Find five mistakes and correct them.

A: How many is milk? Is it expensive?
B: No, it isn't. It about 50 pence a pint.
A: How much is eggs?
B: They're £1 for 6.
A: What about rice? Are they cheap and expensive?
B: It's not expensive at all – it's very cheap.

Unit 4   Lesson A   QUICK CHECK

(i) Complete the sentences.

1. My red shirt is .... Poland. It's got a label: 100% cotton, made .... Poland.
2. My tie's made .... silk. .... green.
3. Julia's got a blue jacket made .... Scotland. It's made .... wool and it's quite formal. She's also got a casual jacket for summer, made .... cotton.

(ii) Study the examples and complete the list.

Examples: *clothes for children = children's clothes*
a skirt belonging to Julia = Julia's skirt

1. Clothes for men = ...
2. A tie for a man = ...
3. A shirt belonging to Mark = ...
4. Clothes for women = ...
5. A dress for a woman = ...
6. Shoes belonging to Suheila = ...

Unit 4   Lesson B   QUICK CHECK

Match the questions with the right answers.

1. Where do you buy T-shirts?
2. Why do you buy hats at the market?
3. How often do you buy shoes?
4. Where does Lee buy ties?

a. Because they're cheap.
b. I buy them at the market.
c. In the duty-free shop.
d. Twice a year.

Unit 4   Lesson C   QUICK CHECK

Complete these sentences using each verb once. Use the right form of the verb in the sentence.

give	receive	say	mean

1. He .... his wife roses on her birthday.
2. Scientists .... that blue roses are ready for the flower shops.
3. A red rose .... *I love you* in Canada.
4. I never .... flowers on Father's Day.

Unit 5   Lesson A   QUICK CHECK

Complete the sentences.

A: Do you .... up quickly in the morning?
B: Yes, I .... What about you?
A: No, I .... Not usually. I wake up, but I don't get .... right away. My wife .... up slowly too. I .... a shower first. Then my wife .... a shower. I get dressed, she .... dressed, and then we .... our breakfast together.

Unit 5   Lesson B   QUICK CHECK

Put the words in the right order.

1. use   you   your   Do   dictionary?   do   Yes   I.
2. songs   she   Does   to   English   listen?   she   No   doesn't.
3. words   new   Do   write   you   down?   do   I   Yes.
4. you   do   often   How   eat   bed   in?   Sometimes.
5. she   up   How   does   often   wash?   Quite   often.
6. the   sleep   does   on   with   often   he   How   lights?   Never.

TRUE TO LIFE ELEMENTARY   © Cambridge University Press 1995

QUICK CHECK EXERCISES

(i) Read the answers. Write the questions.

1. ....?
   I go shopping once a week.
2. ....?
   I buy food at the supermarket.
3. ....?
   No, I never stand in queues.
4. ....?
   I buy food twice a week.

(ii) Read the statements. Write the opposite.

Example: *I join the queue.* **I don't join the queue.**

1. I talk in English a lot.
   ....

2. She sings English songs.
   ....

3. Men shake hands in my country.
   ....

4. Sven goes shopping every week.
   ....

(i) Read the dialogues. Choose a or b.

1. A: I think he's lively.
   B: Me too.
   Does *Me too* mean:
   a. I think so a lot. *or* b. I think the same as you do.
2. A: I think you're very serious, Lynn.
   B: I think so too.
   Does *I think so too* mean:
   a. I think the same as you do. *or* b. I think a different thing from you.
3. A: Jim, I think you're artistic.
   B: No, I'm a practical person, really.
   Does *I'm a practical person, really* mean:
   a. I'm very practical. *or* b. I think a different thing from you: I think I'm practical.

(ii) Complete the sentences.

Example: My ears are not large, they're ...*small*........ .

1. My friend is not shy. She's ....
2. Your son is not selfish. He's ....
3. My daughter's young, but my grandmother's
   ....
4. His friend always seems sad. He's not very
   ....
5. You have a wide forehead, but your brother has a
   .... forehead.

Read each sentence. Is it similar to a or b?

1. Her skirt is too short.
   a. Her skirt is not long enough.
   b. Her skirt is quite short.
2. He has very short hair.
   a. His hair is too short.
   b. His hair is not very long.
3. These gloves are too big for me.
   a. My hands are too big for the gloves.
   b. My hands are too small for the gloves.
4. My boss is not very old at all.
   a. My boss is not old enough.
   b. My boss is quite young.
5. Your son is too shy.
   a. Your son is not confident enough.
   b. Your son is a very shy person.
6. Your clothes are too casual.
   a. Your clothes are not formal enough.
   b. Your clothes are very casual.

(i) Write down what you say if you agree with the sentences.

1. I think it's important for a friend to be kind.
   You agree: ....
2. She's very interested in rock music.
   You agree: ....

(ii) Find words in the ads which mean the same as:

A man with *long hair* = a ....-................. man.
A person who *doesn't smoke* = a ....-................. .

(i) Choose the right answer, a or b.

1. How often does he play the guitar?
   a. Yes, he can play the guitar.
   b. He plays the guitar every night.
2. Can she play a musical instrument?
   a. She can play the piano, but she never does.
   b. She can repair musical instruments.
3. Where does he repair his car?
   a. He can repair a car.
   b. He repairs it in his garage.
4. Can he use a computer?
   a. No, he can't.
   b. His computer's at home.

(ii) Write the questions.

1. ....?
   Yes, he can play the drums.
2. ....?
   Of course I can cook. I'm a very good cook!
3. ....?
   My mother can type very fast.

Study the three uses of *can*.

Use *can* to talk about:
1. ability/skill
2. permission
3. request – use *can* or *could* (the past form of *can*)

Read the sentences. Are they examples of 1, 2 or 3?

1. Maria can play the piano. ....
2. Can you drive me home, please? ....
3. You can get married at 16 in my country. ....
4. She can play the saxophone, but she doesn't do it often. ....
5. People can vote at the age of 18. ....
6. Can I have a kilo of apples? ....
7. If the secretary says yes, you can use the photocopier. ....
8. Can the secretary type fast? ....
9. Could you help me, please? ....

Complete the sentences.

1. I go to work now – as a child I .... to school.
2. He goes to work now – as a child he .... to school.
3. A: Tell me about your past. .... you a happy child?
   B: Yes I .... very happy.
4. I can't remember numbers now, but I .... remember them when I was a child.
5. When Jim was young, he .... a lot of problems at school. Now he doesn't have any at all in his job!

Match the questions and answers.

1. What do you like about your city?
2. What don't you like about your city?
3. What do you know about Alaska?
4. What's your opinion of the people in this city?
5. What do you think of our nightclubs?

a. Not much, but I think it's beautiful.
b. I hate the traffic and the pollution.
c. They're wonderful.
d. I like the restaurants and the nightlife.
e. I think they're very polite and friendly.

Complete the sentences.

A: I hate my job.
B: What .... you like .... it?
A: I don't like .... at night. I like .... with people, but in this job I work with machines. I hate .... with machines all the time! But I like the pay.

Unit 8 Lesson C   QUICK CHECK

(i) Choose an expression from the box. Complete the sentences.

I don't like insects, and I just hate .... But I love .... I like .... with my dog but I don't like .... for a walk with her. She runs around the park a lot and I don't like .... for her.

waiting	flies	going	my dog
playing			

(ii) Match each answer with the right question from the box. Questions 5 and 6 are missing. Write them.

1. ....?
   Yes, I had a cat.
2. ....?
   Minny.
3. ....?
   Fish, bread – and milk.
4. ....?
   In a box beside the window.
5. ....?
   No, my mother didn't like it.
6. ....?
   It was not very friendly.

What did it eat?   What was its name?
Where did it sleep?
When you were a child, did you have a pet?

Unit 9 Lesson A   QUICK CHECK

Complete the answers.

Example: *Where was your school? It was in the city.*

1. What did you have for lunch yesterday? I .... soup.
2. Was it a big school? No, it .... very small.
3. What was the name of your friend? It .... Abbi.
4. Was she clever? No, she .... but she .... very nice.
5. What did you do together? We .... our lunch together every day.

Unit 9 Lesson B   QUICK CHECK

(i) Study the examples, then complete the sentences.

Now	In the past
We move a lot.	*We mov**ed** a lot.*
He moves a lot.	*He mov**ed** a lot.*
I miss my family.	*I miss**ed** my family.*
He misses his family.	*He miss**ed** his family.*

1. She doesn't miss her old school now, but when she first went to college, she really .... it a lot.
2. Every year we stay at my cousin's house; but one year, in 1987, we .... in a hotel.
3. Did he change jobs last year? Yes, he .... jobs in November.
4. She doesn't usually like moving, but last year when they .... she was quite happy.
5. Where did your parents live when they were children? They both .... in Kenya.

(ii) Put the words in each sentence in the right order.

1. Where your school was?
2. What colour your home was?
3. What the names of your friends were?
4. What you annoyed about your school?
5. What you did like at school?
6. Where you did live as a child?

Unit 9 Lesson C   QUICK CHECK

(i) Look at the example. Use the words in the box to complete the sentences.

Example: *I phoned **my wife**. I phoned **her**.*

1. He telephoned Mia. He telephoned ....
2. His mother wrote the letter. His mother wrote ....
3. Mia looked at her husband. Mia looked at ....
4. He looked at his children. He looked at ....

them	him	it	her

(ii) Reread the text in Exercise 1. Then complete the answers with *did* or *didn't*.

Example: *Did he telephone Mia? Yes, he did.*

1. Did she look nervous?   ....
2. Did he have a broken ankle?   ....
3. Did Mia show him a letter?   ....
4. Did he read it all?   ....
5. Did he pay for the phone call?   ....

Unit 10 Lesson A   QUICK CHECK

Find and correct one mistake in each sentence.

Last night, there is a frightening sound at my door. I sit in my chair and didn't open the door. Then I go out of the room and I telephoned my friend. Five minutes later, the doorbell ring. My friend came in and say, 'It's only a cat!'

TRUE TO LIFE ELEMENTARY   © Cambridge University Press 1995

Fill in the missing sentences.

Example:

Present statement	Past statement	Past question
A shot rings out.	*A shot rang out.*	*Did a shot ring out?*

1. They're farmers. .... Were they farmers?
2. He's a storyteller. .... Was he a storyteller?
3. .... He told them a story. ....?
4. She finds the food. ....?
5. They leave the house. ....?
6. .... She ran to him. ....?

Here are twelve verbs from this unit. Add the parts that are missing.

Present tense		Past tense	
I ring	She or he rings	I rang	He or she rang
I sit	She or he	I sat	He or she ....
I think	She or he	I	He or she ....
I meet	She or he	I	He or she ....
I do	She or he	I	He or she ....
I catch	She or he	I	He or she ....
I hear	She or he	I	He or she ....
I run	She or he	I	He or she ....
I come	She or he	I	He or she ....
I say	She or he	I	He or she ....
I go	She or he	I	He or she ....
I write	She or he	I	He or she ....

(i) Here is a rule for using the present simple or the present continuous. Use appropriate expressions from the box to complete the sentences. Add an example sentence for each rule.

Rule:
Use the present simple for things that happen .... or ....
Example sentence: ....
Rule:
Use the present continuous for things that are happening ...., or for temporary or .... situations.
Example sentence: ....

developing	usually	now	three times a day	every month	all the time

(ii) Put the verbs in brackets into the correct form.

Example: *I can't answer the phone, I 'm repairing .... (repair) the car.*

1. He can't answer the door, he .... (have) a shower.
2. You can't phone them, they .... (have) dinner.
3. She can't speak to you, she .... (talk) on the phone.
4. We can't go out with you, we .... (write) a letter.

TRUE TO LIFE ELEMENTARY   © Cambridge University Press 1995

Unit 11 Lesson B QUICK CHECK

Write the verbs in the correct tense.

1. I'm a student, but now it's the holidays, so I
.... (work) in a restaurant.
2. He .... (study) English to go to Australia
for a conference.
3. At the moment, she .... (learn) Chinese
for fun, and she's enjoying the classes.
4. This month, they .... (live) in their
mother's flat while she's on holiday.
5. Are you doing anything at the moment? I
.... (watch) television in the kitchen.

Unit 11 Lesson C QUICK CHECK

(i) One word is missing in the sentences. Add the
missing word.

1. Unemployment going up in our country.
2. The popularity of sports is staying same.
3. Fortunately, water pollution going down.

(ii) Put in the connecting expressions.

1. The cost of living is going up, and unemployment is
going up ....
2. Sport is popular, and .... education.
3. Films are popular, and .... are videos.
4. The cost of living is going up. Unemployment is
.... going up, very quickly.

Unit 12 Lesson A QUICK CHECK

(i) Which is right: a or b?

1. a. We're going on holiday next month.
b. We usually go on holiday next month.
2. a. My brother always comes to see me in August this
year.
b. My brother is coming to see me in August this
year.
3. a. I meet my sister at the theatre at eight o'clock this
evening.
b. I'm meeting my sister at the theatre at eight o'clock
this evening.

(ii) Correct the sentences.

1. She going to Luxembourg this summer.
2. They is meeting their friends at the cinema.
3. On Sunday, I'm go to a party.
4. He's no eating meat these days.
5. What they doing on Saturday?

Unit 12 Lesson B QUICK CHECK

Complete the questions.

1. What are .... at 12 today? I'm meeting
Jon for lunch.
2. Why is Sonia .... the phone? Because
Penny can't answer it, she's busy.
3. Who .... this client? Petra's
seeing her at 3 pm.
4. ...... Petra coming into the .... today? No, she's
flying to Bucharest.
5. .... ? They're meeting
in his office.

Unit 12 Lesson C QUICK CHECK

(i) Complete the sentences. Change them into
negative sentences.

1. I'm going ...... get a job.
I'm ....
2. She...... going to use a dictionary.
She ....
3. They .... to read the newspaper every day.
They ...., ...

(ii) Complete the questions. Choose an appropriate
answer for each question from the box.

1. .... you going to write to me?
....
2. .... are you going to do?
....
3. .... is she going to come to class?
....
4. .... anyone going to write to me?
....

Because it's interesting.
I'm going to use my dictionary.
Yes, Martin is.   Yes, I am.

(i) Study the comparative forms of these words and complete the missing ones.

cold colder	nice nicer	hot hotter	dry drier
green	late	wet	pretty ....
rich	fine	flat	hilly ....
poor	simple	big	noisy ....
cheap	free	thin	lovely ....

beautiful	more beautiful	less beautiful
varied	more varied	less varied
popular	....	....
interesting	....	....
expensive	....	....
modern	....	....
industrialised	....	....
polluted	....	....
crowded	....	....

(ii) Complete the sentences.

1. Canada is .... bigger than Portugal.
2. China is a .... bigger .... Spain.
3. Holland is .... smaller than Brazil.
4. Scotland is a .... smaller than England.

(i) Complete sentence b so that it means the same as sentence a.

Example: a. *Tokyo is more crowded than Brasilia.*
b. *Brasilia is not as crowded as Tokyo.*

1. a. London is bigger than Lisbon.
   b. Lisbon is not ....
2. a. The city centre is dirtier than the suburbs.
   b. The suburbs are not ....
3. a. Bazaars are livelier than department stores.
   b. Department stores ....

(ii) Write a question, using both.

Example: Kyoto Rome old: *Are both cities old?*

1. Sydney Vancouver beautiful: ....?
2. Greece Thailand popular: ....?
3. A shop a bank impressive: ....?
4. John James lively: ....?

(i) Add one word to each sentence to make it correct.

They are best family on our list.
This is worst coffee in town.

This is best place to eat.
Coffee at Dino's is cheaper coffee at the Coffee Corner.

(ii) Write in the superlatives.

large larger	beautiful more beautiful	big bigger ....
poor poorer	varied more varied	bad worse ....
good better	popular more popular	

(i) Complete the verbs.

Present simple	Past simple	Present perfect (long form)	Present perfect (short form)
I try	I tried	I have	I've tried
You do	You did	You have done	You've ....
She watches	She watched	She	She ....

(ii) Choose the correct answer for each question.

1. Have you ever tried horse riding? ....
2. Has your sister ever done any karate? ....
3. Did you like sailing as a child? ....
4. Did they go scuba diving last year? ....
5. Have they ever tried motor racing? ....
6. Do you go hang gliding at the weekends? ....

Yes, they have.   No, I didn't.   No, I don't.   Yes, I have, several times.
Yes, they did, twice.   No, she hasn't.

For each question, choose the correct answer from the box.

1. Have you played tennis this month? ....
2. Have you felt tired this week? ....
3. Have you done any sailing this year? ....
4. Have you had a cold this year? ....
5. Have you felt stressed this week? ....

No, I haven't had time to be ill.   Yes, I've played quite a lot.
Yes, I've worked very late every evening this week.   No, I've felt fine, really relaxed.
No, I've had some problems with my boat.

Which is correct, a or b?

1. a. I haven't find.
   b. I haven't found.
2. a. You haven't done.
   b. You haven't did.
3. a. They hasn't learned.
   b. They haven't learned.
4. a. We haven't watched TV.
   b. We haven't watch TV.
5. a. She hasn't learned much this week.
   b. She haven't learn much this week.

Unit 15 Lesson A QUICK CHECK

(i) Choose a or b.

1. *I keep losing my bag* means:
   a. I lose it all the time.
   b. I lost it once or twice in the past.
2. *Have you ever lost your bag?* means:
   a. Did you lose your bag last year?
   b. In your life up to now, have you lost your bag once, or several times?
3. *I sometimes lose my bag* means:
   a. I lose it often.
   b. I lose it from time to time.

(ii) Which expressions in the box go with these *-ing* forms? There are three expressions for each form.

1. I keep forgetting …
2. I keep breaking …
3. I keep tidying …

windows	the garden	birthdays
my passport	the living room	my leg
cups	my son's desk	my keys

Unit 15 Lesson B QUICK CHECK

(i) The two parts of each sentence are muddled. Rewrite the sentences so that they make sense.

[H/W]

1. Before leaving their desks,   they put it in the bin.
2. Before writing to customers,   they put them away.
3. After reading a letter,   they tidy them up.
4. After using the books,   they find their addresses.

(ii) Use the verb in brackets to complete the sentences.

1. Old envelopes are good .... (put) under the leg of an old chair.
2. Pieces of paper are useful .... (make) paper airplanes.
3. Newspapers are handy .... (kill) flies.

Unit 15 Lesson C QUICK CHECK

Complete the sentences.

1. W................ letters takes longer than using the phone.
2. P................ business appointments in a diary is a good idea.
3. L................ to use a computer well is important these days.
4. St................ information on a computer is very useful.

Unit 16 Lesson A QUICK CHECK

Put *who*, *where* or *that* into these sentences.

1. My neighbourhood has lots of restaurants .... my friends eat.
2. The doctors .... work in the medical centre are very good.
3. The petrol stations .... are near my home stay open at night.
4. I like the park .... there are lots of flowers.
5. The friend .... lives near my house is a teacher.

Unit 16 Lesson B QUICK CHECK

(i) Look at this correct question and answer.

Where's the new restaurant?
I don't know, I haven't seen it yet.

Correct the mistakes in each of these answers.

1. What do you think of the new doctor?
   I don't know, I not meet her yet.
2. Can I borrow your dictionary?
   Sorry, I didn't finish with it yet.
3. Have you finished your letter?
   No, I haven't even start it yet.
4. Do you like your new car?
   Well, it didn't arrive yet.
5. Has Juan come back?
   No, yet.

(ii) Complete the sentences.

1. I've just start_ _ a new job.
2. Have you m_ _ your new neighbour yet?
3. Have you s_ _n their new baby?
4. He'_ just fall_ _ off his bicycle.
5. They'_ _ just b_ _ _ _t a new car.
6. We'_ _ just c_ _ _ back from our holidays.

TRUE TO LIFE ELEMENTARY   © Cambridge University Press 1995

QUICK CHECK EXERCISES

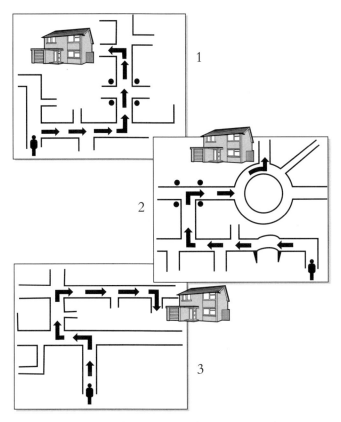

Write directions for the people to get to the buildings.

Complete these sentences.

Example: *I'm a careful person; I do things* carefully.

1. She's a good driver; she drives her car

   ....

2. He's a skilful footballer; he plays football

   ....

3. Puzzles are easy; I can usually do them

   ....

4. They're confident pianists; they play ....

Rewrite each rule so that it has the same meaning.

Example: Rule: *Don't speak impolitely to customers.*
          Rewritten rule: **Speak politely to customers.**

1. Don't walk quickly down the stairs.
2. Don't drive impatiently in the car park, and don't park untidily.
3. Don't behave badly when there are visitors.
4. Don't chat noisily in the corridors.
5. Don't dress casually for work.

Read the answers. Write the questions.

1. ....?
   Yes, I think it's very important to be polite.
2. ....?
   It's important because politeness shows people that you care about them.
3. ....?
   Yes, young people are less formal than their parents.
4. ....?
   The main rule is to think about other people.

Study the example. Change the advice, to make it less strong.

Example: *Don't drink the water!*
          (= an instruction, or a very strong recommendation)
          You shouldn't drink the water or *I don't think you should drink the water.*
          (= it's not a good idea – a gentler recommendation)

1. Don't eat salads.
2. Don't sleep on a long flight.
3. Don't eat too much.
4. Don't put your bag under the seat.
5. Don't stand up before the aircraft has come to a complete stop.

Complete the sentences.

1. A traveller .... take travellers' cheques. (It's a good idea.)
2. Visitors .... buy a visa before travelling. (It's required.)
3. My sister .... get a new passport before leaving. (It's required.)
4. The French .... have a passport to go to Germany. (It's not required.)
5. Air travellers .... arrive at the airport too late. (It's not a good idea.)

Unit 18 Lesson C   QUICK CHECK

Put each word into a circle.

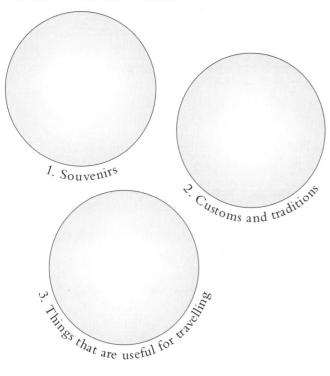

1. Souvenirs

2. Customs and traditions

3. Things that are useful for travelling

singing   a toothbrush   a postcard   a national
holiday   a pot   a carpet   a doll   a queue
a suitcase   a credit card   a dance   a book   a first-
aid kit   bottled water

Unit 19 Lesson A   QUICK CHECK

(i) Complete the short or long forms.

I'd like = I would like
............'d like = She .... like
We'...... like = We would ....
They'd like = They would like
He wouldn'...... like = He would .... like
Why .... you like to be a pilot?
Why ....'t you like to live in Paris?

(ii) Choose the correct answer: a, b or c.

1. Would you like more time to relax?
   a. Yes, I would like.   b. Yes, I would.   c. Yes, I'd.
2. Would you like to work seven days a week?
   a. No, I don't like that.   b. No, I not like.   c. No, I
   wouldn't.
3. Would your sister like a long holiday?
   a. Yes, she does.   b. No, she wouldn't.   c. No, she
   would.

Unit 19 Lesson B   QUICK CHECK

Reorder these sentences.

1. I be teenager like a again to wouldn't.
2. you forgetting keep Would things?
3. have money Why like to would your father more?
4. green like that's world I'd live to a in.
5. someone listen to Perhaps would me.

Unit 19 Lesson C   QUICK CHECK

Complete the sentences by writing a word from the
box that has a similar meaning.

1. The word *beautiful* is similar to ....
2. The word *image* is similar to ....
3. The word *top* in *top model* is similar to ....
4. The word *hard* in *life is hard* is similar to ....

difficult	picture	pretty	best

Unit 20 Lesson A   QUICK CHECK

(i) Complete these polite expressions.

I'm s _ _ _ _   p _ _ _ _ _   E _ _ _ _ _ m_

Add one of the expressions to make these sentences
more polite.

1. Can I try it on, ...?
2. ...., but I bought this clock and
   now it's stopped.
3. .... about that, can I have a look at it?

It's stopped is the short form. The long form is: *It* ....
stopped.

(ii) Fill in the missing words.

.... me. My clock ....
working. Can you give me a ...., please?
I'm t................. sorry. Can I see your r.................?

Unit 20 Lesson B   QUICK CHECK

Match the complaints with expressions in the box.

1. This doesn't fit.   4. This isn't real.
2. This doesn't work.   5. This is too cold.
3. This isn't fresh.

a watch	a bowl of soup	a skirt
a cake	a travel iron	a diamond necklace
a jacket	fish	bread	a hotel room
a Walkman	a T-shirt

Unit 20 Lesson C QUICK CHECK

(i) Put *formal* or *informal* into the spaces.

Sorry is often used in .... spoken or written English.
Apologise is usually used in .... spoken or written English.
Regret is usually used in .... spoken or written English.

Put *speaking* or *writing* in the spaces.

Sorry is used more when ....
Apologise is used more when ....

(ii) Choose an appropriate expression to complete the sentences.

1. We're sorry, but ....
2. The company regrets that
   ....
3. The company apologises for
   ....
4. I'm sorry to ....

> the service has been delayed
> put you to so much trouble
> the delay to the 8:05 service to Reading
> we can't come

Unit 21 Lesson A QUICK CHECK

Complete the following sentences with *need(s)* or *don't/doesn't need.*

1. A rich person .... money.
2. A sick person .... a doctor.
3. You .... education for a good start in life.
4. They .... a ball to play soccer.
5. Rich people .... to work.
6. A young child .... love.

Unit 21 Lesson B QUICK CHECK

Put in the missing words.

1. They live .... a good part of town.
2. Our attitude .... money tells us about ourselves.
3. He always worries .... money.
4. Money is an important thing .... anybody's life.
5. She always dresses .... a red suit.
6. There is a fear .... not having enough money.
7. People have a strong need .... earn money.

Unit 21 Lesson C QUICK CHECK

(i) Complete the sentences with *need* or *need to.*

1. Do you .... a holiday? Yes, I'm really tired.
2. Does he .... go to the bank? Yes. He hasn't got any money at all.
3. Do you .... get a job? No, I just want a change from housework.
4. Does she .... a new pen? No, her old one still works.

(ii) Complete the sentences with *want* or *want to.*

1. Do you .... study English next year? Yes, I do.
2. Do you .... a piece of cake? Yes, please.
3. Do you .... go to the park this afternoon? Yes, I'd like that.
4. Do they .... a new TV? I don't think so.

Unit 22 Lesson A QUICK CHECK

Complete the questions and reorder the answers.

Q: What's Moscow .... in .... ?
A: cold freezing It's
Q: .... summer like in Vancouver?
A: and dry warm It's pretty
Q: What's it .... in Cairo in January?
A: It's San Francisco to bit in June similar a

Unit 22 Lesson B QUICK CHECK

Complete these sentences.

1. When you get cold, p........... on a coat.
2. .... on a coat when you get cold.
3. Make .... you have a hat when you go out in the sun.
4. .... to take your coat when it's wet.
5. .... your umbrella when it's wet.
6. Don't .... the sunscreen when it's sunny.
7. Don't .... to put on your sunscreen when it's sunny.

Unit 22 Lesson C QUICK CHECK

There are two mistakes in each sentence. Correct them.

1. If there's storm, I feeling nervous.
2. If it very windy, I worried about possible damage.
3. If there floods, the best thing do is to go to the top floor.
4. If you're on tenth floor, not use the lift.

Unit 23 Lesson A   QUICK CHECK

Complete the sentences.

1. A festival that is old and hasn't changed is a
   t......................... one.
2. A festival that is quite recent is a m.........................
   one.
3. At festival time, people sometimes give g........... and
   light c.............. .
4. They also cook special foods and have big meals,
   called f................. .
5. Festivals get more c............................ as time passes:
   people buy and sell more things, like cards.

Unit 23 Lesson B   QUICK CHECK

(i) Answer these questions.

1. Which question do you think is more polite, a or b?
   Question a. Can you come for dinner on Saturday?
   Question b. Would you like to come for dinner on
   Saturday?
2. Which answer do you think is more polite, a or b?
   Answer a. I can't that night.
   Answer b. I'd love to come, but I can't, I'm going to
   my mother's.

(ii) Complete these sentences.

1. .... you like to come to the cinema
   tonight?
2. I'd really like to, but I'm .... I can't. I'm
   going to my evening class.
3. Well, ... you .... meet
   us at the café after your class?
4. Yes, ... love to.

Unit 23 Lesson C   QUICK CHECK

Complete the sentences.

1. .... set the table? Yes, please, that's
   very kind of you.
2. .... do the washing up? No, thanks,
   .... do it.
3. .... get you a ....?
   No, it's OK, I never read the paper these days.
4. .... water the plants? It's OK, I
   .... it.
5. .... cook the meal? Yes, please, that
   would ....

Unit 24 Lesson A   QUICK CHECK

With *I*, *you*, *we*, *they*, *she* and *he*, we usually use the
long form *will* in questions about the future but we
use the short form *'ll* in spoken statements.

Complete these examples.

1. .... you have to work harder next year? Yes
   .... have to work much harder.
2. When .... she be 70? .... be 70 next
   year.
3. .... they travel a lot? No, ...
   probably stay at home.
4. .... he have a better job when he's 35? Yes,
   .... be the manager.

(ii) Complete these sentences.

1. .... she want to be a doctor? Yes, so
   .... have to take her exams.
2. .... he like to live in Greece? I think so, so
   .... need to learn Greek.
3. .... they hope to have a car? Yes, but
   .... need to save more money.

Unit 24 Lesson B   QUICK CHECK

(i) Fill in the gaps and answer the question.

1. *I won't* is the short form; *I will not* is the long form.
   He'll is the short form; the long form is
   ....
2. Which two of the following short answers go with
   this question:
   Will you phone me at 9?
   a. Yes, I will.   b. No, I'll not.   c. Yes, I'll.   d. No, I
   won't.

(ii) Write the questions.

1. ....?
   No, he won't be rich in ten years from now.
2. ....?
   Yes, she'll be a good teacher, she's lively.

Unit 24 Lesson C   QUICK CHECK

Write the opposite of these sentences.

1. The future will be exciting in this country.
2. Children won't need to learn languages.
3. The population of the world will increase.
4. There won't be many more cars in the world.
5. There will be some more *Quick Checks* in this book.

TAPESCRIPTS

UNIT 1 FINDING OUT

LESSON A

Exercise 3

1.
INTERVIEWER: Hello.
YAPRAK: Hello.
INTERVIEWER: What's your name?
YAPRAK: Yaprak.
INTERVIEWER: Yaprak? That's an interesting name. How do you spell it?
YAPRAK: Y A P R A K.
INTERVIEWER: Y A P R A K … Where are you from, Yaprak?
YAPRAK: Turkey.
INTERVIEWER: Oh, from Turkey.

2.
INTERVIEWER: Hello.
ARTURO: Oh, hello.
INTERVIEWER: I'm David. What's your name?
ARTURO: Arturo.
INTERVIEWER: Is that A R …?
ARTURO: Yes, A R T U R O.
INTERVIEWER: And where are you from, Arturo?
ARTURO: I'm from … Mexico.
INTERVIEWER: Oh, Mexico. Beautiful country!

3.
INTERVIEWER: Hello.
HELGA: Hello.
INTERVIEWER: Your name is …?
HELGA: Helga Magret.
INTERVIEWER: How do you spell that?
HELGA: H E L G A. Just say Helga, that's enough.
INTERVIEWER: Hm. And where are you from, Helga?
HELGA: Denmark.

4.
INTERVIEWER: Hello there.
KENJI: Oh, hello.
INTERVIEWER: I'm David. What's your name?
KENJI: Kenji.
INTERVIEWER: Oh, Kenji? How do you spell that, Kenji?
KENJI: K E N J I.
INTERVIEWER: And where are you from, Kenji?
KENJI: From Japan.
INTERVIEWER: Whereabouts in Japan?
KENJI: Er, from Tokyo.

LESSON B

Exercise 2

What is there in the room? Well, there's a computer on the table … there's a radio, and … a television. There's a carpet, … um … a painting … and … there's a light. There are chairs and tables, plants, books and two windows.

Exercise 3

Think of a building in your town or city. Answer the questions about your building.
Listen to this example.
Is there a lift?
(You say) *Yes, there is* or *No, there isn't.*
Are there any parking spaces?
(You say) *Yes, there are* or *No, there aren't.*
Ready? Listen and answer.
1. Is there a lift?
2. Are there any parking spaces?
3. Is there a first floor?
4. Is there an information desk?
5. Are there any stairs?
6. Are there any carpets?
7. Is there a third floor?
8. Is there an escalator?

LESSON D

PART 1

Exercise 2

1.
A: What does *pay phone* mean?
B: You put money into the phone. Put the coins in, then talk.
A: How do you spell it?
B: Two words. P A Y pay. P H O N E phone.
A: Could you repeat that, please?
B: Sure. P A Y pay. P H O N E phone.
A: Thank you.

2.
A: How do you say *dictionario* in English?
B: Dictionary.
A: Could you write that on the board, please?
B: Yes, of course. It's in your book.
A: What page is it on?
B: Um, page four.

PART 2

Exercise 1

A: Excuse me, where's the lift?
RECEPTIONIST: It's at the end of the corridor.
A: Where are the toilets?
RECEPTIONIST: They're one floor up, along the corridor.
B: Excuse me, where's the library, please?
RECEPTIONIST: It's along the corridor, on the left, next to the lift.
C: And where's the computer room, please?
RECEPTIONIST: It's one floor up, opposite Room A.

UNIT 2 WHAT HAVE YOU GOT?

Exercise 2

Think about other countries.
1. Have you got any brothers or sisters in another country?
2. Have you got any sons or daughters in another country?
3. Have you got any friends in another country?
4. Is your mother or father in another country?
5. What about your grandparents? Are they in another country?

LESSON B

Exercise 1

MARTIN: What have you got in your handbag, Sheila?
SHEILA: Well, I've got a comb … and a pen. I've got a handkerchief and my credit card.

WILLIAM: What have you got in your briefcase, Ken?
KEN: Um, I've got … er, I've got some money, my car keys, my house keys, my mobile phone, … erm, and a handkerchief.

Exercise 3

INTERVIEWER: Right, er, how many phones have you got, Peter?
PETER: Um, ooh, I've got, er, three phones.
INTERVIEWER: Um? Sheila?
SHEILA: Um, I've got … two.
INTERVIEWER: And, er, how many radios have you got?
SHEILA: Er, um, I've got lots.
PETER: Hmm. I haven't got any.
INTERVIEWER: OK, and, er, and how many plants have you got?
PETER: Oh, I've got loads – I've got lots and lots of plants.
SHEILA: Yes.
INTERVIEWER: And Sheila?
SHEILA: I've got lots too.
PETER: Lots.
INTERVIEWER: Right, er, so how many beds have you got?
PETER: Five. I've got five beds.
SHEILA: Beds?… er …
INTERVIEWER: Sheila?
SHEILA: Er, I've got … three.
INTERVIEWER: OK, and how many books have you got?
SHEILA: Books? Well, I've got lots.
PETER: Er, yes, I've got lots … lots.

Exercise 4

INTERVIEWER: Now, have you got a phone in the bathroom?
PETER: No.
SHEILA: No, I haven't got a phone in the bathroom.
INTERVIEWER: Have you got a television in the bedroom?
PETER: No.
SHEILA: Oh, I'm afraid I have. I have … I've got one.
INTERVIEWER: Ah! Peter, no?
PETER: No. Definitely not.
INTERVIEWER: Have you got any plants in the kitchen, Peter?
PETER: Yes, yes, all over the kitchen.
INTERVIEWER: And Sheila?

SHEILA: Yes, I've got one too.
INTERVIEWER: One?
SHEILA: Well, just one plant, yes, above the sink.
INTERVIEWER: And finally, have you got any beds in the sitting room?
PETER: No … Er, no, no.
SHEILA: No.

LESSON D

REVIEW OF DATES, MONTHS, YEARS

Exercise 1

ALEX: When's your birthday, Sam?
SAM: Oh, it's on the second of December. What about you?
ALEX: My birthday's on the third of March. What about you, Penny? When's your birthday? Is it in August?
PENNY: Yes, that's right … on the sixth of August.

REVIEW OF UNIT 1

Exercise 2

1.
MR LEE: Excuse me, where's the Director's office, please?
WOMAN 1: Yes, it's along the corridor, next to the lift.
MR LEE: Ah, right.

2.
MAN: Come in!
MR LEE: Ah, good morning. My name's Lee. Um, are you the Director?
MAN: No, this is level one. He's on three. Opposite the computer room.
MR LEE: Thank you.

3.
WOMAN 2: Yes?
MR LEE: Ah, good morning. Erm, I'm Stanley Lee. Are you the Director?
WOMAN: Oh, good heavens, no. There are no women directors here. The Director's office is one floor down. It's at the end of the corridor, on the left.
MR LEE: Oh … OK. Um, thanks.

4.
WOMAN 3: Come in!
MR LEE: Um, is the Director in here?
WOMAN 3: No, of course not. He's much further on.

UNIT 3 WHAT WOULD YOU LIKE TO EAT?

LESSON A

Exercise 1

1.
What do you have for breakfast?
Just some croissants or rolls and butter, and lots of coffee, of course.

2.
What do you have for breakfast?
Oh, coffee, yoghurt, some cheese with a bit of bread.

3.

What do you have for breakfast?

I have a big breakfast at seven o'clock every morning: cereal and milk, two eggs, tea and toast.

4.

What do you have for breakfast?

I have rice … and … a lot of fruit, bananas, for example, or apples, pineapple, peaches …

Exercise 2

Version 1

MAN: Is that Room Service?

WOMAN: Yes, sir.

MAN: I'd like to order breakfast, please.

WOMAN: What's your room number, please?

MAN: 308.

WOMAN: Thank you. What would you like?

MAN: I'd like some fruit juice. Um, what have you got?

WOMAN: Orange, pineapple, tomato.

MAN: Orange juice, please.

WOMAN: Anything else?

MAN: Yes, I'd like scrambled eggs with tomato.

WOMAN: Any cereal, cornflakes?

MAN: No, thanks, but I'd like some toast.

WOMAN: Coffee, tea?

MAN: Coffee, please, with cream.

WOMAN: And what time would you like your breakfast, sir?

MAN: Er … about 7.30 is fine, thanks.

WOMAN: So that's orange juice, scrambled eggs with tomato, toast, coffee and cream, room 308, at 7.30.

MAN: That's it. Thanks very much.

Version 2

MAN: Is that Room Service?

WOMAN: Yes, sir.

MAN: I'd like to order breakfast, please.

WOMAN: What's your room number, please?

MAN: 308.

WOMAN: Thank you. What would you like?

MAN: I'd like some fruit juice. Um, what have you got?

WOMAN: Orange, pineapple, tomato.

MAN: Orange juice, please.

WOMAN: Anything else?

MAN: Yes, I'd like scrambled eggs with tomato.

WOMAN: Any cereal, cornflakes?

MAN: No, thanks, but I'd like some toast.

WOMAN: Coffee, tea?

MAN: Coffee, please, with cream.

WOMAN: And what time would you like your breakfast, sir?

MAN: Er … about 7.30 is fine, thanks.

Exercise 4

WAITER: What would you like for breakfast, madam?

MOTHER: I'd like some cereal, and some coffee. With hot milk, please. And my daughter would like two eggs, an apple, some toast with butter and a glass of water.

DAUGHTER: No, no, mother. No eggs, please. I'd just like a banana and some rolls – with jam.

Exercise 1

1.

Fruit: b for banana, a for apple, p for peaches, s for strawberries … BAPS.

2.

Vegetables: peas, beans, potatoes, carrots – P B P C.

3.

Fish: Twelve o'clock salmon, three o'clock tuna, six o'clock sardines, nine o'clock prawns.

4.

Salad: Good morning, what would you like? We've got lettuce, onions, cucumbers and peppers. That's right, lettuce, onions, cucumbers and peppers.

5.

Meat: chicken, lamb, beef, duck.

Exercise 2

1.

My favourite food is probably pasta which I like to cook myself. Also, I like rice and I like potatoes, which I grow myself and tomatoes, and strawberries.

2.

I like very spicy food. I like Indian food. I like food from Thailand, I like Malaysian food. I also like very sweet things. I love ice cream – any flavour. I also like cakes with cream in them. I like chocolate cake and chocolate biscuits and I like chocolate bars as well.

Exercise 2

1.

In Malaysia, where I come from, the food grown in our country is very cheap. People eat fish, vegetables which they grow, and a lot of rice. But all the food that has got to be imported into the country, like strawberries, apples, pears, all European types of fruit and vegetable, is very expensive.

2.

In Chile, food is cheap, specially fresh produce. Fruit grown in the country is very tasty. Vegetables are very cheap and abundant, meat and fish are cheap. Wine is also produced in Chile and you can find very good wine, quite cheap as well.

REVIEW OF UNIT 1

Exercise 1

1.

ma ma MA ma: I'm an actor. I'm an actress. I'm a doctor. I'm a teacher. I'm a builder. I'm a waiter. I'm a waitress. I'm a lawyer. I'm a dentist.

2.

ma ma MA ma ma: I'm a sales person.

3.

ma ma ma ma Ma: I'm an engineer.

Exercise 2

1.

In my country, the United States, because there is no system of national health, perhaps the most expensive bills for a family are for medical needs – doctors and dentists. Almost any professional service is expensive in America. Certainly lawyers' fees, er accountants, anyone in that kind of field. In the trades, it depends. Sometimes it's expensive, sometimes it is not so expensive.

2.

I come from Sri Lanka. In my country, it is very expensive for the average family to have a doctor or a dentist or lawyers. But if you want a man to do all the handy jobs around the house, that is not so expensive. You can get someone in to come and help with all the chores in your house, and that's not expensive. But if you want anyone to do a professional job, that is very expensive.

3.

I come from Northern Ireland. In Northern Ireland, we're very lucky, and we've got a national health service. So it's very cheap to go to the doctor or the dentist because you don't have to pay very much at all. In Northern Ireland, builders seem to be quite cheap as well. But maybe that's because they're not very good. Car mechanics are quite cheap too, and my car keeps breaking down a lot.

REVIEW OF UNIT 2

Exercise 1

A: Have you got any money?
B: I've got a bit.
A: Have you got any change for the phone?
B: Um … I've got a fifty.
A: Oh … have you got any tens?
B: Wait a minute. I've got some somewhere … Oh, yeah, I've got two. Here you are.
A: Oh, great, thanks.

Exercise 2

A: Are there any parking spaces?
B: There are some under the building.
A: Mm. Are there any toilets on this floor?
B: Er, no, there aren't any. There are some toilets on the next floor up.
A: Where are the pay phones?
B: Sorry, there aren't any.
A: OK. Thanks.

UNIT 4 A SENSE OF COLOUR

LESSON A

Exercise 1

MARK: That's a nice jacket, Julia. Lovely blue. Where is it from?
JULIA: Hm … It's got a label … Made in Scotland. 100% pure new wool. Your new tie's nice too, Mark. Is it silk?
MARK: Yes, 100% silk. Made in China. The same colour as your skirt, Suheila.
SUHEILA: Is it? No, not really – my skirt's a different green! It's from Egypt.
JULIA: Really? It's beautiful. What's it made of?
SUHEILA: It's cotton.

LESSON B

Exercise 1

Version 1

1.

I buy my shirts, er, my trousers, and my jackets in a department store. Er, I buy a lot of clothes in a department store. It's fast and easy. Er, but I buy my shoes in a shoe store.

2.

My wife buys my clothes for me. Er, she buys sweaters in a department store and T-shirts in the markets. Er, I go to the shoe shop to buy my shoes.

3.

I buy my clothes from different places. Um, I sometimes buy old clothes in an antique shop. I buy a lot of clothes in markets because they're cheap. Well, in department stores, clothes are usually very expensive.

Version 2

1.

Buying clothes for me is not a great treat. So I like to do it as fast and efficiently as I can. So most of my clothes I buy in a department store. Shirts, trousers, a jacket – things, er … general kind of clothing. Shoes I buy in a shoe store.

2.

I buy, er, some clothes in markets but, er, the person who does most of the shopping for me is my wife. And she's an expert in finding clothes in different parts, in different shops … and I think she gets them from specialist shops. She finds sweaters in a department store, T-shirts in the markets. Shoes are rather difficult to find because I have to go to the shoe shop to try them on and I'm very indecisive so it takes me a long time to make a decision about the right pair of shoes.

3.

I buy my clothes from lots of different places. I quite like second-hand clothes. For instance, I might go to an antique shop and buy a dress that was first worn in the 1920s. I also buy things in markets because it's a lot cheaper than going to department stores.

Exercise 4

1.

Where do you buy your ties, Lee?
I buy them at the market, because they're cheap and colourful.

2.

I buy my shoes from a department store, but my mother buys her shoes at the market.

3.

How often does Leah buy jackets?
She buys jackets twice a year – in the summer, and in the winter. I sometimes buy a jacket in the winter – never in the summer.

4.

Where do your parents buy their clothes?
They buy clothes from Marks and Spencer's, but they buy shoes from a little shoe shop near their house.

5.

Do you and your friend buy your hats at the same shop, Franz?
No, of course not. I buy my hats at the supermarket. She buys her hats at a hat shop, or sometimes at the market.

TRUE TO LIFE ELEMENTARY   © Cambridge University Press 1995

TAPESCRIPTS

LESSON D

REVIEW OF UNIT 2

Exercise 1

1.

WOMAN: Have you got my bag? It's made of leather and it's black.

2.

MAN: Excuse me, have you got my bag in the Lost Property? It's bright red with a white shoulder strap, … er, it's sort of plastic.

3.

WOMAN: It's quite big, it's got a handle and wheels.
EMPLOYEE: What's it made of?
WOMAN: Well, it's a sort of fabric, dark blue, with a bit of brown leather.

1.

WOMAN: Have you got my bag? It's made of leather and it's black.
EMPLOYEE: What's it got inside?
WOMAN: Oh, um … some pens … and a lot of papers and letters from work.

2.

MAN: Excuse me, have you got my bag in the Lost Property? It's bright red with a white shoulder strap, … er, it's sort of plastic.
EMPLOYEE: What's in it?
MAN: A wallet, with some money, not much, er, sunglasses, er, combs, some keys, cheque book … that sort of thing.

3.

WOMAN: It's quite big, it's got a handle and wheels.
EMPLOYEE: What's it made of?
WOMAN: Well, it's a sort of fabric, dark blue, with a bit of brown leather.
EMPLOYEE: What's inside it?
WOMAN: Oh, clothes, mainly, jeans, T-shirts, shorts, some books, that's about all.

REVIEW OF UNIT 3

Exercise 1

WAITRESS: Yes, what would you like?
CUSTOMER: Um, for starters … I'd like chicken soup with noodles.
WAITRESS: I'm sorry, soup's off this evening.
CUSTOMER: Off? What do you mean off?
WAITRESS: Off. I'm sorry, we haven't got any soup this evening.
CUSTOMER: Oh. OK, I'll have, er, chicken with plum sauce.
WAITRESS: That's off too, sorry.
CUSTOMER: OK. Well, I'll have a main course.
WAITRESS: Yes, what would you like?
CUSTOMER: Er … what's this, number two?
WAITRESS: Er … ah, chicken with honey sauce.
CUSTOMER: Mm, sounds … sounds nice. Chicken with honey sauce.
WAITRESS: Oh, I'm so sorry. No honey sauce this evening.
CUSTOMER: No honey sauce? No chicken with honey sauce?
WAITRESS: I'm sorry. Um, how about chicken pie with peas and chips? The chips are nice.
CUSTOMER: Er … well, OK, but without peas.
WAITRESS: Without peas? No peas?
CUSTOMER: Yes.

WAITRESS: Oh, sorry, the pie is with peas.
CUSTOMER: Look, what have you got?
WAITRESS: Well, there's chicken and, um, egg custard.
CUSTOMER: OK. I'll have that.
WAITRESS: What would you like first, the chicken or the egg?

UNIT 5 GOOD HABITS, NEW ROUTINES?

LESSON A

Exercise 3

SPEAKER 1
When I get up in the morning, I go straight to the bathroom. I run the bath, I have a bath, and I have two cups of coffee and a slice of toast.

SPEAKER 2
When I get up, the first thing I do is go to the bathroom and have a quick wash. Then I go downstairs, and make myself some breakfast, which is tea and two slices of toast. Then I go back to the bathroom and have a shower. Then I dress, and then I leave the house.

LESSON B

Exercise 2

Conversation 1
A: Have a chocolate.
B: I don't eat between meals.
A: Don't you? Oh, I eat little snacks all day.
B: Well, it's a very bad habit.
A: Yes, I know, but chocolate is so nice.

Conversation 2
C: You talk and talk. You never listen!
D: But I don't talk a lot at all. I really don't.
C: Well, you never listen.
D: Don't be silly, I listen to people all the time. It's my job.

Exercise 3

I have fifteen students in my elementary class. They come from many countries from Europe, but also from Japan and South America. They learn in very different ways. Pedro, for example, he uses his dictionary a lot. He writes new words down all the time. And Ruiko writes words down too. She writes them in one book, then she writes them again in columns, with different colours to help her remember. She writes a translation beside each word. Susanna is very different. She never writes anything. I say to her, 'Susanna, how can you remember?' But she says she's here to talk English, not to write. She loves talking. She doesn't worry about mistakes. Otto always comes late. He misses half the lesson and doesn't say much when he is here, but he listens to English songs a lot, and he sings them too.

Exercise 2

Version 1
1.
I go shopping once a week, and I always go in my car to the supermarket. You can get everything there and the quality of the food is high.

2.
In my country, you go to the market every day. You go very early and you buy the fruit and vegetables and meat that you need for the day.

3.
I usually go shopping on Saturdays. I go to the big central market where there is all the fresh produce, fruit and vegetables. I also go to the supermarket.

4.
I go to the supermarket about once a week in my car. I buy all the things that are heavy – large packets of washing powder, heavy bags of potatoes, that kind of thing. I also use my local shops. Every day I go to the bakery and buy a nice loaf of bread or a cake.

Version 2
1.
When I go shopping, I go shopping once a week and I always go in my car. I always shop at a supermarket, because you can get everything all together and the quality of the food is very high. I don't go shopping for clothes very often. And when I do, I always go into the centre and go to a department store. And always, I pay by credit card.

2.
In my country, you go to the market very very early and buy only the fruit and vegetables and meat that you need, or fish, for that particular day. For clothes, you usually buy material from the shops and get your tailor to make your dresses for you. Or, occasionally, you might go to a department store and buy some clothes.

3.
In my country, I usually go shopping on Saturdays. I go to the big central market where I can find all the fresh produce, fruit and vegetables, there. For meat, fish and chicken, I go to the butchers or to the fishmonger. I also go to the supermarket to buy packed food which will last for longer, or frozen food as well. For clothes, I buy them in the specialist shops – the shoe shop, the tailors, or where they sell shirts. And I always pay with a cheque or with cash.

4.
I go to the supermarket about once a week in my car. When I take the car, I buy all the things that are too heavy to carry – for instance, bottles of wine, beer, large packets of washing powder, heavy bags of potatoes, that kind of thing. I also use my local shops. Every day, I go to the bakery and buy a nice loaf of bread or a cake perhaps. I also go to my local greengrocer, because he has very good fruit and vegetables. He also has fresh eggs from the farm.

REVIEW OF UNIT 4

Exercise 2

A: What've you got, oh, what've you got?
   What've you got, oh, what've you got?
B: We've got rhythm, we've got blues,
   We've got a hat and … brand new shoes.
A: They've got rhythm, they've got blues,
   They've got a hat and … brand new shoes.
B: What d'you wear, oh, what d'you wear?
   What d'you wear, oh, what d'you wear?
A: We wear whites and we wear greens,
   We wear a shirt and … our blue jeans.
B: They wear whites and they wear greens,
   They wear a shirt and … their blue jeans.
A: What d'you wear, oh, what d'you wear?
   What d'you wear, oh, what d'you wear?
B: We are formal, we wear suits,
   We wear coats and … polished boots.
A: They are formal, they wear suits,
   They wear coats and … polished boots.
B: What d'you want, oh, what d'you want?
   What d'you want, oh, what d'you want?
A: We want English and we want love,
   We want the earth and … the stars above!
B: They want English and they want love,
   They want the earth and … the stars above!

UNIT 6 THE WAY YOU LOOK

Exercise 1

Version 1
SPEAKER A
My friend Nasreen is very young. She looks very confident. People think that she's serious but really she's a very happy person and also kind.

SPEAKER B
My friend Susan looks happy … I think she's very confident. But she's a practical person, really, and very kind.

SPEAKER C
My friend Ken looks serious but in fact he's a lot of fun, and very lively. He's a writer and has a lot of interesting stories to tell.

SPEAKER A: My friend is number 2.
SPEAKER B: My friend is number 1.
SPEAKER C: My friend is number 3.

Version 2
SPEAKER A
My friend Nasreen is very young and healthy. She looks very proud and confident. A lot of people think that she's serious but really she's a very happy person and also kind.

SPEAKER B
My friend Susan looks proud. I think she's very ambitious. But she's a practical person, really, and very kind.

SPEAKER C
My friend Ken looks serious but in fact he's a lot of fun, very generous and very lively. And he's very intelligent and artistic. He's a writer and has a lot of interesting stories to tell.

SPEAKER A: My friend is number 2.
SPEAKER B: My friend is number 1.
SPEAKER C: My friend is number 3.

LESSON B

Exercise 1

MAN: I think I'd like um, a very pretty little girl, um, with big, brown eyes and dark hair, and … um … small, artistic hands.

WOMAN: Oh, I don't know, really. What would I like? Um, … maybe … a boy … with straight, fair hair and, um, er, strong legs.

Exercise 2

1. My feet are too big.
2. My arms are too short.
3. The shoes are not big enough.
4. My shoulders are too wide.
5. The sleeves are too long.
6. The jacket's not big enough.

LESSON D

REVIEW OF UNIT 5

Exercise 2

WOMAN: At the weekend? I … er … stay in bed until 11 o'clock. Then I get up, I have a long breakfast, I read the newspapers … I have lots of time for a change, it's so nice. Sometimes, if I'm feeling really active, I clean the flat and wash all my clothes. Then, on Saturday afternoon … I go out and do some shopping, and in the evening, I usually meet my friends, and we go out to eat, or we go to a film, or a concert … I love weekends.

MAN: Oh, I don't know. I do different things. I usually buy food for the week on Saturdays, and I … erm, often ask my friends to have a meal with me on Sunday evening. I watch sport on TV … I don't play any sports, but I always watch football on Saturday afternoon.

UNIT 7 WHAT CAN WE DO?

LESSON B

Exercise 1

Version 1
1.
INTERVIEWER: In your country, at what age can you vote?
WOMAN: Nowadays, you can vote at 18.

INTERVIEWER: I see. And at what age can you get married?
WOMAN: I'm not sure. I think … 16?

INTERVIEWER: Um. Er, at what age can you open a bank account?

WOMAN: I think you can open a bank account at any age.

INTERVIEWER: Mm. Er, in your country, at what age can you drive a car?

WOMAN: You can learn to drive a car at the age of fifteen and a half. You can apply for your licence at 16.

2.
INTERVIEWER: In your country, at what age can you vote?
MAN: You can vote when you're 18.

INTERVIEWER: And at what age can you get married?
MAN: You can get married when you're 18.

INTERVIEWER: At what age can you open a bank account?
MAN: Ah! Well, I'm not absolutely sure, but I think it is 18 again.

INTERVIEWER: Do you know at what age you can drive a car?
MAN: Ah, yes, this I know: it's 18.

Version 2
1.
INTERVIEWER: Lorelei, in your country at what age can you vote?

LORELEI: For many years the age at which you could vote was 21, but they changed it about 20 years ago to 18. So now you can vote at 18.

INTERVIEWER: I see. And in your country, at what age can you get married?

LORELEI: I'm not sure. I imagine … 16?

INTERVIEWER: Uhuh. Er, at what age can you open a bank account?

LORELEI: I had a bank account as a child, so I think you can open a bank account at any age.

INTERVIEWER: In your country, at what age can you drive a car?

LORELEI: You can learn to drive a car, you can have a provisional licence at the age of 15$\frac{1}{2}$. You can apply for your licence when you're 16, but in some states, farming states, you can drive at the age of 14, so that you can drive farm machinery, like tractors.

2.
INTERVIEWER: Jean-Pierre, in your country, how old do you have to be before you can vote?

JEAN-PIERRE: You have to be 18.

INTERVIEWER: Uhuh, and what age could you get married at?

JEAN-PIERRE: You can get married when you are 18, but there have been cases of people getting married when they were only 16 and you need the approval and the permission from your parents.

INTERVIEWER: Um. How old do you have to be before you can open a bank account?

JEAN-PIERRE: Ah, well I'm not absolutely sure, but I believe it is 18 again.

INTERVIEWER: Do you know how old you have to be before you can drive a car?

JEAN-PIERRE: Ah, yes, this I know. You have to be 18.

LESSON C

Exercise 1

1.
I was a very happy child and I loved animals, and in fact I still do like animals and I am still happy. But I think when I was a child I had a lot more energy than I have now. I'm always tired now.

2.

Well, when I was a child I was on my own all the time, I was always on my own, but now I'm never on my own; I see people all the time.

LESSON D

REVIEW OF UNIT 5

Exercise 1

1.

I get very annoyed with people who drop litter. It just … I mean it makes such a mess everywhere and it makes the countryside … and the town look so untidy. I think it's, it's very rude not to think about how the place looks and other people's feelings … and and it just makes me very angry.

2.

My flatmate annoys me most of all when he doesn't wash up after his meals, which is every meal. So that's the main thing that annoys me in my house.

Exercise 3

I get up in the morning,
I have a cup of tea,
I sit and read the paper,
I get to work at three.
So that's the way the day goes,
Yes, that's the way the day just … goes.

I get a cup of coffee,
I tidy up my desk;
I look at all my letters,
It's time to have a rest.
And that's the way the day goes,
Yes, that's the way the day just … goes.

I make a few quick phone calls,
I write a word or two;
I have a chat with old friends,
I sit and think of you.
So that's the way the day goes,
Yes, that's the way the day just … goes.

I get home in the evening,
I'm tired, it's getting late;
I sit and watch a programme,
And go to bed at eight.
And that's the way the day goes,
Yes, that's the way the day just … goes.

UNIT 8 LOVE IT OR HATE IT!

LESSON A

Exercise 2

1.

What I like about Egypt is the sense of history. The Pyramids are fantastic. And the Sphinx is like something out of this world. The Cairo Museum is fascinating, but you need at least a week to be able to see everything.

2.

What I like about America is the fact that they have no sense of history. Everything about Americans is to do with the future. They love money, they love power, they love fast cars, they love sunshine, and I love those things too. So we go well together.

3.

What I like about Australia is the outdoor life. People seem very relaxed all the time, erm, because they're able to spend so much time outdoors and enjoy the sunshine, erm, and the sea …

4.

I like Greece and I like the Greek people. And I like the way they have so much time for children. I have two children and every time we go to Greece they're involved in everything we do – in restaurants, in … on the beach, everywhere we go, the children are involved. And the Greek people like children so it makes having a holiday there great fun.

LESSON B

Exercise 1

Version 1

INTERVIEWER: Lyn, what do you like about your city?
LYN: Well, I like the open spaces, the parks and the woodlands. I also like the fact that there are people from all over the world.
INTERVIEWER: And what do you like about a birthday?
LYN: I really like having a party.
INTERVIEWER: What do you like about your bedroom?
LYN: I like my bed.
INTERVIEWER: Mm. And…what do you like about your job?
LYN: Well, I really like the women that I work with.

Version 2

INTERVIEWER: Lyn, what do you like about your city?
LYN: Well, I like the open spaces, the parks and er ….·and the woodlands … And the other thing I really like is the fact that in London you have people from all over the world so you get a variety of cultures in restaurants and, and, the kind of people that you meet.
INTERVIEWER: And what do you like about a birthday?
LYN: I think my favourite thing about a birthday is having a party. I really, really like to have a party and invite not too many people so that I can have a chance to talk to them all.
INTERVIEWER: Mm. What do you like about your bedroom?
LYN: In my bedroom I, I like my bed. It's, er, it's high up on the wall – it's about eight feet off the ground and I have to climb up a ladder to get into it. (Really!) I really like that … yeah.
INTERVIEWER: Mm. And … what do you like about your job?
LYN: Well, I like the women that I work with. I like the sense of, er, comradeship, really. And, to be truthful, I like the fact that I don't really have to think about it very much. I just get on and, er, get through the day and then go home.

Exercise 2

1. What do you like about your city?
2. What do you like about a birthday?
3. What do you like about your bedroom?
4. What do you like about your job?
Or: What do you like about your life?

LESSON D

REVIEW OF UNIT 6

Exercise 2

SPEAKER 1
Well there aren't enough bedrooms. And the bathroom's too small. There are too many stairs going to the front door and there's not much light in the living room.

SPEAKER 2
Our bathroom's much too small. And there's not enough light for the garden.

UNIT 9 THOSE WERE THE DAYS

LESSON A

Exercise 2

Version 1
INTERVIEWER: Eileen, can you remember at least five different telephone numbers?
EILEEN: Yes, I can.
INTERVIEWER: Uhuh, how about you, Michael?
MICHAEL: Yes, I can remember lots.
INTERVIEWER: What did you have for lunch three days ago?
EILEEN: Um … chicken, I think. Yes, a chicken sandwich.
INTERVIEWER: And you, Michael?
MICHAEL: Er … I can't remember.
INTERVIEWER: What items of clothing did you have when you were about 10 years old?
EILEEN: Um, let's see … um … oh, yes, I remember now, I remember I had a brown and white dress.
INTERVIEWER: Hmm.
MICHAEL: I remember my school jacket. Dark green.
INTERVIEWER: Hmm. Can you remember all the words of your country's national song?
EILEEN: No, I can't. I can't remember any of the words!
MICHAEL: Yes, I can.
INTERVIEWER: What was your favourite toy when you were a baby?
EILEEN: Oh, I can't remember.
INTERVIEWER: What about you, Michael?
MICHAEL: When I was a baby? Er … a wooden train.
INTERVIEWER: Can you remember anyone with glasses when you were a child under 10 years old?
EILEEN: My father and two cousins.
MICHAEL: My grandfather.
INTERVIEWER: Who was your favourite actor or actress when you were 15?
EILEEN: Ooh … Gregory Peck. And the woman was … Ingrid Bergman.
MICHAEL: Er … Marlon Brando.
INTERVIEWER: Hmm. And can you remember a special smell from your childhood?
EILEEN: Yes, a hospital smell.
INTERVIEWER: And you, Michael?
MICHAEL: I remember the smell of fresh grass, mmmm …

Version 2
INTERVIEWER: Eileen, can you remember at least five different telephone numbers?
EILEEN: Yes, do you want me to tell you them?

INTERVIEWER: No, it's all right. Er, how about you, Michael?
MICHAEL: Yes, it's no problem for me, I can remember lots.
INTERVIEWER: What did you have for lunch three days ago?
EILEEN: Um … a chicken sandwich. I always have that on Mondays.
INTERVIEWER: And you, Michael?
MICHAEL: Er … I can't remember.
INTERVIEWER: Right, now, what items of clothing did you have when you were about 10 years old?
EILEEN: Um, let me see … um … oh, yes, I remember now, I remember I had a brown and white dress. I hated it – it was so awful. I never wanted to wear it.
MICHAEL: I remember my school jacket. Dark green. That's all I can remember.
INTERVIEWER: Can you remember all the words of your country's national song?
EILEEN: Oh, my goodness, no!
MICHAEL: Well, I can.
INTERVIEWER: What was your favourite toy when you were a baby?
EILEEN: Oh, I can't remember. I didn't have a lot of toys.
INTERVIEWER: What about you, Michael?
MICHAEL: When I was a baby? Erm … a wooden train.
INTERVIEWER: Can you remember anyone with glasses when you were a child under 10 years old?
EILEEN: My father and two cousins.
MICHAEL: My grandfather had glasses; I remember they were always on the table beside his chair.
INTERVIEWER: And, er, now, who was your favourite actor or actress when you were 15?
EILEEN: Ooh … Gregory Peck. He was a great actor. And the woman was … Ingrid Bergman.
MICHAEL: Er … Marlon Brando, I think. I can't remember very clearly.
INTERVIEWER: Now, can you remember a special smell from your childhood?
EILEEN: Yes, a hospital smell. I don't know what it was, but it was a hospital smell.
INTERVIEWER: And you, Michael?
MICHAEL: Cut grass. The smell of fresh grass.

Exercise 3

Close your eyes and relax. Imagine your life is a road. Walk back along the road of your life slowly starting with today, then yesterday, then last year. Keep walking slowly. Stop when you get to your years at secondary school. Turn off the road and walk up to the school building. Look at it. Look around the school yard, the shapes, colours. Go inside, walk along the corridors to your classroom. Go inside your classroom. Look around for your desk. Sit down. Look around you at your classmates in the desks near you. Look at their faces, say hello to them. Who are they? Look at their clothes, their faces … Now slowly get up and leave. Walk out of the room, out of the school … back along the road, back to this room. Now open your eyes.

LESSON B

Exercise 2

HELENA: Well, I was born in England and I lived in a small village in Buckinghamshire until I was 18. When I finished school, I went to the States for three months – I was a swimming teacher in a children's camp in North Carolina.

And then I returned to England and went to university in Oxford for three years. After that I moved to Japan. I lived there for two years. I was an English teacher in a school in Nagasaki in the south of Japan. I really enjoyed that. Then I came back to England and did a teacher training course and after that I went back to Japan, back to Nagasaki for another three years. When I finally came back to England, I worked in a Japanese bank in London for a couple of years, and then I got a job in publishing. My job involved a lot of travelling and I went to Japan, the USA, Canada, Malaysia, Morocco, Portugal … I really went to a lot of places. Now I have my own business in England – but I still travel a lot. Only last month I went to Mexico …

LESSON C

Exercise 2

telephoned   looked   seemed   wasn't   arrived   showed
tried   finished   noticed

I .... Mia yesterday from Hong Kong. She was fine. Her new hairstyle .... great and the kids .... fine too, apart from Janine's broken ankle. The plaster .... heavy on the screen, but I'm sure it .... Mia said I .... tired, but that's not surprising – I .... in Hong Kong ten hours late. She .... me a letter from my parents and I .... to read some of it, but it was impossible to see all the words. My mother's handwriting is so bad these days. I'm sure the cost of that call was enormous. It's a good thing I can put it on the company account. When I .... closely at her, just before we finished talking, I .... she looked nervous about something. I wonder what it was …

I telephoned Mia yesterday from Hong Kong. She was fine. Her new hairstyle looked great and the kids seemed fine too, apart from Janine's broken ankle. The plaster looked heavy on the screen, but I'm sure it wasn't. Mia said I looked tired, but that's not surprising – I arrived in Hong Kong ten hours late. She showed me a letter from my parents and I tried to read some of it, but it was impossible to see all the words. My mother's handwriting is so bad these days. I'm sure the cost of that call was enormous. It's a good thing I can put it on the company account. When I looked closely at her, just before we finished talking, I noticed she looked nervous about something. I wonder what it was …

LESSON D

REVIEW OF UNIT 8

Exercise 1

He likes Ted. She likes Fred.
He likes Ann. She likes Dan.
I like … holidays in the Mediterranean.

He likes rocks. She likes clocks.
He likes bikes. She likes hikes.
I like … Jose.

He likes suits. She likes boots.
He likes hats. She likes cats.
I like salmon pâté sandwiches.

He likes rice. She likes ice.
He likes meat. She likes wheat.
I like …

UNIT 10 ONCE UPON A TIME

LESSON A

Exercise 2

1.
The child sat and waited a long time. She ate all her sandwiches and thought sadly of home. At last an old woman came towards her and said: 'Follow me.' They walked down the street and turned into the doorway of a little cottage. There was a fire burning in the hearth and there was a lovely smell of something cooking in the oven. The woman said, 'I'm your Aunty Daisy. Sit down and we'll have something to eat.'
2.
They met for the first time at a railway station. They did not speak to each other but caught the next train to Cairo. The train stopped suddenly and all the lights went out. He panicked. She lit a match. He lit his cigarette with the match. She said, 'This is a no-smoking compartment.'

LESSON B

Exercise 1

Adesose Wallace comes from Nigeria. He was born in Elorin in the northwest of Nigeria and he's from a family of six children. He's an artist – he tells stories, he plays musical instruments, he sings and he does a bit of dancing. He learnt all this from his mother and from the rest of his family. He enjoyed listening to stories when he was a child in Nigeria. When the sun went down in the evenings, they sat underneath the trees and his mother told lots and lots of stories. Today, Adesose tells lots of stories to children in many, many schools. Here's one of the stories he tells.

Exercise 2

Part 1
Once upon a time, long ago, there was a very, very old man and his wife. They had seven children.

One day the old woman went into the kitchen to prepare a meal for the children. And what happened? Suddenly she saw that there were no bananas, no potatoes, there was no rice, not one bit of the lovely food that the children liked to eat. So she was very worried. She quickly ran to her husband:
   'Baba! Baba! We are in trouble.'
   'Mmm. What is the problem?'
   'There's no food for the children.'

Part 2
Luckily the mother found some food for the children. So that was the end of the problem. The father called all the children together. He said: 'Stay inside the house, children. Don't go outside.' Then the old man and the old woman left the children and went to the city.

Part 3
Everything was fine for one day, two days, three days. The children stayed inside the house, playing and laughing and having a good time. The next day, they went outside to play and then … ssss … Suddenly, the wind started blowing. As the wind blew, all the treetops started moving from left to right. Now all the children were scared.

   The children ran into the house, locked all the doors up, all the windows. And then suddenly the rain started. Ah, that was

Ojumbala, the rain god. Now, Ojumbala was behind the window.

Part 4
Suddenly, Ojumbala came into the house.

Ahaha – he started catching the children all over the house. But the little one, the clever little brother … he ran into the bedroom, under the bed. He hid himself there. And what happened to those children? Ojumbala ate all of them … but not the little one, of course, the clever little one. Ojumbala atc all six children, and he was so full he could not move.

By this time, the old man and the old woman thought: 'Well, it's time to go home.' The old man said: 'Hmm, let's go now. I hope the children are safe.'

The old man and his wife arrived home.

'Ayamada! Ayamada! Where are you, children? Hello!'

It was very quiet, so they quickly moved towards the door, opened the door …

'Eh, who is this? Ojumbala? Ojumbala, what are you doing here?'

Ojumbala couldn't move.

Straightaway, the old woman started shouting: 'Oh, my God! Oh, my God, my children! What are we going to do? Ojumbala …'

The old man quickly ran into the kitchen and brought out a very big knife. And he said: 'Ojumbala, if you don't tell me what happened to my children today, I am going to hit you, Ojumbala.'

Ah, and he started hitting Ojumbala. And Ojumbala fell to the ground.

And then he started squeezing his stomach, he started squeezing … and squeezing, and squeezing … and the children came out. Out they came, one by one. And there were six of them. 'Ojumbala, where is the little child?'

Suddenly the clever little child came out from under the bed. And the old woman saw this baby, she was so happy, she just gave him a big hug. And all the children were very, very lucky because they were saved.

LESSON D

REVIEW OF UNIT 9

Exercise 2

SPEAKER 1
I live in Paris now, but when I was a child I lived in a small town in Brittany. My grandmother loved telling me stories about what the town was like when she was a child. They lived in a village outside the town, and … every week they went to town, to the market … to sell their eggs, I think, or maybe it was vegetables and, er, homemade butter. The roads were not paved then, of course, they were just small, dusty little lanes and when it rained they were very muddy – it was very hard for the horse and cart … My grandmother remembered everything so clearly, the big market – it looked big to her when she was so small – and the dark, cluttered shops … And she remembered that one day she went with her father to the school. It was a Saturday and there was no school of course, but she looked with longing at the little desks and the pictures on the wall and there was a big map of the world at the front … She couldn't go to school because they lived too far away.

SPEAKER 2
Well Bucharest was a really elegant city a hundred years ago. People called it 'the little Paris'. It had wide roads … if you see

prints of it in the nineteenth century, there were wide boulevards crowded with carriages. And lots of trees. So it was shady and cool even in the summer. There were beautiful buildings, the opera, theatres, big restaurants, and er … there were a lot of parks and shady squares. Some of the big old buildings are still there, and there are still a lot of shady squares. And … still a lot of trees. But they didn't have all these concrete buildings that we've got now. The buildings were made of stone, and they were lovely.

UNIT 11 WHAT'S GOING ON?

LESSON A

Exercise 2

1.
I'm standing in front of Government House. They're coming down the street now. They're shouting as you can hear, but there is no violence. They're all walking in an orderly way, with the police walking beside them. They're stopping now, and one of them is going up to the door …

2.
The couple are coming down the steps now, the band is playing, the crowd is waving flags. The President is stepping forward to greet them, they're shaking hands. And now a little girl is giving the Prime Minister a bouquet of flowers, and she's bending down to thank the little girl. And now the Prime Minister is walking towards the crowd, she's talking to them, shaking hands …

LESSON B

Exercise 1

Version 1
1.
I'm doing my first job. I'm working for a big company, and I'm living on a boat because flats are too expensive in the city.

2.
I'm a student at the university, so this is a temporary job for me. I'm working in a big restaurant, and I'm really tired, because I'm working until late at night.

3.
Well, I'm a teacher and I'm having a wonderful time on holiday at the moment. I'm seeing a lot of interesting things, and I'm spending a lot of time on the beach, of course. It's great.

4.
We're going on holiday to Spain this year, so I'm learning Spanish by myself. I listen to cassettes at home, while the children are at school. It's hard, but I'm enjoying it.

Version 2
1.
This is my first job, so I'm learning a lot every day. I'm working for this really big company to get some experience. I want to go back to university next year. I'm enjoying it, but everything is really expensive in the city. I'm living on a boat for the moment, because flats are just too expensive.

2.

I'm doing my first job at the moment. It's a temporary job, er, to help me out as I'm a student. And I'm working in this really big restaurant. And I'm really enjoying it, but sometimes I have to stay really late, until one o'clock at night. Um, and then I'm really tired. But er, I really enjoy working and it's a really good experience.

3.

Well, I'm a teacher, and er, I'm having a wonderful time on holiday at the moment. I must say I'm really enjoying the rest. Er, I'm spending loads of time on the beach, er, having lovely food and drink and seeing really interesting things as well. I'm really interested in architecture and I like going to cafés, and, er, well, for one thing it's great not being in the classroom all day.

4.

We're going on holiday to Spain this year, southern Spain. And so when I'm at home, doing the washing up and clearing up the kitchen when the kids are at school, I listen to these Teach-Yourself-Spanish tapes, which are really good. Um, it's, er, it's clever because you get a chance to repeat sentences … and, um, some of the conversation is very fast and it's hard to pick up the pronunciation, but I think I'm doing quite well; things like a 'b' for 'v' and Andalucia instead of Andalusia – it's quite hard but I'm enjoying it.

LESSON C

Exercise 2

1.

In my country, the cost of living is going up. So is unemployment. The number of years that people spend in education is also going up. The level of water pollution is going up. The popularity of sports is going up.

2.

The cost of living in my country is certainly going up and, er, at the same time, unemployment is going up as well. And that's why many people spend more time in education. So the number of years people spend in education is going up, because if people face unemployment after school they stay in education as long as they can. Fortunately, the level of water pollution is going down, and that is because the government is taking steps to reduce the levels of pollution. The popularity of sports? Well, I don't know about that. I think it is staying the same.

3.

In my country, the cost of living is going up, but more slowly than in the past. Unemployment is also going up, very quickly. The number of years people spend in education is going up, as education becomes more and more important. The level of water pollution is unfortunately going up, but so is awareness of the problem. That's also going up. The popularity of sport is staying the same, I think. Sports have always been popular, especially football and baseball.

LESSON D

REVIEW OF UNIT 9

Exercise 2

1. broke, spoke, woke, made
2. rang, sang, brought
3. sent, mended, went
4. hid, did, rode
5. watched, caught, bought
6. thought, drank, stank
7. sold, told, spelled
8. grinned, began, ran

REVIEW OF UNIT 10

Exercise 1

A: Did you read about that Australian man in the Himalayas who got lost in the middle of winter and survived on chocolate bars?

B: No.

A: Well, it was in the paper the other day … he survived for 43 days … up in the Himalayas, and he was dressed in light clothing, and he only had snow and two chocolate bars.

B: Sounds impossible. How did he stay alive?

A: Well, it said in the paper that he kept moving around to keep his temperature up …

B: But 43 days is a month and a half!

A: Yeah, I know, but they said he had a strong personality … that helped …

B: But he only had two chocolate bars. It's impossible.

A: Yeah, and snow to drink … but perhaps he found other things to eat under the snow or something … he was very thin and weak when they found him …

B: Oh, yeah … I think he also had part-time jobs with both the newspaper and the chocolate company …

A: You never believe anything, that's your problem!

UNIT 12 MAKING PLANS

LESSON A

Exercise 2

Version 1

1.

JOHN: What are you doing this weekend, Gill?

GILL: I'm going on holiday to Cornwall with my husband. We're going for a week. What are you doing, John?

JOHN: I'm going to a hotel, with my family.

2.

IRENE: What are you doing this weekend, James?

JAMES: Not much. My friend's coming on Saturday, and we're having a meal, and then going to a film. What about you, Irene?

IRENE: Well, I'm working on Saturday. And on Sunday, I'm making lunch for my mother, because it's Mothers' Day.

Version 2

1.

JOHN: So, what are you doing this weekend, Gill? Anything interesting?

GILL: Well, I'm actually going on holiday. My husband's an engineer, and it's the end of a big job for him in Kuwait, so we're going down to Cornwall for a week, to a little cottage.

JOHN: Sounds great … very relaxing.

GILL: What are you doing, John? Are you going away anywhere?

JOHN: Me, um … well, it's my birthday on Friday, so in fact, I'm going away with my, er, family, to a hotel. It's really nice there … it's not very far, it's in a little village near the town where we live … only takes half an hour to get there.

2.

IRENE: What are you doing this weekend, James?

JAMES: This weekend? Oh, nothing much, really. I'm having a pretty quiet weekend. My friend's coming up on Saturday, and we're going out for a meal together at a little Indonesian restaurant near my place, and, er, after that we're going to a film. I think that's about it. What about you, what are you doing, Irene?

IRENE: Er … well, actually, I'm working all day on Saturday. Very boring, I'm afraid. And Sunday's Mothers' Day …

JAMES: Is it? Oh, I forgot all about that!

IRENE: Yeah, it is, so I'm making lunch for my mum at her house. It's a sort of a tradition, I do it every year on Mothers' Day.

LESSON B

Exercise 2

1.

CALLER: Can Mrs Roman go to a meeting at 3 pm on Wednesday?

2.

CALLER: Hello, this is Mr Brown's secretary. Can either Petra or Marion see Mr Brown at 10 am on Tuesday?

3.

CALLER: This is John Peters speaking. I'm coming to the city on Friday and I'd like to meet Marion Dorkas at 9.30 in the morning. Is she free at that time?

4.

CALLER: Hello there, Guy here. Can you tell me: are Marion and Jon free for lunch on Monday?

5.

CALLER: Hello, Herr Göninge's office here. Herr Göninge's having some trouble with his travel plans. Could he change his meeting with Mrs Roman from Tuesday morning to Monday morning, at the same time?

6.

CALLER: Hello, it's Keith here. Is Jon busy at 11 on Friday morning?

7.

CALLER: Can Marion come to a meeting on Thursday afternoon?

LESSON C

Exercise 2

Dear English class,
I arrived in Canada a week ago and already I think that my English is improving! I'm living in a small flat near the centre of Toronto. It's cheap and quite comfortable.

In your letter you ask what I'm going to do to improve my English. Well, I'm not going to visit the university to see what English courses they offer there because I'm so tired of classrooms. I'm going to read magazines every day. I'm also going to try to get a part-time job because then I can speak conversational English a lot more. I'm going to spend a lot on courses because they are so important. There are some good bookshops here so I'm going to look for one or two books or cassettes to use by myself. Also, I'm going to find a Canadian boyfriend, that's a good way to learn English.

How are you getting on? I was sorry I had to leave in the middle of the course. Are you going to write to me again? Hope to hear from you all soon.

LESSON D

REVIEW OF UNIT 11

Exercise 2

Try to save a precious moment from the past year for the future. Think of a moment that you would like to remember and that you are happy to talk about in class. Go back in your mind now to that moment.

[1] Where are you? What is around you?
Jot down a few words about where you are.
[2] How many other people are there with you?
Jot down their names.
[3] What are you wearing?
What are other people wearing? Jot down a few words about your clothes and their clothes.
[4] Are you eating or drinking? Jot down a few words about the food or drink.
[5] What sounds can you hear? Jot them down.
[6] What can you smell or see? Jot down a few words about that.
[7] What are you doing?
What are other people doing?
Jot down a few words about what you're doing, and what other people are doing.

UNIT 13 BETTER AND BETTER

LESSON A

Exercise 1

INTERVIEWER: OK, first of all, Sue and Pat. Question number 1. Is Greenland bigger than Australia?

SUE: We think yes – that Greenland is bigger than Australia.

INTERVIEWER: No, you're wrong. Australia's much bigger than Greenland. Question number 2. Is China bigger than Brazil?

PAT: Yes … we think China is much bigger than Brazil.

INTERVIEWER: You're right. Question number 3. Is India bigger than Canada?

SUE: Er … we're not sure whether it is bigger. No, we're not, no, it's not bigger than Canada.

INTERVIEWER: And you're right. It's not bigger than Canada. Number 4. Is Italy larger than Japan?

PAT: Yes, definitely. Italy is much larger than Japan.

INTERVIEWER: And you're wrong. Italy is not larger than Japan. Sorry. Last question. Is Mexico smaller than Indonesia?

SUE: Well, we're not sure about this; we think Mexico is smaller than Indonesia.

INTERVIEWER: No. Mexico is not smaller than Indonesia. Sorry.

INTERVIEWER: So. Question 6. Is France larger than Spain?
LAURA: Er, yes, yes, it's a bit larger.
DIETER: Yeah, only just a little bit though.
LAURA: Yes, so France is a bit larger than Spain.
INTERVIEWER: That's absolutely right.
DIETER: Well done!
INTERVIEWER: Question 7. Is Iceland smaller than Cuba?
LAURA: Er, no.
DIETER: That's tricky.
LAURA: No, it's much bigger.
DIETER: Oh, OK.
LAURA: No, Iceland is much bigger than Cuba.
INTERVIEWER: In fact, Iceland is smaller than Cuba. It's a little bit smaller than Cuba. Right, question 8. Is Turkey larger than Egypt?
DIETER: Ooh, er, well, I would say quite a lot larger.
LAURA: Yes, Turkey is larger than Egypt.
INTERVIEWER: No, you're wrong. In fact, Egypt is quite a bit larger than Turkey. Question 9. Which is larger: Kenya or Chile?
LAURA: Chile's larger isn't it?
DIETER: Er … yes.
LAURA: Yes, Chile is larger.
INTERVIEWER: You're absolutely right. Chile is nearly twice as large as Kenya. And the last, question 10. Which is smaller: Thailand or New Zealand?
LAURA: Ooh, it's very close, I think Thailand's a bit, bit smaller than New Zealand.
DIETER: Yes, there's two islands on New Zealand. Yes, Thailand is smaller than New Zealand.
INTERVIEWER: In fact, New Zealand is smaller than Thailand. So the answer there was New Zealand. It's quite a bit smaller than Thailand.

Exercise 2

Version 1
Country 1 is a lot bigger than Greenland. And it's also … much bigger than India. But it's … a bit smaller than Brazil. It's got many interesting animals, like kangaroos.

Country 2 is much smaller than Turkey, but it's a bit bigger than New Zealand. It's also … a bit smaller than Japan. It is the home of spaghetti.

Country 3 is much, much bigger than India, but it's … a bit smaller than Canada. And it's also a bit larger than Brazil and … a lot larger than Australia. It's in Asia. There's a very long wall in this country.

Version 2
Country 1 is a lot bigger than Greenland, a bit smaller than Brazil, and much larger than India. It's in the southern hemisphere and is an island with interesting animals, including kangaroos. It has a population of about 18 million people.

Country 2 is much smaller than Turkey, but a bit bigger than New Zealand. It's a bit smaller than Japan. It's in Europe and is near the Adriatic Sea. In fact there's sea around most of this country. And … it's the home of spaghetti.

Country 3 is much, much bigger than India, but a bit smaller than Canada. It's bit larger than Brazil and a lot larger than Australia. It's in Asia and near to Russia. It has a very large population and a very old culture. There is a very long wall in this country.

Exercise 3
Listen to seven questions; write down your answers.
1. Is your city older than Brasilia?
2. Is your city more interesting than Istanbul?
3. Is your city cleaner than Istanbul?
4. Is your city more polluted than Brasilia?
5. Is your city quieter than Istanbul?
6. Is your city noisier than Brasilia?
7. Is your city more crowded than Brasilia?

REVIEW OF UNIT 11
Exercise 2
1. Are you feeling lonely? (feeling)
2. Are you filling your life with television? (filling)
3. Are you leaving enough time for work? (leaving)
4. Are you cleaning your flat every week? (cleaning)
5. Are you beginning to make friends? (beginning)
6. Are you sleeping well at nights? (sleeping)
7. Are you living a healthy life? (living)
8. Are you eating enough? (eating)
9. Are you keeping warm? (keeping)
10. You're not slipping into bad habits, are you? (slipping)

REVIEW OF UNIT 12
Exercise 1
A: What are you doing this evening?
B: I'm going to the cinema.
A: Who are you going with?
B: With Midori.
A: What are you doing after that?
B: After that? We're having a meal in town.
A: Are you going by bus?
B: No, we're going in my car.
A: What are you doing on Sunday?
B: On Sunday? Nothing, I'm staying at home.
A: When's your mother arriving?
B: She's arriving on Monday. My father telephoned after she left Singapore.

UNIT 14 A SPIRIT OF ADVENTURE

Exercise 1
1.
I jumped out and I felt so free … I could feel the wind on my face. Then, when it opened I knew my first dive was OK. I looked down. I could see lots of things on the ground. It all seemed to happen so quickly, but it was a fantastic feeling … I came down and landed on the ground … I landed on my feet … I've never had another feeling like that.

2.
The very first time was special, really beautiful. I was terrified, but I jumped from the plane into the air. I could feel the wind

on my face. I felt so free, like a little bird. Then I pulled the cord and my parachute opened. I knew my first dive was OK. I looked down. I could see lots of things on the ground. Then it all seemed to happen so quickly. I came down towards the ground and I landed on my feet. I've never had another feeling like that. I picked up my parachute and walked towards the others ... I was so happy.

Exercise 2

Version 1

WOMAN: Have you ever tried sky diving?

MAN: No, never. I've never tried sky diving.

WOMAN: Hmm. How about water skiing? Have you ever tried that?

MAN: Yes, I have, once. Um, I was about 15. What about you? Have you ever tried scuba diving?

WOMAN: No, I haven't. I don't like water. What about ... karate? Have you ever tried that?

MAN: I tried it once, but I didn't like it much. Have you ever done any motor racing?

WOMAN: No, I haven't. I hate motor racing.

MAN: Er, what about ... um ... horse riding? Have you ever tried horse riding?

WOMAN: Er ... yes, I have. I tried it once when I was about 10.

MAN: How did you feel?

WOMAN: Very, very nervous.

Version 2

WOMAN: Have you ever tried sky diving?

MAN: No, never, and I don't want to, thank you, I prefer to stay alive.

WOMAN: How about water skiing? Have you ever tried that?

MAN: Yes, I have, once, when I was about 15. Um, I fell in the water all the time. And it was expensive. What about you? Have you ever tried scuba diving?

WOMAN: No, I don't like water. What about ... karate? Have you ever tried that?

MAN: I tried it once, but I didn't like it much. Have you ever done any motor racing?

WOMAN: No, I haven't, it doesn't interest me at all, too noisy.

MAN: What about horse riding? Have you ever tried that?

WOMAN: Er ... yes, I have, I tried it once when I was about 10.

MAN: How did you feel?

WOMAN: Very nervous because I didn't want to fall off.

LESSON D

REVIEW OF UNIT 13

Exercise 2

INTERVIEWER: Which animal is the easiest to keep, do you think?

WOMAN: Easiest to keep? Erm, probably a cat, because they only need a bit of food each day and they're pretty independent.

INTERVIEWER: Which animal is the most intelligent?

MAN: Well, some people say that a pig is very intelligent because they have a large brain for an animal, but I've never had one as a pet, so I don't know really.

INTERVIEWER: Which pet has the longest life?

WOMAN: I think some parrots live for a long time, especially the larger ones, but I'm not sure why, ... er, maybe it's because they eat the right things, like fruit and nuts.

INTERVIEWER: Which animal is the noisiest?

MAN: My dog ... definitely my dog!

INTERVIEWER: Why is she so noisy?

MAN: It's a he not a she, erm, I don't know, but he barks all the time ... perhaps it's because I'm out a lot, I dunno.

UNIT 15 DOES BEING TIDY SAVE TIME?

LESSON A

Exercise 3

1.
Yes, I have, I lost it once when I was in Pakistan. I can remember I spent hours at the embassy, getting a new one ... it was terrible.

2.
No, I don't. I'm usually too tired to sit and watch anything after work.

3.
No, I don't, because I've got an address and phone book.

4.
Yes, regularly ... in fact I broke a bottle yesterday and ... er ... I broke a plate last week.

5.
Sometimes I do, yes, but I keep a spare car key at home for emergencies.

6.
No, never. In fact, I've never forgotten anyone's birthday in the family.

Now listen to the questions.

1.
Have you ever lost your passport?
Yes, I have, I lost it once when I was in Pakistan. I can remember I spent hours at the embassy, getting a new one ... it was terrible.

2.
Do you sometimes watch TV in the evenings?
No, I don't. I'm always too tired to sit and watch anything after work.

3.
Do you keep losing addresses and phone numbers?
No, I don't, because I've got an address and phone book.

4.
Do you keep breaking things?
Yes, regularly ... in fact, I broke a bottle yesterday and ... er ... I broke a plate last week.

5.
Do you sometimes lock your car keys in the car?
Sometimes I do, yes, but I keep a spare car key at home for emergencies.

6.
Have you ever forgotten your wife's birthday?
No, never. In fact, I've never forgotten anyone's birthday in the family.

LESSON C

Exercise 3

Version 1

INTERVIEWER: What do you like about your computer, Jackie?

JACKIE: Well, it's good for keeping lists of names and addresses – all sorts of things.

INTERVIEWER: How about you, Franz?

FRANZ: I left school before computers came in, so I don't even know how to turn one on!

INTERVIEWER: But do you think they're useful for some things?

FRANZ: Well, I guess they're useful for storing names and figures. But if the computer goes down, everything is lost. It's better to write things on paper, it seems to me.

JACKIE: Then there's the problem with children. Definitely, for children, using computers a lot is bad. They play games all the time.

FRANZ: And it's not very good for your eyes. And you can sit badly at the desk, and get a bad back.

Version 2

INTERVIEWER: How much do you use computers, Jackie?

JACKIE: Well, I used a computer for the first time, um, about two months ago. But now I use it every day, my computer. I just can't manage without it.

INTERVIEWER: What sort of things do you do on the computer?

JACKIE: Well, I play games ... but I suppose I do ... I write letters ...

INTERVIEWER: Yes.

JACKIE: ... most of the time I write letters.

INTERVIEWER: You use it for names and addresses?

JACKIE: Yes, it's good for, for lists. For keeping lists of names, addresses, all sorts of things, yes.

INTERVIEWER: How about you?

FRANZ: Well, I'm afraid I don't even know how to turn one on, actually, if I'm honest. I left school just before computers came in, so I'm really, really unknowledgeable about computers.

INTERVIEWER: But do you think they're useful for some things?

FRANZ: Well, I guess they are useful for storing lots of things, and names and figures ... but it seems to me that when a computer goes down, everything's lost. It seems to me it's better to have it written on paper, really.

JACKIE: Also, I think definitely for children, er, using computers a lot is bad. Because they forget how to use their mind. And also they want to play games all the time, and not do any work.

INTERVIEWER: It's not very good for your eyes, is it, if you keep looking at the screen for too long? (Good point, yeah.) And also, you might sit badly at the chair or at the desk or at the keyboard (That's true). You have to be careful not to do it for too long.

LESSON D

REVIEW OF UNIT 13

Exercise 2

Part 1

A: Is Newcastle larger, do you think?

B: I'm not sure, but all the new buildings they are planning are going to be really high.

A: Yes, I know what you mean. The new office buildings here in Darwin are getting big too, these days.

B: But you have great weather in Darwin. Last year was wet in Newcastle, so the beaches were really quiet and the shops really busy.

A: At least you have great shops, the shopping centre here is really small, compared to Newcastle.

B: But you live in a very beautiful spot and your house is large compared to ours.

A: Yes, but your house is nice to look at, more traditional.

B: Well, yes, maybe, but it's certainly safer to live in Darwin.

A: Do you think so? The crime problem is bigger here these days, you know.

Part 2

1. Newcastle is large.
2. Last year was wet.
3. The shopping centre is small.
4. Your house is nice.
5. It's safe to live here.
6. The crime problem is big.

UNIT 16 OUR NEIGHBOURHOOD

LESSON B

Exercise 1

Version 1

WOMAN: I live in a village, and our next door neighbours have just moved. So now we've got new neighbours. In the family there's a granny and two children, and the mum and dad. And we have just got a new road outside our house. And what else has happened? Oh, yes, a new pub has just opened. Yes, it's great, it's just up the road.

MAN: Well, the most interesting thing that's just happened in my street is the new pelican crossing. There's a school, you see, opposite a shopping street and it was quite dangerous. So we're all very pleased. The quality of things in the shops has improved now, so we're all very happy.

Version 2

WOMAN: I live in a village and our next door neighbours have just moved. So we have, erm, now got new next door neighbours. A new family has just moved in. And in that family, um, there's the granny who has just moved in as well, and the two children, and the mum and the dad. And also we have just had a new road outside our house. There were some men who turned up, and they've just put a new surface on the road. And what else has happened? Oh, yes, er, a pub has just opened. Yes, it's great, it's just up the road, and er ... that's quite new for our village.

MAN: Well, the most interesting and good thing that's just happened in my street is that there's been a new pelican crossing put in. Because there's a school, you see, opposite a shopping street and there's a sweet shop there and the children have have often been injured in car accidents and it's been very dangerous. So that's really good news, we're all very pleased, us in the neighbourhood scheme anyway. And, er, the other thing of course is that since then, the business in the shop has improved and therefore, the quality has improved, so we're all very happy.

LESSON C

Exercise 1

Right, well, you go straight ahead and then turn left. Turn right. And then go down the street and turn right at the traffic lights. Then you take the first street on your right. Cross the bridge. Then you go to the roundabout and take the first street. And it's the third street on the left.

LESSON D

REVIEW OF UNIT 14

Exercise 1

1.
Clue 1: air   2: airplane   3: jump   4: parachute   5: land
2.
Clue 1: animal   2: shoes   3: rider   4: four legs   5: Whoa!
3.
Clue 1: finishing line   2: flag   3: turn   4: fast   5: driver
4.
Clue 1: a watch   2: down   3: air   4: water   5: dive
5.
Clue 1: flame   2: basket   3: gas   4: up   5: hot air
6.
Clue 1: ball   2: walking   3: green   4: hole   5: 18 holes

REVIEW OF UNIT 15

Exercise 2

INTERVIEWER: Chris, what's the biggest regret you've had in your life?

CHRIS: Er … I guess, not studying hard enough at school. Not learning sciences properly, not learning languages. I feel I wasted a lot of time there.

INTERVIEWER: How about you, Kate?

KATE: Erm, I think not keeping up my piano lessons at school. You know, giving up the piano was a big regret. I can't play at all now, and that's a pity.

INTERVIEWER: Er, and what's been the happiest moment in your life up to now, Kate?

KATE: Um, gosh, that's hard. Seeing my little boy, who is three and a half, in his school concert made me very happy and proud. He sang a little song … it was so lovely.

INTERVIEWER: How about you, Chris?

CHRIS: Oh, dear! Oh, I don't know. Erm, I just can't think of anything. I'm sort of happy most of the time, I think …

UNIT 17 IT'S WORTH DOING WELL

LESSON A

Exercise 2

If you have more ticks for questions 1, 2 and 3, you are usually good with numbers. If you have more ticks for questions 4, 5 and 6, you are usually good with words. If you have about the same number of ticks, you are a balanced person, good with both numbers and words.

LESSON C

Exercise 2

Version 1

MAN: I don't think it's very important to be polite. People are sometimes too polite. I think it's better to say what you mean.

MAN: I don't think being polite is very important. It's an old English habit and I think it's a waste of time.

WOMAN: Politeness is very important because it shows people that you care about them and about their feelings. This is very important.

Version 2

MAN: I don't think it's very important to be polite. I think it's nice to be polite but I sometimes think that people are too polite and perhaps they ought to say what they mean more.

MAN: I don't think being polite is very important at all. I think it's one of these English old-fashioned habits that really should be, er, banned, personally. I think it's a waste of time.

WOMAN: Politeness is one of the most important things because it shows people how you think about them and it shows that you care about them and that you care about their feelings. And this is most important.

LESSON D

REVIEW OF UNIT 15

Exercise 1

1. I like being early for work.
2. I like working with tidy people.
3. I like work which gives me regular hours.
4. Work practices in the modern office are very important.
5. Being a manager is a hard job today.
6. Be a good worker so your manager can see how important you are.
7. I want to be in a top position in the company.
8. Working late is a problem for parents with young children.
9. I hate leaving work early when the traffic is terrible.
10. Leave work early and start late – that's what I think.

UNIT 18 ON YOUR TRAVELS

LESSON A

Exercise 2

WOMAN: On a long flight, you should take loose clothes.

MAN: I think on a long flight, you should take boiled sweets for the take off.

WOMAN: Mmm. And you should drink … water?

MAN: I agree … to reduce the effects of dehydration.

WOMAN: Ah, but you shouldn't drink … alcohol.

MAN: I couldn't agree more.

WOMAN: Mmm, definitely. And you should … sleep?

MAN: If you can. And as you've already said, wear comfortable clothes.

WOMAN: Ah, you put you should wear comfortable clothes?

MAN: I did, yes.

WOMAN: And then I put: You shouldn't eat too much.

MAN: No, or try and open the window …

WOMAN: Mmm … that's true. And then at the end I put: When arriving in a hot country after a long flight, you should have a short sleep.

MAN: Certainly. Or sunbathe.

WOMAN: Yes, that's a good idea.

MAN: On a long flight, you should take a very good book to read.

WOMAN: I think you should take a toothbrush.

MAN: Oh, yes. You should drink lots of water and fruit juice.

WOMAN: Oh, yes, plenty of water, that's, that's a very good idea.

MAN: Yes. You shouldn't drink too much alcohol.

WOMAN: You're right. I agree.

MAN: Good. Now you should try and sleep as much as possible.

WOMAN: And you should raise your ankles, because sometimes your feet and ankles swell when you're flying.

MAN: Good idea. Also on a long flight, you shouldn't stay awake for the whole flight. What do you think?

WOMAN: It depends on the film that they're showing. And I think you shouldn't eat too much. That's important.

MAN: Ah, right. Now, when arriving in a hot country after a long flight, I think you should drink lots of water and have a sleep.

WOMAN: Yes, have a salty drink, because it's a hot country, and then have a shower to cool you down.

MAN: Good idea. And of course phone home.

LESSON C

Exercise 2

Version 1

A: A bad tourist is somebody who is very loud, and who doesn't eat the food in another country.

B: A good tourist is somebody who respects the traditions in a different country.

C: A bad tourist is someone who doesn't respect old buildings. When I was in Egypt, I saw some tourists at the Pyramids, and they tried to take a little bit of a Pyramid home with them. I think that's a bad tourist.

D: A bad tourist isn't really interested in the country they're visiting. They want their own language, their own food.

Version 2

A: A bad tourist is somebody who is very loud, and, erm, therefore you notice them all the time. And also who refuses to eat the food in another country.

B: I think a good tourist is one that respects the, er, traditions and ways of the country that they're visiting. They shouldn't be visiting the country if they don't want to take part in the way that that country is.

C: I think a bad tourist is someone who doesn't respect the property that they're looking round. When I was in Egypt, there were two Americans walking around the Pyramids, and one of them went up and tried to chip a piece of it off, to take home. I think that's a bad tourist.

D: I think a bad tourist isn't really interested in the country they're visiting. A bad tourist seems to want their own country, erm, with the same language, the same food, the same interests, but with maybe the sun.

Exercise 3

SPEAKER 1: Tourism is very good for my country. Because I come from Ireland and it is an island. So it's good for us to have people from other countries coming in.

SPEAKER 2: I think tourism is good because people from different countries meet each other, and talk and get to know a little bit about each other's country. But sometimes too many people means … you don't really know what the country's like, because it's full of tourists.

SPEAKER 3: I think tourism is good for countries because it provides the country with lots of money. But it can also spoil the character, sometimes of small villages.

LESSON D

REVIEW OF UNIT 17

Exercise 2

Dear Mr Johns,

Thank you for your letter. We are always very happy to get letters from our customers. However, we were sorry to hear about your bad experience with our shop assistant. He behaved very rudely. I can only say that this is not what we usually teach the staff in our company, and we have reprimanded him severely.

We are enclosing a free voucher. Please use it when you are next in one of our shops.

Yours sincerely,

UNIT 19 A LOOK AT LIFE!

LESSON A

Exercise 4

SPEAKER 1: I'd like more time to do the things I enjoy – playing tennis, writing short stories … but with a young family it's really hard to find the time. I'm always tired, and there's so much to do – driving the kids here and there, cooking, helping my mother, who is very old now, studying part-time at college …

SPEAKER 2: I'd really like to have a long holiday. It's hard travelling all the time. OK, it's nice visiting lots of different countries, and all my friends think my job's exciting. But I never stay very long in any place, so I don't get to know the countries, really. I'm tired of giving people cups of coffee.

LESSON B

Exercise 2

Poem 1

A world that's safe …

I'd like to live in a world that's safe.

I'd like to live in a world that's clean.

I'd like to live in a world that's kind.

I'd like to live in a world that's green.

Poem 2
The world I'd like to live in
I'd like to live in a world that's kind to children,
A world that's got new ideas,
A world that laughs and smiles.
I'd like to live in a world that gives a helping hand,
A world that's got fresh air,
A world that's got time to listen.
That's the world I'd like to live in.

LESSON C

Exercise 3

Part 1

Version 1

SPEAKER 1: I wonder what the conclusion was? 'The most beautiful face is similar to the face of …' What do you think?

SPEAKER 2: I think it's a very balanced face. The left side is exactly like the right side. I read somewhere that that can be perfection …

SPEAKER 1: I think they probably discovered that the most beautiful face is similar to that of a top model. Or maybe a traditional beauty, the Mona Lisa, for example.

SPEAKER 2: Yes, I agree … faces seem to come in and out of fashion.

Version 2

SPEAKER 1: I wonder what the conclusion was? I wonder what they thought the most beautiful face is similar to that of. What do you think?

SPEAKER 2: Erm … I think it must be a very symmetrical face … (Yes) because I read somewhere where you did a test, if you took both left sides of somebody's face, it can either show what is wrong with a face, or show perfection. (Yes) So I think maybe …

SPEAKER 1: I mean I think … think it's probably more likely that, they discovered that the most beautiful face is similar to that of, say, the top model of the time. (Yes) Or maybe even a traditional beauty, like the Mona Lisa.

SPEAKER 2: Yes … I think the most beautiful face could well have been, um, something that was the, the style of the time, because faces seem to come in and out of fashion.

SPEAKER 1: Yes.

Part 2

After studying the most beautiful face, they discovered that it is similar to the face of a young child. In a young child, the eyes are lower in the head. The lips of the most beautiful face were also similar to those of a baby, not similar to the lips of an average person.

LESSON D

REVIEW OF UNIT 18

Exercise 3

MAN: I lost my cash! I lost my cheques!
WOMAN: I lost my shoes! I lost my watch!
MAN: I lost my shirts! I lost my shorts!
WOMAN: I lost my chocolates! I lost my cheese!
MAN: I lost my reservation! I lost my ship!
WOMAN: I lost my charm! I lost my chance!
MAN: I lost my child! But I found her again.

UNIT 20 I'M SO SORRY!

LESSON A

Exercise 4

WOMAN: Excuse me. I bought this watch last week and now it's stopped. Can you replace it for me?

SHOP ASSISTANT: I'm terribly sorry, madam. I have to get the manager. Would you mind waiting here for a moment?

WOMAN: Look! This came from your shop and it's not working. I want a refund.

SHOP ASSISTANT: Wait a moment. I have to find the manager.

LESSON B

Exercise 3

Version 1

INTERVIEWER: Tris, do you usually complain a lot in hotels, restaurants, or trains?

TRIS: Oh, absolutely. Every time. Because if you've paid, you should get your money's worth.

INTERVIEWER: And do you stay calm and polite? Or do you get angry?

TRIS: Oh, I get angry. I think it's the only way to get a refund. And it always works.

INTERVIEWER: Kate, when you're visiting other countries, do you complain a lot … or do you keep quiet?

KATE: I usually keep quiet, because I don't know the language well enough. And I don't know the culture very well – it's sometimes very different.

INTERVIEWER: And what about in your own country? Do you complain when things aren't satisfactory?

KATE: Oh, yes, I complain a lot.

Version 2

INTERVIEWER: Tris, do you normally complain a lot when something isn't satisfactory, like in hotels, restaurants, trains?

TRIS: Absolutely. Every single time. Because I feel if you've paid, you deserve to get your money's worth. And if you get, erm, anything less, then you're perfectly … within your rights to complain … until you get satisfaction. I really think that.

INTERVIEWER: Yeah, and do you stay calm and polite when you complain? Or do you get angry and sarcastic?

TRIS: Well, I'd love to think that I stayed calm and rational and polite, but I think actually the only way to really, successfully get your, your way with these people is to go from calm and polite into towering rage. That works. (Right) Yeah. Sarcasm not so much. But if they … if you get angry customers, I think that's when you get the refund.

INTERVIEWER: Kate, when you're visiting other countries, do you complain about things … or, or do you tend to keep quiet?

KATE: Um … I tend to keep quiet. (Right) Um, partly because, erm, I don't know the language well enough and I think if you do complain, you have to do it articulately and clearly. And also, erm, in another country the, the culture might be quite different. And, and it may be acceptable.

INTERVIEWER: Mm. What about in your own country? Do you complain if things aren't satisfactory?

KATE: Oh, yes. Yes, I complain a lot. Vehemently.

UNIT 21 ALL YOU NEED IS LOVE ... OR MONEY

Exercise 4

Version 1

JIM: Well, I don't know about you, but I think about money all the time.

JANE: Is this because you haven't got any money at the moment?

JIM: You're right, I haven't got any at all at the moment. But what about you, Jane, are you good with money?

JANE: Well, I do worry about money, especially in the last two years, since I bought my flat. Do you worry about money, Mike?

MIKE: Yes, I do worry about money, but that's because I'm married and I've got two children ... and quite a large car. I worry about paying the bills. My wife says I shouldn't worry. We've been married for twelve years and we've always had enough money.

JANE: Well, I worry terribly about money. I can't seem to save any money. When I save a bit, it all goes very quickly.

MIKE: Do you think that's because your parents were like that?

JANE: That's possible. They didn't have much money, and I don't think they saved very much.

MIKE: My parents always told me to be careful with money. And to try to save. They said, 'Money doesn't grow on trees'.

Version 2

JIM: Well, I don't know about you, but I am obsessed with money, at the moment, anyway. I find myself constantly thinking about money, about how I can make more money, how I can save what money I have ...

JANE: Is this because you're very broke at the moment?

JIM: This is because I am particularly broke at the moment, but erm, but I mean what about you? I mean are you, are you good with money?

JANE: Erm, well I do worry about money, and more so in the last couple of years since I bought my own flat. Because that's sort of a commitment. And, um, it's important to me and I want to keep the flat on. Do you worry about money, Mike?

MIKE: Um, I do worry about money, but then I have quite a lot of commitments. I'm married and I have two children and quite a large car. So I worry about being able to pay the bills, but then again, my wife says that I shouldn't worry, because, er, we've been married for twelve years now and we've always had enough money.

JANE: You survived ... yes, it's funny because I, I do worry terribly about money ... I always have. Erm, and, I don't know, it's, erm, however much you try and save, which I do try and save, I don't know about you, but it never seems to work. Something comes along and takes that little bit you've saved.

MIKE: Do you think that's because your parents were like that, or, or were they not like that?

JANE: Could be, actually. Yes, there never was much money around. And I don't think they ever managed to save very much.

MIKE: Yes. My parents always told me to be concerned about money. And try and save. And that, erm. And they said, 'Money doesn't grow on trees'.

Exercise 1

1.
I'm Janina. I want to study Spanish, but I don't really need it for my job. I just want to go on holiday in Mexico or Mejico, I should say.

2.
I'm Olga. I want a child, but I don't want to lose my job and I need the money.

3.
My name's Jim. I don't need to go to university because I'm 75 years old, but I want to be a student again, and I certainly don't want to sit at home in front of the TV for the rest of my life.

REVIEW OF UNIT 19

Exercise 1

1. It's your key.
2. I lie in bed every night.
3. I liked it when we were at the shop.
4. That's not too safe. I'm scared.
5. I like a credit card.
6. He likes meat.

Exercise 2

Some of my friends are psychologists, dentists, artists, typists, scientists, poets and economists.

REVIEW OF UNIT 20

Exercise 1

1.
Watch out! You've knocked over the vase!
I'm sorry, that was totally accidental!

2.
Your daughter ran in front of my car!
I'm very sorry. I'm sure she didn't realise it was dangerous.

3.
Your children have made a mess of this room!
Oh dear, I'm sorry. They've never been very tidy, I'm afraid.

4.
Slow down! I can't type as fast as that!
I'm so sorry. I should be more patient.

5.
Now look what you've done! You've put all my letters into the wrong files!
Sorry. I guess that was rather stupid.

6.
Oh, you've got a letter from *Travel Magazine*. What does it say?
It says: The editor regrets that it wasn't possible to include your article in the January magazine.

7.
You didn't tell me you couldn't come.
Oh, I'm terribly sorry. I just didn't think it was very important.

8.
Look, I'm sure you'll be all right at the interview. Just don't show that you're nervous.
Well, I'm sorry, but I can't. I'm not very confident.

Exercise 2

Listen and reply with a short apology.
1. Watch out! You've knocked over the vase!
2. Now look what you've done! You've put all my letters into the wrong files!
3. Your children have made a mess of my room!
4. You didn't tell me you couldn't come.

UNIT 22 THE RIGHT CLIMATE?

LESSON A

Exercise 1

INTERVIEWER: What's it like in these places in January?
METEOROLOGIST: In the northern hemisphere first, well … Anchorage in Alaska, right up north in America, has an average temperature in January of about –11 Celsius … er, Rome in Italy is a lot warmer at about 8 degrees, and in Istanbul, Turkey, it's about 5 degrees on average in January.
INTERVIEWER: What's it like in the southern hemisphere in January?
METEOROLOGIST: Well, in the southern hemisphere, January is a summer month … so in Johannesburg in South Africa, for example, the average is about 20 degrees in January … erm … in Buenos Aires, in Argentina, it's a little warmer at 23, and in Mawson, right down in Antarctica, January has an average temperature of zero degrees … rather cold I'm afraid.

Exercise 3

Version 1
A: What's winter like in Anchorage, Alaska?
B: Well, in Anchorage, the winter's very long, and the days are very short. The winter months are very cold, freezing cold in fact. There's a lot of snow and ice. The average temperature's minus 11.
A: What about Sydney in Australia? What's winter like there?
C: In Sydney, there's no snow or ice. It's sometimes chilly in the evenings. Er, there's not too much rain in the winter and it can get windy from time to time. But with an average winter temperature of about 13 degrees, it's really quite warm.
A: What's Jakarta like in winter?
D: For Indonesia, and especially Jakarta, we don't need to use the word 'winter' at all. The average temperature stays the same all year round, at about 27 degrees. In August, it's hot and humid. But there's less rain than in other months.

Version 2
A: What's winter like in Anchorage, Alaska?
B: Well, in Anchorage the winter's very long and the days get, er, very short. In winter months like December, January, February, it's very cold, freezing cold in fact. There's a lot of snow and ice and when people go out, frostbite is always a danger. In January, the average temperature is about minus 11, and with winter winds it can get much lower. You need to be strong to live in those temperatures.
A: What about Sydney in Australia? What's winter like there?
C: In Sydney, it's true to say there isn't really a winter in the usual sense of the word because there is no snow or ice. It sometimes gets chilly in the evenings or in the early morning, but most people don't have heavy overcoats. There's usually less rainfall in the winter than in the summer

and it can get windy from time to time, but with an average winter temperature in August of about 13 degrees, it's really quite warm and on some days it can feel like a European summer's day.
A: What's Jakarta like in winter?
D: Talking about, er, Indonesia and especially Jakarta, we don't need to use the word 'winter' at all because the city is quite close to the equator and the average temperature stays the same all year round at about 27 degrees. So in August it's hot and humid … quite tiring for the traveller from the northern hemisphere. One good thing about August in Jakarta, however, is that it's traditionally the driest month, on average in fact drier, for example, than London is at the same time of year.

LESSON D

REVIEW OF UNIT 20

Exercise 2

1. I'm really sorry I've been away all week. But a friend of mine suddenly had a free ticket to Spain. So I had to go.
2. I'm so sorry I haven't done the homework you set for last week but my children have been ill and there simply hasn't been time.
3. I'm so sorry I'm late for class. I was on my way here and I realised I'd left the gas on, and I had to go back.
4. Oh, I do apologise. I've forgotten my book! I thought I'd got the right one with me, but the one I need is still on the kitchen table.

UNIT 23 CELEBRATIONS

LESSON B

Exercise 1

JENNY: Hello.
ELLI: Hello, it's Elli here. Is that Jenny?
JENNY: Oh, hi, Elli. Yes, it is. How are things?
ELLI: Fine, thanks. How about you?
JENNY: Oh, fine. Things are a bit busy at work at the moment.
ELLI: Really? Look, I'm having a party for my birthday – on Saturday, at Mario's Café. Would you like to come?
JENNY: Oh, it's your birthday! Happy birthday!

Exercise 2

ELLI: … I'm having a party for my birthday – on Saturday, at Mario's Café. Would you like to come?
JENNY: Oh, it's your birthday! Happy birthday! Yes, I'd love to come! At Mario's, what time?

Exercise 3

ELLI: Hello, it's Elli here. Is that Giles?
GILES: Oh, hello, Elli. How are you?
ELLI: Fine, thanks. How about you?
GILES: Oh, fine … I'm working hard, as usual.
ELLI: Me too. Look, I'm having a party for my birthday – on Saturday, at Mario's. Can you come?
GILES: Oh, I'm sorry, I'd really love to come, but I've got to work at the restaurant on that night. Thanks very much for inviting me.

Exercise 1

1.

A: Ah, you look really worn out. Shall I get you a cup of tea?

B: Oh, yes, please, I'd love one.

2.

A: Good morning, breakfast is cooking. Sit down.

B: Wonderful! Um, listen, shall I go out and get you a newspaper while you're cooking?

A: Er, well, we've got five minutes, yes, would you? I'd love one.

B: Fine. OK.

A: OK. Great.

3.

A: Mmm, that's good, isn't it?

B: It was a lovely lunch. Thank you very much indeed. Erm, look, there's so much washing up. Shall I do the washing up for you?

A: Oh, no, no, no, no, no, don't be silly. No, no, I enjoy washing up. No, let me do it.

B: Please let me, I'd be delighted. It's the least I could do.

A: Maybe if you dry …

B: Right.

4.

A: Listen to that dog!

B: Oh, I know, three o'clock, you see. That's when I normally take him out.

A: It's his walk time. Shall I take him?

B: Oh, would you mind?

A: Yes, I've got Wellingtons, I could just take him now.

B: Oh, that would be lovely. The lead's on the back of the kitchen door.

A: OK.

5.

A: Oh, that smells great.

B: Thanks.

A: Is it Chinese?

B: Yes, it is.

A: Oh, I love Chinese food. Shall I set the table?

B: Oh, that would be wonderful. Erm, let's eat in the, the sitting room.

Exercise 3

Version 1

1.

The best thing about being a host in St Lucia is that you can show everybody where to go. You can show them where to find the best fruit. You can show them the best beaches. And you can cook them a really great meal.

2.

One of the best things about Indian culture is the hospitality you offer to your guests. Anyone who comes to your home is a guest. You make sure they are comfortable and give them something to eat. You should offer them something, even just a glass of water. You should do it in a nice way – then the guests know that you are happy to see them.

Version 2

1.

The best thing about being a host in St Lucia is that you get a chance to show everybody where to go. You can show them where to find the best mangoes and bananas and coconut; you can show them the best beaches, the quietest spots. When they get home, you can cook them the best meal, flying fish, dashin, yam and sweet potato; you can take them to the highest point, the Pittons in St Lucia and show them the whole of St Lucia in one view.

2.

One of the best things about Indian culture is the hospitality that you show to your guests. Whoever comes to your home is your guest, and it's your responsibility to make them feel comfortable and to feed them. Even if you're not a wealthy family, you offer them what you have. And make them feel comfortable in your home. So you may cook them some food, or offer them some fruit, or even just a glass of water. But you must do it with graciousness. And so that they feel that you are pleased to see them. You must welcome them at all times.

REVIEW OF UNIT 21

Exercise 1

Part 1

black	It's black.
blue	It's blue.
bright	It's bright.
brave	She's brave.
place	It's a place.
plant	It's a plant.
price	That's the price.
print	That's a beautiful print.

Part 2

1. I want some sunglasses – the sun's too bright.
2. This room needs a bit of colour – I'd like a nice, big plant.
3. I really need a new car, but the problem is the price!
4. No, I don't want white, I really want blue.

Part 3

Example: You hear: *spend*
    You say: *I want to spend, spend, spend.*

1. spend I want to spend, spend, spend.
2. smile I want to smile, smile, smile.
3. sleep I want to sleep, sleep, sleep.
4. snore I want to snore, snore, snore.
5. stop I want to stop, stop, stop.

All right then, let's stop.

Exercise 2

I've got a guitar and I really want to play.
I've got a nice flat and I really want to stay.

I've moved to the city and I really love the place;
I've got a big garden and I really need the space.

I'm going on a holiday, I'm travelling to Spain;
I don't want to drive, so I'm going on the train.

I've got lots of money and I really want to spend.
But I'm all on my own and I really need a friend.

I'm out in the evenings and I dance till I drop;
I love modern music and I don't want to stop.

Do you like lots of fun? Do you like a happy style?
Then forget all your troubles and smile, smile, smile!

UNIT 24 LOOKING AHEAD

LESSON B

Exercise 3

A: About sixty years ago when my father was about 20, he was at a fairground with his girlfriend. There was a fortune teller there in a little tent. She was a bit unusual because she studied not only your hands, or the palms of your hands, I should say, but also your feet. Apparently, you can tell a lot from people's feet and in the deserts some people can read the character of a person from the footprints they leave in the sand.

B: Really?

A: Anyway, the fortune teller studied my father's hands and feet, and then made these predictions about his future: You'll marry a woman with dark hair and blue eyes. Your wife will be the same age as you.

B: Was she right?

A: Well, yes, the fortune teller was right – my mother has got dark hair and blue eyes and is only eleven days older than my father. In fact she was the girlfriend at the fairground. She also said: You'll sell things for a large company.

B: Wasn't your father a salesman?

A: Yes, she was right again. Ten years later, my father got a job selling beds for a large company. In fact, he stayed with the same company for 30 years. She also said: You'll have two children – two sons. Again, correct – I've got one brother and no sisters. Then she said: Your health will not be good, your heart will be a problem for you, but you'll live to be 73 years old. Well she was correct yet again; my poor father had a lot of illness, including heart trouble, and he lived to be 73. But … she was wrong in one way: she was wrong in her last prediction … he's still alive. He'll be 77 this year!

LESSON C

Exercise 1

Version 1

A: Well, to succeed in the future, children will need lots of imagination. They'll need to read a lot.

B: I agree, but they'll also need a lot of money, because things will get more and more expensive.

C: Mm. And also languages. They'll need to speak more than one language.

B: Yes, you're right, that'll be really important.

D: I also think children will need to know a lot about computers.

C: Yes, and to enjoy their hobbies as well, because they'll live longer and have a lot of free time.

B: And to enjoy all that free time, they'll need to be fit.

D: Yeah, and they'll need to tackle the problem of pollution. The world's getting more polluted all the time …

Version 2

A: Well, I think if children are going to do well in the future, they're going to have to develop an imagination. I think that's one of the biggest things they'll need, er, because there's just too much television and I think a really positive step forward would be getting, getting much more of an imagination going – more reading, that sort of thing.

B: I, I agree but I think children er … will need in the future, to succeed, an awful lot of money, because things are just going to be so expensive.

A: Yes … Also languages. (Mm) To be able to speak more than one language, certainly.

B: That will be an asset, won't it?

C: It will certainly make you more employable.

D: I also think children will definitely need to be completely computer literate. (Oh, yes) I mean, even today, kids are learning it from school, but they will definitely need quite advanced levels of computer technique, I think …

C: Yes, they will, and, er, to enjoy sport and leisure, as well, I think … and fitness.

B: That will be important, won't it, because they'll need to keep really fit, yeah.

D: And they'll need to be more ecologically aware because the world, after all, is becoming worse and worse in terms of pollution and stuff like that …

C: Yes, they'll have to all be green.

LESSON D

REVIEW OF UNIT 23

Exercise 1

1.

WOMAN: Double 5 094, hello.

SUE: Hello, it's Sue here.

WOMAN: Hi!

SUE: I've moved into my new place. I'm having a party on Saturday. Can you come?

WOMAN: Oh, I'd love to come, but I can't. We're going to be away on Saturday.

SUE: Oh, what a shame.

WOMAN: Sorry.

2.

MAN: Hello.

SUE: Hello, it's Sue here. I've moved into my new place, and I'm having a party on Saturday. Can you come?

MAN: Oh, Sue, Saturday … Erm, well, I'm not sure if I can get out of a previous date.

SUE: Well, do try. It's at eight o'clock. But you could come later.

MAN: Well, I will try, because I'd rather come to your party, and I'll ring you back.

SUE: Thank you, bye.

MAN: Bye.

3.

CHRIS: Hello?

SUE: Hello, Chris, it's Sue here. I've moved into my new place.

CHRIS: Oh, great! Was the move OK?

SUE: Yes, very easy. I'm having a party on Saturday, to celebrate. Can you come?

CHRIS: Yes, I'd love to. What time?

SUE: Oh, 7, 7.30 … any time after 7, really.

ACKNOWLEDGEMENTS

Authors' acknowledgements

We would like to extend warm thanks to Ruth Gairns and Stuart Redman, whose help and support we very much appreciated throughout our work on this shared project.

We are grateful to our readers, whose detailed and constructive comments were extremely valuable to us: Gillian Lazar, Susan Garvin, Virginia Garcia, Diann Gruber, Carol Herrmann, Philip Town, Anthony Nicholson and Antonio Marcelino Campo.

At Cambridge University Press, we would like to express our thanks to our commissioning editor, Peter Donovan, to our editor, Kate Boyce, whose expert guidance and remarkable problem-solving ability smoothed so many difficulties, to James Dingle for his help with the pilot edition, and to the rest of the staff, especially Jeanne McCarten, for their continued support. Our thanks go to Helena Gomm for her editorial skill, patience and good humour, to our design team, Nick Newton and Randell Harris, to our recording producers, Peter Taylor and James Richardson, and to the staff at AVP.

Stephen Slater is very grateful both to his colleagues at CALUSA (the Centre for Applied Linguistics in the University of South Australia) for their encouragement and patience, and to all the members of his family in Australia and England who so generously gave up their time to enable him to work on this project.

And finally, a big thank you from Joanne Collie to all the members of her family for their creative ideas and their support.

The authors and publishers would like to thank the following institutions and teachers for their help in testing the material and for the invaluable feedback which they provided:

Insearch Language Centre, UTS, Sydney, Australia; Transfer, Paris, France; Centro Linguistico di Ateneo, Parma University, Parma, Italy; Cambridge Institute of English, Reggio Emilia, Italy; Regency School, Turin, Italy; The Cambridge School, Verona, Italy; Latvia University, Riga, Latvia; Languages International, Auckland, New Zealand; Cambridge English Studies, La Coruña, Spain; Universidad de Navarra, Pamplona, Spain; École d'Ingénieurs, Geneva, Switzerland; Dilko English, Istanbul, Turkey; Chichester School of English, Chichester, UK.

The authors and publishers are grateful to the following illustrators:

Peter Byatt: pp. 168/9, 170; Jerry Collins: pp. 6, 163, 165, 171, 173, 174, 176/7, 178, 179, 186, 187, 189, 191, 195, 213; Joanna Kerr: pp. 116, 197; Celia Witchard: pp. 164, 184, 196.

Design and DTP by Newton Harris

Recordings produced by Martin Williamson, Prolingua Productions, at Studio AVP, London